POLITICS AND THE PAUL'S CROSS
SERMONS, 1558–1642

Politics and the Paul's Cross Sermons, 1558–1642

MARY MORRISSEY

OXFORD
UNIVERSITY PRESS

OXFORD
UNIVERSITY PRESS

Great Clarendon Street, Oxford OX2 6DP

Oxford University Press is a department of the University of Oxford.
It furthers the University's objective of excellence in research, scholarship,
and education by publishing worldwide in

Oxford New York

Auckland Cape Town Dar es Salaam Hong Kong Karachi
Kuala Lumpur Madrid Melbourne Mexico City Nairobi
New Delhi Shanghai Taipei Toronto

With offices in

Argentina Austria Brazil Chile Czech Republic France Greece
Guatemala Hungary Italy Japan Poland Portugal Singapore
South Korea Switzerland Thailand Turkey Ukraine Vietnam

Oxford is a registered trade mark of Oxford University Press
in the UK and in certain other countries

Published in the United States
by Oxford University Press Inc., New York

© Mary Morrissey 2011

British Library Cataloguing in Publication Data

Data available

Library of Congress Cataloging in Publication Data
Library of Congress Control Number: 2011929282

Typeset by SPI Publisher Services, Pondicherry, India
Printed in Great Britain
on acid-free paper by
MPG Books Group, Bodmin and King's Lynn

ISBN 978–0–19–957176–5

3 5 7 9 10 8 6 4 2

In Memory of Jeremy Maule

Acknowledgements

Second only to the debt acknowledged in the dedication, I owe my thanks to Professor Patrick Collinson, who has been a generous advisor and a patient referee. Colleagues at the University of Aberdeen (particularly the members of the Centre for Early Modern Studies), at Nottingham Trent University, and the University of Reading (particularly those involved in the Early Modern Research Centre), have all jollied this project along even when I dragged it into the Slough of Despond. I am very grateful for the help, advice, and company that they have given me. The team of editors on the *Oxford Edition of the Sermons of John Donne*, under the general editorship of Peter McCullough, have become a source of intellectual encouragement and friendship. They too have helped to get this book finished. Alan Cromartie is a useful resource for early modern studies, and I acknowledge that I exploit him in this regard. The staff at Oxford University Press, particularly Andrew McNeillie and Ariane Petit, have been a great help to me in preparing this book for the press. I also thank the anonymous readers of the typescript for their comments and advice. All errors remaining are my own.

The staff of several libraries have been unfailingly obliging to me while I was researching this book, and I would like to thank librarians in University of Reading Library, Cambridge University Library, the British Library, the Bodleian Library, Lambeth Palace Library, the Huntington Library, the Folger Shakespeare Library, the Guildhall Library, and the former Corporation of London Record Office, and Mr Jo Wisdom, Librarian of St Paul's Cathedral.

Finally, while I cannot claim that Cait and Aideen have helped me to write this book, I name them here because I never neglect an opportunity to mention them.

Contents

List of Illustrations   viii
List of Abbreviations   ix
Notes on the Text   x
Preface   xi

1. The History of a Sermon Series   1

2. From Pulpit to Press   35

3. Controlling the Sermons   68

4. Controlling the Pulpit   102

5. The Monarch and Paul's Cross: Preaching on Political Anniversaries   130

6. Preaching against the Church of Rome: Anti-Catholicism and Anti-Popery   160

7. Preaching against the Puritan Movement   191

    Epilogue   222

Bibliography   229
Index   249

List of Illustrations

1. John Gipkyn, 'Old St Paul's' diptych (1616), left-hand inner panel   9

2. John Gipkyn, 'Old St Paul's' diptych (1616), right-hand inner panel   14

3. Vignette of Saint Pauls included in the map of Middlesex, from John Speed, *The Theatre of Empire of Great Britain* (1611)   15

List of Abbreviations

APC	*Acts of the Privy Council of England, 1542–1631*, ed. J. R. Dasent, 46 vols (1890–1964)
ARCR	A. F. Allison and D. M. Rogers, *The Contemporary Printed Literature of the English Counter-Reformation between 1558 and 1640*, vol. II: *Works in English* (Aldershot: Scolar Press, 1994)
BL	British Library, London
Bodl.	Bodleian Library, University of Oxford
CSPD	*Calendar of State Papers, Domestic Series, of the Reigns of Edward VI, Mary, Elizabeth and James I,* 12 vols, ed. Robert Lemon (vols 1, 2) and Mary Anne Everett Green (vols 3–12) (1856–70); *Calendar of State Papers, Domestic Series, of the Reign of Charles I,* 23 vols, ed. John Bruce (vols 1–13) and William Douglas Hamilton (vols 13–23) and Mrs S. C Lomas (vol. 23).
CUL	Cambridge University Library
HMC	Historical Manuscripts Commission, Appendices to the Reports
LMA	London Metropolitan Archive
LPL	Lambeth Palace Library
PRO	Public Records Office
Register of Sermons	Millar MacLure, *Register of Sermons Preached at Paul's Cross, 1534–1642*, rev. Peter Pauls and J. C. Boswell (Ottawa: Dovehouse, 1989)
STC²	*A Short-Title Catalogue of Books Printed in England, Scotland & Ireland and of English Books Printed Abroad, 1475–1640*, compiled by A. W. Pollard and G. R. Redgrave; 2nd edn., revised and enlarged by W. A. Jackson, F. S. Ferguson, and Katherine F. Pantzer, 3 vols (London: Bibliographical Society, 1976–91)
Wing	*Short-Title Catalogue of Books Printed in England, Scotland, Ireland, Wales and British America and of English Books Printed in Other Countries, 1641–1700,* compiled by Donald Wing, 2nd edn., revised and enlarged, 3 vols (New York: Modern Language Association of America, 1972–88)

Notes on the Text

Dates are Old Style, but the year is taken to begin on 1 January.

Place of publication is London, unless otherwise stated.

In quotations, the original spelling and punctuation is retained, except that i/j and u/v have been modernized. All abbreviations are preserved, except that tildes and fossil-thorns are expanded silently. Black letter type is rendered as roman type, and roman type used in black letter publications is represented by underlining. Quotations from manuscripts have abbreviations expanded and superscriptions lowered silently.

To avoid the reproduction of lengthy sermon titles in the notes, early modern texts are referred to by their short-titles with date and STC^2/Wing reference.

English words used as terms of art in preaching rhetoric are placed in inverted commas where necessary.

The extracts from the Bible on which the sermon is based (the 'text') is quoted as it is written in the printed text/manuscript of the sermon. This is to preserve the wording used by the preacher, which sometimes differs from standard translations, because the 'division' of the sermon, and consequently its structure, depends on the exact wording of the 'text'.

Preface

I have been advised to include in the Preface those things to which my readers' attention should be drawn. So, firstly, I need to say that Paul's Cross was an outdoor pulpit that stood in the northern part of the churchyard of old St. Paul's cathedral in London, from which sermons of about two hours duration were delivered on Sunday mornings (usually at 10 a.m.). Most of the eminent preachers, in this age of eminent preaching, took their turn at Paul's Cross. (The exception, to my great regret, is Lancelot Andrewes.) A considerable number (roughly 250) of the sermons preached at Paul's Cross were subsequently printed or survive in manuscript copies, and those texts form the core of this study. A *Register of Sermons preached at Paul's Cross*, originally compiled by Millar MacLure and revised by Peter Pauls and J. C. Boswell, is the invaluable companion of any scholar working on this material.[1]

But I should also alert my reader to the fact that many Paul's Cross sermons are not considered here. In his 1620 *Sermon at Paules Crosse, on Behalfe of Paules Church*, Bishop John King of London distinguished his sermon from those preached 'every Sabbath day, out of this chaire', which delivered a message of 'Moyses or Christ, Law or Gospell'.[2] Most Paul's Cross sermons, even within the limited sample of those that survive today, were not about politics or religious controversy. Most were concerned with catechetical information and with exhortations to piety, charity, and obedience to one's superiors, and they are not central to the study that follows. The neglect of these more characteristic sermons (such as the sermons on trade and business ethics preached before Bartholomew Fair; the notorious 'Jeremiads' or 'national warning sermons'; the great meditations on the Passion preached on Good Friday; and the delightfully complicated sermons that 'rehearsed' the Passion and the Spital sermons on Low Sunday), I hope to remedy before too long. And that other great sermon series through which the politics, religion, and culture of early modern London were shaped, the 'Spital sermons' preached every Easter in Spitalfields to the city's most wealthy and most vulnerable members (the aldermen and the orphans of Christ's Hospital), is a subject that I have begun to investigate and hope to describe more fully in the future. There is much to say about Paul's Cross and the sermon culture of early modern London, and this study hopes to contribute to that subject as it is now taking shape.[3]

---

[1] Millar MacLure's original register was an appendix to *The Paul's Cross Sermons, 1534–1642* (Toronto: University of Toronto Press, 1958). This was revised and published separately as *Register of Sermons Preached at Paul's Cross, 1534–1642*, rev. Peter Pauls and J. C. Boswell (Ottawa: Dovehouse, 1989).

[2] John King, *A Sermon preached at Paules Crosse, on Behalfe of Paules Church* (1620), *STC*[2] 14892, pp. 31–2.

[3] Most significant for the study of London's preaching culture is the work of Emma Rhatigan on Lincoln's Inn ('Donne's Readership at Lincoln's Inn', in Jeanne Shami, M. Thomas Hester, and Dennis Flynn (eds), *The Oxford Handbook for John Donne Studies* (Oxford: Oxford University Press,

The decision to begin with the minority of sermons that concern political and religious controversies is motivated by a wish to provide the reader with the most intelligible starting place for understanding the part that the Paul's Cross sermon series[4] played in the religious life, and religious conflicts, of London from the accession of Elizabeth I to the outbreak of Civil War. There is an element of pragmatism also: after several years when I offered detailed readings of individual sermons at seminars and conferences only to face as my first question, 'Can you tell us something about Paul's Cross?', it occurred to me that there was no point telling people about one Paul's Cross sermon until I had provided sufficient contextual information about Paul's Cross for the surviving sermons to make sense. I attempt to do that here: to offer as much information as I can glean from the sources about who appointed the preachers; about the physical environment in which the sermons were preached and the auditors listened to them; how the sermons came to be printed and the other forms in which they might be extant today; how much 'freedom' the preacher had in tackling political or religious controversies; about the other uses of the space surrounding the pulpit, and how that might affect the hearers' understanding of the sermons.

I have chosen my dates partly in order to avoid two large and complex subjects: the pivotal role of Paul's Cross in the mid-Tudor Reformation has already been told.[5] The role of Paul's Cross in the politics of the English Civil Wars and Interregnum has not been told at all, because the continuation of the sermon series after 1642 has not been recognized: I offer the briefest sketch of this subject in the Epilogue. This leaves me with the eighty-four years between 1558 and 1642 to consider. In these years Paul's Cross went from being a pulpit from which the evangelically-minded minister could exhort Londoners to accept Protestantism, to being a place where an ambitious young cleric could make a reputation that would help him to a patron and a living, until finally the pulpit was torn down and the sermons transferred into the cathedral where they became the Sunday morning custom of the city's governors.

That there is a narrative (albeit of a rather conventional 'rise and fall' type) to this account of Paul's Cross is deliberate, and where possible the chapters that follow retain a chronological structure. I wish to emphasize that the administrative

---

forthcoming), and of Arnold Hunt, whose *The Art of Hearing: English Preachers and Their Auditories, 1590–1640* (Cambridge: Cambridge University Press, 2010) was unfortunately not available in time for its findings to be incorporated in this study. More generally, publications like the forthcoming *Oxford Handbook of the Early Modern Sermon*, eds Hugh Adlington, Peter McCullough, and Emma Rhatigan, will prove indispensible in creating a detailed picture of early modern preaching, preachers, and auditors.

[4] The Paul's Cross sermons are described as a series throughout this study. This is partly to avoid the suggestion that the sermons were an institution with a legal identity, like the court sermons organized through the Chapel Royal. The Paul's Cross sermons were not completely ad hoc, however: they were almost always preached at the same place and time, and an organizational structure grew up around them. Even after the demolition of the pulpit and the end of episcopacy, the sermons were referred to as 'Paul's Cross sermons', if only for accounting purposes.

[5] In particular, see Susan Bridgen, *London and the Reformation* (Oxford: Clarendon Press, 1989), and Ethan Shagan, *Popular Politics and the English Reformation* (Cambridge: Cambridge University Press, 2003).

mechanisms and the political and religious complexion of the sermons changed over time. Too often Paul's Cross is assumed to have been a stable 'institution', run by a unitary 'government' which could 'tune the pulpits' to perfection: the story of Paul's Cross (no institution, but rather a custom that was given funding) is far less tidy. It is one of ad hoc arrangements achieving a kind of permanence while they served a function. The series operated through, perhaps despite, a tussle between several authorities: the royal government, the dean of Paul's, but particularly the bishop, and the Corporation of London. Usually, the political interests of these parties were aligned: they wanted 'orthodox' preaching that cast no aspersions on the authorities and taught the people their duty. But sometimes their interests differed, and that created the possibility that something impolitic, or unorthodox, or newsworthy, might be said at Paul's Cross. Paul's Cross was a popular venue partly because for much of its history it was a place from which explosive things might be said.

I don't wish to suggest that the bishop, the Corporation, or the Privy Council thought that Paul's Cross was a kind of 'fourth estate', or that the 'stakeholders' in this sermon series thought that the cut and thrust of debate in public a 'good thing'. Rather, I am suggesting that before Archbishop William Laud and Charles I became involved with it, the authorities that shared control over Paul's Cross had conflicting interests and policies, and none of them were capable of exerting consistent and complete control over the pulpit. Because of that, Paul's Cross was a platform that *might* be available to the wide spectrum of opinion that was contained, albeit uneasily, within the Elizabethan and Jacobean Church. Consistent control over Paul's Cross, pulpit and sermons, came about when the Laudian Church authorities found themselves dealing with a sympathetic bench of aldermen, and the Laudians seemed to have been successful in appointing only preachers who agreed with them. The result was a narrowing of the sermons' audience.

Understanding the administrative structures and political forces that impinged on the preacher will not of itself explain the sermons that we read. This book attempts to be both a historical study of the Paul's Cross sermon series *and* a literary study of the sermons. It is not 'interdisciplinary' in the sense that it seeks to conflate the purposes of literary and of historical scholarship, but I hope that it is interdisciplinary in so far as it offers historical answers to historical questions while providing literary analysis of texts that have been hitherto neglected by scholars in my discipline. For this reason, a vital element of this study is the recovery of sermon genres and the basic 'parts' of a sermon as a literary form. The premise on which I build my argument, particularly in Chapters 5 to 7, is that preachers used the literary conventions for preaching as one of the resources that allowed them to intervene in political controversies without breaking the fundamental rule that the preacher's message comes from God, not the monarch. The preachers of 'political anniversary' sermons found in exhortations to thanksgiving a way of reminding their hearers of the benefits of good government; the preachers of anti-Catholic sermons used the 'confutational' genre so that they could avoid complex theological questions and concentrate on the more readily intelligible questions of loyalty and trustworthiness. When Richard Bancroft used those arguments and that genre to preach against puritanism and Martin Marprelate, he did not need to spell out to his hearers that he thought the puritans were no better than the papists. So I ask my readers to pay particular attention to the details offered of the ways that a preacher 'divides' his text, of the 'doctrines' he reveals through the 'explication' of the text and the way he 'applies' those doctrines to the hearers before him. And I direct the reader to Chapter 2 for an account of what I take these preaching terms to mean, and how we can use them in the analysis of sermons, by genre or by individual text.

Lastly, I will contradict my own good advice to undergraduates and end with a quotation, because the principle on which this study rests has already been stated with great eloquence by Brian Cummings. He writes:

Religious writing appears to be marginal to both religion and writing, a limited activity of pious, sectarian, and personal motivation. Such assumptions misconstrue both religion and writing. Writing was produced in the context of a religious crisis which overwhelmed political and social culture. Only by an odd prejudice of literary history can such matters be regarded as peripheral to literary production. Moreover, a large majority of the writings of the sixteenth and seventeenth centuries was religious. That such writing is not usually described as literature distorts literary history. To define religious writing as non-literary is to beg the question of what 'literature' means, and to call most 'literary' works of the period non-religious completes a circular argument.[6]

---

[6] Brian Cummings, *The Literary Culture of the Reformation: Grammar and Grace* (Oxford: Oxford University Press, 2002), pp. 5–6.

1

The History of a Sermon Series

Why's *Peter's* Golden, *Paul's* a Leaden Cross?
Why, because Golden words *Paul's* Cross ingross.[1]

Most students of early modern England will encounter some reference to the
weekly sermons delivered from the pulpit that stood in St Paul's Churchyard,
known as Paul's Cross. Because of the number of these sermons that were printed
(approximately 250 before 1661), they constitute a valuable source for the study of
early modern religion and religious controversy. The fame and calibre of the
preachers who appeared there (Hugh Latimer, John Foxe, John Jewel, Richard
Hooker, John Donne) ensures that any student of early modern preaching will
encounter a Paul's Cross sermon. And the number of politically sensitive sermons
preached from that pulpit (Jewel's 'Challenge' sermon of 1559, Richard Bancroft's
anti-Puritan sermon of 1589, William Barlow's sermon on the execution of the Earl
of Essex, and Richard Gardiner's 1642 Accession Day sermon) has induced many
writers on the politics of Elizabethan and early Stuart England to include a Paul's
Cross sermon among their sources. The undoubted importance of these sermons
has led many to think of Paul's Cross as one of the institutions of early modern
English government.

But Paul's Cross was not an institution, nor a changeless custom; it was a series
of sermons identifiable for being preached in the same place on a regular basis. The
series gained a degree of stability through public support and funding, which
allowed a set of arrangements to grow up that ensured the sermons' continued
performance. The Paul's Cross sermons served a need and continued for as long as
that need existed. It is important to make this point at the outset, because the view
of Paul's Cross that we have inherited from its earliest historians, John Stow (1524/
5–1605) and William Dugdale (1605–86) in particular, is static and nostalgic. This
has led Paul's Cross's only modern historian to see it as an essentially medieval
institution, a 'ritual, as old as a folkmoot, as fresh as a ballad or a news-sheet, as
unchanging as a mass', as representative of an era when 'England was, even theoreti-
cally, one audience listening to one voice'. Consequently, for Millar MacLure 'the
period between More and Milton, Latimer and Laud, represented the middle and old
age of Paul's Cross.'[2]

---

[1] *John Owen's Latine Epigrams Englished by Thom. Harvey, Gent.* (1677), Wing O825E, p. 88.
'Peter's Cross' is the Cheapside Cross.
[2] Millar MacLure, *The Paul's Cross Sermons* (Toronto: University of Toronto Press, 1958), pp. 116, 167.

MacLure is mistaken in seeing the Paul's Cross sermons as a ritual, and in thinking of the reign of Elizabeth and James as its 'middle and old age'. Only a chronological description of the arrangements for the performance of these sermons can demonstrate how far the fame and political importance of Paul's Cross in the Elizabethan and early Stuart periods was a recent development, and how far its continuance was contingent on its convenience for the various authorities who shared responsibility for it. The Paul's Cross sermons were continued not out of habit or out of respect for custom, but because they were found to be useful. They served different, and not always complementary, functions for the church authorities, the City government, the citizens of London, and the visitors to the city; and those needs were not stable over the more than one hundred years between the Reformation and the Civil War. Proof that Paul's Cross was a functional part of London's religious, political, and cultural life, and not merely a sentimentally preserved relic of its past, is provided by the ease with which contemporaries allowed the pulpit to be demolished in the 1630s: once the sermons stopped serving the ecclesiastical, civil, and religious functions they had accrued in the previous decades, the pulpit was allowed to be torn down during the building work on the cathedral with not a single contemporary comment to tell us exactly when that happened. To describe Paul's Cross is to describe the history of its component parts (the pulpit cross, the cathedral churchyard) and the reasons the various parties involved (the authorities who exercised control over the choice of preachers, the preachers who spoke, and the audience who attended) had for investing in its continuance.

THE PULPIT CROSS AND ITS NEIGHBOURS

According to the best historian of Paul's Cross, William Sparrow Simpson, 'a pulpit cross, from which the Word of God might be preached to a congregation gathered in the open air, under the blue vault of heaven, was by no means an uncommon adjunct to a church' in the Middle Ages.[3] Sparrow Simpson also says that 'a full history of Paul's Cross would be a history of religion in England. Every great event, political and religious, whilst the Cross was standing, found here its eloquent defender or denouncer.'[4] Both statements are true: there was nothing unusual about a pulpit cross per se, but Paul's Cross became one of the most influential pulpits in England. It was second only to the court pulpits in its potential to influence ecclesiastical policy, and it surpassed the court pulpits in its capacity to reach a wide, non-elite audience. The reasons why this pulpit cross became so important lay in its situation and the growth of its immediate surroundings as the hub of early modern London's news-gathering networks.

The pulpit cross stood in 'the Cross Yard', the area to the north-east of Old St Paul's, between the choir and St Faith under St Paul's to the east and the northern

---

[3] W. Sparrow Simpson, *Chapters in the History of Old S. Paul's* (1881), p. 149.
[4] Sparrow Simpson, *Chapters*, p. 211.

transept of the cathedral.[5] Although this area was still used for burials (as late as 1581, the Privy Council wrote to the Dean and Chapter to force them to reform the 'overcommon burialles in Paules Church Yarde'),[6] it also acted as an essential link for the movement of news and people through the city. The cathedral, from the great west door to the great north door that opened onto the 'Cross Yard', formed a convenient shortcut between Ludgate Hill and Cheapside, and so the 'middle aisle' became famous for the collection of gossip in the city, as any reader of Renaissance city comedy knows.[7] 'Walking, jangling, brawling, fighting, bargaining &c, namely in sermons & service time' were the abuses that Bishop Pilkington blamed for the lightning strike of 1561 that destroyed the steeple.[8] The proclamation of 1561 for 'the reverend usage of all churches and churchyards' mentions St Paul's in particular and orders fines for those who 'walk up and down, or use any kind of disturbance, or spend the time in the same about any bargain, or other profane causes' during preaching or prayer 'within the said church of St. Paul's, or churchyard of the same'.[9] Servants seeking work gathered in the middle aisle, or 'Paul's Walk': Sir John Falstaff claims to have 'bought' Bardolph in St Paul's.[10] The '*si quis*' door, in the north aisle, had long been used as the place where clerics seeking work advertised their availability. According to John Earle, Paul's Walk also became 'the Market of young Lecturers, whom you may cheapen here at all rates and sizes'.[11] The cathedral precinct was also home to a commercial theatre company for much of the time between 1575 and 1606–8. Although the exact location of the theatre used by the Children of Paul's is uncertain, it was probably on the south side of the cathedral, opposite the

[5] For a detailed map of the position of Paul's Cross, see Peter W. M. Blayney, *The Bookshops in Paul's Cross Churchyard* (London: Bibliographical Society, 1990), Figs. 1, 10, 11. Figure 1 is reproduced in *A Short-title Catalogue of Books Printed in England, Scotland and Ireland, and of English Books Printed Abroad*, A. W. Pollard and G. R. Redgrave, 2nd edn. (London: Bibliographical Society, 1991) (*STC* [2]), vol. 3, facing p. 243.
[6] *Acts of the Privy Council, 1581–2*, p. 399.
[7] The third act of Ben Jonson's *Everyman Out of his Humour* is set in the middle aisle of St Paul's: *Ben Jonson*, eds C. H. Herford and Percy Simpson (Oxford: Clarendon Press, 1925–52), vol. 3. So too is the first scene of Thomas Middleton's *Michaelmas Terme*, ed. Theodore B. Leinwand, in *Thomas Middleton: The Complete Works*, gen. eds Gary Taylor and John Lavagnino (Oxford: Oxford University Press, 2007), I.1.137. Thomas Dekker offers mock advice to the London visitor about how to conduct himself in Paul's Walk: *The Guls Horne-booke* (1609), *STC* [2] 6500, sigs D[r]–D3[v].
[8] James Pilkington, *The True Report of the Burnyng of the Steple and Church of Poules in London* [1561], *STC* [2] 19930, sig. A8[r].
[9] *Documentary Annals of the Reformed Church of England*, ed. Edward Cardwell, 2 vols (Oxford, 1839), vol. 1, pp. 276–9, p. 277. The cathedral nave had been used for business dealings well before the Reformation. In particular, scriveners assigned themselves places in the nave from the early fourteenth century: Derek Keene, 'From Conquest to Capital: St Paul's, c. 1100–1300', in Derek Keene, Arthur Burns, and Andrew Saint (eds), *Saint Pauls: The Cathedral Church of London 604–2004* (New Haven: Yale University Press, 2004), pp. 17–32, pp. 27–8.
[10] William Shakespeare, *Henry IV, Part II*, ed. A. R. Humphreys, 2nd ser., (London: Routledge, for Arden, 1966). The editor quotes the proverb that one should not 'make choice of 3 things in 3 places, of a wife in Westminster, of a servant in Paules, of a horse in Smithfield'.
[11] John Earle, *Microcosmographie, Or A Piece of the World Discovered* (1628; 1633 edn.), *STC* [2] 7444, sig. L8[r].

Cross Yard.[12] If Paul's Cross was a natural extension of Paul's Walk, it is no wonder that the pulpit cross was used for publishing libels. In 1580, Thomas Millington, grocer, gave 'a libell to the preacher at Pawles Cross againste the Magistrates of this cittye', for which he was committed to Newgate. In 1607, a Catholic libel was 'cast in the Lord Mayor's pew at Paul's Cross . . . to feign her late Majesty to be in hell tormented by many devils, which caused his Majesty to waver in opinion, with other fictions not fit to be inserted', and in 1629 two libels were found at Paul's Cross, both addressed to the king, and complaining that he had lost the love of his subjects and would be dethroned by God.[13]

The idea of Paul's Cross as a semi-official medium of communication (Thomas Carlyle called it 'a kind of *Times Newspaper*' and H. Gareth Owen updated this to the 'Broadcasting House of Elizabethan England'[14]) is usually related to the use of the site for folkmotes in the twelfth century,[15] but these had ended long before the pulpit cross was erected.[16] Paul's Cross's importance to gossip and news-gathering networks was the result of its proximity to the home of early modern England's book trade. The north side of the Cross Yard backed onto the walls of the precinct and beyond it lay Paternoster Row. These two areas are best known as the home of London's stationers. Peter Blayney's work on the stationers' shops of Paul's Churchyard reveals how close the pulpit stood to the heart of London's print publishing industry. He writes:

There were bookshops in other parts of the precinct . . . But during the second half of the sixteenth century, Paul's Cross Churchyard became the unrivalled centre of retail booksell-ing in London, and consequently in England. Other than St Paul's School, the Sermon House, and the cathedral itself, by the time of the Civil War virtually every frontage in the Cross Yard either was, or had been, a bookshop.[17]

---

[12] Reavley Gair suggested that the theatre may have been in the undercroft of the Chapter House, which is also where the sermons were preached in bad weather before 1598. This seems unlikely. The more likely place is the Almonry, which ran along Paul's Alley adjacent to the Chapter House Cloister: Reavley Gair, *The Children of Paul's: The Story of a Theatre Company, 1553–1608* (Cambridge: Cambridge University Press, 1982), pp. 44–56; Roger Bowers, 'The Playhouse of the Choristers of Paul's, c. 1575–1608', *Theatre Notebook* 54 (2000), 70–85; Herbert Berry, 'Where Was the Playhouse in Which the Boy Choristers of St Paul's Cathedral Performed Plays?', *Medieval and Renaissance Drama in England* 13 (2001), 101–16, pp. 109–13.

[13] City of London, London Metropolitan Archive, Repertory of the Court of Aldermen (Rep.) 20, f. 104ᵛ; HMC, *Downshire*, vol. 2, p. 22; *CSPD, 1628–9*, pp. 550, 552.

[14] Thomas Carlyle described Paul's Cross as 'a kind of *Times Newspaper*, but edited partly by Heaven itself': *Cromwell's Letters and Speeches: vol. 1* in *Complete Works*, 30 vols (1870), vol. 14, pp. 65–6; H Gareth Owen, 'Paul's Cross: The Broadcasting House of Elizabethan London', *History Today*, 9 (1961), 836–42.

[15] Millar MacLure, *The Paul's Cross Sermons*, 5; G. H. Cook, *Old S Paul's Cathedral* (London, 1955) p. 68.

[16] Caroline M. Barron, *London in the Later Middle Ages: Government and People, 1200–1500* (Oxford: Oxford University Press, 2004), p. 23. As a result of the folkmote, however, the Cross Yard was the subject of jurisdictional disputes between the dean and chapter of the Cathedral and the London Corporation: see Peter W. M. Blayney, 'John Day and the Bookshop That Never War', in Lena Cowen Orlin (ed.), *Material London, ca. 1600* (Philadelphia: University of Pennsylvania Press, 2000), pp. 322–43, pp. 338–40.

[17] Blayney, *The Bookshops in Paul's Cross Churchyard*, p. 5.

We might even postulate an element of symbiosis in the relationship between the booksellers of Paul's Churchyard and the preachers who delivered sermons at the Cross. Printed sermons, along with other forms of religious writing, make up about half the press's output before 1660,[18] but sermons only became a really significant print genre in Elizabeth's reign; approximately 1,200 sermons in 513 sermon-books were printed.[19] It was the later years of Elizabeth's reign that saw the greatest expansion in the publication of sermons, and for the years 1583 to 1640, Peter Blayney has calculated that at least 1,328 sermon-books (1,851 including second and subsequent editions) were printed.[20] Paul's Cross contributed a significant number to the tally of printed sermon-books in the decades before the Civil War: to date, 202 sermons-books printed between 1580 and 1640 containing one or more Paul's Cross sermons have been identified.

Paul's Cross was also well positioned for the oral media of communication still so important in early modern England. The area around the pulpit cross was one of the very few large, open spaces in a very overcrowded city, and so it was an ideal site for the publication of proclamations: in 1562, Elizabeth's recovery from illness was ordered by the Council to be 'published to morrow at Poules Crosse' and news of the defeat of the Armada was proclaimed by Alexander Nowell, Dean of St Paul's, on 20 August 1588, the first public notice of the defeat.[21] James I's accession also seems to have been proclaimed from Paul's Cross. In his Accession Day sermon of 1617, John Donne reminded his hearers of their fears on the death of Elizabeth; Paul's Cross was then '*the Sanctuary* whither we all resorted this day, to receive the assurance of our safety, in the proclamation of his undoubted title to his Kingdom'.[22] At some stage, probably during Laud's primacy, this use of the pulpit for what were essentially secular purposes declined. On 5 December 1630, the peace with Spain was proclaimed 'neere Paules Crosse', but not it seems from the pulpit itself.[23]

Such proclamations were sufficiently common for an assumption to develop that Paul's Cross would be the platform from which political announcements related to religion would be first made. The letter-writer John Chamberlain reports the various expectations of what Bishop John King would say in the 1620 sermon that James I attended. (Many thought it would be about the 'Spanish Match', but Chamberlain guessed rightly that it would be about the rebuilding of St Paul's.)

---

[18] Patrick Collinson, Arnold Hunt, and Alexandra Walsham, 'Religion Publishing in England, 1557–1640', in John Barnard, D. F. McKenzie with Maureen Bell eds, *The Cambridge History of the Book in Britain*, vol. 4: *1557–1695* (Cambridge: Cambridge University Press, 2002), pp. 29–66, esp. 29.

[19] Alan Fager Herr, *The Elizabethan Sermon: A Survey and a Bibliography* (Philadelphia: University of Pennsylvania Press, 1940), p. 117. This figure includes reprints before 1610.

[20] Peter W. M. Blayney, 'The Alleged Popularity of Playbooks', *Shakespeare Quarterly*, 56(1) (2005) 33–50, esp. pp. 43–4, appendix.

[21] 'Order for a Form of Prayer of Thanksgiving for the Queen's Recovery, 1562', in *Documentary Annals of the Reformed Church of England*, ed. Edward Cardwell, vol. 1, pp. 281–2. John Stow, *Annales, or A General Chronicle of England. Begun by John Stow, continued. by Edward Howes, Gent.* (1631 [1632]), *STC²* 23340, p. 750.

[22] *The Sermons of John Donne*, ed. G. R. Potter and E. M. Simpson, 10 vols (Berkeley: University of California Press, 1953–62), vol. 1, p. 219.

[23] Stow, *Annales* (1631[1632]), *STC²* 23340, p. 1046.

When reporting the news that Prince Charles and the Duke of Buckingham were travelling to Madrid in February 1623, Chamberlain wrote that he planned to go to Paul's Cross: the Privy Council were to be there and 'yt may be the preacher hath order to say somwhat in this busines'.[24] At times, the pulpit might also become available to those with political messages that were unwelcome to the royal government, something explored in greater detail in Chapter 3.

There were many subjects that were neither purely political nor religious, and for these Paul's Cross proved an invaluable means for the authorities to communicate with ordinary residents of London. In 1547, the Corporation decided that the preacher at Paul's Cross should be 'made pryvie before his sermon to the boke devysed by this courte for the declaracon of the Cyties diligence for the comforthe of the pore at Saynt Barthilmewes Spyttell to the intent that he maye there manyfeste the same at the crosse to the hole congregacon'.[25] Although public gatherings of all kinds were cancelled during outbreaks of the plague,[26] the Corporation and Privy Council appear to have found that the usefulness of Paul's Cross outweighed the danger, at least during less serious outbreaks. The national and civic government's priorities are clear from the following letter from the Privy Council of 1592 advising the cancellation of the lord mayor's feast:

You shall do well to cause the preacher at Paules Crosse on Sonday nexte before the feaste to notefye to the people the reasons why those feastes are for this tyme forborne, and to let them understande of your meaninge not to omitt the same for sparinge of chardge, but by reason of the infection and inconvenyence that maie come by drawinge of assemblie of people togeather, and to converte the same or some good porcion thereof to a use more acceptable to God and for the good of the cittie.[27]

It is not unknown for printed sermons to refer to the plague being present in the city, and others refer to it having abated recently—something that must have played a part in the popularity of 'Jeremiads' with preachers and hearers.[28]

The disadvantage of a pulpit standing in one of the city's few open spaces was that it became an ideal place for a disorderly crowd to gather. The entrances into the cathedral precinct were gated, and had been since the thirteenth century.[29] This

---

[24] *The Letters of John Chamberlain*, ed. Norman Egbert McClure, 2 vols (Philadelphia: American Philosophical Society, 1939), vol. 2, pp. 297, 480–1.

[25] City of London, London Metropolitan Archive, Letter Book Q, f. 214ʳ. The entry is dated 25 September.

[26] Paul Slack, *The Impact of Plague in Tudor and Stuart England* (Oxford: Clarendon Press, 1985), 228–37.

[27] *APC*, 1592, p. 232.

[28] The plague is said to be currently in the city in Thomas White, *A Sermo[n] preached at Pawles Crosse on the Sunday the Thirde of November 1577 in the Time of the Plague* (1578), *STC²* 25406; Christopher Hooke, *A Sermon Preached in Paules Church in London* ([1603]), *STC²* 13703, sig. A4ʳ; Richard Stock, *A Sermon Preached at Paules Crosse, the Second of November 1606* (1609), *STC²* 23276, p. 10; John Jones, *Londons Looking Backe to Jerusalem* (1633), *STC²* 14722, p. 42. (Jones' sermon was preached in 1630.) Anthony Fawkner, *Comfort to the Afflicted* (1626), *STC²* 10718, and Thomas Fuller, *A Sermon Intended for Paul's Cross* (1626), *STC²* 11467, refer to the severe outbreak of 1625/6 as having abated recently.

[29] William Dugdale notes that in the thirteenth year of Edward I's reign, permission was given for the churchyard to be enclosed and the gates closed every night: *The History of St Pauls Cathedral in*

made the crowd gathered at Paul's Cross easier to control. In one of the worst incidents of riot at Paul's Cross, on 13 August 1553, Dr Gilbert Bourne, Mary's chaplain, was attacked by the crowd, who were 'showtyng at hys sermon, as yt [were] lyke madpepull'. Bourne was pulled out of the pulpit and nearly struck by a dagger. The next week, Dr Thomas Watson, chaplain to the bishop of Winchester, preached in what was clearly intended to be a show of strength by the government. Members of the Privy Council were there along with the lord mayor and alderman and the city's guilds sitting in order. A troop of two hundred men accompanied the preacher to the pulpit and stood around it all through the sermon.[30] Although such incidents were rare, the possibility of disorder beginning at the Cross was one that Elizabeth's government took seriously. The Earl of Essex and his supporters timed their ride into London to coincide with the end of the sermon at Paul's Cross, where a crowd would be already gathered.[31] On 16 February 1601, a week after the Earl of Essex's rebellion, the Privy Council were informed that six hundred soldiers had been stationed in St Paul's Churchyard, probably beside the pulpit cross, as one of two 'places of assembly' from which the City authorities could 'make head to any sudden commotion'.[32] After 1634, the sermons were no longer preached in the Cross Yard because of the building work on the cathedral,[33] so the most politically volatile events, sermons preached on the Accession Days of 1640 and 1642, were preached in the confined space of the cathedral choir.

The other use of the precinct's gates was more benign. Collections for charitable causes were common, particularly but not exclusively after the Easter Passion and Rehearsal sermons (as well as after the Spital sermons).[34] In 1538, when a collection

---

London, from its Foundation until these times (1658), Wing D 2482, p. 17. For the background on this, see Caroline M. Barron, 'London and St Paul's Cathedral in the Later Middle Ages', in Janet Backhouse (ed.), *The Medieval English Cathedral: Papers in Honour of Pamela Tudor-Craig* (Donington: Shaun Tyas, 2003), pp. 126–49, pp. 129–30.

[30] *The Diary of Henry Machyn, Citizen and Merchant-taylor of London, from A.D. 1550 to A.D. 1563*, ed. John Gough Nichols (1848), 41; *Chronicle of the Grey Friars of London*, ed. John Gough Nichols (1852), p. 83. See also Millar MacLure, *Register of Sermons Preached at Paul's Cross, 1534–1642*, rev. Peter Pauls and J. C. Boswell (Ottawa: Dovehouse, 1989), pp. 34–5. An unsympathetic account of Watson's sermon (the writer finding it 'neither eloquent nor edifieng') is found in British Library MS Harleian 353, ff. 141ʳ⁻ᵛ.

[31] Arnold Hunt, 'The Religious Context of the Essex Revolt', in Lori Anne Ferrell and Peter McCullough (eds), *The English Sermon Revised: Religion, Literature and History, 1600–1750* (Manchester: Manchester University Press, 2000), pp. 86–114, p. 96.

[32] HMC, *Salisbury*, vol. 11, p. 59. The day before, Bancroft reports that there were plans for 500 armed men 'all the day in St Paul's churchyard, where the preaching place is' (HMC, *Salisbury*, vol. 11, p. 59).

[33] Dugdale, *History of St Pauls Cathedral*, p. 159. Dugdale's statements about the end of Paul's Cross are inaccurate and misleading: see below.

[34] Most of the references found to charitable collections relate to the Easter sermons, but in 1596, the Corporation ordered a weekly collection 'at every sermon hereafter at Paules Crosse during the pleasure of this courte': LMA, Rep. 23, f. 563ᵛ. This was in response to a Privy Council 'motion' for such a collection. Privy Council requests were quite frequent in Elizabeth's reign, but are much rarer thereafter: this may reflect the custom becoming sufficiently established that prompts from the Privy Council were unnecessary. The Privy Council usually wrote to the bishop of London (to remind the preacher to mention the collection) and to the lord mayor (to arrange for the collection to be made). Most are for collections to redeem those captured by the Turks, or to repay those who redeemed captives: *APC, 1581–2*, p. 375; *APC, 1590*, p. 225; *APC, 1591*, p. 281; *APC, 1592–3*, p. 207; *APC,*

for charitable causes was taken up at the sermon, 'two persons' were placed 'at everie dore' to 'gather up the devotions of the people'. In 1590, when the Privy Council ordered a collection to be made at Paul's Cross for the redemption of Turkish prisoners, they suggested that 'either at the dores of the Churchyard where the people usually goe forth a collection to be made, or otherwise as they sit'.[35]

The pulpit itself was no mere relic, timeless and unchanging. The first cross, erected before 1241, was being used as a pulpit by at least 1387,[36] by which time the churchyard on this side of the cathedral became known as the 'Cross Yard'. In 1449, that cross was replaced with the pulpit known to Elizabethan and early Stuart Londoners; Bishop Thomas Kempe of London, who paid for the work, had his coat of arms placed on the 'leaded cover'.[37] When the foundations were discovered in 1878, they suggested a substantial building made up of a pulpit with an unroofed ambulatory around it, in all forming an octagon about thirty-seven feet in diameter. The pulpit itself was a wooden structure, roofed, but with open sides, in all seventeen feet across.[38] Our most detailed image of Paul's Cross comes from John Gipkyn's diptych, commissioned by Henry Farley in 1616 and now in the possession of the Society of Antiquaries. These pictures are inaccurate in many particulars, especially regarding the architecture of the cathedral, but they do represent the pulpit and its immediate surrounds quite faithfully (Figure 1).[39] For example, they show the space immediately surrounding the pulpit as it was in the mid-Jacobean period. That space had been quite open in the sixteenth century: in 1599, the German visitor Thomas Platter said, 'the congregation mostly sits or stands beneath an open sky, coming and going at will.'[40] In 1595, a low wall was built around a section of the ambulatory, so that the pulpit was 'partly inclosed with a wall of bricke' when the Cross was 'new repayred [and] painted'.[41] This wall seems to have been extended so as to encompass the pulpit in 1608, when a man called John Hurlebutt, haberdasher and citizen, was granted a lease for the 'keepinge of the preachinge place . . . and the roomes about the same preachinge place latelie by the said John Hurlebutt inclosed with bricke & timber, upon the stayres

---

1597–8, p. 408; *APC, 1599–1600*, p. 157; *APC, 1600—1*, p. 270. In November 1586, the Privy Council requested a collection to relieve soldiers who had fought in the Low Countries: *APC, 1586–7*, p. 253; in April 1596, the Corporation ordered a collection at the Easter sermons for 'the relief of the moste pore and needieste persons as want succour and reliefe within the severall wardes of this cittie': LMA, Rep. 23, f. 520ᵛ. The collections yielded around £70. For this sum in the context of Londoner's other charitable giving, see Ian Archer, 'The Charity of Early Modern Londoners', *Transactions of the Royal Historical Society* 12 (2002), 223–44, p. 241.

[35] *APC, 1590*, p. 225. The collections were handed to, and disbursed by, the Chamberlain of the City.
[36] Barron, 'London and St Paul's Cathedral in the Later Middle Ages', p. 140. On the Medieval history of Paul's Cross, see also Sparrow Simpson, *Chapters in the History of Old S. Paul's*, Ch. 9.
[37] Dugdale, *History of St Pauls Cathedral*, p. 128.
[38] F. C. Penrose, 'On the Recent Discoveries of Portions of Old St Paul's Cathedral', *Archaelogia*, 47 (1883), 381–92, p. 385.
[39] Pamela Tudor-Craig and Christopher Whittick, *'Old St Paul's': The Society of Antiquaries' Diptych, 1616* (London: London Topographical Society, 2004), colour plates II and III, p. 27.
[40] *Thomas Platter's Travels in England, 1599*, trans. and intro. Clare Williams (London: Jonathan Cape, 1937), p. 177.
[41] Stow, *Annales* (1631[1632]), *STC²* 22340, p. 770.

Figure 1 **John Gipkyn, 'Old St Paul's' diptych (1616), left-hand inner panel.**

leadinge to the said Preachinge Place'. Hurlebutt's wall in effect turned the ambulatory around the pulpit into an enclosed space, or 'room' in which people might sit for the sermon, and this is clearly visible in the Society of Antiquaries' diptych. Hurlebutt was given the right to charge for entrance into this space. The condition of the lease was that he 'receive & take noe extraordinarie Fees or exactions but onely such Fees as are and shalbe due and by use and ancient Custome shall and may be warranted or avouched without any further exaction in that behalf'.[42] Paul's Cross was a far more confined and orderly space, therefore, by the early Jacobean period.

Preaching at the Cross was, nonetheless, an open-air event, with all the attendant problems. Although the acoustics in the churchyard may have been helped by the walls of the cathedral, preachers had difficulty being heard by an audience on three sides. John Whitgift gave Paul's Cross as an example of a pulpit where 'those behind, or on the sides, cannot so well hear as those that be before'.[43] This was to remain a problem throughout the time that the sermons were preached outside the cathedral: John Hales of Eton prefaced his Paul's Cross sermon with an elaborate apology for his inability to make himself heard by all his auditors: 'seen I may be of many, but to be heard with any latitude and compass, my natural imperfection doth quite cut off'.[44] John Chamberlain reported on 1 July 1622 that 'on the first Sonday of this terme the bishop of London preached at Paules Crosse, where there was a great assemblie but a small auditorie, for his voyce was so low that I thinke scant the third part was within hearing'.[45] The effort required of a preacher to make himself heard by the auditory was obviously considerable: in 1599, Thomas Platter, reports that the preacher 'always has a bottle of wine and some bread behind him near the pulpit, where at his request, he is refreshed with food and drink', because the size of the auditory meant 'the preacher must speak all the louder, so that all may hear and understand'.[46]

Rain also hindered preachers and auditors from time to time.[47] It has been thought that in cases of very bad weather the sermons were delivered in St Faith

---

[42] City of London, Guildhall Manuscript 25630, vol. 5 (Dean's Registers, 1604–14) ff. 170v–172r; I would like to thank Peter McCullough for this reference. The lease on this enclosed space was granted to Nicholas Wainewright, haberdasher, on 11 April 1634, by which time the churchyard was fenced in and the pulpit abandoned. He was to pay only 12d p.a. rent, so this must represent an investment by Wainewright on the assumption that the sermons would return to the churchyard: City of London, Guildhall Manuscript 25630, vol. 8 (Dean's Registers, 1631–42), ff. 302r–v.

[43] *The Works of John Whitgift*, ed. Rev. John Ayre, 3 vols (Cambridge, 1851–3), vol. 2, p. 463.

[44] John Hales, 'Choice sermons preach't on several eminent occasions', in *Golden Remains* (1659), Wing H267, p. 26.

[45] *Letters of John Chamberlain*, vol. 2, pp. 442–3. Montaigne's sermon argued for payment of the unpopular 'benevolence' and towards the rebuilding of St Paul's, both controversial and unpopular subjects. Even crowded indoor venues could make hearing difficult: John Manningham reports of a sermon he attended at the Temple (by Francis Marbury), in 1602, 'I may not write what he said, for I could not heare him; he pronounces in manner of a common discourse. We may streache our eares to catch a worde now and then, but he will not be at the paynes to strayne his voyce, that we might gaine one sentence': *The Diary of John Manningham of the Middle Temple, 1602–3*, ed. Robert Parker Sorlein (Hanover, NH: University Press of New England, 1976), p. 115.

[46] *Thomas Platter's Travels in England, 1599*, p. 177. The physical effort involved in preaching for two hours without amplification should not be forgotten: even from the relative comfort of an indoor pulpit. Richard Greenham is reported to have been 'so earnest, and took such extraordinary pains in his preaching, that his shirt would usually be as wet with sweating, as if it had been drenched in water': Samuel Clarke, *The Lives of Thirty-Two English Divines*, 3rd edn. (1677), Wing C4539, p. 12.

[47] Bodleian Library MS Tanner 50 is a manuscript of notes from sermons preached at Paul's Cross in 1565 and 1566. The writer appears to have taken notes as he listened to the sermon and later made a fair copy of these notes, because on f. 63v, he tells us 'the rayne combred me here, so that I could not wryt anythinge of his arguments'. He notes that on 17 March 1566, the sermon (by 'Mr Harres of New Colledge Oxford') took place 'in Poulls churche because of the foull wether': f. 29v.

under St Paul's, the parish church built under the cathedral choir and otherwise called 'St Faith in the Shrouds'. This may be a mistake: Strype records that 'in the foul and rainy weather, these solemn sermons were preached in a Place called '*The Shrowds*', and Margaret Cornford took this to mean St Faith in the Shrouds.[48] But the few title pages of printed sermons mentioning the 'shrouds' of the cathedral do not mention St Faith,[49] and St Faith occupied only one of the 'shrouds'. In his presentment to the 1598 episcopal visitation, the verger John Howe says that the 'Shrowdes and Cloysters under the convocation howse' were the place where 'not longe since the Sermons in foule weather were wont to be preached'.[50] The 'convocation house', or rather the chapter house where convocation met, was on the south-western side of the cathedral between the south transept and the nave; it had an undercroft accessible through the cathedral, and this was also referred to as 'the shrouds'.[51] This is undoubtedly where the sermons were preached in wet weather before 1598. Thereafter, the sermons were preached within the cathedral if they could not be preached in the churchyard. Sir Richard Paulet records hearing the Bishop of Bangor preach 'in Poules because the wether was to wett to be at the Cross' in March 1610. A printed sermon of 1618 was preached in the church because of the 'tempest'; John Donne's 1622 sermon on the Gunpowder Plot was 'intended for Paul's Cross, but by reason of the weather, was preached in the church'.[52] Given that the nave of the church was not used for religious services, it is most likely that the sermons were preached in the choir. This is significant because it helps to explain why the sermons were transferred to the choir of the cathedral when building work closed the outdoor pulpit in 1634 without any comments being made by the auditors.[53] Also important is the fact that the choir was a far

[48] John Strype, *A Survey of the Cities of London and Westminster . . . by John Stow . . . Now Lastly Corrected, Improved and very much Enlarged . . . by John Strype* (London, 1720), p. 149; Margaret E. Cornford, *Paul's Cross, A History* (London: SPCK, 1910), p. 11. On the parish church of St Faith under St Paul's or 'Saint Faith in the Shrouds', see Carol Davidson Cragoe, 'Fabric, Tombs and Precinct, 1087–1540', in Keene, Burns, and Saint (eds), *Saint Pauls*, pp. 127–42, pp. 131, 136.

[49] Few sermons were printed before alternative arrangements were made for preaching in wet weather, but those that do (Hugh Latimer's 'Sermon of the Plough' of 1548 and Thomas Lever's 1550 sermon) don't mention St Faith by name. Latimer's sermon is described as being delivered 'in the Shroudes at Poules Churche in London' and Lever's is said to have been preached 'in the shroudes': *27 Sermons preached by the Right Reverende . . . Hugh Latimer* (1562), *STC²* 15276, f. 13ʳ; Thomas Lever, *A Fruitfull Sermon made in Paules Church at London in the Shroudes* [1551], *STC²* 15543.

[50] City of London, Guildhall Manuscript 9537, vol. 9, 'The Answeres to all such Articles given to be enquired of in the first Visitation of the Reverend Father in God Richard, Lord Busshopp of London', ff. 42ᵛ–61ᵛ, f. 60ʳ. Substantial extracts from these presentments are printed in *Registrum Statutorum et Consuetudinum Ecclesiae Cathedralis Sancti Pauli Londiniensis*, ed. W. Sparrow Simpson (1873).

[51] Carol Davidson Cragoe, 'Fabric, Tombs and Precinct, 1087–1540', in Keene, Burns, and Saint (eds), *Saint Paul's*, pp. 131, 139, Fig. 68.

[52] Hampshire Record Office MS 44M/F2/15/2, transcription by Dr Eric Lindquist of MS 44M/69/F2/15/1, p. 15. I am grateful to Dr Lindquist for permission to use this transcription. Michael Wigmore, *The Way of All Flesh: A Sermon Prepared for Pauls Crosse, and Preached in the Church, by Reason of a Tempest, the 13. of December. Anno Dom. 1618* (1619), *STC²* 25618; *Sermons of John Donne*, ed. Potter and Simpson, vol. 4, p. 235. Thomas Fuller's *A Sermon Intended for Paul's Crosse, but Preached in the Church of St Paul's, London* (1626), *STC²* 11467, and Thomas Myriell's *The Christians Comfort* (1623), *STC²* 18321, were also appointed for Paul's Cross, but, for no specified reason were preached in the cathedral.

[53] Dugdale, *History of St Pauls Cathedral*, p. 134.

more confined space than the churchyard, and so the auditory would have been smaller in consequence: the preacher of a 1624 printed sermon remarked that the 'violence of a wet season' denied his sermon 'some Auditors, which it might have had'.[54] The move meant that the sermons were being performed, albeit occasionally, in a more easily controlled, and more definitely ecclesiastical space, even before the end of Elizabeth's reign.

The arrangements for seating the sermons' auditors also evolved in the sixteenth century. Before Hurlebutt's wall enclosed the pulpit, a seat on one of the 'forms' or benches laid out for the purpose could be had, probably for hire. These benches were presumably taken from inside the cathedral, but we do not know who was responsible for taking them out and returning them.[55] Members of the livery companies could make special arrangements for the days when they attended the sermons. In 1605, the Saddlers' Company recorded payment of 18d to 'a woman at Poles Crosse for setting out a forme for the Companye'.[56] When Hurlebutt's wall created a 'room' for auditors immediately beside the pulpit, seats there were rented out: in 1622, Simonds D'Ewes, anxious to hear John Donne's sermon on the *Directions for Preachers*, took particular care to arrive early and 'by great good fortune and little cost, stood close by him within the Crosse, and ther wrote as much as I desired'.[57] Other regular attendees might make their own arrangements: in 1629, a servant reported that he was regularly sent by his master to keep a place for him at Paul's Cross.[58] The demand for places does not seem to have abated over the Elizabethan and early Stuart periods, particularly for prestigious or newsworthy sermons; latecomers, even if they were gentlemen, might well find that there was standing room only. In 1611, William Devick went to hear Theophilus Higgons's recantation sermon (the subject of much gossip). 'I came too late', he reports, 'to have any place'.[59]

Arrangements for seating members of the government, both civic and national, also grew more elaborate over the Elizabethan period. Before 1483, the lord mayor and aldermen were protected from the weather only with a cloth or awning; in that year a gallery was built against the wall of the north choir aisle.[60] This too became insufficient, because in 1567, the Corporation ordered the chamberlain of the city

---

[54] Robert Bedingfield, *A Sermon Preached at Pauls Crosse the 24. of October. 1624* (Oxford, 1625), *STC²* 1792, sig. ¶2ᵛ.

[55] William Stepney's dialogue about attending a Paul's Cross sermon has one of the speakers say, 'Let us go, for it is time, or else we shall have no place, for all the formes will be taken up': *The Spanish Schoole-master. Containing Severall Dialogues, According to Every Day in the Weeke* (1591), *STC²* 23256, p. 126; Sparrow Simpson records that 'it is said that they [the congregation] paid a penny or a half penny a piece for the privilege of using these forms' (*Chapters in the History of Old S. Paul's*, p. 159). This seems likely given that there seems to have been a customary rate for space at the Paul's Cross sermons in 1608 when the pulpit was enclosed by Hurlebutt's wall.

[56] W. Sparrow Simpson, *Saint Paul's Cathedral and Old City Life* (1894), p. 91.

[57] *The Diary of Sir Simonds D'Ewes (1622–1624)*, ed. Elisabeth Bourcier (Paris, Didier, 1974), p. 97. Infuriatingly, D'Ewes goes on to say 'therfore I speake noe moore of it, having it in my booke at the end of Mr Jefferayes sermon', which notebook has not survived.

[58] *CSPD, 1628–9*, p. 552.

[59] HMC, *Downshire*, vol. 3, p. 31.

[60] Barron, 'London and St Paul's Cathedral in the Later Middle Ages', p. 140, n. 77.

to pay for the gutter to be diverted so that rainwater did not fall on them during the sermon and that the bench be 'enlarged as muche as yt convenyently may be so that they may quyetly syt duringe the tyme of the sermons there'.[61] In 1569, a far more substantial 'sermon house' was built, paid for by the lord mayor, so that the lady mayoress and the aldermen's wives could also be accommodated during the sermons. It required moving the pulpit one yard to the east to make extra room, as well as using the 'voyde roome next to the place' where the lord mayor and aldermen sat.[62]

The place where the lord mayor, aldermen, and their wives sat may have been one of two 'sermon houses' built against the cathedral wall, the other accommodating the 'Doctors of Law', that is, Doctors of Civil Law. In his visitation presentment of 1598, one of the cathedral vergers reported that in the past, two vergers had the 'keepinge of twoe places as the place where the Judges sitt to heare the sermons At Paules Crosse and the steeple'.[63] But the Corporation was also paying a 'poore man' to clean the sermon house where they sat, and these payments continued until the end of our period (they appear to have been paid, presumably out of benevolence, after the 'sermon house' was pulled down).[64] The vergers and the 'poor man' paid by the Corporation must have been cleaning different areas. The existence of two 'sermon houses' also explains an apparent anomaly in the records: on 9 April 1634, the Court of Aldermen gave order that the 'the Seates for the Lord Maior Aldermen and officers of this citty in Paules Church yard be removed and carried away in regard of the Masons workeing there for the repaire of the Church'. A year later, in June 1635, workmen were paid for 'carrying the lead timber etc that was pulld down of the roomes where the prebends of the church the doctors of law and the parishioners of St Faiths did sett to hear sermons at St Paul's Cross'.[65] It seems most likely that there were two 'sermon houses' pulled down at different times

---

[61] LMA, Letter Book V, f. 139[v]. The entry is dated 13 November 1567.

[62] LMA, Letter Book V, f. 224[r]. See also LMA Rep. 16, ff. 447[r], 448[r]. The initial order for the 'survey' was made on 17 February 1569, the order for the Chamberlain to begin the work on 1 March. The foundations of the pulpit were found to be only twelve feet from the foundations of the old cathedral, so that those sitting in the 'sermon house' built into the buttresses would have been much closer to the pulpit than the Society of Antiquaries' diptych would suggest: W. Sparrow Simpson, *Documents illustrating the History of S Paul's Cathedral* (1880), pp. xv–xvi.

[63] City of London, Guildhall Manuscript 9537, vol. 9, f. 52[r].

[64] *Chamber Accounts of the Sixteenth Century*, ed. Betty R. Masters (London Record Society, for the Corporation of London, 1984), p. 28 (for 1584–5), p. 80 (1585–6). City of London, London Metropolitan Archive, City Cash Book 1, ff. 52[r] (1632–3), f. 142[v] (1633–4), f. 235[r] (1634–5); City Cash Book 3, f. 47[r] (1639–40); City Cash Book 4, f. 44[v] (1640–1), f. 140[v] (1641–2), f. 215[r] (1642–3); City Cash Book 5, f. 53[r] (1643–4). The same entries record payments to the vergers of St Paul's for opening and closing St Dunstan's Chapel for the lord mayor and aldermen. The cleaning of the pulpit itself was done by the vergers of St Paul's, for which they received 12*d* a week after 1626, through the legacy of Thomas Chapman the younger: W. Sparrow Simpson, *Documents illustrating the History of St Paul's Cathedral*, pp. 140–1, See also *CSPD, 1635–6*, p. 66.

[65] LMA, Rep. 48, f. 270[v]; City of London, Guildhall Manuscript 25,473/2, f. 37[r]. John Gipkyn's diptych may not be accurate in its depiction of the sermon houses. For example, he extends the sermon houses to the end of the north choir aisle, and so does not show the door into St Faith under St Paul's, which lay in the middle of the north choir aisle. The door to St Faith is visible on Wenceslas Hollar's engraving of St Paul's from the North (Dugdale, *History of St Pauls Cathedral*; see also Tudor-Craig and Whittick, Fig. 12, p. 27) and in the small vignette of St Paul's and Paul's Cross in John Speed's *Theatre*

Figure 2 **John Gipkyn, 'Old St Paul's' diptych (1616), right-hand inner panel.**

of Great Britain (1611), *STC²* 23041, map of Middlesex (see also Tudor-Craig and Whittick, Fig. 13, p. 28). Speed's rather crude woodcut does show the 'sermon house' to be more like an assemblage of small buildings, with different sized windows, rather than a single building that Gipkyn showed. There is, nonetheless, some indication that there was more than one sermon house in Gipkyn's diptych: there are two different coloured backgrounds visible on the lower level (three bays red and two green).

Figure 3 Vignette of Saint Pauls included in the map of Middlesex, from John Speed, *The Theatre of Empire of Great Britain* (1611).

(Figures 2 and 3). This suggests that the buildings erected for the different parts of the Paul's Cross auditory were larger and more substantial than has been hitherto supposed. We can see, therefore, that throughout the Elizabethan and Jacobean periods the pulpit and the accommodation for the auditory were repeatedly renovated to become grander and more permanent, as well as more comfortable for the social elite and less accessible for others.

THE AUDIENCE

We know of some regular attendees at the Paul's Cross sermons, such as the London aldermen and liverymen. We know of occasional visitors, such as Simonds D'Ewes or John Chamberlain, who have been quoted earlier.[66] But we have no description of the social make-up of the whole audience at a Paul's Cross sermon on any particular occasion; nor have we any sources telling us explicitly about changes in the composition of the auditory over time. What follows, therefore, is an attempt to join up some rather distant dots in order to form a picture of who heard the sermons delivered from the pulpit cross.

The monarch was the least regular but most prestigious member of the auditory: Elizabeth, James I, and Charles I attended one sermon each at Paul's Cross during their reign (Elizabeth for the celebration of the defeat of the Armada in 1588, James to begin the campaign for rebuilding the cathedral in 1620, and Charles I both to celebrate the birth of Prince Charles and to re-start his father's rebuilding campaign in 1630). These visits will be dealt with in more detail in Chapter 5. The royal government was more often represented by members of the Privy Council, although it is unclear whether attendance was regular or confined to occasions when it might be useful as a means of emphasizing the royal government's support for the religious or civic authorities. The growing importance of Accession Day sermons at Paul's Cross in James I's reign meant that this became an occasion on which attendance by at least some members of the Privy Council was expected. John Donne's 1617 Accession Day sermon was delivered before 'the Lords of the Council, and other Honorable Persons'.[67] In 1619, John Chamberlain reports that 'all the counsaile about this towne were at a poore sermon at Paules Crosse' for the Accession Day. In 1623, however, only seven Privy Councillors were there. 'They made but a poore shew', he said, 'seven or eight at most, among whom the Lord President was the prime man, none of the Grandes (as the Lord Archbishop, Lord Keper, Lord Treasurer, Lord Marshall) affoording their

---

[66] Chamberlain's reports of Paul's Cross sermons are almost certainly first hand. On 18 February 1613, he writes to Dudley Carlton that 'on Sonday I was fetcht from Powles (where I was set at the sermon) to see the bride [Princess Elizabeth] go to church: *Letters of John Chamberlain,* vol. 1, p. 423.
[67] *Sermons of John Donne,* ed. Potter and Simpson, vol. 1, p. 183.

presence'.[68] We know of few Accession Day sermons from the reign of Charles I, and have no evidence that members of the Privy Council continued to attend the sermons at the Cross.

Commentators also noted occasions when the presence of the Privy Council was particularly strong or evidently political. On Whitsunday 1559 (14 May), Edmund Grindal, soon to replace Edmund Bonner as bishop of London, proclaimed from Paul's Cross the restoration of 'King Edward's service book'. According to one observer, 'the Lord Keeper and the whole council' were there, perhaps partly to compensate for the fact that 'never a bishop or Canon of St Paul's was present'. The diarist Henry Machyn offers a more detailed list: 'the quens consell, the duke of Norfoke, my lord keper of the seylle, and my lord of Arundell, my lord treysorer, my lord marques of Northamton, my lord admerall, my lord of Sussex, my lord of Westmorland, my lord of Rutland, and mony mo lords and knyghtes, my lord mare and the althermen'.[69] Chamberlain also tells us that 'most of the counsaile' were at Paul's Cross on 11 April 1619 to attend John King's sermon of thanksgiving on the King's recovery from illness, along with the lord mayor and aldermen, the guildsmen, and several bishops.[70]

Other senior courtiers might attend a sermon at Paul's Cross for similarly political motives. Dr Watson's sermon on 20 August 1553 (the week after the attack on Dr Gilbert Bourne) was heard by 'the marques of Winchester the Earle of Bedforde the Earle of Pembroke the Lord Wentworthe the Lord Riche', as well as the lord mayor and aldermen and Edmund Bonner, Bishop of London, along with at least '120 of the garde . . . with their holberde'.[71] In August 1599, John Chamberlain reports that 'the Lord Generall with all the great officers of the field came in great bravery to Powles Crosse', no doubt to quell anxiety caused by the false alarm that the Spanish were at Brest, the rumours of which were then 'hottest'.[72] Courtiers might also have attended out of curiosity, as when Theophilus Higgons, a clergyman who had converted to Catholicism and become a Jesuit, recanted this conversion at Paul's Cross. The sermon, which took four hours to deliver, was a talking-point in London. Sir William Browne reported that the audience was the largest ever seen at Paul's Cross, and included lords of the Privy Council and several bishops.[73] Even if the Privy Council rarely attended formally as a body, senior courtiers were sufficiently regular to be included in the vignette on the Paul's Cross sermons found in Claudius Hollybrand's *The French Schoolemaster* (1573). In the dialogue for Sunday, one speaker says to the other, 'what Lord is that which is above in the gallery? doe you not know him?', and the reply is, 'It is my Lord of N. and

---

[68] There may have been particularly strong representation by the Council in that year, because the sermon was preached during the 'Long Progress' by the King to Scotland; *Letters of John Chamberlain*, vol. 2, pp. 225, 487.

[69] *CSP Foreign*, vol. 1, p. 287, 28 May 1559. *Diary of Henry Machyn*, p. 197. Machyn misdates the sermon to 15 May.

[70] *Letters of John Chamberlain*, vol. 2, pp. 227, 229.

[71] British Library MS Harl. MS 353, f. 141ʳ.

[72] *Letters of John Chamberlain*, vol. 1, p. 83.

[73] HMC, *Downshire*, vol. 3, p. 33.

that Lady which sitteth by him is my Lady the Admirall, the Dutchesse of N. the Countess of N, the Marquesse of N. My Lady Treasurer'.[74] The greater number of sermons preached at Court in the reign of James may have lessened courtiers' visits to Paul's Cross (Sir Francis Bacon said it prevented the Privy Council's attendance at the Spital sermons),[75] but there is no indication that they stopped going altogether.

Like the Privy Councillors, the presence of the bishop of London was notable enough to be mentioned by diarists and letter writers when he attended on important occasions. His presence was also common enough to be included as a feature of the sermons mentioned in the dialogue on Paul's Cross in William Stepney, *The Spanish Schoolemaster* (1591). The speaker asks 'what Doctor is he that sitteth at the high window?', and is told, 'he is the bishop of London, and the other that sitteth with him is the Deane of S. Pauls.'[76] There does not seem to have been an expectation that the bishop attend every week: several complaints made to the bishop against Paul's Cross preachers make clear that the bishop was not there in person. Many Elizabethan and early Stuart bishops of London were also court preachers and had obligations to fulfil there. Some attended Paul's Cross as preachers, rather than auditors, as we shall see. Similarly, Elizabethan and early Stuart deans of St Paul's were occasional, but not infrequent, preachers at Paul's Cross. Members of the cathedral chapter were notably absent at the start of Elizabeth's reign because of lingering opposition to the doctrine preached there: the cathedral was slow to accept changes to the liturgy in the reign of Edward VI, swift to restore Catholic practice under Mary, and slow again to abandon it in 1558–9.[77] From at least 1562, the minor canons and vicars choral were required to attend Paul's Cross sermons, but this was an obligation placed on them by the bishop of London, not the cathedral statutes.[78] We do not know how long this practice continued: attendance at Paul's Cross in particular is not mentioned in later visitation articles (attendance at the divinity lectures and sermons in the cathedral is), which may reflect the expansion of sermon provision within the cathedral.

Other members of the national elite attended sermons at Paul's Cross on an irregular basis. Members of Parliament sometimes heard sermons there: in a sermon of 10 May 1579, John Stockwood appealed to MPs present to use the parliament then sitting to make greater provision for preaching in England. The printed

---

[74] Claudius Hollybrand, *The French Schoolemaster* (1573; 1649 ed.), Wing S293B, f. 47ᵛ.

[75] *The Letters and Life of Francis Bacon*, ed. James Spedding, 7 vols (London: Longman, 1862–74), vol. 6, p. 167. Bacon may be inventing a tradition here: the Privy Council did attend the Spital sermons in 1617, on Bacon's prompting, probably because of the King's absence in Scotland. Anthony Munday notes their presence there and says 'in my remembrance, nor else (in my reading) I finde not the like' (*The Survey of London . . . Inlarged by the Care and Diligence of A.M. . . . Finished by the Study and Labour of A.M H.D and others* (1633), *STC²* 23345, p. 177.

[76] William Stepney, *The Spanish Schoolemaster* (1591), *STC²* 23256, p. 126.

[77] Susan Bridgen, *London and the Reformation* (Oxford: Clarendon Press, 1989), pp. 447, 436; David J. Crankshaw, 'Community, City and Nation, 1540–1714', in Keene, Burns, and Saint (eds), *Saint Paul's*, pp. 45–70, p. 50.

[78] 'Grindal's Regulations for S. Paul's Cathedral, 1562', in Walter Howard Frere (ed.), *Visitation Articles and Injunctions of the Period of the Reformation*, 3 vols (London: Longmans, 1910), vol. 3, p. 116.

version of Daniel Featley's *The Angel of Thyatira Indited* has a marginal note saying that MPs were present at the sermon: the appeal for strong action against Roman Catholics was no doubted targeted at them.[79] In 1627, the Reader of Middle Temple was ordered to 'repair to the sermon at St Paul's Cross, wearing his cap in such decent and orderly manner as anciently hath been used' on the Sunday before he began his reading.[80] Ordinary members of the Inns and students like Simonds D'Ewes and John Manningham were also occasional members of the auditory at Paul's Cross: Thomas Gataker writes with pride that in his time as lecturer at Lincoln's Inn, few members went to hear other preachers, although 'some few would now and then step to *Paul's Cross*'.[81]

In marked contrast to the irregular attendance of Privy Councillors, bishops, deans, and lawyers, the lord mayor and aldermen of London are referred to as attending the sermons weekly, and so they are without doubt the most visible and consistent members of the auditory at Paul's Cross. Regular attendance by the members of the Corporation dates back to the 1420s, and the sermons, along with services in the cathedral, had been a part of the Corporation's formal observance of feast days since before the Reformation. Thereafter, Paul's Cross gained importance at the expense of the cathedral, as some older customs that took place there were abandoned and replaced with sermons. For example, before the Reformation, the high point of the Corporation's attendance at the cathedral had been the three processions, on the Monday, Tuesday, and Wednesday after Whitsunday, each taking slightly different routes, involving different followers, but all ending at St Paul's where the procession was censed (by a clerk or chorister dressed as an angel) and the *veni Creator* was performed by the choir and organ. In April 1548, this practice was replaced with 'three solemn sermons'.[82] It was curtailed again in 1552, when the holiday was shortened to include only the Monday and Tuesday. But the two sermons were duly preached, and the venue for this new custom was Paul's Cross.[83] The ceremonial importance of the event is clear from the arrangements made for the lord mayor and aldermen's attendance. In 1564, the Court of Aldermen ruled that 'as meny of my masters thaldermen for the tyme beinge as convenyentlye maybe shall there attende upon the Lorde

---

[79] John Stockwood, *A Very Fruiteful Sermon Preched at Paules Crosse* (1579), *STC²* 23285, pp. 8–10; Daniel Featley, *Clavis Mystica* (1636), *STC²* 10730, p. 473.

[80] *Minutes of the Parliament of the Middle Temple*, ed. C. T. Martin, in C. H. Hopwood (ed.), *Middle Temple Records*, 2 vols (London, 1904), vol. 2, p. 986. This appears in a series of 'Orders to be observed in the Houses of Court' for Hilary Term, 1627, and is the only mention of Paul's Cross in the *Middle Temple Records*. 'Anciently' may be meant here in the sense of 'formerly', and so it is unclear how old the custom was. Roger Ley's 'Gesta Britannica', written in the 1660s, says that the judges attended sermons at Paul's Cross, but it is not clear how accurate this is and for how much of the pre-Civil War period (British Library MS Stow 76, f. 228ᵛ).

[81] Thomas Gataker, *A Discours Apologetical* (1654), Wing G319, p. 43.

[82] Barron, 'London and St Paul's Cathedral in the Later Middle Ages', pp. 142–3; LMA, Letter Book Q, f. 94ᵛ.

[83] The *Greyfriars' Chronicle* reports among other unwelcome changes in 1552 'at Wytsontyde was but ii sermons; they ware lyke-wyse at the crosse, and he that prechyd the sonday [Nicholas Ridley, Bishop of London] prechyd the ii other, and but ii dayes kept holy days' (*Chronicle of the Grey Friars of London*, p. 74).

Mayre of the cytye,'[84] and in 1569, the aldermen were ordered to attend in their scarlet liveries for Whitsunday and Monday and in violet on the Tuesday, and their wives were also to attend.[85] The fate of the old processions through the city is unclear,[86] but the changes wrought by the Reformation to the Whit-tide holidays had strengthened the role of Paul's Cross in the Corporation's religious observances.

Indeed, arrangements for the lord mayor and aldermen's attendance at the Paul's Cross sermons became increasingly elaborate from Elizabeth's to James's reign. Before the Reformation, the custom had been for the Corporation to gather first in the chapel of St Dunstan's, which they used as a kind of robing room.[87] From about 1600, they seem to have adopted the practice of hearing prayers in the choir before leaving the cathedral for the 'sermon house' in the churchyard.[88] This meant that the Corporation sat in the choir of the cathedral every Sunday, and appropriate arrangements developed to accommodate them. In February 1607, the Corporation ordered an annuity of twenty shillings to be paid to the vergers of St Paul's:

> in regard they shall everye Sabaoth and usuall festivall day hereafter as the L Maior and Aldermen shall repayr thither to here devyne service or sermons keepe or cause to be kept the usuall places within the Quire for his lordships, thaldermen, and principall officers of this Cittye that shall attend uppon his Lordship, and not to suffer anye others to sitt or bee placed therein.[89]

In 1613 the Corporation were given designated seating in the choir; this appears to have been part of an attempt by Dean Overall to use the civic ritual growing up around the Paul's Cross sermons to strengthen the Corporation's weak links with the liturgical life of the cathedral itself.[90] The City's sword was carried before the

---

[84]   LMA, Rep. 15, f. 328ʳ.

[85]   LMA, Letter Book V, f. 236ʳ.

[86]   *The Ordre of my Lord Maior, the Aldermen, and the Sheriffs, For Their Meetings and Wearing of their Apparell Throughout the Whole Year* (1621), *STC*² 16728, simply says that for Whitmonday and Tuesday 'the Lord Mayor and Aldermen must meete with my L. at Pauls in their Scarlet Gownes without clokes, to heare the sermon', pp. 22–3.

[87]   LMA, Letter Book Q, f. 214ʳ; Guildhall Manuscript 9537, vol. 9, f. 47ʳ. St Dunstan's chapel lay behind the choir, at the south corner of the east end of the church, according to Wenceslas Hollar's plan, published in Dugdale's *History of St Pauls Cathedral*.

[88]   LMA, Rep. 31, part I, f. 38ʳ. The entry for 26 January 1613 summarizes a letter to the Corporation that probably came from Dean Overall. It says that it is 'not above twelve or fourteene yeares sythence they [the lord mayor and aldermen] usually came to prayers in the quire' before attending the sermons at Paul's Cross 'which course this court thinck fitt to be continued'. This was also the pattern of events on James I's visit in 1620, unlike Elizabeth's, so it appears to have become the custom by then.

[89]   LMA, Rep. 27, f. 335ᵛ.

[90]   LMA, Rep. 31 part I, f. 38ʳ (26 January 1613), notes that the court had been informed that the 'long pillows which are usually sett before the lord mayor and aldermen in the quire at Powles are very much rent and decayed', that they were paid for by the chapter and belonged to the church. The Dean of Paul's, the only probable source of this 'information' also asks the committee to 'bestowe a faire cloth to be hanged before the high alter'. A committee is set up to arrange for new 'pillowes of velvet' with the city's arms embroidered on them, to pay for the lord mayor's seat in the choir to be 'raised and made more gracefull and comely', and to consider the cost of the new altar cloth that the Dean requested. On 25 February, the Court agreed to the paying for a new altar cloth: LMA, Rep. 31, part 1, f. 52ʳ. The City Cash Books record payment to the vergers for setting out the cushions used by the Corporation and for replacing them in the cupboard in St Dunstan's chapel. The order authorizing these payments is from October 1613: City Cash Book 1, f. 230ʳ; City Cash Book 2, ff. 40ᵛ, 130ʳ, 205ʳ; City Cash

lord mayor in the churchyard, cathedral nave, and choir, something that brought the Corporation into conflict with the Laudian Church authorities in 1633.[91] By the mid-Jacobean period, Paul's Cross had become so much the focus for the religious element of civic ritual that in May 1619, when the principal officers of the city were belated given mourning cloth after the death of Queen Anne, they wore it to a sermon at Paul's Cross, to which they processed in a more public way than usual. The aldermen, recorder, and other officers were ordered to meet in the Guildhall chapel by seven in the morning, where they heard prayers, and then 'in comelye and decent order in their mourninge garments' went to the sermon at Paul's Cross, the pulpit being hung with black for the occasion.[92]

Paul's Cross was also central to the Corporation's religious observances on the most important feast in the Church calendar: the Easter Spital sermons. The prestige of this series is unmistakeable from Stow's description of it in the *Survey of London*. He writes that 'time out of minde, it hath beene a laudable custome' to have 'some especial learned man' preach the Passion sermon on Good Friday at Paul's Cross, and 'the like learned men' were to preach the three sermons at St Mary's Spital on the Monday, Tuesday and Wednesday after Easter Sunday, and finally for 'one other learned man at *Paules* Crosse, to make rehearsall of those foure former Sermons, either commending or reproving them, as to him by judgment of the learned divines was thought convenient. And that done, he was to make a sermon of his owne studie, which in all were five sermons in one'.[93]

These were the most prestigious sermons in the year, with the two Paul's Cross events in particular being an opportunity for virtuosic displays by the preacher. The timing of the 'Passion sermon' (at the liturgically significant hour of one o'clock, unlike the weekly sermons that took place at 10 a.m.) suggests that it was also functioning as a replacement for traditional Good Friday devotions like 'Creeping to the Cross'.[94] The sermons had no less civic pageantry than was used at

---

Book 3, ff. 42ᵛ, 135ʳ; City Cash Book 4, ff. 39ᵛ, 135ʳ, 211ʳ; City Cash Book 5, ff. 47ʳ, 148ʳ, 253ᵛ. John Donne alludes to this in his 1626 funeral sermon for Sir William Cokayne, preached in the cathedral on 12 December. He says that those 'who have now the administration of this Quire' (i.e. the residentiary canons) are glad 'that our Predecessors, but a very few yeares before our time . . . admitted these Honourable and worshipfull Persons of this City, to sit in this Quire, so, as they do upon Sundayes' (*Sermons of John Donne*, eds. Potter and Simpson, vol. 7, p. 275). I would like to thank Peter McCullough for alerting me to this reference.

[91] City of London, London Metropolitan Archive, Corporation of London Remembrancia, vol. 7, ff. 128ʳ, 131ʳ; LMA, Rep. 47, f. 210ʳ.

[92] LMA, Rep. 34, f. 136ᵛ; *Letters of John Chamberlain*, vol. 2, p. 241.

[93] *A Survey of London by John Stow*, ed. Charles Lethbridge Kingsford, 2 vols (Oxford: Clarendon Press, 1908), vol. 1, p. 167.

[94] *The Ordre of my Lord Mayor, the Aldermen & the Shiriffes, for their Metings and Wearynge of theyr Apparel Throughout the Yeare* (1568), STC² 16705.7, reports that the lord mayor and aldermen meet at Paul Cross 'at one of the clocke to heare the sermon'. This is repeated in the 1621, 1625, and 1629 editions. On 3 April 1572, the Court of Aldermen minute a request from Laurence Chaderton, the preacher for the Passion sermon that year, 'that my lord maior & his brethren shall appoynt them selves to be at powles by xii of the clock at the furthest for to here his sermon' (LMA, Rep. 17, f. 297ʳ). Simonds D'Ewes reports that he heard a sermon 'in the afternoone at Paules Crosse' on Good Friday in 1624 (*The Diary of Sir Simonds D'Ewes*, p. 188).

Whitsunday, according to Stow. The lord mayor and aldermen processed to the pulpit cross at St Paul's and to St Mary's Spital with their wives, wearing violet livery on Good Friday and scarlet on Low Sunday.

The Corporation's financial commitment to the Paul's Cross sermons is described below, but no less significant is the place that they assigned to their attendance in urban pageantry. It is not surprising, therefore, that Thomas Middleton set one of the episodes of *The Triumphs of Truth*, the Lord Mayor's Show for 1613, in Paul's Churchyard. Time, gesturing to the pulpit cross in his speech says:

> *Seest thou yon place, thither I'll weekly bring thee,*
> *Where Truth's celestial harmony thou shalt hear,*
> *To which I charge thee bend a serious ear.*[95]

The lord mayor and aldermen were expected to attend Paul's Cross very regularly, but formal attendance by the guildsmen may have been restricted to holidays and special occasions. Like the Privy Councillors and bishops, they are among those mentioned by Machyn as present 'in ther best leveray, syttyng on forms, [every] craft by them-selff' at the sermon on 20 August 1553 by Dr Watson: this was an ostentatious display of loyalty on the part of the citizens in response to the riot of the previous week.[96] From at least 1596, the guildsmen were present at the Easter sermons, the high-point of the liturgical year: in that year, the Corporation established a rota of the 'great' and 'inferior' companies to take their turns appointing 'eight discreat persons of the livery' of that company to take up the charitable collections.[97] The proliferation of political anniversary sermons in the reign of James I (Accession Day, the anniversary of the Gowrie Conspiracy, and the Gunpowder Plot) meant that there were more occasions in the year for formal attendance by London's citizens in their guilds. The Saddlers' Company attended the Sunday after the Gunpowder Plot, and regularly attended Paul's Cross to hear the Gowrie Conspiracy sermons until 1616.[98] The Stationers' Company had a similar arrangement: they 'attended on their stand' (a large bench), and on forms obtained from the cathedral when James I came to Paul's Cross to hear Dr John King preach.[99] The Merchant Taylors Company made regular payments 'for keeping the Companies seats at Paules Cross' for political anniversaries sermons up unto the year that the pulpit was closed.[100] The guildsmen were present, in their liveries, on the occasions when the monarch came to Paul's Cross; they also attended formally for the mourning of Queen Anne.

---

[95] Thomas Middleton, *The Triumphs of Truth* (1613), ed. David M. Bergeron, in *Thomas Middleton: The Complete Works*, p. 973, ll. 484–6.

[96] *Diary of Henry Machyn*, p. 41.

[97] LMA, Rep. 23, ff. 520ᵛ, 594ᵛ.

[98] W. Sparrow Simpson, *Saint Paul's Cathedral and Old City Life*, p. 91.

[99] Edward Arber, *A Transcript of the Registers of the Company of Stationers of London, 1554–1640* (1875–94), vol. 5, p. xlii.

[100] City of London, Guildhall Manuscript 34048 (Merchant Taylors Company, Master and Wardens Account Books), vols 15, 16, and 17. I would like to thank Emma Rhatigan for alerting me to this source.

Paul's Cross was obviously a place where the constituent members of London's population, civic and ecclesiastical, could demonstrate their loyalty to the regime by their presence. But what of weekly, informal attendance by London citizens, and by the rest of the population who were not freemen of the city's companies? We know that sufficient numbers attended the sermons for it to be considered a notable gathering, even on ordinary Sundays: Thomas Platter described the auditory as 'so vast that the aforesaid big church will not hold it'.[101] But we have only two figures for the numbers that attended, and, although they are consistent, they are probably not strictly accurate. A visitor to England in 1545 said that 6,000 people attended the sermons at Paul's Cross; in 1560, John Jewel told Peter Martyr Vermigli that 'six thousand persons, old and young, of both sexes' could be found singing psalms after the sermon at Paul's Cross in that year.[102] Visitors to London were brought to the Paul's Cross sermons, as appears from William Stepney and Claudius Hollyband's use of it as the setting for their Sunday dialogues in their language-learning manuals. English visitors to the city also attended. In a 1602 sermon, Robert Wakeman says:

I had thought (Right Honorable, right worshipfull & dearly beloved in Christ Jesus) when I first made choice of this text to have applied this sermon of *Jonas* to this renowned city of *London* being the *Metropolis* of al *England* as *Nineveh* was of *Assyria*, because in my simple judgment this argument heere handled may very well befit this place & these times. But considering with my selfe that many of this greate assembly are inhabitants of other places of this land, I doe rather thinke it best to apply it to the people of *England* in general; that what is spoken of them, every man in particular may accompt as spoken unto himselfe.[103]

Wakeman's claim is borne out by the sermon notes of men like Robert Saxby, an East Anglian clothier who spent time in London in 1629 and took notes of several sermons he heard in the city, including one from Paul's Cross.[104] In popular literature, Paul's Cross also features as a place where crowds of London's inhabitants were to be expected. In the 1576 play by George Wapull, *The Tide Tarrieth No Man*, Greediness goes to Paul's Cross because so many gather there 'such may be my hap: | Of my ill debtors there to spye some'. In his satiric *Black Book* (1604), Thomas Middleton has the devil bequeath to 'Benedick Bottomless, most deep cutpurse' the benefit of 'pageant days, great market days, ballad places' and 'the sixpenny rooms in playhouses', and exhorts him not to 'stick, Benedick, to give a shave of your office at Paul's Cross in the sermon time'.[105]

---

[101] *Thomas Platter's Travels in England, 1599*, p. 177.

[102] *The Zurich Letters, AD 1558–1579*, ed. Hastings Robinson, 2 vols (Cambridge, 1842–5), vol. 1, p. 71; Sebastian Muenster, *Angliae Descriptionis Compendium*, cited in *Thomas Platter's travels in England, 1599*, p. 52. Peter McCullough estimates that 5,000 people could have attended the sermons in the 'preaching place' at Whitehall, which makes the figure of 6,000 for Paul's Cross seem not impossible (*Sermons at Court: Politics and Religion in Elizabethan and Jacobean Preaching* (Cambridge: Cambridge University Press, 1998), pp. 43–4).

[103] Robert Wakeman, *Jonahs Sermon, and Ninivehs Repentance* (1606), *STC²* 24948, p. 55.

[104] Cambridge University Library MS Add. 3177, f. 26ᵛ.

[105] George Wapull, *The Tide Tarrieth No Man* (1576), ll. 1079–90, in *English Morality Plays and Moral Interludes*, eds. Edgar T. Schell and J. D. Shuchter (New York: Rinehart and Winston, 1969), p. 345. Debtor later reports that he was arrested during the sermon, ll. 1299–1302. I would like to

There can be no doubt that in the reigns of Elizabeth I and James I, the Paul's Cross sermons attracted a large and heterogeneous audience. That does not mean, however, that this remained true through the reign of Charles I. It seems most likely that the audience at the Paul's Cross sermons began to dwindle from the early 1620s onward: although the national and civic elite continued to attend, with the Corporation's patronage increasing if anything, the ordinary hearers attending in a private capacity became fewer. The reasons for this shift can be found in the role that Paul's Cross played in the religious life of the city during the implementation of the 'Elizabethan settlement'.

In the early years of Elizabeth's reign, with many non-preaching and barely conformable ministers still in benefices around the city, Paul's Cross was one of the few pulpits that could accommodate a large auditory and where the bishop of London could choose the preacher. Not surprisingly, efforts were made to ensure that as many Londoners as possible could attend the sermons there. Edmund Grindal and Edwin Sandys, the first Elizabethan bishops of London, preached at Paul's Cross themselves, and one of them may have been responsible for the order that Morning Prayer in London parishes be over in time for the parishioners to attend the sermons at Paul's Cross. An episcopal injunction to this effect was current in 1579, and it was repeated in Aylmer's injunctions from the visitation of 1583.[106] This was obviously a stop-gap measure to ensure some access to preaching for parishioners with non-preaching ministers, but it was far from a solution for the whole city. In 1581, London's senior clerics tried a more ambitious scheme: with the backing of the Privy Council, Bishop John Aylmer and Alexander Nowell, Dean of St Paul's, wrote to the Corporation requesting their financial support. Their plan was to group the city's parishes together and 'assigne for every convenient division that may be had . . . a learned man' to preach in 'a certaine Church to be named and at a certain hower whereunto such other paroches next adjoyning may conveniently repaire'. The scheme failed for lack of financial support from the Corporation, who claimed that the citizens were already funding a preaching ministry through parish lectureships and by providing exhibitions for scholars at the universities.[107]

The lord mayor's reply also points out that Aylmer and Nowell had not counted all of the preaching provision in the city, including the lectures 'at the temple and Innes of Courte nor in the Cathedrall Church of Powles'. Institutions like the Inns of Court had lecturers by the 1580s, and the provision of sermons in the cathedral

---

thank Charlotte Steenbrugge for alerting me to this reference. Thomas Middleton, *The Black Book* (1604), ed. G. B. Shand, in *Thomas Middleton: The Complete Works*, p. 217.

[106] *Narratives of the Days of the Reformation, chiefly from the Manuscripts of John Foxe the Martyrologist*, ed. John Gough Nichols (1859), p. 23; City of London, London Metropolitan Archive, Consistory Court of London, Act Books, 1583, MS DL/C/300, pp. 530–1.

[107] LMA, Remembrancia, vol. I, ff, 112ᵛ–114ᵛ. On the Corporation of London's support for preaching in the city, see Arnold Hunt, 'The Art of Hearing: English Preachers and Their Audiences, 1590–1640', University of Cambridge, PhD thesis, 2001, pp. 98–100.

itself increased significantly between 1598 and 1636.[108] Indeed, the provision of sermons for the city's population increased rapidly in the years after the clerics' scheme collapsed. Individual guilds and companies funded annual sermons, like the one John Donne delivered to the Virginia Company in 1622, and charitable bequests for sermons were increasingly popular.[109] In 1571, a Paul's Cross preacher claimed that in London 'the word of God is plentifully preached', but that was merely the beginning of the heyday of 'sermon-centred piety' in London.[110] Paul Seaver has shown the popularity of the parish lectureship, and he has estimated that the number of active lectureships in London jumped from between 50 and 60 in the middle of James's reign to reach a peak of 107 around 1625. There could have been as many as 100 sermons preached every week in London in the mid-1620s.[111] The Corporation's sponsorship of sermons was also increasing: by the 1630s, they were funding an annual sermon at the election of the lord mayor in the Guildhall and a weekly sermon in the Guildhall chapel on Thursday mornings, as well as administering the endowments for the Paul's Cross sermons and the annual Whitsunday sermon at the New Churchyard.[112] There must have been some competition for auditors, even if some people attended more than one sermon a week, and Paul's Cross appears to have lost some of its 'casual' audience to parish lecturers. It still had an unrivalled reputation as a venue for 'newsworthy' sermons and prestigious preachers: in 1598, Stephen Gosson claimed that comments he made in a Paul's Cross sermon were repeated to him 'fortie miles hence'; nearly forty years later, a Paul's Cross preacher predicted that his 'words now utterd against vaine talke shall anone become ye subject of vaine talke'.[113] But by the 1620s, Paul's Cross features less frequently in the notes taken by 'sermon-gadders' than it had done in the 1560s.[114]

---

[108] The visitation returns from 1598 (Guildhall Manuscript 9537, vol. 9) mention the famous divinity lectures as the only weekly sermon. In Laud's visitation of 1636, there is said to be a sermon every Sunday afternoon, and two sermons on holy days. The divinity lecturer preached three times a week in term time: HMC, *9th Report*, p. 154. Contemporaries do not always distinguish between sermons preached in the cathedral and at Paul's Cross. For example, in 1602, John Manningham said Dr John Dove's previous sermon 'at Paules' had been on divorce, but that sermon, *Of Divorcement* (1601), is described as a Paul's Cross sermon on its title page (*Diary of John Manningham*, ed. Sorlein, p. 115). Between 1634 and 1642, when the Paul's Cross sermons were preached in the cathedral choir, most sermons 'appointed for the Cross' mention the fact on their title pages.

[109] *Sermons of John Donne*, eds. Potter and Simpson, vol. 4, no. 10; Stanley Johnson, 'John Donne and the Virginia Company', *ELH* 14(2) (1947), 127–38, p. 134.

[110] E. B., *A Sermon Preached at Pauls Cross on Trinity Sunday, 1571* (1576), *STC²* 4183, sigs F2^{r-v}. This sermon is probably by Edmund Bunny, rather than Edward Bush as noted in *STC²*.

[111] Paul Seaver, *The Puritan Lectureships: The Politics of Religious Dissent, 1560–1662* (Palo Alto, CA: Stanford University Press, 1970), pp. 127–8.

[112] The Corporation funded an annual sermon at Michaelmas in the Guildhall at the election of the mayor from at least 1563 (see *Chamber Accounts of the Sixteenth Century*, p. 123) and a weekly sermon in the Guildhall Chapel on Thursday mornings, before the market at Blackwell Hall (from 1631, see City Cash Book 2, f. 35^v). They administered the endowment for the Whitsunday sermon in the New Churchyard left by Lord Mayor Thomas Rowe in 1569: see LMA, Letter Book V, f. 246^r.

[113] Stephen Gosson, *The Trumpet of War* (1598), *STC²* 12099, sig. G5^r; Folger Shakespeare Library MS V.a.1 (Sermons by unknown preachers), ff. 59–73, 'at the Crosse on February 2, 1636', f. 64^v.

[114] See Arnold Hunt, 'The Art of Hearing', pp. 142–50.

THE PREACHERS' APPOINTMENTS AND PAYMENT

Who decided which preachers appeared at Paul's Cross, and who arranged for them to be reimbursed for their time and trouble? The routine overseeing of the Paul's Cross sermons (appointing appropriate preachers and managing the rota) lay with the bishop of London from the beginning of the sixteenth century, if not earlier. But the bishop's rights over Paul's Cross were sometimes curtailed if political conditions necessitated it: in 1534, the conservative John Stokesley found his right to appoint to Paul's Cross taken by Cranmer; in October 1535, it was given by Cromwell to John Hilsey. In the early years of Elizabeth's reign, Archbishop Parker oversaw the appointments to Paul's Cross and the Spital, usually controlled by the Corporation.[115] Bishop Edmund Grindal of London also assumed some intervention by the Privy Council: in October 1562, before he was to preach at the Cross, he wrote to William Cecil to find out whether the rumour of the death of the King of Navarre was true, and asked 'if there be any other matter which ye wish to be uttered there for the present state'.[116] It was John Aylmer, during his long term as bishop of London (1577–94), who did most to secure the bishop's control over the Paul's Cross sermons, and we hear of no routine oversight by others in the years after his elevation to London. Aylmer's known antipathy to the puritan movement might explain the freedom he had in appointing Paul's Cross preachers: in a letter to the Queen of 1582, complaining of his detractors, he reminded Elizabeth that he had 'ever such a watch upon Paul's Cross, that in my time there came never any Puritan in that place'.[117] Nonetheless, the Privy Council might still cooperate with the bishop of London on particularly sensitive occasions, something Arnold Hunt has demonstrated with respect to the Earl of Essex's rebellion, for example, when Richard Bancroft kept Robert Cecil well briefed on arrangements for preaching at the Cross.[118]

The day-to-day administration of the preaching rota was probably not handled by the bishop himself; he was, after all, a senior cleric with a populous diocese. Few letters of appointment survive, but those we have do carry the bishop's name. Those that mention the recipient's name, however, were sent to men known personally to the bishop, and so our surviving sample may not be typical of those sent out to other preachers.[119] In 1539, Stephen Gardiner reportedly sent his

---

[115] Cornford, *Paul's Cross: A History*, pp. 35–6; Bridgen, *London and the Reformation*, pp. 232–4, 451–2; *Correspondence of Matthew Parker*, eds. John Bruce and Revd Thomas Thomason Perowne (Cambridge, 1853), pp. 239–40, 260–4, 275, 318.

[116] *The Remains of Edmund Grindal, D.D.*, ed. Rev. William Nicholson (Cambridge, 1843), p. 253.

[117] *Memoirs of the Life and Times of Sir Christopher Hatton, K.G.*, ed. Sir Harris Nicolas (1847), p. 244.

[118] Arnold Hunt, 'Tuning the Pulpits: The Religious Context of the Essex Revolt', pp. 97–101.

[119] Four letters of appointment to Matthew Parker survive, one from Thomas Cromwell (*c.*1537), one from Archbishop Cranmer, dated May 1548, another dated January 1550, and one from Nicholas Ridley from 1551 (*Correspondence of Matthew Parker*, ed. John Bruce (Cambridge 1853), pp. ix, 5, 39, 45). A letter from William Laud, from August 1633 (his last month as bishop of London), is addressed to Richard Sterne (*The Works of Archbishop Laud* (Oxford, 1860), vol. 7, p. 47. Sterne became Laud's chaplain the same year. On the other hand, Humfrey Leech recounts an invitation from the bishop ('my very Honourable, and much respected friend') to preach at Paul's Cross that echoes the surviving

chaplain to 'knowe who should occupie the crosse that lent, and to speake for a place for me on one of the sondayes'. The bishop's chaplain 'thought in his mynde, rather to take that daye [the first Sunday] for me' rather than have Robert Barnes preach. Gardiner's chaplain would hardly have acted so assertively in conversation with the bishop of London himself; it seems more likely that he was discussing the rota with another, more junior cleric like himself.[120]

As with other aspects of the Paul's Cross sermons, the arrangements become less haphazard over the course of Elizabeth's reign. It appears that the bishop used the staff at his disposal, primarily his chaplains, to arrange for preachers to appear: the letters of appointment require the preacher to report to the bishop's chaplain. We know that in Aylmer's time it was the bishop's chaplains who ended up filling the gaps in the rota. When the Corporation complained to Aylmer about some comments made by his chaplain in a Paul's Cross sermon, Aylmer cites in mitigation the fact that the man had often preached there when the appointed preacher failed to turn up.[121] Indeed, Aylmer himself did the same, as attested by Thomas Cooper, writing anonymously in *An Admonition to the People of England* (1589). In one of the many responses to the Marprelate pamphlets, he denies that Aylmer is the 'dumb John' of Marprelate's caricature: 'How many sermons hath he preached at Paules Crosse? Sometimes three in a yeare, yea, sometimes two or three together, being an olde man, to supply some yonger mens negligence'.[122] It seems most likely, therefore, that the bishop's chaplains undertook the routine administration of the preaching rota: gathering information about potential preachers, sending letters of appointment, meeting the preachers beforehand, and advising them on subjects to avoid.

These men were also regular preachers at the cross; for the Elizabethan bishops of London in particular, Paul's Cross was treated as their most important pulpit. In 1566, Edmund Grindal wrote to Matthew Hutton, then Master of Pembroke Hall, explaining that Hutton's appointment to Paul's Cross had to be postponed: because a parliament had been called 'the Bishops shall occupie the rowme those Sundays in the myddes of the terme'.[123] In 1577, Bishop Edwin Sandys excused his failure to visit William Cecil on the grounds that he had been preoccupied with the preparation of his sermon of farewell to the diocese of London, delivered from Paul's Cross.[124] In a famous, caustic letter to the lord mayor of 1582, John Aylmer

---

letters of appointment. This may indicate that letters were routinely sent out in the bishop's name. However, as this incident is found in Leech's 'motives' tract for conversion to Catholicism, it may be that he wished to exaggerate his relationship with the bishop (*A Triumph of Truth* (1609), *STC²* 15363, p. 76).

[120] Stephen Gardiner, *A Declaration of such True Articles as George Joy hath gone about to Confute as False* (1546), *STC²* 11588, f. V^r.

[121] LMA, Remembrancia, vol. I, ff. 117^v–118^r. The preacher was Laurence Dyos (also spelt Deios).

[122] [Thomas Cooper] *An Admonition to the People of England* (1589), *STC²* 5682, pp. 60–1. I would like to thank Alan Cromartie for this reference.

[123] *The Correspondence of Dr Matthew Hutton, Archbishop of York* (1843), p. 54.

[124] *CSPD, 1547–1580*, p. 545. Sandys sermon is printed in *Sermons Made by the Most Reverende Father in God, Edwin, Archbishop of Yorke* (1585), *STC²* 21713, pp. 372–84. It is one of several Paul's Cross sermons printed in this volume.

describes his 'chaire' as 'the pulpit at Poules Crosse', rather than the 'cathedra' in St Paul's. Many post-Reformation deans of St Paul's were also assiduous preachers at the Cross, most notably Alexander Nowell and John Donne.

The willingness of other preachers to deliver Paul's Cross sermons should not be assumed, and the difficulty facing the bishop and his chaplains in finding fifty-two preachers willing and capable of delivering a two-hour sermon should not be underestimated. Unlike the court, which had regular preaching only during Lent (this was extended to all year round under James I's reign), even in Edward VI's reign a preacher was expected at Paul's Cross every week.[125] The bishop and his chaplain had various resources on which they could rely to find preachers. From the beginning of the sixteenth century there was a small but growing supply of scholars from Cambridge and Oxford, as it was a condition for the degree of B.Th. in Cambridge that the candidate should preach a sermon at Paul's Cross.[126] In Oxford, it was considered sufficiently demanding to be treated as equivalent to the Latin sermon demanded of those commencing a B.D.[127] Another source of competent preachers arose from the obligations on fellows of some of the newer colleges to preach at Paul's Cross. Men like John Fisher and John Colet made a particular virtue of preaching *ad populum* and Paul's Cross was one of the venues from which a large audience could be addressed. For this reason, Lady Margaret Beaufort, guided by Fisher, made the performance of a sermon at Paul's Cross one of the conditions set for the Lady Margaret preachership at Cambridge.[128] The example was followed by those formulating the statutes of colleges founded at this time: it was a condition for a doctor holding a fellowship at Corpus Christi and St John's Colleges, Oxford, that they preach a Paul's Cross sermon in the first ten years of their fellowship.[129] It is no exaggeration to say that Paul's Cross owed its

---

[125] The writer of the Greyfriars' chronicle thought it noteworthy that in 1549 'the xiii day of the same monyth [October] was no sermond at the crosse' (p. 64). Peter McCullough discovered the extension of preaching at court beyond Lent and Easter under James I (*Sermons at Court*, pp. 115–25).

[126] This requirement for the B.Th. was in place by the fifteenth century: see Damien Riehl Leader, *A History of the University of Cambridge*, vol. I, to 1546 (Cambridge: Cambridge University Press, 1988), p. 174. See also George Peacock, *Observations on the Statutes of the University of Cambridge* (London, 1841), p. 12. The performance (or promise) of the Paul's Cross sermon is noted in the 'grace books' up until the 1560s; thereafter there are many more entries each year and they become more summary, and so the Paul's Cross sermon is rarely mentioned: *Grace Book [Delta]: containing the Records of the University of Cambridge for the years 1542–1589*, ed. John Venn (Cambridge: Cambridge University Press, 1910).

[127] *Register of Congregations, 1505–1517*, ed. W. T. Mitchell (Oxford Historical Society, 1948), 320; *Register of the University of Oxford*, vol. 2, part I, ed. Andrew Clark (Oxford Historical Society, 1887), pp. 131, 136–7, 140, Register of Convocation, 16 February 1594, fol. 275ʳ.

[128] J. B. Mullinger, *The University of Cambridge, From the Earliest Times to the Royal Injunctions of 1535*, 3 vols (Cambridge, 1873), vol. 1 pt. 2, pp. 440–1; *Endowments of the University of Cambridge*, ed. John Willis Clark (Cambridge, 1904), pp. 65–70.

[129] *Statutes of the Colleges of Oxford* (Oxford, 1853), vol. 2, pp. 60, 78; vol. 3, p. 59. The example for this stipulation may well have come from Bishop John Fisher's draft statutes for St John's College, Cambridge, where preachers were required to preach eight sermons *ad populum* a year at unspecified pulpits. As with the Oxford college statutes, however, Fisher's statutes make provision for fellows absent from the college because they were preaching at Paul's Cross, the Spital or Westminster (*Early Statutes of the College of St John the Evangelist in Cambridge*, ed. J. E. B. Mayer (Cambridge, 1859), pp. 98, 99, 144). Before their abolition, preaching chantry had also provided the occasional Paul's

fame to the Christian humanists who took steps to ensure the supply of preachers, at least as much as it did to the Reformers of the next generation who appeared there so often.

Of course, these regulations did not mean that all of these preachers fulfilled their obligations, and the colleges alone could not provide sufficient preachers to man Paul's Cross all year round. More important to the continuation of the Paul's Cross sermons was the payment that the preachers received for their sermons, and whether that was sufficient to cover their expenses, particularly given the state of clerical incomes at the time. Before the Reformation, the Paul's Cross sermons were funded by bequests left by those wishing to be included in the 'bead roll' read at the end of the sermons, and by gifts from religious gilds or fraternities. The wealthy 'Jesus Gild', for example, paid money towards the Paul's Cross sermons so that the members of the gild would be remembered in the preachers' prayers.[130] The end of prayers for the dead meant the end of the bead roll, and the dissolution of the chantries meant the end of the gilds and fraternities. John Stow notes that a bequest from 1487 of 4d for each preacher at Paul's Cross and the Spital was 'not performed' any longer.[131] The effect on the funding of the Paul's Cross sermons seems to have been quite immediate, with preachers showing reluctance to undertake a task for which they would not be paid. Edmund Bonner was the first to complain of a shortage of preachers: he asked a correspondent in Cambridge to 'exhorte suche as ye knowe apte and mete for that purpose' to preach at the Cross, because 'of late' there 'hath not been many here at paules crosse to preche the word of God'.[132] In 1555, Bonner demanded a subvention from the Dean and Chapter of the cathedral to fund the sermons, but this arrangement did not outlive his time in office.[133] The early years of Elizabeth's reign did not see any improvement in the funding of the sermons. There was an ample supply of preachers nonetheless, because many of the returning exiles were on an energetic campaign of evangelizing that took in Paul's Cross in particular: between April and August 1559, of the nine Paul's Cross preachers we know of, seven were future bishops, and they preached at Paul's Cross repeatedly over the next year.[134] Thereafter, it is unclear whether the preachers were paid and the rota always filled. Manuscript notes from 1565–6

Cross preacher, as the founders of some of these specified that the priest should appear at Paul's Cross or the Spital (Susan Wabuda, *Preaching during the English Reformation* (Cambridge: Cambridge University Press, 2002), p. 167).

[130] 'The Fraternity of Jesus, Other Ordinances enacted for divine service', in *Registrum Statutorum*, ed. Sparrow Simpson, pp. 446–52, p. 451. See also Susan Bridgen, 'Religion and Social Obligation in Early Sixteenth-Century London', *Past and Present* 103 (1984), 67–112, p. 100; Wabuda, *Preaching during the English Reformation*, pp. 52–3.

[131] Stow, *Survey*, ed. Kingsford, vol. 1, p. 246.

[132] Corpus Christi College Cambridge MS 119, item 14.

[133] *Visitation Articles and Injunctions of the Period of the Reformation*, vol. 2, pp. 377–8. This demand is included in the injunctions to the cathedral from the 1555 visitation.

[134] See *Register of Sermons*, pp. 41–2. The entry there for Matthew Parker preaching on 10 February 1559 is an error, as the Cross was closed between December 1558 and the Easter sermons of 1559, because of the royal injunction prohibiting preaching. When opened again for the Easter sermons, the pulpit was found to be 'very filthy' (Stow, *Annales*, p. 637).

suggest that sermons were preached most weeks and that the preachers were mostly London ministers and senior clerics.[135] The Lent 'preaching season' at court probably provided some help: in 1597, Bishop William Bilson reported 'that being stayed [from going home] by my Lord of Canterbury to preach before her Majesty at the last Lent; he thought it requisite likewise to appear at Paul's cross'.[136] It seems that for the early and middle years of Elizabeth's reign, Paul's Cross relied on the evangelical zeal of preachers living near London or senior clerics visiting there, because its endowments were severely depleted. In 1591, William Fisher declared in his sermon that the 'learned men, from both universities' who preached at Paul's Cross were 'hardely, and unwillinglye . . . drawn hither' because of the cost involved. Fisher thought that £52 a year would provide enough financial support for the preachers, and urged the Corporation to contribute, seeing that a 'reverend Bishop' had already promised to provide 'a good parte' of the cost involved.[137]

That bishop was undoubtedly John Aylmer, who made determined, and ultimately successful, efforts to ensure that Paul's Cross had the preachers and the funding that would ensure its continuity. He complained in the 1586 convocation that some senior clerics had failed to preach at Paul's Cross when required.[138] In December 1592, he complained to the Privy Council that 'men out of both universities and other places that bee calld to preache there, are soe hardly drawne unto that place that those which by my appoyntment have the chardge to call the said preachers . . . cannot have twoe amongst tenne of them that be soe sent for'.[139] Aylmer's letter may have been written at a moment of particular difficulty for him: he goes on to say that in 1580 he had deputed the task of appointing the Paul's Cross preachers to one William Cotton, who 'either wearied by the refusall of the preachers appoynted or not greatefully remembringe his faithfull promise to mee' was now refusing to do so any longer. In 1586, Aylmer had also made an arrangement with a local clergyman to fill in for any preachers who failed to show up, but this part of the system was not working well either, as Aylmer's

---

[135] Bodleian Library MS Tanner 50. Between June 1565 and November 1566, Alexander Nowell, Dean of St Paul's, preached twice; the Bishop of Winchester preached once. Four archdeacons (Robert Crowley of Hereford, Thomas Lever of Coventry, Watts of Middlesex, and Thomas Cole of Essex), two chaplains to bishops (Padye, chaplain to the bishop of Winchester and Bitley, chaplain to the archbishop of Canterbury), and two cathedral prebendaries (Turner, a prebendary of Canterbury cathedral, and Bullingham, a prebendary of St Paul's) preached. William Day, Provost of Eton, preached twice and James Calfhill, Reader of the Divinity lecture in St Paul's, preached once. Otherwise, there were eight preachers described as holding London benefices and eight described as being from Oxford or Cambridge, including John Whitgift of Peterhouse.
[136] John Strype, *Historical Collections of the Life and Acts of the Right Reverend Father in God, John Aylmer* (Oxford, 1821), pp. 360. Cross-referencing the *Register* of Paul's Cross sermons with Peter McCullough's calendar of court sermons reveals no other coincidences like this except for John Jewel's repetition of the 'Challenge' sermon at court in March 1560. This may be due to the fact the bishops were less likely to print their sermons and so we have less information about how often they appeared at Paul's Cross.
[137] William Fisher, *A Godly Sermon Preached at Paules Crosse the 31. day of October 1591* (1592), *STC²* 10919, sigs C4ʳ–C6ʳ.
[138] Strype, *Life of Aylmer*, p. 201.
[139] British Library MS Add. 32092, f. 140ʳ.

chaplains were doing that instead.[140] The Privy Council referred the matter to Archbishop Whitgift. Whether this gave Aylmer the additional backing he needed, in March 1594 he was able to institute an order binding the St Paul's prebendary of Harleston 'for the supplieng of the want of preachers at Powles Cross'. The prebendary was to perform the administrative duties associated with appointing the preacher and he was to supply any vacancy at the Cross by either preaching himself or finding a deputy.[141] This arrangement did not outlast Aylmer's time as bishop. His successor, John Fletcher, had to order his archdeacons to note down the 'speciall men within your precinct as are able to furnish the preachinge at Powls Crosse, the more principale for the terme, the second sorte for *non terminus*'.[142]

Aylmer's last action on behalf of Paul's Cross was leaving £300 in his will, along with £100 given him from the will of the Countess of Shrewsbury, to create an endowment that would secure the stipend for the Paul's Cross preachers; this put the sermon series on a sound financial footing again, and complaints about the unwillingness of preachers to appear at Paul's Cross ceased. Aylmer left his endowment to the Chamber of London to administer, and in doing so acknowledged the Corporation's financial acumen and reliability, as well as their sustained interest in the sermon at Paul's Cross. The Corporation administered this money (which arrived into the Chamber of London in 1606, and, with interest, amounted to £480), and the legacies, many of them left by London citizens, that followed it. These benefactors were remembered by name in the sermon or in the prayer before it, which in a sense created a 'reformed' version of the old 'bead-roll'.[143] Not all churchmen thought this altogether appropriate: when replying to objections made to his *Collection of Private Devotions* (1627), John Cosin acidly remarks that it is 'strange' some should object to references to the saints when 'they can be well enough content that a girdler, and a grocer, the lady Ramsey, and Mr Johnson, should be every Sunday commemorated in a prier at Paules Crosse'.[144] Cosin had clearly heard this prayer more than once, for these were indeed major benefactors,

---

[140] City of London, London Metropolitan Archive, Vicars General Books, 'Stanhope', vol. I, f. 144ʳ. Anthony Anderson, the preacher concerned, had been involved in a dispute over the vicarage of Stepney, and his willingness to fill in at Paul's Cross may have been influenced by Aylmer's ability to help him with this. Aylmer was also the 'setter up' of William Cotton, at one time Aylmer's chaplain and the man supposed to administer the rota: Aylmer appointed him to the lucrative living of St Margaret Fish Street; see H. Gareth Owen, 'The London Parish Clergy in the Reign of Elizabeth I', Ph.D. thesis, University of London, 1957, pp. 198–9.

[141] *APC*, 1592, p. 383; Vicars General Book, Stanhope, vol. 2, ff. 163ᵛ–164ᵛ.

[142] Hertfordshire Records Office, ASA 5/5 No. 201, 2 January 1594/5.

[143] Very few sermon-books include this 'bead roll' of benefactors. An exception of Samuel Collins, *A Sermon preached at Paules Crosse* (1607), *STC²* 5564, pp. 86–9.

[144] *The Correspondence of John Cosin*, ed. George Ornsby, 2 vols (Durham, 1869), vol. 1, p. 135. For a list of the endowments, see P. E. Jones, 'St Paul's Cross and Preachers', Corporation of London Record Office Research Papers 4.13, 1934, pp. 7–11; Richard Newcourt, *Repertorium Ecclesiasticum Parochiale Londiniense* (1708), vol. 1, p. 4. The benefactors are mentioned within a Paul's Cross sermon in Thomas Jackson's *London's New-Yeeres Gift* (1609), *STC²* 14303, f. 8ʳ, and Thomas Myriell, *The Devout Soules search* (1610), *STC²* 18323, pp. 80–1. Minutes of the Court of Aldermen meeting for 13 May 1602, records the receipt of Katherine Bailife's legacy and notes that 'the said Katherin Bailif shalbe remembred amongst other the Benefactors rehearsed at Paules Crosse.' LMA, Corporation of London Rep. vol. 34, f. 444ʳ.

though not all of them were London citizens: The 'girdler' was George Palyn, who left £200 in 1611, the grocer was Sir Thomas Russell, who left £10 p.a., but Mr Robert Johnson was archdeacon of Leicester (he left £100 to Paul's Cross in 1610). Interestingly, the name that Cosin omits is Bishop Aylmer's.

Once they began administering Aylmer's endowments, the Corporation's oversight of, and support for, the funding of the Paul's Cross sermons steadily increased. In dealing with the endowments, they paid careful attention to the needs of the preachers: three times a committee of aldermen met to consider how Aylmer's bequest could be best spent.[145] Combining it with £10 p.a. from the will of Thomas Russell, administered by the Drapers' Company, the Corporation could give 26s 8d to all unbeneficed preachers appointed to Paul's Cross.[146] In 1609 they received a petition from 'Mr Specht, preacher', suggesting that all preachers, beneficed or not, should receive 20s for a Paul's Cross sermon. The argument of the petition seems to have been that many beneficed clergy had small livings and families to support, and they sometimes had to travel greater distances than university-based students: at any rate, these were the arguments recorded for the decision to use the increased funds brought by Robert Johnson's benefaction of 1610 to pay all Paul's Cross preachers whose income was less than £100.[147] The preacher's allowance went up in 1612 (to 33s 4d), and again in 1616 (40s) and 1640 (£2 9s). Paul Seaver has estimated that the value of the average salary of London lecturers (comparable in many ways to the unbeneficed clergy preaching at Paul's Cross) was £21/8 in 1600–9, £29/7 between 1610 and 1619, £33 in the 1620s, and £37/7 in the 1630s. This means that until the 1630s, when the rate of benefactions slowed, a Paul's Cross sermon was worth about 7% of the annual income of a lecturer.[148]

As well as administering the benefactions that paid the preachers, the Corporation also responded to preachers' complaints about the accommodation and 'entertainment' provided for them. In 1608, the City began to pay for five nights' lodging for the preacher and his servant, with dinner at the lord mayor's table. In 1610, a request by John Fleming, the man who lodged the preachers, that money be provided for the preachers' 'diet' was accepted. Fleming's request may have been part of a campaign: in a sermon of June 1609, George Webbe had acknowledged that lodging was provided for the preachers but asked that 'some good Shunamite' among the citizens provide for the preacher's diet.[149] Evidently, preachers were not slow to make demands on the city: in a sermon of 1635, William Evans complained that 'food we have, that are called to this place, and wee thanke you for it. But

---

[145]   LMA, Rep. 27, f. 221ᵛ (19 June 1606), f. 230ᵛ (1 July 1606); LMA, Rep. 28, f. 57ʳ (9 July 1607).
[146]   LMA, Rep. 28, f. 145ʳ.
[147]   LMA, Rep. 29, ff. 79ᵛ, 203ʳ, 259ᵛ.
[148]   Seaver, *The Puritan Lectureships,* p. 150.
[149]   LMA, Rep. 28, f. 145r; Rep. vol. 29, f. 65v. George Webbe, *Gods Controversie with England* (1609), *STC²* 25162, pp. 37–8. The house where the preachers lodged became known as the 'Shunamite's house', according to Izaak Walton in his *Life of Hooker: The Lives of John Donne, Sir Henry Wotton, Richard Hooker, George Herbert, and Robert Sanderson,* ed. George Saintsbury (Oxford: Oxford University Press, 1927), p. 176. The stipend allowed 'the shunamite' was increased on several other occasions: P. E. Jones, 'St. Paul's Cross and Preachers', p. 11.

raiment, a gowne we want, we are faine to seek for, and sometimes to goe without'. It was not until 1637 that this request was answered, but the Corporation did pay for 'two new Gownes of Turky Grogrome' for the Paul's Cross preachers, to be kept in the house where the preachers lodged.[150] The lord mayor and aldermen also responded positively to at least some of the many dedications they received to printed Paul's Cross sermons: a gift of £5 was given to Matthew Law, stationary and verger of St Paul's, when he presented them with a copy of William Worship's *Patterne of an Invincible Faith* (1616). In 1636, John Gore received a gift from the Corporation in consideration of the dedication to Christopher Clitherow that he placed in the printed version of his *The Oracle of God*.[151]

By the end of James I's reign, a Paul's Cross sermon was an attractive proposition for a newly ordained minister: it paid well, and brought a new preacher to the attention of more potential patrons than was possible at any venue other than the court. This is reflected in the printed sermons: the lord mayor and aldermen receive as many dedications of Paul's Cross sermons as the bishops do, and both groups figure far more highly than any other (although those with livings often dedicate the printed sermon to their patron).[152] Rather than an expensive obligation, preaching at Paul's Cross had become a sign of ambition, good or bad. Thomas Fuller reported that Robert Abbot gained preferment because of a performance at Paul's Cross.[153] John Earle's 'bold Forward man', 'if hee bee a scholler . . . ha's commonly stept into the Pulpit before a degree; . . . and his next Sermon is at *Pauls* Crosse, and that printed'.[154] Appointments to Paul's Cross were now too useful to stand apart from the patronage system: in an epistle dedicatory to his 1607 sermon, John Pelling remarks that his patron, the earl of Hertford, had secured him the appointment to preach at Paul's Cross, doubtless by appealing to the bishop.[155]

If the reign of James I—when the sermons were well funded, preachers ambitious to appear there, and hearers still flocking to the sermons—marks the high point in the history of Paul's Cross, then the accession of Charles I marks the beginning of the end. Few members of the senior clergy from those years appeared there at any stage of their career. The exceptions are equally telling: Arthur Lake, an

---

[150] William Evans, *The Christian Conflict, and Conquest* (1636), *STC²* 10595, p. 10; City Cash Book 2, f. 213ʳ.

[151] LMA, Rep. 32, f. 323ʳ; City Cash Book 2, f. 46ᵛ. John Gore, *The Oracle of God* (1635 [1636]) Wing G 1294. The City Cash book entry does not mention the sermon's title, but this is the only printed sermon by Gore with a dedication to the lord mayor or aldermen. In 1637, the Corporation gave Oliver Whitbie a gift of £5 for his dedication of the printed version of *Londons Returne, after the Decrease of the Sicknes* (1637), *STC²* 25371, to 'the Lord Mayor, Aldermen Recorder and Sheriffs of this Cittie'; City Cash Book 2, f. 136ʳ. But the copy of this sermon now extant carries a dedication to John Pultney, esq., with whom Whitbie says he stayed while the plague was in the city. Whitbie may have had two variants of the printed copy produced, with two different dedications, but no variants are listed in *STC²* for this sermon.

[152] Seventeen dedications to the lord mayor of London and/or aldermen and sheriffs have been found among the sermons extant, and seventeen dedications to a bishop or archbishop.

[153] Thomas Fuller, *The Church History of Britain; from the Birth of Jesus Christ untill the year M.DC. XLVIII* (1655), Wing F 2416, Cent. XVII, Book X, p. 72.

[154] Earle, *Microcosmosgraphie*, sig. Mᵛ.

[155] John Pelling, *A Sermon of the Providence of God* (1607), *STC²* 19567, sigs A3ʳ⁻ᵛ.

old-fashioned 'preaching pastor'[156] and Bishop of Bath and Wells, was one of only
two bishops to appear at Paul's Cross in Charles's reign. The other was William
Laud, who preached during his time as bishop of London. Otherwise, Robert
Sanderson, John Donne, and Henry King are the only clerics of reputation (then or
now) who appeared at Paul's Cross after 1625. Henry King only appeared once
after 1625, while Sanderson was then the humble Rector of Boothby Pagnell in
Lincolnshire. That leaves John Donne, Dean of St Paul's, as the only senior cleric
and respected preacher who took his turn at Paul's Cross.

The calibre of men appointed for most Sundays seems to have declined also, with
far fewer bishop's chaplains and archdeacons appearing in the *Register of Sermons*.
Fewer Paul's Cross sermons were printed in Charles's reign, and we find fewer
references to sermons in letters or diaries, all suggestive of the declining status of the
sermon series. Given the Laudians' stated opposition to 'sermon-centred piety', it is
not surprising that the Paul's Cross sermons, which did not take place in a church
and were divorced from any liturgical context, did not appeal to them. Indeed, as
the moving force behind Charles I's renovation of St Paul's, William Laud was
party to the decision to demolish the pulpit cross, and was therefore instrumental in
ending the series as it had been known. In 1633, work began on the cathedral, and,
according to William Dugdale's *History of St Pauls Cathedral*, 'the Houses adjoyning to, and neer the Church, being compounded for, and pulled down; and a great
part of the Church-yard paled in, for the Masons to work in; whereby the Sermons,
which usually had been at the *Cross*, were removed into the Quire'.[157] Contrary to
Dugdale's claim that the pulpit cross survived until the 1643 ordinance against
'monuments of superstition and idolatry', it is most likely that it was taken down in
1634 or 1635 along with the 'sermon houses'. It was certainly gone by 1641, when
Henry Peacham remarks that Paul's Cross 'the most famous preaching place' has
been pulled down 'with an intent to be built fairer and bigger when the Church
shall be finished'.[158] But this never happened. That this should be the case, and
that it should happen with almost no contemporary comment, demonstrates how
rapidly the cultural significance of the Paul's Cross sermons had shrunk. Confined
to the choir of the cathedral, a sermon series that had once addressed the London
community was then addressing only the London government. To find the reasons
why they did not object to the end of Paul's Cross sermons, and why the rest of its
auditory had stopped going there, we need to trace in detail the arguments that
were presented in the sermons themselves.

---

[156] The phrase is Kenneth Fincham's, *Prelate as Pastor: the Episcopate of James I* (Oxford: Oxford
University Press, 1990).
[157] Dugdale, *History of St Pauls Cathedral*, p. 134.
[158] [Henry Peacham], *A Dialogue between the Crosse in Cheap and Charing Crosse . . . by Ryhen
Pameach* (1641), Wing P944, sig. A4[r].

2

From Pulpit to Press

Any claim for the political impact of public sermons must take into account the fact that the original oration survives only in a written or printed copy, which will vary to some extent from the words spoken at the time. How then do we know whether the words reported to us are the ones that had a political impact, and how can we judge what it was about a sermon that was found objectionable or controversial? This chapter will demonstrate that an assessment of the Paul's Cross sermons' interventions in Elizabethan and early Stuart politics need not be unduly hampered by such uncertainties if we understand correctly the relationship between the original speech and the textual versions of it that survive. An examination of the typical methods of sermon composition, delivery, and recording can help us to distinguish the parts of each sermon most likely to be lost, or added, in the transition to paper. We can then include these factors into our consideration of the sermon's impact. Such calculations are already the stock-in-trade of historians and literary critics working on speeches, plays, and masques—all genres whose study involves the same uncertainty about changes made in the transition from speech to written form. It is our lack of familiarity with the conventions of sermon composition that makes this task seem greater for the study of preaching. Of course, practices varied between preachers and over time. No one would argue that the differences between a sermon as it was preached and as it survives in print or in manuscript form are negligible or non-existent. What is argued here, however, is that the differences between the oral, written, and printed copies of a sermon did not prevent contemporaries from seeing them as different versions of the same oration. This ought to provide us with a starting point from which we can construct an interpretative method for the analysis of the Paul's Cross sermons as events that we now encounter through manuscript and printed copies.[1]

---

[1] A briefer, but more general account, of the printing of sermons can be found in H. S. Bennett, *English Books and Readers* (Cambridge: Cambridge University Press, 1965), vol. 2, pp. 148–56. A far more extensive study of printed sermon-books has been conducted by Ian Green, *Print and Protestantism in Early Modern England* (Oxford: Oxford University Press, 2000), esp. pp. 194–216. The findings of Arnold Hunt in his *Art of Hearing: English Preachers and Their Auditories, 1590–1640* (Cambridge: Cambridge University Press, 2010) adds considerably to our knowledge of this subject.

PREACHERS' AND HEARERS' SERMON NOTES

Unlike plays and masques, the full text of a Paul's Cross sermon did not usually exist on paper prior to its performance in public. The evidence we have suggests that almost all early modern preachers spoke from notes rather than a full text.[2] There were practical reasons for this: many preachers delivered an hour-long sermon to their congregations once a week, and the production of a full text of each sermon would have created excessive demands on their time; a Paul's Cross sermon was twice as long, and so would have taken even longer to prepare. For Anthony Anderson to have 'penned, and then conned my Sermon by hearte' would have been 'a heavy laboure, bothe lothsome, & needlesse I praise God of his mercies'.[3] This does not mean that Paul's Cross sermons were extempore performances.[4] Preachers like Anderson wrote notes of the structure of their sermons, and memorized those. In his very popular handbook on preaching, the moderate puritan writer Richard Bernard advises against being 'tied' to words and suggests as a help to memory that the preacher 'note the chiefe heads of thy speech briefly in a little peece of paper, a word or two for every severall thing'. These preparatory notes can be brought into the pulpit, if a little disguised:

If any should thinke this a disgrace, it is not unknowne, how both in the University & other places, many very learned and woorthy Divines use this helpe: either taking up a little paper books bound like Testaments, or the Bible with a paper fastned in it: and these no whit at all lesse esteemed.[5]

Feats of memory were prized, nonetheless, as is indicated by Bernard's suggestion that notes be hidden. Miles Mosse boasts that he cannot reproduce his sermon exactly as he preached it because *'writing nothing at large, nor carrying with me any helpe of my notes into the pulpit; some things might easily be forgotten, which I premeditated, some things might be added, which I premeditated not'*.[6] Others, like John Warner, Bishop of Rochester, prepared notes more extensive than the 'word or two for every severall thing' that Bernard suggested, as the extensive

---

[2] John Sparrow, 'John Donne and Contemporary Preachers: Their Preparation of Sermons for Delivery and for Publication', *Essays and Studies* 16 (1931), 144–78.

[3] Anthony Anderson, *A Sermon Preached at Paules Crosse* (1581), *STC²* 570, sig. A2ʳ.

[4] All writers on preaching, conformist and puritan, before the Civil War disavow extempore preaching: even a firebrand like Samuel Hieron criticized the preacher that 'vents raw, sudden, undigested meditations' as well as the one who polishes his sermon for literary effect alone: *The Dignity of Preaching*, in *Works* ([1620?]), *STC²* 13377.5, pp. 585–6. Richard Bernard stated emphatically that 'preaching is not a labour of the lippes, and an idle talke of the tongue' but 'an uttering of God truth . . . acquired through Gods blessing by diligent labour and study': *The Faithful Shepherd* (1607; 1621 edn.), *STC²* 1941, pp. 108–9. William Perkins says that 'in preparation, private study is with diligence to be used', and gives advice on making a commonplace book to this end, on methods of interpreting the Bible and on constructing a sermon: William Perkins, *The Art of Prophecying*, in *Works*, 3 vols (1616–18), *STC²* 19651, vol. 2, p. 651. In fact, most of the work is given over to these subjects, although it is now the passages warning against human wisdom and the rhetorical arts that are quoted most often.

[5] Richard Bernard, *The Faithfull Shepheard* (1607), *STC²* 1939, sig. M3ʳ.

[6] Miles Mosse, *Justifying and Saving Faith* (Cambridge, 1614), *STC²* 18209, sig. 2¶2ʳ.

manuscript notes for his sermons attest.[7] Very occasionally, we come across a preacher who spoke from a prepared script, but this seems to have been from necessity rather than choice. Izaak Walton repeats an anecdote about Robert Sanderson, whose friend Henry Hammond convinced him to try relying on his memory on one occasion:

> And at Dr *Sanderson's* going into the Pulpit, he gave his Sermon (which was a very short one) into the hand of Dr *Hammond*, intending to preach it as 'twas writ; but before he had preach'd a third part, Dr *Hammond* (looking on his Sermon as written) observed him to be out, and so lost as to the matter, that he also became afraid for him; for 'twas discernable to many of the plain Auditory; But when he had ended this short Sermon, as they two walk'd homeward, Dr *Sanderson* said with much earnestness, *Good Doctor give me my Sermon, and know, that neither you nor any man living, shall ever persuade me to preach again without my Books.* To which the reply was, *Good Doctor be not angry, for if I ever perswade you to preach again without Book, I will give you leave to burn all those that I am Master of.*[8]

Sanderson's embarrassment at his faulty memory is evident from Walton's narrative.

The notes that the preacher prepared for delivering his sermon are, in effect, the earliest draft of the sermon that might survive and be available to us. Preachers usually kept these notes for use in future sermons and as a record of what they had delivered. Occasionally, these notes became the basis of a printed sermon-book if no other, better copy-text survived, as was sometimes the case with posthumous publications.[9] Anthony Burgess, the editor of John Stoughton's sermons, explains to the reader that Stoughton had left some of his sermons fully written out and ready for the press. Burgess had to piece together some of the other sermons by combining the notes that Stoughton had left with notes made by hearers. Stoughton's notes comprised diagrammatic summaries, which the editor includes as a preface to the sermon as proof of authenticity; these are described as '*the heads of the Sermons (which were all that were left perfected by the Author)*'

---

[7] Bodleian MSS Eng.th.b.4–7, Sermon Notes by Dr John Warner, Bishop of Rochester. These include notes on sermons heard by Warner, in Oxford and elsewhere, and notes on some of his own sermons. Some are very short, taking up no more than four sides of paper; others are extensive, such as the notes on a sermon that he preached at Paul's Cross, 21 April 1611: Bod. MS Eng. th.b.5, ff. 95–102. Preparatory notes towards a sermon by William Chappell, Provost of Trinity College Dublin, were printed posthumously as *The Use of Holy Scripture Gravely and Methodically Discoursed* (1653), Wing C1958. The notes are very unlike Warner's, being rather schematic and containing almost no continuous prose.

[8] Izaak Walton, *The Lives of John Donne, Sir Henry Wotton, Richard Hooker, George Herbert, and Robert Sanderson*, ed. George Saintsbury (Oxford: Oxford University Press, 1927), p. 385.

[9] Several Paul's Cross sermons were first published posthumously, and some of these were worked up by editors from notes left by the author. Emmanuel Utie describes his edition of Roger Fenton's sermons as having 'the proportion of his former workes, thou not lin'd with those fresh colours, yet his without addition or correction': R. Fenton, *A Treatise. . . . With 6 Certaine Sermons Preached in Publike Assemblies* (1617), *STC²* 10805, sig. Aᵛ. Hamlett Marshall, editor of a Paul's Cross sermon by John Spenser, writes that Spenser's sermons were 'penned for his own private use, then with any purpose to have printed eyther before or after his own death': *A Learned and Gracious Sermon Preached at Paules Crosse* (1615), *STC²* 23096, sig. ¶4ʳ. Utie and Marshall describe themselves as the author's junior colleague (curate or 'minister', presumably lecturer) and no doubt acquired the author's papers for this reason.

placed as *'a methodicall Analysis prefixed'* before the sermon as reconstructed from notes.[10]

More usually, if a preacher wished to make his sermon public after its delivery, he would make, or have made, a full manuscript copy. Several such manuscript copies of unprinted Paul's Cross sermons are extant.[11] Unfortunately, none of the manuscripts provide explanations for the production of the full-text copy, but we can reconstruct these reasons from other sources. We can assume that it was a sufficiently onerous task not to be undertaken without reason: John Donne commented that it took him about eight hours to copy a sermon out in full.[12] A preacher whose sermon was found offensive or controversial was usually commanded to present a copy to the bishop of London for examination. (This topic will be dealt with in greater detail in Chapter 3.) A more common reason for writing out a full copy of a sermon was the request of friends or potential patrons who had been in the auditory. Roger Ley dedicated his first Paul's Cross sermon to Mr Robert Ducie, Alderman of London, who, Ley says, was present when it was preached. Similarly, Henry Greenwood 'presumed to present' to Sir and Lady Lestrange Mordaunt the doctrine 'that lately in publike place was sounded in your eares'.[13] These copies might then circulate among networks of associates: John Chamberlain sent copies of popular or newsworthy sermons to Dudley Carleton, particularly those by Lancelot Andrewes. On 30 December 1609, he told Carleton that he was 'promised some notes' of Andrewes' Christmas sermon 'and then your part is therein'. Accessing these manuscript copies depended on the usefulness of one's associates and acquaintances, however. Of John Donne's 1617 Accession Day sermon at Paul's Cross, Chamberlain told Carleton, 'I know not how to procure a copie of Dr Donne's sermon yf yt come not in print, but I will inquire after it'.[14] The circulation of manuscript copies of sermons happened in less socially exalted circles too: George Creswell reports that he made the initial copy of his sermon 'at the *request*

---

[10] John Stoughton, *XV Choice Sermons Preached upon Select Occasions* (1640), *STC²* 23302, sigs A4^{r-v}. The 'methodolicall' analyses preface 'Five Sermons on II Cor. V. XX' (sigs A2^r–A4^r) and 'Six Sermons on 1 Cor. II.II' (sigs A3^r–A4^r).

[11] The most famous manuscript copy of a Paul's Cross sermon is that of John Donne's 1622 Gunpowder Plot sermon, edited by Jeanne Shami: *John Donne's 1622 Gunpowder Plot Sermon: A Parallel-Text Edition* (Pittsburgh: Duquesne University Press, 1996). Manuscript copies of sermons not mentioned elsewhere in this study include a sermon by 'Mr Lambe' (possible John Lambe), preached on 20 August 1629 (Bodl. MS Eng.th.e.14, pp. 249–370); the Accession Day sermon for 1620, by John Harris (Lambeth Palace Library MS 447); an undated sermon by John Jegon (LPL MS 113, ff. 35^r–44^r). The Passion sermon for 1588, by 'D Bright', probably Arthur Bright, survives in St Paul's Cathedral, MS 38.F.22, ff. p. 1^r–16^r, on which see Peter McCullough (ed.), *Lancelot Andrewes: Selected Sermons and Lectures* (Oxford: Oxford University Press, 2005), p. 463. The rehearsal sermon for 1605 by R. Barlow (who has not been identified, but may be Ralph Barlow, later Bishop of Tuam) survives in Huntington Library MS Ellesmere 1172, along with Barlow's summary of the Good Friday sermon by 'Dr Fentoun' (possibly Roger Fenton). A sermon by John Dove preached on 1 June 1606 is extant in Folger MS V.a.251, and a Paul's Cross sermon by an unknown preacher from 2 February 1636/7 is in Folger MS V.a.1, ff. 59^r–73^r. My sincerest thanks go to the archivists and librarians who assisted me in consulting these manuscripts.

[12] John Donne, *Letters to Severall Persons of Honour* (1651), Wing D1865, p. 154.

[13] Roger Ley, *The Bruising of the Serpents Head* (1622), *STC²* 15568, sig. A2^r; Henry Greenwood, *Tormenting Tophet, or a Terrible Description of Hel* (1615), *STC²* 12336, sig. A3^v.

[14] *The Letters of John Chamberlain*, vol.1, pp. 292, 295; vol. 2, p. 74.

of a religious knight (*an Alderman of the Citie of* London)' but was thereafter 'desired (*nay, importuned*)' by other acquaintances to have it printed.[15] In the case of the Rehearsal sermons, it appears to have been a courtesy for the Spital preachers to provide the 'Rehearser' appointed for Paul's Cross with a copy of his sermon, as the rehearser had to summarize the Spital sermons.[16] Many of these manuscript copies went no further than the collections of the preachers and their friends, and appear to have been intended for nothing more. Some were probably also intended to become the copy-text for printers: John Donne had the presentation copy of his 1622 Paul's Cross Gunpowder Plot sermon made on the king's request, and it is probable that print publication was intended even though this did not happen at that time.[17]

Those present at the sermon who were unable to acquire the preacher's copy could make notes of their own, a practice that modern scholars now associate with 'the godly' but which was too common to be restricted to them. We have already encountered note-takers like the clothier Robert Saxby, or John Manningham of Middle Temple (whose rather ungodly diary includes scurrilous anecdotes as well as sermon notes). Henry Smith recommended the practice to his auditors as the method used by 'some of the Universitie, which did never heare good sermon, but assoone as they were gone, they rehearsed it thus'.[18] John Rogers recommended note-taking at sermons to a gentlewoman called Anne Smithe, impressing on her that 'so manie sermons thou hast well hard as thou hast thy notes to shew in thy bookes'.[19] In his pedagogic writings, John Brinsley recommended the taking of sermon notes as a means of teaching the Christian religion to grammar school boys. The lowest forms were expected to take down only three or four notes, but the older boys were expected to note down 'all the substance and effect of the Sermon', and to note down in the margin all the scriptural references given by the preacher. They would then be able to make a 'repetition' of the sermon 'yea to doe it with admiration for children'.[20]

Sermon notes by hearers survive in a great variety of forms, some written up later in neater or more extended form, others left in tiny notebooks as they were jotted down during the sermon. Some notes give a full summary of the sermon's

---

[15] George Creswell, *The Harmonie of the Lawe and the Gospell* (1607), STC^2 6038, sig. A3ʳ.

[16] Thomas Goff tells us that he gave notes of his sermon to the rehearser: *Deliverance from the Grave* (1627), STC^2 11978, sigs A2ʳ⁻ᵛ. This practice probably explains the survival of a manuscript version of Lancelot Andrewes' 1588 Spital sermon in St Paul's Cathedral MS 38.F.22.01, a manuscript book containing the three Spital sermons for that year. On this manuscript, and the differences between the two versions of Andrewes' sermon, see McCullough (ed.), *Lancelot Andrewes: Selected Sermons and Lectures*, pp. 462–6.

[17] Jeanne Shami, 'Donne's 1622 Sermon on the Gunpowder Plot: His Original Presentation Manuscript Discovered', *English Manuscript Studies, 1100–1700*, 5 (1995), 63–86, p. 64; Jeanne Shami (ed.), *John Donne's 1622 Gunpowder Plot Sermon*, pp. 11–14.

[18] Henry Smith, *Thirteene Sermons upon Severall Textes of Scripture* (1592), STC^2 22717, f. 18ʳ.

[19] Bodl. MS. Rawl. D. 274, 'Theological Common-place book of John Rogers', p. 379.

[20] John Brinsley, *Ludus Literarius: or, The Grammar Schoole* (1612), STC^2 3768, pp. 255–9, 255–6. See also John Brinsley, *A Consolation for our Grammar Schooles* (1622), STC^2 3767, p. 56. The repetition, or 'rehearsing', of sermons in homes after a sermon is a practice associated with puritan piety: Patrick Collinson, 'Elizabethan and Jacobean Puritanism as Forms of Popular Culture', in Christopher Durston and Jacqueline Eales (eds), *The Culture of English Protestantism, 1560–1700* (London: Macmillan), pp. 32–57, pp. 47–50.

argument, and may have been taken by an assistant or relative of the preacher, possibly to assist print publication later.[21] Most sermon notes by hearers can be distinguished from preachers' notes by their incompleteness: most hearers could not copy down exactly every word of a sermon or speech.[22] Instead, hearers did as Brinsley advised his grammar school boys: they concentrated on getting a summary of the sermon's main argument (Brinsley's 'substance and effect') and the scriptural references given.[23] We can demonstrate this with an example from John Manningham's diary, which include notes of John Spenser's sermon preached at Paul's Cross on 10 October 1602.[24] This sermon was not printed until 1615, so Manningham cannot have referred to the printed edition when he made his diary entry. The notes are extensive, beginning with some points that Spenser made in his introduction about the sinfulness of the times and the nature of parables (p. 90). The five main points (or 'doctrines', as they were called) that Spenser presented are noted down in diminishing fullness, with the fourth having only one sentence (pp. 91–5). Manningham seems to have lost the thread of the sermon at this point, because he then noted down only a couple of stray points from the final sections of Spenser's sermon. The first, a complaint about England's covetousness, is a long paragraph; the other, a digression on a rumour that papists were buying up church livings and making use of the funds to support the Jesuits, is almost as long in Manningham's notes as it is in the printed version of Spenser's sermon (pp. 94–5; Spenser, p. 38). The section where Manningham is closest to the sermon as it was printed is the 'division' of the biblical text, the place where a preacher provided a summary of the sermon's points in the order in which they would be handled. The printed version reads:

---

[21] Ian Green has conducted an extensive survey of the different types of sermon notes extant from the sixteenth and seventeenth centuries, and has detailed the different forms in which notes by preachers and hearers survive: 'Continuity and Change in Protestant Preaching in Early Modern England', Friends of the Dr Williams's Library Sixtieth Lecture (London: Dr Williams's Trust, 2009). I am very grateful to Professor Green for allowing me to consult his paper prior to publication.

[22] The exceptions are, of course, those sermons taken down 'by characterie', i.e. in shorthand. Although no Paul's Cross sermon-books are described as deriving from shorthand notes, the practice was not unknown. One reason for using 'characterie' was to get as full a copy of a sermon as possible to use as a copy-text for printing, with or without the author's permission. Three sermons by Henry Smith, by far the most popular Elizabeth preacher, were printed from copies taken 'by characterie' (*STC²* 22660, *STC²* 22664, *STC²* 22693 et seq.) At least one of these, *A Sermon of the Benefite of Contentation* (1590), *STC²* 22693, was produced, the epistle informs the reader, even though 'it were not the authors minde or consent that it shoulde come foorth thus in market' (sig. A3ʳ). The practice continued into the seventeenth century, even though preachers were less shy of publication than Smith had been. William Bridge's *The True Souldiers Convoy* (Rotterdam, 1640), *STC²* 3732, is based on notes 'taken by Characters, whilest it was preached' and it had 'not being ordered to the presse by the author himselfe' (sigs A1ᵛ, G3ʳ).

[23] There are few cases of a sermon surviving in versions derived from the author (a printed sermon-book or authorial manuscript) and in notes taken by a hearer, so there are few cases where such comparisons are possible. A more famous example is provided by the sermon notes on two sermons by John Donne (P&S vol. 5, nos. 18 and 19): P. G. Stanwood, 'John Donne's Sermon Notes', *Review of English Studies* 29(115) (1978), pp. 313–20. On the process of taking notes on sermons see W. Matthews, 'Shakespeare and the Reporters', *The Library* 4th ser., 15 (1935), 381–498, pp. 490–8.

[24] *The Diary of John Manningham*, ed. Robert Parker Sorlein (Hanover, NH: University Press of New England, 1976); John Spenser, *A Learned and Gracious Sermon Preached at Paules Crosse* (1615), *STC²* 23096.

In which words is comprehended the summe of the whole: 1. The church of Israel is proposed under the figure of the Lord's vineyard. 2. Is set downe the Lords care of provision for his Vineyard: *What could I have done for my Vineyard, which I have not done?* 3. The end of God's care and benefites, fruits, good works, (*I looked for grapes*). 4. The Churches unthankfulnes, (It *bringeth forth wilde grapes*) 5. and lastly, the judgement which passed on it, (*Judge, I pray you*). (sig. B2ʳ)

In Manningham's notes, this reads as follows:

The things considerable in the text are, first, the churche, resembled by the vine; 2. Godes benefites towards the churche expressed in the manner of his dressing the vine; 3. the fruit expected; grapes: judgment and righteousness; 4. the fayling and ingratitude, by bringing forth sower and wild grapes; oppression and crying; 5. Godes judgment, vers. 6. (pp. 90–1)

Most of Manningham's sermon notes follow the same pattern: he almost always records the biblical text on which the preacher spoke and the 'division' of the biblical text; he attempts to follow the main points (or 'doctrines'), in order, but when he gets lost he just takes down stray points or anecdotes that interested him.[25] Another example is provided by a sermon preached on 23 September 1565 by John Bullingham, a prebendary of St Paul's: manuscript notes by two hearers of the sermon survive. While one notetaker (the writer of Bodleian Library MS Tanner 50) makes better sense of the sermon than the other (Lambeth Palace Library MS 739), both hearers include the 'division' of the text and the two copies of the 'division' are substantially the same, differing mainly in the wording used.[26]

Notes of sermons taken from printed sermon-books are very different: having access to the entire text of the sermon, and perhaps permanent ownership of it, the reader did not need to record the structure of the argument in summary, and so did not note the biblical text or its division. There was also time to copy out every word of passages that were of particular interest. An example of this is found in notes on John Wilkinson's 1620 sermon *Rabboni, or Mary Magdalens teares,* in Bodleian Manuscript Rawlinson D.1350. The heading gives the date of the sermon's printed edition, so the source is in no doubt. There is no summary of the sermon's argument; instead, passages of rather purple prose from different parts of the sermon have been written out in full, with references to the pages of the printed edition.[27]

---

[25] Other good examples are Manningham's notes on an otherwise unknown Paul's Cross sermon by Roger Fenton, preacher at Gray's Inn, pp. 134–9; 'one Barlowe, a beardless man of Pembroke hall in Cambridge', pp. 164–7; and Thomas Holland, pp. 196–201. One of the shortest summaries is on p. 134, where the sermon of 'a good plaine fellowe' in the Temple Church is recorded only in the text, the division, and one sentence. The one occasion where the division is not noted is when 'Dr Dawson' preached at Paul's Cross. Manningham notes the text and then remarks that 'all the while he prayed he kept on his velvet night cap untill he came to name the Queen, and then of went that to, when he had spoken before both of and to God with it on his head'. This extraordinary performance obviously distracted Manningham, as the first page of his notes consist of unconnected and very short jottings (p. 131).

[26] Bodl. MS Tanner 50 ff. 3ʳ⁻ᵛ; LPL MS 739, ff. 2ʳ–4ᵛ.

[27] Bodl. MS Rawlinson D.1350, ff. 53ʳ–55ᵛ. Another good example is the extract from John Milward's Gowrie plot sermon of 1607, *Jacob's Great Day of Trouble, and Deliverance* (1610), *STC*² 17942, found in BL Add. 12,515. Milward's encomium to Elizabeth is written out in full as 'A note of Queene Elizabeth and King James', ff. 22ᵛ–23ʳ.

PRINTED SERMON-BOOKS

The sermon had its widest reach, and potentially greatest impact, when it was published in print, and the Paul's Cross sermons were increasingly popular as printed commodities over the period studied. Only four sermons from the 1550s were printed, in three sermon-books, and only one from the 1560s. That number climbs to eleven for the 1570s, fifteen (in ten sermon-books) for the 1580s, and fifteen (in fifteen sermon-books) for the 1590s. During the reign of James I, the high point of the Cross's prestige, the most dramatic publication rates are seen: forty sermons (in thirty-nine sermon-books) were printed between 1600 and 1609; sixty-two between 1610 and 1619, and fifty between 1620 and 1629. Thereafter, the popularity of Paul's Cross diminished: twenty-eight sermons (in twenty-six sermon-books) were printed in the 1630s, and only fifteen sermons described as being appointed for Paul's Cross appeared (in thirteen sermon-books) in the twenty years before 1661.[28]

The process by which Paul's Cross sermons came to be printed was much the same as that for any other work.[29] A publisher had to be willing to take on the financial risk involved, and to make a payment to the preacher in exchange for the manuscript of the sermon.[30] What preachers were paid for the copy of their sermon is not known, but the existence of a posthumous publication like John Stoughton's *XV Choice Sermons Preached upon Select Occasions* (1640), which was published for the financial benefit of his widow, suggests that they were paid something.[31] The numbers of Paul's Cross sermons printed, particularly in the Jacobean period, would indicate that they were considered a sound economic venture, and so publishers may have been willing to pay for the copy. A sermon-book with a single sermon fitted neatly into the gap between the 'penny godly' and the larger, Latin treatises and commentaries that many English printers and booksellers considered too expensive to produce and sell.[32] The average quarto Paul's Cross sermon-book took up between five and thirteen sheets of paper and probably

---

[28] The figures given are for the years in which the sermons were printed, not when they were preached. Except for those first published in collections, most of the Paul's Cross sermons that were printed appeared within two years of their delivery.

[29] The best guide to the process of print publication is Peter W. M. Blayney, 'The Publication of Playbooks', in John D. Cox and David Scott Kasten (eds), *A New History of Early English Drama* (New York: Columbia University Press, 1997), pp. 383–422, pp. 389–415.

[30] 'Publisher' is used here to mean the person who arranged for the printing of the sermon-book and financed the venture. As Peter Blayney has pointed out, these were usually, but not always, wholesale booksellers rather than members of a separate profession (ibid. p. 391).

[31] John Stoughton, *XV Choice Sermons Preached upon Select Occasions* (1640), *STC*[2] 23306, sig. A3[r]. This collection is a reissue with a new title page of two others, *Choice Sermons preached upon Selected Occasions*, *STC*[2] 23302, and *XI Choice Sermons*, *STC*[2] 23304. This would suggest that Stoughton's sermons did not sell very well.

[32] John Barnard, 'Introduction', in John Barnard, D. F. McKenzie, with Maureen Bell (eds), *The Cambridge History of the Book in Britain*, vol. IV: *1557–1695* (Cambridge: Cambridge University Press, 2002), pp. 1–25, pp. 5–9. On the 'penny godlies', cheap broadsides, and ballads with a pious or providential theme, see Tessa Watt, *Cheap Print and Popular Piety, 1550–1640* (Cambridge: Cambridge University Press, 1991).

retailed at four or six pence (more than a 'penny godly' but comparable to a playbook).[33] Most were not marketed to the poorest book-buyers, however, judging by their format and typeface. Paul's Cross sermon-books from the 1550s and 1560s were usually printed in black letter (the typeface that was most widely legible, even to those with only basic literacy skills), as were nine of the ten sermon-books containing Paul's Cross sermons preached in the 1570s. Only six (out of ten sermon-books) were printed in black letter in the 1580s, and only three (out of fifteen sermon-books) from the 1590s.[34] Only three Paul's Cross sermons thereafter were printed in black letter.[35] The smallest format in which Paul's Cross sermons were printed is octavo, with the majority of single sermon-books from the 1600 onwards being in quarto format and collections of two or more sermons in quarto and, for larger collections, in folio.[36]

Another indication of the profitability of sermon-books is the readiness of publishers to arrange for print publication without the permission of the preacher, using either notes taken by hearers at the sermon or the preacher's own notes or full-text copy of the sermon. The popular Ipswich preacher Samuel Ward appeared at Paul's Cross in 1616, and in the printed version of this sermon, *Balm from Gilead to Recover Conscience*, Thomas Gataker, his friend and editor, tells the reader that Ward was asked to prepare the sermon for the press but refused out of modesty.[37] In the end, however, '*to prevent the wrong that by imperfect Copies printed he might otherwise sustaine*', he left his notes and deputed care of the publication to Gataker who, '*being present at the speaking of it, with the Authors Notes, and his owne helpes, hath done his endeavour to penne it as neare as he could, to that which by the Authour himself was then delivered*'. Should we doubt this story, the dedicatory epistle to another of Ward's sermons makes clear that the threat was real. Ambrose Wood, 'Ward's affectionate friend', admits he was responsible for printing the sermons 'which I copied partly from your mouth, and partly from your notes' without

---

[33] Peter Blayney calculated that the average playbook was printed on nine sheets of paper, so a sermon-book with a single sermon, title page, and dedication is roughly comparable in size ('The Publication of Playbooks', p. 406). On the retail price of playbooks, see pp. 411–12. For the retail price of sermon-books, see David McKitterick, ' "Ovid with a Littleton": The Cost of English Books in the Early Seventeenth Century', *Transactions of the Cambridge Bibliographical Society*, 11 (1997), 184–234, p. 220; Green, *Print and Protestantism in Early Modern England*, p. 39.

[34] These figures give the numbers of sermons preached in each decade; all sermons in this sample were printed in the same decade that they were preached.

[35] Those three are William Barlow, *A Sermon Preached at Paules Crosse* (1601), *STC²* 1454, on the Earl of Essex's execution in 1601 (a sermon printed swiftly and intended to reach as wide an audience as possible); Greenwood, *Tormenting Tophet* (which also makes use of italic and roman typefaces for quotations and their translation), and Robert Johnson, *Dives and Lazarus*, 4th edn. (1623), *STC²* 14694.3, a sermon whose tone and subject is similar to that of the 'penny godlies'. Unusually for a Paul's Cross sermon-book, many of which did not have a second edition, this sermon had eight editions up to 1628.

[36] David L. Gants notes that two-thirds of single sermon-books printed between 1614 and 1618 were in quarto format: 'A Quantitative Analysis of the London Book Trade, 1614–1618', *Studies in Bibliography*, 55 (2002), 185–213, p. 190 and Table 3. Tessa Watts notes that sermons were not generally published as 'penny godlies', a possible exception being the very popular *Trumpet of the Soule* by Henry Smith: *Cheap Print and Popular Piety, 1550–1640* (Cambridge: Cambridge University Press, 1991), pp. 314–15.

[37] Samuel Ward, *Balme from Gilead to Recover Conscience* (1617), *STC²* 25035, sigs A3^{r–v}.

Ward's permission but with the 'approbation and earnest intreaty of such, whose judgments you reverence, and whose love you embrace: who also have made bold here and there to vary some things; not to any great consequence, if I can judge'.[38] George Bury's 1607 sermon was offered to the press in similar circumstances by an anonymous 'C.B', who admits his 'boldnesse in committing this Sermon to the generall view . . . without his [the author's] leave' because 'it hath received the current stampe of approbation in the judgement of the wisest' and of the dedicate, Sir William Walgrave, 'an auricular judge of the gracefull delivery'.[39] The publication of marketable sermons without the preacher's permission was common enough to force Thomas Playfere to offer inducements to the public to buy the right edition: his Spital sermon, *The Pathway to Perfection*, was issued with his hugely popular *The Meane of Mourning*. An unauthorized version of the latter sermon, printed 'falsly, and in most places so quite contrary to my meaning', went through three editions in 1595. Playfere was 'enforced of necessitie' to have a corrected version of *The Meane of Mourning* printed and

thought good likewise to let this [*The Pathway to Perfection*] goe with it. . . . so if any one who hath cast away his money upon the former editions, wil bestow a groate upon the true copie now set out by my selfe, hee may have this sermon with it for nothing, in surplussage over and besides the bargaine.[40]

Having secured a copy of the sermon, the publisher needed to get permission from the censors, the chaplains of the bishop of London, or archbishop of Canterbury, for printing the sermon. Many sermon-books were licensed in the normal way,[41] with the publisher paying for the text to be scrutinized by the censors. The dedication to George Gifford's 1591 Paul's Cross sermon is signed by 'T.C.', almost certainly Tobie Cooke, the publisher. He tells us that the copy-text derives from notes taken by hearers that were 'conferred and laid together' and then corrected by the preacher. The 'coppie comminge to my handes, I have', he says, 'by publicke authoritie printed it'.[42] Given the sensitivity of the subject matter in an age of religious controversy, it is no surprise that some sermons were censored. Michael Wigmore's *The Way of all Flesh* has omissions from the version

---

[38] Samuel Ward, *A Coal from the Altar* (1615), sig. π^r. This is *STC²* 25039. The second edition appeared the following year and was corrected and 'much amended' by the author: *STC²* 25040. Thomas Cheshire tells the reader that he had decided to print his 1640 Paul's Cross sermon because a bad edition had been printed. This edition did appear: on the copy of the sermon in the Thomason tracts (Thomason E. 177[3]), there is a manuscript annotation on the title page that reads 'difrent from the former vide Epist: to the Reader', suggesting that Thomason was aware of a previous edition.
[39] G[eorge] B[ury], *The Narrow Way, and the Last Judgement* (1607), *STC²* 4179.5, sigs A2^{r-v}. The preacher's name is taken from *STC²*.
[40] Thomas Playfere, *The Pathway to Perfection* (1596), sigs A2^r–A3^r. This is *STC²* 20020. It was issued with *STC²* 20015, *The Meane in Mourninge, By T. Playfere* (1596). *STC²* 20014, 20014.3, and 20014.5 are the unauthorized editions. None carry the author's name and all have the title *A Most Excellent and Heavenly Sermon: Upon the 23 Chapter of the Gospell by Saint Luke*. All three were printed for Andrew Wise and are dated 1595.
[41] See S. Mutchow Towers, *Control of Religious Printing in Early Stuart England* (Woodbridge: Boydell Press, 2003).
[42] George Gifford, *A Sermon Preached at Pauls Crosse* (1591), *STC²* 11862.3, sigs A2^{r-v}.

preached because 'some things were exempted by the supervisor as bitter; others spoken in the Pulpit and left out of the copy'.[43] Unfortunately, we know nothing more about this incident.

Comments made in the epistles to some of the Paul's Cross sermon-books suggest that the preachers sometimes played an active part in gaining permission to have their sermons printed.[44] The reason may be the close relationship between at least some of the preachers and the authorities: the preachers at Paul's Cross were appointed by the bishop of London's chaplains, the same men who acted as press censors. The chaplains would have met the preacher before his sermon, and, in the 1630s, may have demanded to see a copy of the sermon before it was preached (something that will be discussed in Chapter 3). They, or the bishop of London, may also have been present at the sermon when it was delivered, and may have indicated to the preacher that print publication would be welcomed. In the dedication to his *Sermon of the Providence of God*, preached in October 1607, John Pelling explains that his patron 'procured the right reverend father in God, the Lord Bishop of London . . . to require it [the copy of the sermon] of me', perused it and 'by his authoritie hath allowed it'.[45] For the bishop's own chaplains, the process was even simpler. In a dedicatory epistle to John Aylmer, Robert Temple writes that 'according to your Lo. Pleasure (right reverend Father) I have copied out this Sermon, and let it go to the presse'.[46] This did not mean that the normal process of obtaining authorization for printing was short-circuited for all Paul's Cross sermons. In the epistle to his *Description New Jerusalem*, preached in 1601, Henoch Clapham writes that after delivering the sermon he '*sent it to the examination, and so it was returned authorized to the presse*'. Clapham was a former separatist, only recently reconciled to the Church of England when he preached this sermon at Paul's Cross; he was to continue to cause problems for the bishop of London thereafter. The authorities may have taken more than usual care with him.[47]

The copy of the sermon then had to be entered into the Stationers' Register to secure the publisher's right to have it printed. Records are far from complete, but it seems that this happened quite quickly for many Paul's Cross sermons: a lapse of

---

[43] Michael Wigmore, *The Way of All Flesh* (1619), *STC²* 25618, sig. A3ʳ.

[44] This appears to have been relatively common, particularly for authors of religious books. See Cyndia Susan Clegg, *Press Censorship in Elizabethan England* (Cambridge: Cambridge University Press, 1997), pp. 63–5; Arnold Hunt, 'Licensing and Religious Censorship in Early Modern England', in Andrew Hadfield (ed.), *Literature and Censorship in Renaissance England* (London: Palgrave Macmillan, 2001), pp. 127–46, pp. 131–5.

[45] John Pelling, *A Sermon of the Providence of God* (1607), *STC²* 19567, sig. A3ᵛ. Pelling's sermon was entered in the Stationers' Register on 18 November 1607 with Thomas Ravis, Bishop of London, listed as the licenser: Edward Arber, *A Transcript of the Register of the Company of Stationers, 1554–1640* (1875–94), vol. 3, f. 160ᵛ.

[46] Robert Temple, *A Sermon Teaching Discretion in Matters of Religion* (1592), *STC²* 23869, sig. A2ʳ.

[47] Henoch Clapham, *A Description of New Jerusalem* (1601), *STC²* 5336.5, sig. A4ʳ. Alexandra Walsham, 'Clapham, Henoch (fl. 1585–1614)', *Oxford Dictionary of National Biography*, (Oxford: Oxford University Press, 2004; online edn., Jan 2008, <http://www.oxforddnb.com/view/article/5431>, accessed 2 February 2008.

between two and four weeks between preaching and entry for publication is not uncommon.[48] Thomas Adams' four Paul's Cross sermons were all entered in the Stationers' Register within three months of being preached, but the last of these, *The Temple*, a sermon on the anniversary of the Gowrie Conspiracy preached in 1624, was entered a mere six days after its delivery.[49] The shortness of this period suggests that publishers moved quickly with a sermon they thought profitable or newsworthy. Adam's sermon on the Gowrie Conspiracy unites a warning against idolatry with an assertion of God's care for Protestant England, a heady mixture in the summer of 1624 when Prince Charles was urging war against Spain. Entering the copy also protected the publisher from pirate publications: pirate editions of sermons, especially by famous preachers like Henry 'Silver-tongued' Smith, lecturer at St. Clement Danes, are extant, suggesting that there was competition for 'vendible' sermons.[50]

Finally, the publisher had to find a printer to set the text and print the copies. Although it is a commonplace to say that early modern authors were rarely assiduous in seeing their works through the press, at least some of the Paul's Cross preachers appear to have seen and corrected proofs of their sermon-books before publication.[51] For those with benefices outside London, this would have required some effort: the Paul's Cross preachers were provided with accommodation from the Thursday night before their sermon until the Monday after dinner (which took place around midday) following the sermon. This hardly left time to produce a copy of their sermon, let alone find a publisher and see the sermon through the press. They could only correct proofs if they came back to London or made other arrangements to see them. As we have seen, Samuel Ward, preacher at Ipswich, left the printing of his Paul's Cross sermon in the care of his friend Thomas Gataker, then Rector of Rotherhithe in Surrey (but also a guest lecturer in Lincoln's Inn, his former post). Presumably Gataker was better placed to see the work through the press. Occasionally, preachers elected to have their sermons printed closer to home at one of the university presses (although the publisher sometimes also made arrangements for selling through a London bookseller).[52]

---

[48] R. C. Bald has shown that sermons by John Donne and William Laud were also entered within a month of being preached: 'Dr. Donne and the Booksellers', *Studies in Bibliography*, 18 (1965), pp. 70–80, p. 75.

[49] Thomas Adams, *The Temple* (1624), *STC²* 129; it was entered on 11 August.

[50] Pirate editions of collections of sermons by Henry Smith are listed as *STC²* 22783.3 and 22783.5.

[51] Errata lists are one sign of this, and are to be found in the first editions of several sermon-books: Thomas Aylesbury [Ailesbury], *A Sermon Preached at Paules Crosse* (1623), *STC²* 1000; Robert Barrell, *The Spiritual Architecture* (1624), *STC²* 1498; Robert Bedingfield, *A Sermon Preached at Pauls Crosse* (Oxford, 1625), *STC²* 1792; Edward Chaloner, *Six Sermons* (1622), *STC²* 4936; William Foster, *The Means to Keep Sinne from Reigning* (1629), *STC²* 11204; Joseph Hall, *The Passion-sermon* (1609), *STC²* 12693.7; Roger Ley, *Two Sermons* (1619), *STC²* 15569; Charles Sonibancke [Sonnibank], *The Eunuches Conversion* (1617), *STC²* 22927.

[52] Thomas Barne and Robert Bedingfield are described as students on the title pages of their printed sermons: Thomas Barne, *A Sermon Preached at Pauls Cross* (Oxford, 1591), *STC²* 1464.8; Robert Bedingfield, *A Sermon Preached at Pauls Crosse* (Oxford, 1625), *STC²* 1792. Thomas Holland, Regius Professor of Divinity in Oxford and Rector of Exeter College, had both editions of his Paul's Cross sermon printed there, although the second edition had a London bookseller: Thomas Holland, [[H] -e paneguris]

Even if preachers were able to visit or communicate with the printer frequently, the printer might not have been able to comply with the author's demands for commercial reasons. John Andrewes tells his readers that he has not 'conclouted *the* Margent *with many* Quotations; *because I found it somewhat* cumbersome *to the* Compositors'. The printer of Elias Petley's *The Royall Receipt* found a way around another expensive aspect of printing a sermon: he informs the reader that as well as the errata he lists there are other '*literall, figurative,* and *punctuall* faults, which the Ingenuous will either mend or pardon. For Greeke I had none: such Notes as I might not omit, I have expressed in Italian Letter'.[53] The printer Henry Bynneman provides an unusually detailed account of the difficulties he faced with one of Thomas White's sermons. He writes:

I crave pardon (Christian Reader) for that the Writer being full of other businesse him selfe, wherby he could not followe this, and his hande beeing very harde & small, hath bin the cause of some escapes in the print: Yet let it not discourage thee, but take thy pen and bestow the paynes to correct them, and I hope the profite shall make thee recompence. I have not altogether satisfied the Author neither in disposing many things, yet I have done my best, but the matter being not much amisse, our labour is not lost.[54]

The author clearly saw a copy of the sermon and provided a list of corrigenda for the printer. Something in the layout (the 'disposing') of the sermon was disliked, but the printer clearly thought they were minor matters (there is 'not much amisse'). George Creswell also saw proofs of his sermon before it went to press, and his printer alerts the reader to an error in the typesetting, rather than resetting the text:

Understand, Christian Reader, that part of the matter contained in the ninetenth and twentith pages aforegoing, was (by him that copied out this Sermon, for the Presse), set downe in the Margent, without certain direction for us, where to bring it into the body of the Book. And consequently, for want of a guide, we have somwhat failed (as we understand since) of the due order observed by the Authour, in his originall Copy: which was as followeth . . . .[55]

D. Elizabetha (Oxford, 1600), *STC*[2] 13596.5; *Paneguris D. Elizabethae* (Oxford, 1601), *STC*[2] 13597; John Gumbleden signs the epistle of his sermon from his 'study in Longworth, Berkshire'; although printed at Oxford, it was sold by William Web, a London bookseller: *Gods Great Mercy to Mankinde* (Oxford, 1628), sig. A2[v]. Miles Mosse, based in Combes in Suffolk, had his sermon printed in Cambridge, as did John Fosbroke, described on the title page as rector of St. Andrew's Craneford in Northampton; Mosse's sermon was sold in London through Matthew Law: Miles Mosse, *Justifying and Saving Faith* (Cambridge, 1614), *STC*[2] 18209; John Fosbroke, 'England's Warning', in *Six Sermons* (Cambridge, 1633), *STC*[2] 11199.

[53] John Andrewes, *The Brazen Serpent* (1621), *STC*[2] 591, sig. A3[v]; Elias Petley, *The Royall Receipt* (1623), *STC*[2] 19801, sig. H2[r].

[54] Thomas White, *A Sermon preached at Pawles Crosse* (1578), *STC*[2] 25405, sig. A4[r]. The printer's name is not on the title page but is listed in *STC*[2].

[55] George Creswell, *The Harmonie of the Lawe and the Gospel* (1607), *STC*[2] 6038, sig. D8[r]. Creswell signs the dedicatory epistle and dates it 8 October 1607; the sermon was preached on 9 August that year. It is therefore very unlikely that the sermon was published without Creswell's permission or that this is a second edition.

The preacher's oversight of the printing of his sermon can be partly explained by the widespread assumption that the paper copy was a record of the sermon as it was delivered from Paul's Cross. In the epistles of sermon-books, preachers often insist that the printed version of the sermon is as close to what was preached as their notes and their memory would allow. In preparing his sermon for the press, William Holbrooke claims to have kept 'as neere as I can to the very words I used in the preaching of it, without addition or detraction'. The same claim is made by Thomas White for the printed version of his 1589 Accession Day sermon.[56] Thomas Playfere (or his printer) goes to great lengths to assure his readers than they will read his *The Pathway to Perfection* as it was preached. In the epistle to the reader, we are told:

> The quotations which are marked without a Parenthesis, as this [abc] were all uttered when the Sermon was preached. The rest which are marked with a Parenthesis, as thus, ([a]), ([b]), ([c]) were thought convenient to be printed, though not the quotations themselves, but only the matter contained in them was preached.[57]

Playfere was not the only one to take such pains to point out relatively small changes: Abraham Gibson tells his readers '*some* Quotations *I have omitted, and interposed in the* Margent, *to the end it may no way be obscure, but plaine to the plainest*'.[58] Even when the changes were too extensive for this kind of specificity, preachers make reference to the types of changes made, again demonstrating an assumption that the printed sermon would be treated as a record of the sermon preached. Additions are usually justified on the grounds that they contain material the preacher intended to deliver, and so were essentially part of the sermon, but that the preacher ran out of time in the pulpit. John Whalley ends his printed Paul's Cross sermon where he ended it when preaching. The last pages contain a note saying: 'But where my wordes were cut off in preaching, my lines must end in writing. Therefore to end, take these uses to thy profit'. This is followed by a list of the 'uses' and 'profits' for the reader.[59] Others took the opportunity of the printed version to make good on what they left out. In the epistle to the reader, Daniel Donne informs us that 'from the Beginning of' his printed sermon 'to the 52. Page, I preached it word for word as it is printed', but that lack of time meant the rest of the printed sermon was given only 'a briefe Paraphrasticall Explication' in the pulpit; he makes up for this in the sermon-book, where this section is expanded to

---

[56] William Holbrooke, *Loves Complaint, for Want of Entertainment* ([1610?]), *STC²* 13564, sig. A4ʳ; Thomas White, *A Sermon Preached at Paules Crosse* (1589), *STC²* 25407, sig. A2ᵛ.

[57] Thomas Playfere, *The Pathway to Perfection* (1596), *STC²* 20020, sig. A4ʳ.

[58] Abraham Gibson, *The Lands Mourning, for Vaine Swearing* (1613), *STC²* 11829, sig. A4ʳ. In the same spirit, Henry Greenwood tells his readers to treat the quotations in Latin and 'other tongues' as 'country stiles, stepping over them thou losest not the way by them, for their exposition follow them': *Tormenting Tophet* (1615), *STC²* 12336 sig. A4ᵛ.

[59] John Whalley, *Gods Plentie Feeding True Pietie* (1616), *STC²* 25294, pp. 67–8. William Fisher also gave an abbreviated form of the points he would have preached in full 'if the time did not exclude me' (sig. D5ʳ). These points fill the pages of the rest of the quire (to D8ᵛ), so there may have also been considerations of space and the cost of additional paper: *A Godly Sermon Preached at Paules Crosse* (1592), *STC²* 10919.

become almost double the length of the rest.[60] Similarly, Francis Marbury managed to deliver only half his sermon at Paul's Cross. In the printed version, he tells the reader: '*This second part was not uttered for lacke of time, but was likewise by authoritie thought fit to be annexed in the print*'.[61] John Stockwood tells his readers that there is 'more here set down, than in deed was uttered at the Crosse, yet was the whole meant there to have bin spoken, had not time cut off so much of it as was handled at another place in the afternoon'.[62] References to oral delivery are also left in sermons: the address to those present at the beginning and the call to prayer at the end in particular. Robert Wakeman leaves us a very specific reference to the conditions in which he delivered his sermon. He tells his readers, much as he would have told his hearers:

And I must confesse that my meditations have beene so farre inlarged in this second point, that (the time beeing almost past and the weather so sodainely unseasonable) I shall not now deliver, without offending your patience, the one quarter of that which I had purposed.[63]

We can see from this that a sermon could be expanded in publication without being considered different in essence from the oration delivered at Paul's Cross. We can therefore conclude that the various forms in which a sermon was recorded and transmitted all retained what was considered essential and identifying about that sermon. And what was essential to each sermon was the structure it derived from the way it interpreted the passage of the Bible on which the preacher spoke. When preachers say that they have revised the sermon, they are at pains to say that this essential structure has been unaltered. Anthony Anderson says that he has 'faithfully here set down' his sermon because 'neither anye Methode is altered, or matter omitted, that by me then was there spoken' even though the 'words' were altered. Similarly, John Foxe says that his 1570 sermon is not 'in speach & forme every thing so precisely as was spoken' but asserts that he has 'not much digressed from the sentence, order, & principall poyntes in the sayd Sermon conteined'.[64] The preacher knew the 'shape' of his oration before he delivered it. The particular 'form of words' might change and digressions might be expanded in the paper copies of the sermon, but this was not seen to alter the sermon beyond recognition. The structure of the sermon and the doctrines it expounded (the 'method' and 'matter', the 'form' and 'principall points', as Anderson and Foxe put it) formed a kind of 'core' that changed little between media. For this reason, we are justified in

---

[60] Daniel Donne, *A Sub-poena from the Star-Chamber of Heaven* (1623), *STC²* 7021, sig. π4ʳ.

[61] Francis Marbury, *A Sermon Preached at Paules Crosse* (1602), *STC²* 17307, sig. E5ʳ. Gabriel Price also appends a 'second part' that was 'not uttered, for lacke of time; yet thought fit by the Author to be annexed in the Print': *The Laver of the Heart* (1616), *STC²* 20306, p. 143.

[62] John Stockwood, *A Sermon Preached at Paules Crosse on Bartholomew Day* ([1578]), *STC²* 23284, sig. A5ʳ. Although a fairly common practice at the time, a sermon preached in two venues like this is uncommon for Paul's Cross. Thomas Burt's *A Nicke for Neuters* (1604), *STC²* 4132, was (according to its title page) 'begun and preached at Paules Crosse . . . and continued & finished in Paules Church'. This is the only other example found by this writer.

[63] Robert Wakeman, *Jonahs Sermon and Ninivehs Repentance* (1606), *STC²* 24948, p. 70.

[64] Anderson, *A Sermon Preached at Paules Crosse* (1581), *STC²* sig. A2ᵛ; John Foxe, *A Sermon of Christ Crucified* (1570), *STC²* 11242.3, sig. A2ᵛ.

following their practice in treating each paper witness as a different version of the same work, not as a separate composition. To give a fuller account of this stability, we must first investigate the method of sermon composition in use at the time.

SERMON COMPOSITION: FROM DESK
TO PULPIT TO PRESS

In a sermon 'purposed' to have been preached at Paul's Cross, Laurence Deios, chaplain to John Aylmer, defines preaching as 'the expounding of scripture and applying of it to the present state, by the working of Gods spirit in the mouth of a man called for that purpose'.[65] The terms of this definition offer us a full account of the theory of preaching espoused by Deios and his fellow Paul's Cross preachers, and they are worth examining in detail.

Firstly, we must pay attention to the strict scriptural emphasis in Deios's definition: preaching is an 'expounding of scripture'. English preachers of the Elizabethan and early Stuart periods preached *on* a text from the Bible: they chose a short passage, usually of no more than three or four verses, sometimes less, and they built the whole of the sermon around it. This extract from Scripture was 'expounded' and 'applied' to 'the present state'. As the preacher began his sermon with God's truth set out in the biblical text, his arguments were made persuasive by his demonstration that they derived from that biblical text. In his 1610 handbook of scriptural commonplaces, William Knight argues for a method of sermon composition in which the meaning of a passage in Scripture is first 'found out by the Grammaticall, Rhetoricall, and Logicall Analysis' and that interpretation is then used as the basis for the subsequent argument. By this method, he says, the preacher will 'teach the people upon those grounds onely, which the holy Ghost hath laide downe to your hand' and the hearers will remember the sermon better. More importantly, 'the things delivered wil be of greater authority in their consciences, leaving them no place for contradiction, because then they shall gainesay the Scriptures'.[66] What the preacher had to say *arose* from his text. As Richard Bernard put it, 'the doctrine is not to bee written from the text, as if the text were drawn to the lesson; and not the doctrine from it.'[67] The sermon drew its authority from the scriptural text, and was convincing insofar as it was clearly derived from the Bible's words.

[65] Lawrence Deios, *That the Pope is That Antichrist* (1590), *STC²* 6475, p. 139. The title page of this sermon-book, containing two sermons by Deios, says the first was preached at Paul's Cross, the second 'purposed also to have bene there preached'. The sermons were printed without the author's permission, according to the epistle, but Deios was a frequent preacher at Paul's Cross: City of London, London Metropolitan Archive, Corporation of London Remembrancia, vol. I, f. 118ʳ.

[66] William Knight, *A Concordance Axiomaticall: Containing a Survey of Theologicall Propositions* (1610), *STC²* 15049, sig. A5ʳ.

[67] Bernard, *The Faithfull Shepheard* (1607), *STC²* 1939 p. 44. The terminology used in seventeenth-century preaching manuals varies between writers. In what follows, I will use the terms given by Richard Bernard, the writer whose models best fit the practice of Paul's Cross preachers.

The first decision the preacher had to make in preparing his sermon, and so the most significant point for any interpretation of a sermon, was the initial choice of biblical text. A Paul's Cross preacher was usually allowed to choose his text.[68] But he would be guided in his choice by exegetical patterns already established, by either the Church Fathers or the Magisterial Reformers. The choice of text was, therefore, determined by the preacher's choice of subject: an exhortation against sinfulness would often take a text from the prophetic books, most notoriously Jeremiah; devotional sermons, Lenten sermons, and sermons on repentance tended to favour the Psalms. The choice of text, and of subject, had to suit the circumstances of the sermon's delivery: it should be 'fit for the hearers . . . agreeing to the persons, the time and the place', as Richard Bernard put it.[69] Robert Sanderson compiled lists of biblical texts suitable for use when preaching on different occasions (weddings, funerals, baptism, etc.), on different topics ('upon victory or good successe', 'against false teachers', or 'in time of war'), and before various auditories (before the king, for judges, and 'texts for Paules Crosse', a rather miscellaneous list of texts with some Jeremiad-like warnings against sinfulness).[70] A more personal choice of text might be made, but the influence of previous interpretations is still apparent: Robert Vase chose the story of Jonah and the vine for his Paul's Cross sermon of 1624 because he, like Jonah, was 'a wrastler' and had to 'study after patience', an interpretation of this episode common since the Middle Ages.[71]

Even smaller extracts from the Bible, down to individual verses, had such well-established interpretations that they were treated as encapsulating the teaching of the Church on particular points: they were commonplaces of arguments, *loci communes* in the strict sense, in that they functioned as summaries of doctrines and arguments that could be applied to particular circumstances.[72] Matthew 22:21 ('Render therefore unto Caesar the things which are Caesar's'), for example, was so generally interpreted as proving that piety did not excuse Christians from political obligations that merely quoting this verse might be sufficient to make the point.[73] Preachers drew on these biblical texts, these 'scriptural common-places' to provide

---

[68] This may have been a change brought by the Reformation. Stephen Gardiner claims that Robert Barnes, preaching at Paul's Cross in 1539, was the first preacher not to choose 'the scripture of the sonday he preached on' (*A Declaration of such True Articles as George Joye hath gone about to confute as false* (1546), *STC²* 11588, f. VIʳ). The one example of a preacher having his text chosen for him is John King's 1620 sermon 'on behalf of Paul's Church', for which the text was given him by the king: *A Sermon at Paules Crosse, on Behalfe of Paules Church* (1620), *STC²* 14982, pp. 32–3.

[69] Bernard, *The Faithful Shepherd* (1621 ed.), *STC²* 1941, p. 116.

[70] BL MS Add. 20,066, 'Notes for sermons by Robert Sanderson', ff. 1–19ʳ.

[71] Robert Vase, *Jonah's Contestation about his Gourd* (1625), *STC²* 24594, sigs A2ᵛ, A3ʳ. John Hayward chose his text for more pragmatic reasons: it was 'offered by order of my private exercise in mine own place': John Hayward, *God's Universal Right Proclaimed* (1603), *STC²* 12984, sig. A2ʳ.

[72] The 'topics', or 'commonplaces of argument', were headings for the types of argument that the speaker could apply to a particular issue. Cicero described them as the 'seats' of arguments: literally, the 'places' in the memory from which arguments could be taken and applied to particular circumstances: Cicero, *Topica*, II.8, trans. H. M. Hubbell (Cambridge, MA: Harvard University Press, for the Loeb Classical Library, 1949), pp. 386–7.

[73] William Barlow chose this text for his sermon on the Earl of Essex's execution. His choice of a text whose relevance to the question of political obligations was firmly established but which did not deal directly with the evils of rebellion was undoubtedly influenced by the authorities' anxiety about

them with proofs for the arguments they presented: for this reason, scriptural quotations like Matthew 22:21 were often called 'proof-texts'. Compilations of such proof-texts were increasingly available to preachers, in concordances or the marginal glosses in the Geneva Bible.[74] The cross-referencing of biblical proof-texts allowed preachers to make a nuanced choice of the text on which they would preach. For example, a sermon on political obedience might take as its text Romans 13 ('Let every soul be subject to the higher powers, for there is no power but of God', &c.); alternatively, a preacher might choose a sermon less overtly on obedience, such as 1 Timothy 2:1–3 ('I exhort therefore before all things that requests, supplications, intercessions, and giving of thanks be made for all men; For kings, and for all that are in authority, that we may lead a quiet and a peaceable life, in all godliness and honesty'). This was the choice made by Richard Gardiner, who had the courage to preach the Accession Day sermon in 1642 but the discretion to choose a conciliatory text.[75]

Having chosen his text, the preacher next had to decide how he would interpret it for his hearers. He needed to 'explicate' it, literally 'unfold' it, by interpreting it in a way that 'opened' or revealed its meanings. He might analyse the words using the resources of his humanist education, addressing grammatical questions about the text—by whom and to whom it was spoken—and literary questions about genre (is it part of a history, poem, or prophecy?) and style (is it meant literally or metaphorically?). He might consider different translations of the text and their relative merits. From this analysis, he would discover the 'doctrines' in his text. These 'doctrines' were the particular teachings that the text contained and that the preacher thought most pertinent to his hearers. Each text could be examined over and over again to furnish new doctrines, and new sermons, because the Bible functioned as an endless resource to be 'mined' by the exegete. Robert Wilkinson preached for his allotted two hours at Paul's Cross on a three-word text ('Remember Lot's wife'); in the dedicatory epistle to the printed version, he reminded his readers of the inexhaustibleness of Scripture:

If any man shall thinke the Text too short for such an Auditorie, let him acknowledge, it is a peece of the bread of life, which while we break it, increaseth in our hands, as the few loaves wherewith our Saviour fed so many thousands; Yea rather let him think that we our selves are too short, too weake, and too shallow to sound but the depth of ordinarie Divinitie, and *Who is sufficient for these things?*[76]

---

support for the Earl within the city: *A Sermon Preached at Paules Crosse . . . With a Short Discourse of the late Earle of Essex* (1601), *STC²* 1454.

[74] Detailed guides to 'proof-texts' became increasingly available to preachers in the seventeenth century. Good examples are Richard Bernard, *Thesaurus Biblicus* (1644), Wing B2035; John Clarke, *Holy Oyle for the Lampes of the Sanctuarie: or, Scripture-Phrases Alphabetically Disposed* (1630), *STC²* 5359; William Knight, *A Concordance Axiomaticall* (1610), *STC²* 15049.

[75] Richard Gardiner, *A Sermon Appointed for Saints Pauls Crosse . . . March 27, 1642* (1642), Wing G231. John White also chose this text for the 1615 Accession Day sermon: *A Sermon Preached at Paules Crosse upon the Foure and Twentieth of March, 1615* in *Two sermons* (1615), *STC²* 25392.

[76] Robert Wilkinson, *Lots Wife. A Sermon Preached at Paules Crosse* (1607), *STC²* 25656, sig. A2ᵛ. Paul's Cross evidently brought out a competitive streak in preachers, and this is seen in their choice of text. John Rawlinson did not let it pass unnoticed that he managed to preach for two hours on only two

To communicate these doctrines most effectively, the preacher needed to show their derivation from his biblical text and also to demonstrate that they were consonant with Scripture generally. The principle of *sola Scriptura* meant that God had given his Church in the Scripture all the knowledge it needed, and each believer all the precepts and examples that they might need to work out their salvation. Therefore, to prove his explication of the text (and therefore to show that his doctrines were properly derived from his text), the preacher needed to collate Scripture, 'collecting' the doctrines, in the phrase of William Perkins, by comparing cryptic or troublesome passages with more perspicuous ones, so that a theologically sound understanding would be established.[77] It is for this reason that John Brinsley described the preacher as 'soundly interpreting and opening the sense of the Scriptures by the Scriptures'.[78] Those things necessary for salvation were written with unmistakeable clarity; more difficult passages could be understood by collation and comparison with other parts of Scripture. Paul's Cross preachers reiterated the patristic commonplaces that the Bible contained 'milk and strong meat', and that it was a river containing shallows where the lamb could wade and depths where the elephant could swim.[79] The preacher could also refer to the expositions of the same text offered by the Church Fathers and the Magisterial Reformers: though they carried less authority than Scripture, their support lent weight to the preacher's interpretation of cryptic passages.

Having explicated the text and arrived at the doctrines to be presented, the preacher then needed to decide on the structure of his oration. Here, too, the biblical text is central to this method of composition. Izaak Walton gives us a useful account of this task as undertaken by John Donne:

> The latter part of his life may be said to be a continued study; for as he usually preached once a week, if not oftener, so after his Sermon he never gave his eyes rest, till he had chosen out a new Text, and that night cast his Sermon into a form, and his Text into divisions; and the next day betook himself to consult the Fathers, and so commit his meditations to his memory, which was excellent.[80]

Having chosen his text, Walton tells us that Donne 'cast his sermon into a form, and his Text into divisions', so that the 'form' the sermon took is linked to the biblical text, which is broken down into sections. Each doctrine derived from the biblical text was referred to a phrase, or possibly just a word, in the text. That link between the biblical text and the doctrines was central to the structure of the sermon. The order in which each doctrine would be explained (the 'form' of the

---

words: *Vivat Rex. A Sermon Preached at Pauls Crosse* (1619), *STC²* 20777, p. 1. He was bested in this by Thomas Walkington, whose text was the single word 'Rabboni': *Rabboni; Mary Magdalens Teares* (1620), *STC²* 24970.

[77] William Perkins, *The Arte of Prophecying*, in *Works* (1616–18), *STC²* 19651, vol. 2, p. 663.

[78] John Brinsley, *The Preachers Charge. And Peoples Duty* (1631), *STC²* 3790, p. 5.

[79] Aylesbury [Ailesbury], *A Sermon Preached at Paul's Cross*, p. 2; Gabriel Price, *The Laver of the Heart* (1616), *STC²* 20306, pp. 1–2; Edward Boughen, *A Sermon Preached at Saint Pauls Crosse* (1635), *STC²* 3408, p. 33. John Dyos reproduces many of these patristic quotations in his *Sermon Preached at Paules Crosse* (1579), *STC²* 7432, ff. 20ʳ⁻ᵛ.

[80] Walton, *Lives*, p. 67.

sermon) might simply follow the order in which the relevant phrases of the biblical text fell. A good example of this is the 'division of the text' in Immanuel Bourne's *The True Way of a Christian*, preached on 2 Corinthians 5:17 ('Therefore if any man be in Christ, he is a new creature: old things are passed away, Behold, all things are become new'):

In which for our methodicall and orderly proceeding, if you observe the words; There is First, an imposition, or setting forth of our new man. *Therefore if any man be in Christ, he is a new creature:* Secondly, a deposition or laying aside of our old man. *Old things are passed away.*

Thirdly, a Reason and confirmation of them both *Behold, all things are become new.*[81]

Bourne then handles each of these points (the 'setting forth of our new man', the 'laying aside of our old man', and 'the confirmation') in detail within the body of the sermon. Alternatively, the preacher might rearrange the phrases of his biblical text to correspond to the order in which he wished to handle each of the doctrines. When preaching the sermon, he would quote the text as it lay in the Bible, but then when 'dividing' it, he would rearrange it so that the phrases of the biblical text corresponded to the order in which he would handle the doctrines to which they were referred. For example, Donne rearranged the two phrases of Matthew 11:6 ('And blessed is he, whosoever shall not be offended in me') when he preached on it at Paul's Cross in 1629. He gives the division as follows:

The words have in them an Injunction, and a Remuneration; A Precept, and a Promise; The Way, and the End of a Christian. The Injunction, The Precept, The Way is, As you love blessedness, *be not offended in me*, Be satisfied with mee, and mine Ordinances; It is an Acquiescence in the Gospel of Christ Jesus: And the Remuneration, the Promise, the End, is *Blessedness*; That, which in it self, hath no end, That, in respect of which, all other things are to no end, Blessedness, everlasting Blessedness, *Blessed is he, whosoever is not scandalized, not offended in me.*[82]

Donne then continues to offer further subdivisions of the phrase to be explicated first, 'be not offended in me', referring it to 'our facility in falling into the *Passive scandall*, the mis-interpreting of the words or actions of other men'. Donne has composed his division in a way that places the emphasis on the second part of the text, on the 'injunction' not to take offence. He has also used his division to introduce the word 'scandalize', and through it the idea of 'passive scandal', taking offence at the harmless actions of others, on which he will dwell for much of the sermon.

---

[81] Immanuel Bourne *The True Way of a Christian to the New Jerusalem* (1622), *STC²* 3419, sig. B2ᵛ. Sometimes preachers displayed their skill in finding unusual means of dividing their text. In *Mystical Bedlam*, Thomas Adams uses the punctuation marks in the text (a comma, colon, and full-stop) to describe man's sinfulness, regeneration, and death: *Mystical Bedlam*, in *Works* (1630), *STC²* 105. In a Paul's Cross sermon of 1616, William Worship compares his text to a drama and divides it according to the Aristotelian parts (*protasis, epistasis, catastrophe*): *The Patterne of an Invincible Faith* (1616), *STC²* 25995, p. 2.

[82] *The Sermons of John Donne*, eds G. R. Potter and E. M. Simpson, 10 vols (Berkeley: University of California Press, 1953–62), vol. 9, pp. 109–10.

This practice of structuring the sermon around the 'division' of the biblical text is characteristic of English preaching at this time, Donne being unusual only in the skill with which he does it. The division served a practical purpose, as it acted as an aid to memory for the preacher and hearers, in the way the *partitio* of classical rhetoric enabled speaker and hearer to remember the form an oration was to take.[83] The scriptural text would have been already familiar to sermon-goers, making it even easier for them to remember the order of the arguments. Richard Bernard advised the preacher to 'gather the parts by circumstances, even as the words lie in order, if it may be, for the better helpe of the meaner sort'.[84] The structuring of the sermon around the biblical text also emphasized that the preacher's sermon revolved around it: the doctrines demonstrably arose from the biblical text, and the whole sermon was therefore an 'unfolding' of one part of the Bible. For this reason, the 'division' of the text, marking out the units into which the biblical quotation would be broken up, is usually a distinct and obvious part of the opening of a sermon. In printed sermon-books, there is often a marginal note to alert the reader to the 'division'. Occasionally, printed sermon-books will make the division even clearer by providing a diagram linking the individual words of phrases in the biblical text with the doctrines derived from them in the order in which they are handled.[85]

'Explicating' and 'dividing' the text was only one half of the preacher's task. Deios says that preaching was the expounding of Scripture and the 'applying of it to the present state'. John Brinsley, similarly, said the preacher opened the sense of the Scriptures 'with Application of them to the use of the Church'. Again, we must bear in mind the inexhaustibleness of Scripture: the Bible's words contain precepts and examples that addressed every failing and every crisis that the individual or the Church might encounter. The preacher's task was to show what guidance Scripture offered for his hearers in their present needs, both in matters of faith and morals. The preacher's choice of a text and his interpretation of it were to be guided by the religious needs of his hearers. Having laid out the doctrines implicit in his scriptural text, he was to elaborate fully on why they were necessary and relevant to his hearers. In short, he 'applied' the doctrines found in the text to 'the present state' and 'the use of the Church'. Richard Bernard explains:

After the deliverie of the doctrine, enforming the auditory that there is such a thing, and what it is, followes the use necessarilie, that the hearers may know what to doe with that which they so understand. These two cannot in nature be sundred; nothing can be taught but there is use and end thereof.[86]

---

[83] Cicero makes the partition the third part of the oration, after the exordium and the narration (or statement of facts). He says that 'a partition correctly made renders the whole speech clear and perspicuous'. In it, the 'matters which we intend to discuss are briefly set forth in a methodical way': *De Inventione*, I.xxii.31, trans. H. M. Hubbell (Cambridge, MA: Harvard University Press, for the Loeb Classical Library, 1949), pp. 62–3.

[84] Bernard, *The Faithfull Shepheard* (1607), *STC²* 1939, p. 21.

[85] Thomas Bedford, *The Sinne unto Death* (1621), *STC²* 1788, sigs A4ʳ⁻ᵛ; Robert Wakeman, *Jonahs Sermon* (1606), *STC²* 24948, sig. ¶4ʳ; George Benson, *A Sermon Preached at Paules Crosse* (1609), *STC²* 1886, sig. B4; Robert Harris, *Gods Goodnes and Mercy* (1622), *STC²* 12831, sig. A3ʳ.

[86] Bernard, *The Faithfull Shepheard* (1607), *STC²* 1939, p. 60.

The 'application' made the teachings of Scripture operative in the hearers' lives, and was therefore at least as important as the explication of the text. In the most influential preaching manual of the period, Hyperius of Marburg wrote, 'to apply aptly and properly the scriptures to present business and affaires is the principall vertue that belongeth to a preacher'.[87] The text could be made relevant to the circumstances of the sermon's delivery by reference to similarities between the occasion (especially on religious or civic festivals) of text and sermon. Even if not applied to the occasion, the text was almost always applied to the 'life and manners' of the hearers through the presentation of moral and social precepts. In English preaching manuals, the 'uses' to which biblical texts tended were usually classified by categories drawn from 2 Timothy 3:16 and Romans 15:4 to give us what were, in effect, sermon genres: confutational (opposing doctrinal error and heresy); instructive (explaining matters of faith or morals), corrective (criticizing sinful practices and habits), and consolation (the 'practical divinity' of helping those afflicted in conscience, or through bereavement, or during times of plague).[88] Individual sermons might not always fit neatly into these generic categories, however, as they often combined the different 'uses' of a text. For example, a sermon might show how a biblical text disproves Catholic teaching (a 'use' of confutation) and follow this by an 'instructive' use of the text in its demonstration of the 'true doctrine'.

Part of the application of the sermon's doctrine involved 'rousing up' the hearers so that they would want to follow teachings they had heard. This 'exhortation' was sometimes a separate final section to the sermon and its defining characteristic was vehemence. The preacher exhorted by presenting compelling arguments for the advice he delivered, showing the hearers the 'means to' and the 'motives' in favour of adopting the advice he presented. In *The Faithful Shepheard*, Richard Bernard advised the preacher to 'use perswasions and exhortations' after he had proved his doctrines. These persuasions include the 'motives' to adopt the given precepts, such as 'the approbation thereof with God, with godly men' and the 'means' available to put them into practice, such as 'Gods assistance, his promise to helpe, the excellency and good even in using these meanes'.[89] The famous 'Jeremiads' preached at Paul's Cross are characterized not just by uses of 'correction', the castigation of the hearer's sinfulness by comparison with the failings of biblical Israel, but also by equally vehement exhortations to godliness. In this way, the descriptions of the punishments visited on the Israelites so typical of these sermons function as 'motives' to the hearers to mend their ways. The preachers married this with an

---

[87] Hyperius (Andreas Gerardus), *De Formandis Concionibus Sacris* (1553), trans. John Ludham, *The Practis of Preaching* (1577), *STC²* 11758, Lib. II, f. 121ᵛ.

[88] The terms used vary, but Bernard, William Perkins, and John Wilkins, the three most influential English writers on the subject, give these four. It was the innovation of Hyperius in *De Formandis Concionibus Sacris* to classify sermons according to these Pauline precepts (ibid. ff. 18ʳ–19ʳ). On the influence of Hyperius, see Jameela Lares, *Milton and the Preaching Arts* (Cambridge: James Clarke, 2001), pp. 49, 56–74; on William Perkins and other English preaching manuals, see pp. 77–80.

[89] Richard Bernard, *The Faithfull Shepheard* (1607), *STC²* 1939, pp. 65–6.

often lyrical presentation of God's patience with sinners, emphasizing that the 'means' to repentance and amendment of life were readily available.[90]

Such exhortatory arguments (means and motives) were not the only tool in the preacher's arsenal: he could also try to move the hearers emotionally by deploying the rhetorical skills he had learned at grammar school and university. Having explained the use of 'means' and 'motives' in exhortation, Richard Bernard also advises the 'use of rhetoricke', and 'all the engins of that Arte and grace in speaking' to persuade the hearers.[91] There was not, as modern scholars have argued, an anti-rhetorical 'plain style' that rejected all the techniques and 'arts of speaking well' on the grounds that they were duplicitous in their appeal to the emotions. That dichotomy, central to the debate on secular rhetoric, was less relevant to preaching, because preaching (unlike secular rhetoric) depended on the operation of the Holy Spirit to affect a change of heart in the hearers.[92] The preacher's task was to do his best to assist the 'motions of the spirit', using all the skills and arts that he was master of. And so preaching theorists, even moderate puritans like Bernard, restricted the usefulness of rhetoric primarily to the task of exhortation, but they did not dismiss it out of hand.

In preparing his sermon, therefore, the preacher studied his text, derived doctrines from his explication of it, and decided on the uses to be made of the doctrines. He divided his text, arriving at a structure built around the biblical 'core' of his oration. Finally, he provided himself with scriptural proof-texts and quotations from the Fathers and modern commentators to support each of the doctrines he presented. He would then write notes of the division and as much of the rest of the sermon as he needed to help his memory in the pulpit. His hearers would follow much the same process in their note-taking: they would note down the scriptural text and then the division. As each doctrine was expounded, they would jot down as much as they could of the arguments, and of the proofs presented, on each point. They would take care to note the 'applications', the uses they were to make of each doctrine. And they might also try to copy down felicitous or memorable phrases used. After the sermon, both preacher and hearers would return to their notes and make a fuller copy of these jottings, expanding the prose and clarifying the doctrines and uses as they had summarized them. Biblical references jotted down would be looked up and the quotations included; the same might be done for references to the Church Fathers. If the preacher intended his manuscript to become the copy-text for a printed version of the sermon, he would

---

[90] On the Jeremiad as a sermon of exhortation, see my 'Rhetoric, Religion and Politics on the St Paul's Cross Sermons, 1603–1625', PhD thesis, University of Cambridge, 1998, pp. 179–201.

[91] Bernard, *The Faithfull Shepheard* (1607), *STC²* 1939, p. 66. Contrary to modern assumptions about 'plain style preaching', puritans placed greater emphasis on exhortation, with its heightened, emotional style, than their conformist colleagues. Griffith Williams complained in his 1614 Paul's Cross sermon that there was too much exhortation, that 'we have some men in our daies, that are *alwaies moving* and *perswading,* but *never teaching* for notwithstanding all their great shew of *doctrine,* they have nothing in their doctrines, but meere exhortations' (*The Resolution of Pilate* in *The Best Religion* (1636), *STC²* 25718, p. 399).

[92] For a fuller treatment of this subject, see my 'Scripture, Style and Persuasion in Seventeenth-Century English Theories of Preaching', *Journal of Ecclesiastical History,* 53(4) (2002), 686–706.

polish the prose style and provide translations for quotations in Latin or Greek. He would be more careful about distinguishing quotations (in English and Latin) by the use of italic script. He might also take the trouble to provide additional marginal references to back up his arguments, particularly in sermons on religious or political controversies. It is not impossible that he would heighten the style of particular passages, particularly of exhortation, to compensate for the loss of emphasis provided by voice and gesture in the pulpit.

It is because the sermon is structured around the 'explication' and 'application' of a biblical quotation that it remains identifiable through the various physical forms in which it survives. Modern readers, like early modern hearers, must undertake the same task of identifying the text, its division, doctrines and their proofs, uses and exhortation, if they are to interpret a sermon properly. Knowing the text, the division, and the doctrines provides us with a 'skeleton', the shape of the oration and the core of its argument. That skeleton may not necessarily give us a summary of the whole sermon: particular points would be expanded or contracted as time and occasion required. We saw from their epistles dedicatory that preachers felt at liberty to expand on sections they felt were curtailed in the version of the sermon that they preached. The preacher would deliver his points in the order given in the division, but this did not mean that he would slavishly follow all the steps for explicating and then proving each doctrine in equal depth every time: unusual or puzzling texts required more explication than well-known and perspicuous ones; texts used by Catholics to support their claims, or by puritans to support their disagreements with the Church authorities, would be supported with proofs to a greater extent than catechetical texts similarly expounded by all Christians. Proofs (or 'confirmations') that supported particular interpretations of the biblical text might be inserted if they facilitated an anti-papist or anti-puritan digression; if they were not considered necessary, they might be left out. Exhortatory passages might be inserted throughout the sermon, at the end of each section (after each doctrine), or they might be held back to a single, extensive, and heightened 'final exhortation'. These were matters of individual style and judgement, and they did not really affect the argumentative core of the sermon: the relationship between the chosen text, doctrines, and uses. Nonetheless, they provided the learned and skilful preachers of the upper clergy, like John Donne, John and Henry King, Joseph Hall, and Robert Sanderson, who were often required to preach on controversial subjects, with techniques and means to make subtle distinctions in the advice they gave their hearers on matters of faith, morals, and politics, as will be demonstrated in the chapters that follow.

The argument presented here for a common method of sermon composition is not meant to imply that there were no perceived differences in style across the English Church. But it was initially a matter of emphasis. J. W. Blench describes three methods of sermon composition in Elizabeth's reign: the ancient (that is, patristic style, the homily), the modern (that is, the medieval scholastic method), and the 'new reformed method of doctrines and uses', which he describes as the form advocated by Perkins and other puritans and considers 'unbearably tedious to the modern reader'. The 'vast majority of the Elizabeth preachers', he says, used a 'modified version of the "modern style" adapted to concur with the parts of a secular rhetoric'.[93] I would argue, rather, that we see a fusing of various techniques to form an 'English Reformed method'. From the 'ancient' homily method described by Blench came the idea of taking a scriptural text (traditionally a whole chapter of the Bible, but by this method merely a couple of verses), and explicating and applying it to the hearers' lives. The system of dividing a 'theme' (or text) according to logical or grammatical categories to form a structure for the oration derived from the 'modern' scholastic method. Unlike much medieval preaching, however, in the best Elizabethan and early Stuart preaching the influence of Humanism is clear in the limited number of subdivisions made. The 'theme' of the scholastic sermon was often a doctrinal proposition; the use of an extract from the Bible in Elizabethan and early Stuart preaching is without doubt a product of Reformation thought. We see this transition in the printed versions of Foxe's *Sermon on Christ Crucified*. The Latin version has 'Thema' in the margin where the text is cited. The English version has 'Text' printed in the margin at the same point.[94]

There was a tendency for this method of sermon composition to develop the same faults as its medieval predecessor, with the text being 'crumbled' into ever smaller parts and each unit subjected to examination with all its ancillary proofs, reasons, applications, and objections. This tendency became associated with the 'left wing' of the Church. In 1614, Griffith Williams complained of puritan preachers who brought their sermons 'to such a forme of doctrines, and reasons, and observations, and use, so that I am sure the like can never be found in the writings of the ancient Fathers, or any of the learned Schoolemen', although this method is, he confesses in a marginal note, 'most plaine and easie, and therefore most profitable for the simpler sort of people'.[95] By the 1650s, when there were moves away from this method of sermon composition, the tendency to 'crumble' the text was one of the faults identified. In his *Ecclesiastes* (1656), John Wilkins writes that 'the common practice of dissecting the words into minute parts and inlarging upon them severally, is a great occasion of impertinency and roving from the chiefe sense'.[96] In a list of commentaries, tracts and sermons appended to William Chappell's *The Preacher* (1656), the sermons of Lancelot Andrewes, Daniel Featley, Joseph Hall, Arthur Lake, William Perkins, and even the puritan 'roaring boy of Banbury', William Whately, are all described as 'elaborate'.[97]

The 'plaine, easy way of *Doctrine* and *use*',[98] should be seen, therefore, as a simplified version of the same method of composition used by Donne, Andrewes, and other regulars at court and Paul's Cross. Less concerned with such elite pulpits, puritan writers on preaching stressed ways to make the sermon intelligible to all

[93] J. W. Blench, *Preaching in England in the Late Fifteenth and Sixteenth Centuries* (Oxford: Blackwell, 1964), pp. 100–2.

[94] John Foxe, *De Christo Crucifixo* (1571), *STC²* 11242.3, sig. B'; A *Sermon of Christ Crucified* (1570), *STC²* 11247, sig. B'.

[95] Williams, *The Resolution of Pilate*, in *The Best Religion* (1636), *STC²* 25718, p. 399. Williams' sermon takes a text (John 19:22) and divides that text as other preachers do: he is not opposed to the method per se, but to the rather pointless multiplication of subdivisions.

[96] John Wilkins, *Ecclesiastes* (1656), Wing W2188, p. 11.

[97] William Chappell, *The Preacher* (1656), Wing C1957, sig. K9'.

[98] Abraham Wright, *Five Sermons, in Five Sundry Styles* (1656), Wing W3685, sig. A3'.

hearers, and advised a simple construction that offers first explication ('doctrines') and then application ('uses') for this reason. But the wish to communicate effectively to all hearers was not necessarily inconsistent with the desire to produce elegant prose. Although Richard Bernard delineates the various stages to the opening, proving and applying of every kind of doctrine, he tells his readers that these procedures should not be followed in a slavish way obvious to the hearers:

> But in all this which I have spoken, my meaning is not, that in preaching, a minister, after hee be entred upon his text, should say: This is the doctrine, this is the proofe, this the use: now to the reasons, now we will make application, and prevent or make objections: which is, I confesse a plaine way to a rude congregation, easie to bee conceived and written of such as attend and will take the paines: but it interrupts the course of the speeche, and it is too disjointed, and lesse patheticall. Therefore albeit for the understanding of the things distinctly by them I have made severall chapters, yet the preacher, which will follow this course, may in speaking knit them altogether in a continued speech after the maner of an oration, keeping the method to himselfe.[99]

The simpler the sermon's structure, the easier it was for hearers to follow: sound advice for the average preacher addressing an ordinary parish audience.

Something more impressive was needed at Paul's Cross, where many of the hearers were learned, a good many literate (given the relatively high literacy levels in the citizen community), and all attending in order to hear the 'best' and 'most learned' preaching the English Church had to offer. Rhetorical decorum dictated that the style of the sermon be suited to its hearers, and anecdotal evidence does suggest that preachers were able and willing to adapt their styles to suit their auditory. Walton reports of George Herbert:

> The text for his first sermon was taken out of *Solomons proverbs,* and the words were, *Keep thy heart with all diligence.* In which first Sermon, he gave his Parishioners many necessary, holy, safe rules for the discharge of a good Conscience, both to God and man. And deliver'd his sermon after a most florid manner; both with great learning and eloquence. But at the close of this Sermon, told them, *That should not be his constant way of Preaching, for, since Almighty God does not intend to lead men to heaven by hard Questions, he would not therefore fill their heads with unnecessary Notions; but that for their sakes, his language and his expressions should be more plain and practical in his future Sermons.*[100]

Contemporaries were clearly aware of these differences, and recognized what was particularly suited to particular audiences. Robert Bolton tells the readers of his *Discourse of True Happiness* that it was originally five sermons:

> but all to a most judicious and intelligent auditorie; therefore there is a continuance of matter, coherence and stile. I must entreate thee, out of thine ingenuous discretion, to distinguish the places where they were preacht, as thou shalt find the direction of my speech, and some particular applications more naturall and necessarilie with individuall reference appropriated thereunto.[101]

---

[99] Bernard, *The Faithfull Shepheard* (1607), *STC²* 1939, pp. 79–80.
[100] Walton, *Lives*, p. 295.
[101] Robert Bolton, *A Discourse about the State of True Happinesse, Delivered in Certain Sermons* (1611), *STC²* 3228, sig. Aʳ.

The Paul's Cross preacher might address many of London's ordinary citizens, but he also addressed many of its governors, as members of the Privy Council or the Corporation. Apostrophes to 'the magistrates' present at the sermon demonstrate how conscious the preachers were of this. Roger Ley said that sermons 'delivered in that audience, are principally for the governours of this honourable cittie'.[102] Conscious of this, the Paul's Cross preachers pulled out all the rhetorical stops, the 'engins of that Arte and grace in speaking'. It is not surprising that they might want their efforts made permanent in manuscript or print form, or that the skill and polish of the sermon is only evident when we have an authorial full-text available. What they could not avoid losing, however, was much lamented: the advantage of the 'voice, gesture, and person of hym that spake it'.[103]

THE 'LIVELY VOICE' AND THE 'DEAD LETTER'

We have little idea of the types of gestures used by early modern preachers.[104] Not surprisingly, the advice offered them concurs with the advice Hamlet gave the actors: too much was bad. The puritan William Ames advised that 'the speech and action ought to be wholly spiritual flowing from the very heart' showing the preacher to be 'a man much conversant in exercises of piety' who was convinced of what he said. Added to this should be 'zeale, charity, mildnesse, freedome, humility, with grace and authority'. This may sound like a recipe for the worst kind of revivalist roaring, but Ames goes on to say that 'the pronouncing of the speeche must be both naturall, familiar, cleere and distinct, that it may be fitly understood'.[105] Accusations of histrionic behaviour were a sure way to insult a preacher. John Earle's 'young raw preacher' reuses sermons he has heard, so that when he preaches 'the onely thing hee ha's made in [the sermon] himselfe, is the faces'. His use of the voice is similarly ill-judged: 'His action is all passion, and his speeche interjections: Hee ha's an excellent faculty in bemoaning the people, and spits with a very good grace'.[106] The Catholic polemicist Thomas Harding was a good deal less good humoured in his caricature of John Jewel's:

rhetorical perswasions in the Pulpit with a holy holding up of your handes, and casting up of your eyes to heaven, and with your lamentable crying out of your Oos, which you use very commonly, weening therby to perswade the simple, your stoute asservations, your favour of the common people and others, that clap you on the shoulder, you vaine pulpit buzzing,

[102] Ley, *The Bruising of the Serpents Head* (1622), sig. A2ᵛ.
[103] Anderson, *A Sermon Preached at Paules Crosse* (1581), *STC²* 570, sig. A2ʳ.
[104] Significant advances on this subject are being made by Catherine Armstrong: see '"Error Vanquished by Delivery": Elite Sermon Performance in Jacobean England', Oxford D.Phil. thesis, 2007, unpublished, and her forthcoming 'Sermons in Performance', in Hugh Adlington, Peter McCullough, and Emma Rhatigan (eds), *The Oxford Handbook of the Early Modern Sermon* (Oxford: Oxford University Press).
[105] William Ames, *The Marrow of Sacred Divinity* (1642), Wing A 3000, pp. 161–2.
[106] John Earle, *Microcosmographie* (1628; 1633 ed.), *STC²* 7444, sig. B3ᵛ.

your *Gloria patri* at Powles Crosse: al this hath made many a one beleve, that M Jewel was a great Clerke, a pillar of the Gospel, a peerlesse felowe.[107]

But judicious use of gesture and voice was clearly expected of the preacher. John Donne was particularly praised for his 'powerfull kinde of preaching by his gestur and rhetoriquall expression'.[108] Thomas Fuller notes as an unusual aspect of Richard Hooker's preaching that he used 'gesture none at all, standing stone-still in the Pulpit', and appears to be at pains to provide an explanation, 'as if the posture of his body were the embleme of his minde, unmoveable in his opinions'.[109] Paul's Cross preachers suggest that such an approach would not have worked in that pulpit, which is not surprising given the nature of this large, outdoor space. In printing his *London's New-Yeeres Gift*, Thomas Jackson laid aside '*the gestures and countenance of a living man*' and says he has '*wrappe myselfe in dead letters, though of less effectual persuasions*'.[110] John Lawrence offers his 'mite', confessing that it has lost something of what it had when it was preached 'for a dead letter cannot be so patheticall as a living voice; neither can the pen so set it forth in writing, as the tongue in speaking'.

The persuasive power of the 'lively voice' was not merely a matter of rhetorical skill, but an effect of the inspiring power of the Holy Spirit active at the time of the sermon. It was the Holy Spirit who gave preacher and hearers the grace to make the right use of the event. Miles Mosse explains it as follows:

Now some things there are, in which I humbly crave favourable interpretation.
1. As first that I doe not put upon this treatise *in the penning, that* vigor *and* vivacitie *which it carried in the* preaching. *For there is even in nature a great difference between the tongue, and the quill, between speaking and writing. The very sound and tune of the voice is melodie to the eare: it beeing the proper* Object *of that* Sense. *And therof it is, that the* special part *of* Oratorie *is said to be* Pronunciation. *And besides that* Vox est ictus animi *passing through the eare, and braine, and blood, it smitheth (as it were) and giveth a stroake upon the verie soule, and so with a kind of violence doth deepely affect it. Therefore it is called* Viva vox, *as that which hath in it a speciall kind of livelinesse. . . . But yet further, besides all the worke of* Nature, *there is in* Preaching, *a speciall gift of* grace: *which enableth a man to speak with such evidence of the* Spirit, *& with such power to the* Conscience, *as no pen of man by writing can expresse: whereof* Preaching *is the most lively and effectuall instrument* of salvation *and so to be respected.*[111]

For most Jacobean preachers, it was within the event of the sermon, when the hearers and preachers were prepared to make spiritual use of what was said, that the Holy Spirit would intervene to make the encounter spiritually profitable. The event of the sermon was as significant as the message the preacher delivered there, for it was *during* the sermon that the Spirit might make the hearer capable of understanding the Scripture

---

[107] Thomas Harding, *A Rejoindre to M. Jewels Replie* (Antwerp, 1566), ARCR 376, sigs. ¶[r–v].
[108] *The Diary of Thomas Crosfield*, ed. F. S. Boas (Oxford: Oxford University Press, 1935), p. 43.
[109] Thomas Fuller, *The Church History of Britain* (1655), Wing F 2416, XVI Cent., Book IX, p. 216.
[110] Thomas Jackson, *London's New-Yeeres Gift* (1609), *STC*[2] 14303, sig. A2[r]; John Lawrence, *A Golden Trumpet, to Rowse up a Drowsie Magistrate* (1624), *STC*[2] 15325, sig. A4[r].
[111] Miles Mosse, *Justifying and Saving Faith* (Cambridge, 1614), *STC*[2] 18209, sigs 2¶[v]–2¶2[r].

through the preacher's words. For some preachers, this meant that the spiritual benefit to be accrued from the sermon-book was consequently less than from the sermon preached. Laurence Chaderton says as much in the epistle to his 1578 Paul's Cross sermon:

But let no man thinke, that the reading of this can be half so effectual and profitable to him, as the hearing was, or might be. For it wanteth the zeale of the speaker, the attention of the hearer, the promise of God to the ordinary preaching of his word, the mighty & inwarde working of his holy spirit, & many other things which the Lord worketh most mercifully by the preaching of his glorious Gospel, which are not to be hoped for by the onely or bare reading of his worde, or the written sermons of his ministers. Nevertheless, I trust that he wil blesse the reading herof, to the prayse of his owne name, and the comfort of his church.[112]

Not everyone agreed: Henry Greenwood compares the way 'the eare conveieth grace to the affections of the soule' with the eye, which 'bringeth much matter to the understanding of the mind', and so both senses 'are great instruments in the furtherance of our soules in the way of Gods Kingdome'.[113] Indeed, the epistles to printed sermon-books suggest that preachers had given some thought to the ways in which their sermons communicated with hearers and readers. Needing to justify publication (the 'stigma of print' was clearly a factor, if only in the rather weak sense that preachers wished to avoid the appearance of pride and ambition), they suggest different uses for the sermon in the oral and print media. John Bridges, whose treatise *A Defence of the Government Established* (1587) was so long it became the butt of Marprelate's humour, showed a similar lack of restraint when rewriting his Paul's Cross sermon of Whitsunday 1571 for the press. This does not mean that he was unaware of the need to retain his audience's attention; if anything, it was an understanding of the different ways one's attention is focused when hearing and reading that justified this prolixity. He was 'content' to 'furnish my former notes with further provision' because such length is 'allowable' in a book but 'not sufferable' and 'a great deale more than tedious' in a sermon. This is because the preacher does not speak to the reader, 'but themselves to them selves that should reade me, should speake it for me', and the reader does so at their own pace: 'when they are wearie, lay me aside a gods name, and make four Sermons (if they please) of one'.[114]

The sermon acquired greater permanence and greater circulation in being printed. Nathaniel Delaune was prompted to print his sermon by friends who 'desired to renew their memorie, and refresh their comfort in reading printed, that which once they heard preached'. Although 'there is a great difference betweene preaching, and printing . . . as betwixt a quicke, and a dead body', as the latter lacks

---

[112] Laurence Chaderton, *An Excellent and Godly Sermon* ([1578?]), *STC²* 4924, sigs. A3ʳ.

[113] Henry Greenwood, *Tormenting Tophet* (1615), *STC²* 12336, sig. A3ᵛ. This is particularly interesting as Greenwood was another writer of plain, popular sermons, and was no less an advocate of 'practical divinity' than Chaderton.

[114] John Bridges, *A Sermon Preached at Paules Cross* ([1571]), *STC²* 2726, sig. A3ʳ. Edward Rainbow also contrasts the way the 'attentive eye' can take in more than the 'listning eare': *Labour Forbidden, and Commanded* (1635), *STC²* 20603, sig. A2ʳ.

'the Action, which is the life of perswasion', he decided to 'wrap my self in dead letters, to help memorie in those that were present, and to extend the benefit of Gods word to others that were absent'. Charles Richardson sent his sermon 'forth into the world, that whereas, while it was delivered by voice, it could extend but to a few, now being committed to the Press, it might be communicated to many'.[115] William Jackson had *The Celestial Husbandry* printed 'because the matter therein being of great use (and a Sermon is but nine dayes wonder,) [I] would not have the funeral so soone'. Similarly, Thomas Myriell claims that it grieves the 'spirituall father, to see that his ofspring, (bred of his braine, and brought forth by his breath) should die as soone as it beings to live'.[116] Preachers were not naïve about their reader's diligence, however: Thomas White notes that some who buy sermons 'let them sleepe in their houses'.[117]

The printed sermon, with its greater permanence and wider circulation, was also used defensively by preachers: to confute erroneous reports of what was preached, and to clarify the sermons' teachings if they were challenged subsequently. Because the printed sermon was accepted as a record of the oration, the preacher could appeal to those not present as well as to those who had heard the sermon in his defence against complaints circulating after the event: it enabled the preacher to make what can only be described as an appeal to public opinion. William Gravet did this in his sermon-book *Of the Holy Scriptures* (1587). In the epistle to the sermon-book, Gravet tells us that his sermon discussed the nature and authority of the Church, a topic '*of most great controversie between the Papists and us*', and that he made particularly use of patristic arguments, especially from St Augustine in that part of the sermon. Not long after, however, another preacher '*shortly after in the same place (as it was reported to me) did bitterly reprove me for so doing*'. Gravet now leaves it up to the 'godly, learned and discreet' readers to judge '*whether he hath in this point, unadvisedly and uncharitably abused me or not*', and this they can do '*by the reading of the very same things, in the same order that they were then uttered*'.[118] Gravet does tell the reader that he has made changes to the sermon in preparing it for the press, but only on this one point and in order to clarify his argument.

---

[115] Nathaniel Delaune [Delawne], *The Christians Tryumph* (1617), *STC²* 6550.5, sig. A2ᵛ. (Delaune's name is misspelt 'Delawne' in *STC²* and *Early English Books Online*; he was the son of William Delaune, formerly Guillaume de Laune.) Charles Richardson, *The Price of Our Redemption* (1617), *STC²* 21015, sig. A3ʳ. The same sentiment is expressed by John Stockwood, *A Sermon Preached at Paules Crosse on Bartholomew day* ([1578]), *STC²* 23284, sig. A3ʳ.

[116] William Jackson, *The Celestiall Husbandrie* (1616), *STC²* 14321, sig. *2ʳ; Thomas Myriell, *The Devout Soules Search* (1610), *STC²* 18323, sig. A8ʳ.

[117] Thomas White, *A Sermon Preached at Pawles Crosse* (1578), *STC²* 25405, sig. A3ʳ.

[118] William Gravet, *A Sermon Preached at Paules Crosse . . . Intreating of the Holy Scriptures* (1587), *STC²* 12200, sig. A2ʳ. This may represent only one episode in a long-running dispute. On 19 July 1573, Richard Crick delivered a notorious sermon from Paul's Cross praising the presbyterian platform advocated in the *Admonition to Parliament*. Gravet reported him to the bishop and Crick was questioned. Gravet says that he had preached at Paul's Cross the Sunday before Crick and had 'proved the ceremonyes used in our Church of England . . . to be thinges in their owne nature indifferent, which I proved by scripture, and by St Augustine'. Crick 'toke certaine of my reasons, & confuted them openlye, which he did in bare wordes, but not in substaunce & matter'. Crick's response is that he 'did never remember the other preacher to speake of it, & I am suer I never went about to confute it': Inner Temple MS Petyt MS 538, vol. 47, ff. 476ʳ–478ᵛ.

Consequently, he goes to considerable lengths to alert the readers to the changes made to the sermon preached, and we see this on page 29, where there is a mark in the text (∵) and a marginal note saying:

This unto the same marke again, I added to that which I spake, bicause since that time, I was in the same place spoken against for using manie testimonies out of the doctors.

In 1636, Griffith Williams also made use of this aspect of the printed sermon-book: his *Resolution of Pilate*, as it is printed, contains criticism of the laity interpreting Scripture, a justification of anti-puritan preaching and a warning against prying into the king's prerogative, all subjects liable to be controversial. He says that '*this Sermon was no sooner preached, but it was much* traduced *by the prejudicate and malitious hearers, to many of my friends and others, which heard it not*'. He decided to print it so that '*they, which heard it not, might reade it, and thereby be satisfied of what I spake*'. Although the printed version is not exactly what was preached, he insists that nothing he said has been left out or altered; he has merely '*added a little more then I spake, the shortnes of the time causing me then, to overpasse more then halfe the matter, that I had collected*. The reader '*may know both what I spake, and what I purposed to speake*'.[119]

The wider circulation of the printed sermon was also of use to more senior clerics, who defended not only their own positions, but also the Church's. For example, Henry King preached at Paul's Cross in 1621 to refute the rumours then circulating that his father, Dr John King, Bishop of London, had converted to Catholicism before his death. As the slander was spreading, so the printed sermon might '*be set in a course to overtake it*'. Indeed, he goes on to say, '*a* Sermon *preached from the* Presse, *sometimes edifies so much the more then from the* Pulpit, *by how much the report is carried forther*'.[120] A more complicated case involved Thomas Bilson, Bishop of Winchester, in 1597. He preached at Paul's Cross in the Lent of that year on Christ's descent into Hell; this was a sensitive subject, not least because the rejection of this doctrine by the separatists Henry Barrow and John Greenwood was part of the case against them that led to their execution in 1593.[121] Bilson's sermon met a swift response from 'a Bachelor of Arts as I heard, even at Paules Crosse', and so Bilson undertook to preach one of the Spital sermons that Easter in order to defend what he had preached. Archbishop Whitgift prevailed upon Bilson to

---

[119] Williams, *The Resolution of Pilate*, in *The Best Religion* (1636), *STC²* 25718, sig. 2H3ʳ. This sermon and *The Delight of the Saints*, an expanded version of another Paul's Cross sermon, are the only sermons in the volume to have a separate dedication and epistle. *The Resolution of Pilate* was entered in the Stationers' Register on 22 July 1614, little more than a month after it was preached (13 June), and may have been printed then, which would explain the separate dedication. There is no extant copy of that edition, if one was made: Vivienne Larminie, 'Williams, Griffith (1587/8–1672)', *Oxford Dictionary of National Biography* (Oxford: Oxford University Press, 2004; online edn., Jan 2008, <http://www.oxforddnb.com/view/article/29507>, accessed 2 February 2008.

[120] Henry King, *A Sermon Preached at Pauls Crosse, the 25 of November. 1621* (1621), *STC²* 14969, sig. L4ʳ.

[121] William Richardson, 'Bilson, Thomas (1546/7–1616)', *Oxford Dictionary of National Biography* (Oxford: Oxford University Press, 2004; online edn., Jan 2008, <http://www.oxforddnb.com/view/article/2401>, accessed 16 June 2009.

publish his sermon and to send a copy to Burleigh 'not distrusting' that he too would 'judge it fitt to be preached and published'.[122] But Burleigh advised Bilson to delay publication until after the parliament, because of the 'great hurle raised' against his preaching 'by certaine popular preachers in that citie',[123] among whom was the semi-separatist Henry Jacobs, who published *A Treatise of the Sufferinges and Victory of Christ* (1598) confuting Bilson.[124] The versions of both of Bilson's sermons finally published, *The Effect of Certaine Sermons touching the Full Redemption of Mankind* (1599), are not, Bilson tells his readers, in 'the same words which I then spake; I wrote them not; but I assure thee before him that knoweth all things, that I have not swarved nor altered anie materiall point from the methode, propositions, proofes and conclusions, which I then used, nor from the wordes as farre as either my notes, or my memory upon the fresh foote could direct mee'. He does admit, however, that he has added 'manie proofes and authorities' omitted in the pulpit for reasons of time, and has answered some objections to his doctrine more fully in print than he did there. Nonetheless, he offers the reader 'the self same in effect, which then I uttered and purposed, if the time would have suffered'. Bilson adds to his treatise a 'conclusion' designed to address Jacob's tract directly, and he tells the reader that he decided to do so 'lest my silence should augment his boldnes' and to give the reader 'a taste of the rashnes and weaknes' of his enterprise.[125] If Bilson's initial sermon was designed to prevent the spread of dangerous doctrinal errors, the controversy that his sermon caused had the opposite effect, and Bilson had to wait until he could print what had by then become a defence of his own sermon.

It is clear, therefore, that the preachers who delivered sermons at Paul's Cross were as aware as modern scholars that the printed sermon-book is not the same as the oration on which it was based. This does not mean that they considered it an entirely separate work; rather, they saw print as a different medium through which they could communicate the doctrines, and the uses of those doctrines, uncovered in their study of the biblical text. Although the absence of the 'lively voice', and the 'promise of God to the ordinary preaching of his word, the mighty and inward working of his holy spirite', in Cartwright's words, meant that the sermon-book could never replace the hearing of sermons, there were compensatory advantages too. Printing a sermon meant more people could have access to it, those that heard it could remember it better by re-reading, and those who had been misinformed of its contents could be corrected.

To conclude, there were several different routes by which a Paul's Cross sermon was made public: through the preacher's notes, through oral delivery, from the

---

[122] British Library MS Lansdowne 84, f. 172$^{r–v}$.

[123] Thomas Bilson, *The Effect of Certaine Sermons Touching the Full Redemption of Mankind* (1599), *STC²* 3064, sig. A4^{v}.

[124] Stephen Wright, 'Jacob, Henry (1562/3–1624)', *Oxford Dictionary of National Biography* (Oxford: Oxford University Press, 2004; online edn., Jan 2008, <http://www.oxforddnb.com/view/article/14566>, accessed 16 June 2009; Henry Jacob, *A Treatise of the Sufferings and Victory of Christ* ([Middelburg], 1598), sig. A2^{r}.

[125] Bilson, *The Effect of Certaine Sermons*, *STC²* 3069, sigs A4^{v}–B2^{r}.

notes taken by hearers, through a manuscript full-text copy made by the preacher and circulated to his acquaintances, and through the printed version on sale to the general public from bookshops. Acknowledging these different media allows us to consider more fully the relationship between the textual witnesses and the original oration. Only one version, the one delivered orally from the pulpit in St Paul's Churchyard, is unavailable to us. But the arguments it contained, embedded as they are in the interpretation of the biblical text, will not have changed beyond recognition in their transition to the paper versions that survive. The Paul's Cross preachers vied for the attention of the sermon-going and the sermon-reading public. They constructed their sermons to make the essence of their arguments easily transferrable between the media available to them.

3

Controlling the Sermons

While acknowledging the political importance of Paul's Cross, modern scholars have rarely considered the difficulties that faced the authorities in controlling this pulpit, or the degree to which the possibility that controversy might begin at Paul's Cross contributed to the pulpit's significance. It is presumed that the Cross can be treated as not just a 'national pulpit', but an arm of government. It was 'the traditional site for the dissemination of the official line on political and religious issues', 'the nation's principal propaganda outlet, where official preachers explained government policy, or denounced heresy or rebellion'.[1] There is also an assumption that the 'heyday' of Paul's Cross was during the reigns of Edward VI and Mary, when the conflicts between Protestant and Catholic clerics and governors were played out publicly from that pulpit. After Elizabeth came to the throne, the hierarchy took control of Paul's Cross and such high-profile disputes were no longer aired from Paul's Cross. Millar MacLure describes Paul's Cross as 'the most important vehicle of persuasion used by the government during the period 1534–1554', and claims that this semi-official status resulted in the demise of Paul's Cross as a site of political controversy. In Elizabeth's reign 'the establishment begins to claim her own, and the preachers begin to speak from a distinctive platform'. By the Stuart period, the Paul's Cross preacher 'became a period piece'.[2] It is true that from the 1530s to 1550s, Paul's Cross was one of the most effective sites used by the royal government for presenting and enforcing doctrinal change; that story cannot be extracted from the larger political narrative of those years, and has been told very well already.[3] But MacLure is wrong to suggest that Elizabeth's succession brought the Cross firmly and unambiguously under the control of the royal

---

[1] Patrick Collinson describes Paul's Cross as a 'national pulpit' in *The Birthpangs of Protestant England: Religious and Cultural Change in the Sixteenth and Seventeenth Centuries* (London: Macmillan, 1988), p. 20. Joseph Black, 'The Rhetoric of Reaction: The Martin Marprelate Tracts (1588–89), Anti-Martinism, and the Uses of Print in Early Modern England', *Sixteenth Century Journal*, 28 (1997), 707–25, p. 711. Eamon Duffy described Paul's Cross as the 'nation's principal propaganda outlet' in a review of Derek Keene, Arthur Burns, and Andrew Saint (eds), *St Paul's: The Cathedral Church of London 604–2004* (New Haven: Yale University Press, 2004), *Sunday Telegraph*, 30 May, 2004, 'Review', p. 13.

[2] Millar MacLure, *The Paul's Cross Sermons, 1534–1642* (Toronto: University of Toronto Press, 1958), pp. 20, 55, 87.

[3] On Paul's Cross and the Reformation, see Susan Bridgen, *London and the Reformation* (Oxford: Clarendon Press, 1989), pp. 232–6, and Ethan Shagan, *Popular Politics and the English Reformation* (Cambridge: Cambridge University Press, 2003), pp. 79–82, 170–2.

government, and that this nullified the potential of that pulpit for religious and political controversy. In 1620, William Clough, the Vicar of Bramham, was reported to have called the king and the lord president fools, and to have said that he 'would get leave to preach at Paul's Cross, and would expose the evils of government'.[4] This suggests that Paul's Cross was also perceived as an influential place from which the authorities might be castigated.

The history of the monarchs' and bishops' attempts to exert control over what was said at Paul's Cross reveals the limitations on their ability to prescribe what was said from there. There were many points at which the authorities could lose control of the pulpit, from their choice of preacher to the dissemination of sermons in manuscript and printed form. Most importantly, we must always remember that 'the government' is only a convenient short-hand when dealing with Paul's Cross: there were several authorities (the Privy Council, the bishops, and the Corporation of London) who exerted a claim on the pulpit, and they did not always share the same policies and objectives. Nor were they unwilling to use the public forum provided by the Paul's Cross sermons to forward their aims to the detriment of their fellow governors. Paul's Cross can be seen as a constitutive element of what Peter Lake and Steven Pincus have termed the 'post-Reformation Public Sphere', which they describe as follows:

Moreover, during moments of perceived crisis or emergency, members of the regime, its supporters, loyal opposition, and overt critics and opponents all resorted to religiopolitical controversy and making public pitches. Print, the pulpit, performance, and circulating manuscripts were all used to address promiscuously uncontrollable, socially heterogeneous, and, in some sense, popular audiences. Such activity implied the existence of, and indeed notionally at least called into being, an adjudicating public or publics able to judge or determine the truth of the matter in hand on the basis of the information and argument placed before them.[5]

These 'public pitches' were made at times of crisis, or perceived crisis, and were 'never assumed to be a normal or regular feature of political life'. They could be dismissed by opponents as 'a form of "popularity", a dangerously seditious appeal to the people inimical to good order and monarchical rule' and had to be defended on the grounds that they demonstrated 'the continuation of loyalty and obedience by other means'. Paul's Cross was one of the media deployed for the making of these 'public pitches'; arguments derived from Christian and Protestant commonplaces were presented to the auditories at the pulpit at various times as proof of the need to eliminate or protect church ornaments, to abolish or retain episcopacy, to punish or to accept 'godly' non-conformity. The legitimacy of the message depended on the auditors' and the authorities' responses: standing in so public a pulpit, the preacher had the full weight of Protestant pastoral theology behind him. A political

---

[4] *CSPD, 1619–23*, p. 187.
[5] Peter Lake and Steve Pincus, 'Rethinking the Public Sphere in Early Modern England', *Journal of British Studies*, 45 (2006), 270–92, pp. 276–7.

power-broker would need to provide an equally, or more compelling, answer if they wished to de-legitimize words spoken from Paul's Cross. But it was far easier to prevent such messages being delivered in the first place, and so control of the appointments to preach at Paul's Cross was the crucial element in the management of this sermon series.

THE ROLE OF THE BISHOPS

William Cecil famously put Paul's Cross on the agenda for the very first day of Elizabeth's reign, when he reminded himself to 'consider the condition of the prechar at Pawles Cross, that no occasion be given by him, to stir any Dispute touching the Governance of the Realm'.[6] The early years of Elizabeth's reign saw the royal government give more persistent and focused attention to Paul's Cross than it was to receive again before the Spanish Match. The first sermon of the new reign was preached by Dr William Bill, the Queen's almoner, on 20 November, three days after the accession.[7] But for the next five months or so, Paul's Cross was empty in accordance with the Queen's inhibition on preaching of 28 December: this is in contrast with the court pulpits, where preaching continued throughout this period. This contrast demonstrates the difficulty the government had in controlling Paul's Cross,[8] particularly with Bonner still officially in his position as bishop of London (until his deprivation on 29 May 1559). Preaching did not resume at Paul's Cross until the Rehearsal sermons were preached on 2 April 1559 by Thomas Sampson, a returned exile and future leader of the puritan movement.[9] From this point until the queen left London on progress in September, Paul's Cross was part of the campaign by Cecil and the Queen's emerging episcopal bench to discredit opposition to the new Supremacy and Uniformity bills then making their uneasy way through the parliament. As John Strype puts it:

Great care was taken, while this important work of the change of religion, and rejection of the papal power was in hand, to have good preaching at St Paul's; and that none but men of

---

    [6] Public Records Office, State Papers, Domestic, 12/I/fol. 3; see also Norman L. Jones, *Faith by Statute: Parliament and the Settlement of Religion, 1559* (London: Royal Historical Society, 1982), p. 31.
    [7] *The Diary of Henry Machyn, Citizen and Merchant-taylor of London, from A.D. 1550 to A.D. 1563*, ed. John Gough Nichols (1848), p. 178.
    [8] Preaching continued in court throughout this Lent, coinciding with the parliament: Peter McCullough, *Sermons at Court: Politics and Religion in Elizabethan and Jacobean Preaching* (Cambridge: Cambridge University Press, 1998), pp. 59–60.
    [9] *Machyn's Diary*, p. 193. The *Register of Sermons* lists two sermons between William Bill's sermon of 20 November and Sampson rehearsal sermon of 2 April, but both may be 'ghosts'. Edwin Sandys reported to Heinrich Bullinger that the Catholic Bishop of Chicester, John Christopherson, preached the Sunday after Bill and 'refuted everything that had been said on the Sunday proceeding' with 'great vehemence and freedom'. Sandys is reporting this second-hand and the incident is uncorroborated from other sources. Norman L. Jones thinks it unlikely that the Bishop would have been allowed air his views from Paul's Cross, but thinks it probable that he may have said something somewhere else (*Faith by Statute*, p. 36). The *Register of Sermons* repeats W. H. Frere's claim (*The English Church in the Reigns of Elizabeth and James I*, 1911) that Matthew Parker preached on 10 February 1559, but this was a sermon at court: McCullough, 'Calendar of Sermons', with *Sermons at Court*.

good wisdom and learning should come up at the Cross, the better to reconcile the people to the work that was doing.[10]

The 'important work of the change of religion' was, as we now know, much more a matter of brinkmanship than Strype's narrative suggests, and Paul's Cross was deployed by the royal government as another means to tilt the odds in their favour. When parliament rose for Easter 1559, the Queen's plans for the Church had almost come unstuck: the bill for the supremacy sent from the Commons to the Lords in February had been revised so drastically that it allowed only minimal changes to the liturgy and failed to define the queen's supremacy over the Church, making future efforts to reform of doubtful legitimacy.[11] Elizabeth needed to discredit and then depose the Marian bishops if she wanted to take control of the Lords. The propaganda instruments used were a disputation between the Catholic hierarchy and the Protestants preparing to replace them,[12] and a sermon at Paul's Cross. The Westminster Disputation began on 2 April, but by the second day, confusion arose over the rules of the debate (some apparently genuine, some deliberately staged) and the proceedings were abandoned. Within hours, two of the Catholic bishops were arrested for their behaviour and sent to the Tower. The government sought to maximize public awareness of their view of the Catholic disputants' behaviour: an account was drafted by the Privy Council for print publication. But before that happened, Dr William Bill was back at Paul's Cross on 9 April, 'and declaryd warfor the byshopes whent to the Towre'.[13] The next day, with the balance of power in the House of Lords significantly altered, a new supremacy bill was introduced.

This was only the beginning of the campaign to win ordinary subjects over to the decisions made in the Houses of Parliament, however, and it was a campaign in which Paul's Cross took the lead. Between April and August, seven of the nine Paul's Cross preachers that we know of were future bishops: Edmund Grindal, soon to be called to London, Robert Horne (to Winchester), William Barlow (to Chichester), Edmund Sandys (to Worcester), John Jewel (to Salisbury), Thomas Bentham (to Lichfield), and John Scory (to Hereford).[14] Four of these were among the disputants at Westminster (Scory, Sandys, Grindal, and Horne).[15] Over the next year, they were

---

[10] John Strype, *Annals of the Reformation*, 4 vols (Oxford, 1824), vol. 1, p. 198.

[11] The account that follows is taken from Jones, *Faith by Statute*, pp. 113–29.

[12] The Protestant disputants included not only many future bishops, but the men who would dominate Paul's Cross in the months that followed: Richard Cox, Edmund Grindal, Robert Horne, Edwin Sandys, and John Jewel: Raphael Holinshed et al., *The Third Volume of Chronicles* (1586), *STC²* 13569, p. 1183.

[13] *Machyn's Diary*, p. 194.

[14] *Register of Sermons*, p. 41. It may not have been planned this way by the Queen or Cecil: the formation of Elizabeth's first bench was a drawn-out process involving compromises between Cecil's support for the 'evangelicals', Elizabeth's preference for the Edwardians who had stayed in England, and the exchequer's plans for the bishops' temporalities: see Brett Ussher, *William Cecil and Episcopacy, 1559–1577* (Aldershot: Ashgate, 2003), pp. 26–64.

[15] John Jewel, *Works*, ed. Revd John Ayre (Cambridge, 1850), vol. 4, p. 1200. Matthew Parker wrote to Peter Martyr Vermigli, saying that the other disputants were (Richard) Cox, (David) Whitehead, (John) Aylmer, and (Edmund) Guest.

to preach at Paul's Cross repeatedly, Grindal making three more appearances, Bentham and Jewel two more each, Sandys and Scory returning just once, while Richard Cox, Bishop of Ely, Miles Coverdale, Thomas Sampson, and Alexander Nowell, confirmed as Dean of Paul's in December 1560, also took their turn there. Paul's Cross was a significant part of this campaign to convert Londoners to the new English Church, which is why Jewel's famous 'Challenge' sermon, first preached in November 1559 was delivered here and at court: like his *Apology* of 1562, this sermon adopted the same argumentative strategy as the Westminster disputation, insisting on Scripture and the practices of the Primitive Church as the only legitimate bases for formulating doctrine and liturgy.

This concerted and sustained government effort to make use of Paul's Cross for gaining acceptance for the emerging settlement was hardly sustainable. Even in 1559, the different priorities of the Queen against those of Cecil and the Marian exiles could find expression there. Following the five-month campaign by the bishops in waiting, the Queen went on progress in late summer 1559, leaving the city in the hands of the Ecclesiastical Visitors then conducting their enquiry into the city's churches. They encouraged the destruction of images and altars in city churches,[16] and were probably responsible for appointing preachers more radical than the Queen may have liked to see appearing at Paul's Cross, including an exiled Scot, John McBray, and an exiled Frenchman, John Veron; certainly, a tone of invective more stridently anti-Catholic than before was allowed to dominate.[17] Something similar happened at court: Peter McCullough has shown that the court preachers of spring 1559 formed 'a remarkably well-tuned choir indeed', but by the end of that year 'factional strife began to mark ecclesiastical as well as civil politics, and the court pulpit rarely sounded univocally'.[18] By the time the queen returned in October, the bishops-elect were again serving repeatedly at Paul's Cross. This lapse in control by the royal government did not nullify the overall campaign of those crucial two years, but it does demonstrate that disagreement between the Queen and the new Church hierarchy prevented Paul's Cross becoming the 'principal propaganda outlet' for the Privy Council.

For the authorities to retain complete control over the message delivered from Paul's Cross required the cooperation of the different elements of government present in spring and early summer 1559: the bishops and the Privy Councillors, the lord mayor and aldermen. We can get a measure of how unusual such control was by looking at the many instances where it collapsed. One of the earliest was in 1565, when puritan dislike of the vestments prescribed in the *Book of Common Prayer* flared into outright opposition and Archbishop Parker knew he had the full support of neither government nor Church hierarchy in his drive to ensure the full conformity that the Queen had demanded. Bishop Grindal of London seems to have been more willing to help the godly ministers than his archbishop, and this extended to his use of the right to appoint preachers to Paul's Cross. Three of the

---

[16] Kenneth Fincham and Nicholas Tyacke, *Altars Restored: The Changing Face of English Worship, 1547–c.1700* (Oxford: Oxford University Press, 2007), pp. 35–7.

[17] Ussher, *William Cecil and Episcopacy*, p. 36.

[18] McCullough, *Sermons at Court*, p. 60.

twenty ministers who asked the Ecclesiastical Commissioners not to press them to conform on the vestments issue in March 1565 preached at Paul's Cross within the year: Thomas Lever preached on 28 October 1565; Dr Thomas Cole, Archdeacon of Essex, appeared on 12 November 1565; James Calfhill on 10 February 1566.[19] Grindal also used his influence to support the appointment of two of the main figures in the controversy and leaders of the emerging puritan opposition, Thomas Sampson and Laurence Humphrey, to the Easter Spital sermons of 1565, despite the fact that Archbishop Parker was then planning to have them deprived of their benefices.

The significance of this episode can only be gauged by remembering the important place of the Spital sermons in the civil ritual of the city: attending sermons at Paul's Cross and the Spital was the London community's way of marking the high point in the Church's calendar. (Only Easter Sunday, when attendance at one's parish church was mandatory, was not celebrated here.) John Stow devotes considerable space to these sermons in the *Survey*, more than to any other aspect of the Paul's Cross sermons.[20] The arrangements for getting to the Spital sermons are described in *The Ordre of my Lord Maior, the Aldermen & the Shiriffes, for their Metings and Wearynge of theyr Apparel Throughout the Yeare* for 1568:

All the Aldermen & Shirifes commeth to my lords place before 8. of the clocke to breakefast, in their scarlet gounes furred, and their clokes and horses.

And after breakefast, take theyr horses and ride to the spittle, and there put on their clokes, and so sit downe in order to heare the sermon, which done, rydeth homewarde in order till they come to the Well with two buckets within bishopsgate, and there so many of the Aldermen as dyneth wyth the shiriffes, taketh their leaue of my lord, & the rest go home with him.[21]

Indeed, on one occasion, the Spital sermons took precedence over Paul's Cross: in 1638, when Easter Tuesday fell on Charles I's Accession Day, the sermon for that occasion, usually preached at Paul's Cross, 'was preached at St Mary Spittle where was present also the liveries of the XII Companies of the City'.[22]

The appointment of the Spital preachers belonged to the Corporation, but they usually sought the bishop's approval for their choices. On 21 March 1565, the Court of Aldermen agreed that the names of Alexander Nowell, Dean of St Paul's, 'doctor Humfre, doctor Sampson & doctor Cole' be put 'to the lorde bysshop of

[19] Bodleian Library MS Tanner 50, ff. 23ᵛ, 26ʳ, 35ʳ. I would like to thank Professor Patrick Collinson for alerting me to this source. Most of the sermon notes in this collection are from Paul's Cross (the exception being a marriage sermon), so this may have been a Paul's Cross sermon moved into the church because of the weather. On the twenty ministers' appeal to the Ecclesiastical Commissioners, see Collinson, *The Elizabethan Puritan Movement* (London: Jonathan Cape, 1967; repr. Oxford: Clarendon, 1990), pp. 74–5.

[20] *A Survey of London by John Stow*, ed. Charles Lethbridge Kingsford, 2 vols (Oxford: Clarendon Press, 1908), vol 1, pp. 167–8; City of London, London Metropolitan Archive, Repertory of the Court of Aldermen 23, f. 126ᵛ.

[21] *The Ordre of my Lord Mayor, the Aldermen & the Shiriffes, for their Metings and Wearynge of theyr Apparel Throughout the Yeare* (1568), *STC*² 16705.7, sigs B2ᵛ–B3ʳ.

[22] City of London, London Metropolitan Archive, City Cash Book 2, f. 211ʳ.

London to the ende that suche three of them as his lordeshipp shall best lyke' might
be invited to deliver the sermons at the Spital that Easter.[23] On hearing of the
appointment of Sampson and Humphrey, Parker wrote to Cecil disavowing any
part in it, and rightly assuming that the appointment came from the lord mayor and
the bishop. Parker warned 'if these solemn sermons should stay for want, now after
so short a warning, it would raise a marvellous speech. I pray you advertise the
Queen's Majesty.'[24] Presumably with the connivance of Grindal, the city authorities kept up their support of the emerging puritan party the following year. On 13
March 1566, Parker wrote again to Cecil, asserting his determination to exercise
control over the appointments to these prestigious sermons in spite of the Corporation: 'some persons appointed shall be disappointed, and others placed, as is
promised me', he writes, and adds a note:

Yesterday, the lord mayor send me such word [of Thomas Cole's appointment]; this day
came the chamberlain and another from him to signify that it would be hard to get any
other; and therefore they wished to have those two, with the bishop of Durham or Mr
Beaumont. I told them the Queen's pleasure resolutely, and if they would seek to her
majesty to be dispensed with, I could not assure them to speed, and so left them to their
consultation, charging them yet that they should not suffer the days to be unoccupied, so to
derive an envy and muttering against their sovereign.[25]

Easter Sunday was not until 14 April, which left the Corporation a full month to
find alternative preachers. By 3 April, Parker could inform Cecil that he had agreed
on preachers' appointments with the lord mayor. There were still some negotiations: the lord mayor asked Parker to 'to obtain of Mr Becon' to preach on the
Wednesday; Parker promised to do so, but advised that if Becon could not preach,
that the Monday preacher also take the Wednesday (the least prestigious) slot
'rather than the day should be void, to raise a speech'. Parker had replaced Bishop
Grindal of London as the adviser to the Corporation on the Spital sermons, at least
for this occasion.[26] Throughout this correspondence there is a clear sense of how
unpopular it would be with Londoners should the disputes over vestments lead to
the cancellation of one or more of the Spital sermons, and that was an element in
the calculations being made by bishop, archbishop, and the Corporation in their
tussle over the choice of preachers.

The Queen allowed Matthew Parker to fight her battle over vestments, and it
was he who intruded on Grindal's right to appoint during 1565–6. But Parker did
not manage to keep all dissenting voices away from Paul's Cross even in these years
of direct oversight. On 18 October 1565, Robert Crowley preached there and
reportedly said that 'the sobryety of apparell of Prests doth not consist in one

[23] LMA, Rep. 13(1), f. 431[r].
[24] *Correspondence of Matthew Parker, DD, Archbishop of Canterbury*, ed. John Bruce and Revd Thomas
Thomason Perowne (Cambridge, 1853), p. 239. The editors wrongly assume that the appointment was to
Paul's Cross, an error repeated in *The Register of Sermons*.
[25] Ibid. pp. 263–4.
[26] Ibid. pp. 275.

certen kinde of apparell'.[27] On 10 February 1566, James Calfhill, divinity lecturer in St Paul's, preached what is ostensibly an anti-Catholic sermon, defending his opposition to crucifixes as 'will worshipe and abhominable'. Calfhill uses the word 'cross' to designate the crucifix, and denounces it on the grounds that having a 'very liknes of Christ', it is 'but an idoll'. Calfhill's purpose was at least as much aimed at Elizabeth and her retention of a cross (or crucifix) in her private chapel despite the sustained objections of her bishops.[28]

The bishop's role as appointer of the Paul's Cross preachers did not, therefore, ensure that the policies of the royal government and the Queen were always given univocal support from this pulpit. Indeed, the bishops as preachers were no less willing to use Paul's Cross to put pressure on the Queen, even on issues where she was singularly unwilling to act despite public opinion. The Cross was used by the bishops in a 'calling into being' of the sort of 'adjudicating public' modelled by Lake and Pincus, or perhaps rather an extending of an adjudicating public already formed around these controversies. In 1567, for example, John Jewel preached a sermon that has been interpreted as a comment against the plan for the Queen to marry the Archduke Charles of Austria.[29] Sometime in late 1576 or early 1577, Archbishop Tobie Matthew also strayed onto the sensitive subject of the Queen's marriage in a sermon at Paul's Cross. We know this from a letter he wrote to the Earl of Leicester, explaining the context in which he mentioned the succession (the continuance of the Protestant religion, threatened by the 'Antichrist of Rome', not 'touching succession of other maters & persons as it is a cause that concerneth the prince & the Piers'), asserting his good intentions and pleading for the 'good opinion' of the Earl and the Queen. The suggestion that Matthew meddled with political matters is, he says, 'a device to disgrace me with her maiestie & discredit me with your good Lordship', but mentioning the succession, even to tell the hearers that it was none of their business, can only have been an attempt to remind the public of this lingering problem, particularly when dealing with it in the context of the persistent threat of 'popery'.[30]

The Queen's marriage was not the only subject on which she disagreed with a considerable part of the 'political nation' in these years. The fate of Mary, Queen of Scots, was another, and on this subject Paul's Cross was again used by her bishops

---

[27] Bodleian Library MS Tanner 50, f. 8[v]. Crowley would publish his opposition to vestments in print the following year: Basil Morgan, 'Crowley, Robert (1517x19–1588)', *Oxford Dictionary of National Biography* (Oxford: Oxford University Press, 2004) online edn., Jan 2008, <http://www.oxforddnb.com/view/article/6831>, accessed 4 June 2009.

[28] J. T. Tomlinson, *Queen Elizabeth's Crucifix* (London: Church Association, 1900).

[29] J. E. Neale places Jewel's sermon on Joshua 6:1–3 at Paul's Cross and dates it to November 1567, at a crucial point in the negotiations over the proposed marriage with the Archduke: *Queen Elizabeth* (London: Jonathan Cape, 1934). Although Neale cites no source for this, it is plausible. The sermon was preached in November, as Jewel says he is preaching on the anniversary of the Queen's accession; it was printed in a collection of sermons preached at court and Paul's Cross, and the tone and content of the sermon makes the former venue very unlikely: *Certaine Sermons preached before the Queenes Majestie, and at Paules Crosse* (1583), *STC*[2] 14596, sig. D5[v]. In late 1567, when the *Defence of the Apology* was about to appear, Jewel might have felt sufficiently secure in the Queen's favour to take this kind of calculated risk.

[30] Folger Shakespeare Library, MS V.b.317, ff. 11[v]–12[v], ff. 12[r–v].

to promulgate a policy she opposed. The relevant sermon was preached by Grindal's successor in London, Edwin Sandys.[31] In the 1585 printed edition, this sermon is described as having been preached when a 'maine treason' was discovered, but its reticence about the perpetrators of the treason makes it unlikely that this was designed to be a public denunciation of condemned traitors. Until recently, it was dated to August–September 1586, and said to relate to the Babington Plot, but that plot was not discovered until July 1586.[32] It seems reasonable to assume that the sermon was preached while Sandys was bishop of London, placing it in the years 1570–6.[33] The reference in the sermon to conspiracies by 'noble personages', and the example of 'Marie, the very sister of Moses' (p. 361: the more usual form was Miriam),[34] suggest that the occasion of the sermon was most probably during the parliament of 1572, when the Ridolfi Plot was debated and parliament sought to convince the Queen to have Mary, Queen of Scots, tried for treason.[35] Sandys attended this parliament and was on the joint committee that drew up two bills against Mary (one for her execution, one for her exclusion from the succession). When told that the Queen would not proceed with the bill for Mary's attainder, the joint committee, including the bishops, decided to put forward a petition to her.[36] The section drafted by the bishops uses the same biblical example as this sermon, David and Absalom; it draws the same lesson that 'it is daungerouse for any Christyan prince and contrary to the worde of God with coullor of mercy and pittie to doe that whereby he shall discourage and kill the

---

[31] Edwin Sandys, *A Sermon preached at Pauls Cross at what time a Maine Treason was Discovered*, in *Sermons made by the most Reverende Father in God, Edwin, Archbishop of York* (1585), *STC*[2] 21713, pp. 359–72.

[32] *Register of Sermons*, p. 65. The editors follow the Parker Society, *The Sermons of Edwin Sandys*, ed. Rev. John Ayre (Cambridge, 1841), pp. 403–17, where the sermon is related to the Babington Plot, but that plot is misdated to 1585. The Babington Plot was not discovered until July 1586: Conyers Read, *Mr Secretary Walsingham and the policy of Queen Elizabeth*, 3 vols (Oxford: Clarendon Press, 1925), vol 2, pp. 47–9. Kathryn Murphy corrects this error and suggests a date in May 1572: 'The Date of Edwin Sandys's Paul's Cross Sermon, "... at which time a maine treason was discoured"', *Notes and Queries* (December 2006), pp. 430–2.

[33] Of Sandys' seven Paul's Cross sermons, three can be dated for certain and these were all preached during his time in London. Those which the *Register of Sermons* could not date it assigned to these years: *Register of Sermons*, pp. 50, 54, 57, 80.

[34] For the text that Sandys refers to (Numbers 12), the Wycliffe Bible (early and late versions) and the Rheims-Douay Bible are the only translations that use Mary (or Marie/Maria) as the usual form for Miriam. This is also true of the other texts where Moses's sister is mentioned (Exodus 6:20 and 15:20; Micah 6:4; 1 Chronicles 6:3). The Bishops' Bible uses 'Marie' once, in a marginal note to Leviticus 18:10; the 1587 Geneva Bible uses 'Marie' in a marginal note to Leviticus 13:20 and 'Maria' in the 'Table of the interpretation of the proper names ... found in the Old Testament'. Miriam is otherwise used in the text of the Old Testament in Coverdale's Bible, the Great Bible, the Bishops' Bible, and the 1587 Geneva Bible: *The Bible in English* database, Version 1.0 (Chadwyck-Healey, 1996).

[35] Sandys seems to have been ill in late 1570, when action was taken against the rebels. In a letter to Cecil dated 25 August 1570, Archbishop Parker wrote that 'the Bishop of London's recovery is doubtful': *CSPD, 1547–1580*, p. 390. It is therefore unlikely that Sandys would have been able to preach a sermon at the time that this 'main treason' was actually discovered. He was well again by 2 April 1571, when he preached at the opening of the 1571 parliament, a sermon in which he also stressed the dangers of the enemies of Protestantism: J. E. Neale, *Elizabeth I and Her Parliaments, 1558–1581* (London: Jonathan Cape, 1953), pp. 184–5.

[36] Neale, *Elizabeth I and Her Parliaments, 1558–1581*, pp. 262–75; *Lord's Journal*, 12 May 1572.

hartes of his owne good subjectes and faithfull councellores' from David's example.[37] This petition was probably drafted on 24 May, the Saturday before Whitsunday, and delivered to the Queen on 26 May, Whitmonday. Sandys almost certainly stayed in London that weekend: as bishop of London he would have officiated in St Paul's on Whitsunday, but the dean would have preached in the Cathedral. I suggest that Sandys preached his sermon on a 'maine treason', in words that echo so closely the petition soon to be delivered to the Queen, at Paul's Cross on Whitsunday 1572.[38]

Sandys was doubtless taking a risk in presenting from a public pulpit an argument that had not yet been presented to the Queen but on a subject to which she had already indicated her opposition. Not surprisingly, Sandys is rather reticent about his theme, even in his choice of text: part of Psalm 4:5, 'Offer the sacrifice of righteousness', a text more associated with exhortations to charity than political questions.[39] Sandys's handling of the theme is similarly indirect: his 'explication' of the biblical text is surprisingly short and an unusual amount of time is devoted to describing its context in the scriptural narrative. David wrote the Psalm, Sandys begins by explaining, in the 'great distress, whereunto he was brought by the monstrous & unnaturall rebellion which his ambitious sonne Absalom raised against him' (p. 359). David turns to God for help, emphasizing his innocence of anything that might justify such a rebellion. And so Sandys draws his first lesson from the sermon, that 'the security of princes doth not rest upon their power, be they never so strongly guarded, but upon their innocencie' (p. 361). Like many traitors, Absalom is a man 'of high place and great authoritie'; even 'Marie the verie sister of Moses and a woman of place and countenance devised a plot to displace hir brother' (p. 361). Absalom was a hypocrite, doing everything to make himself popular with discontented people and feigning religious sincerity, but this was merely to hide his treason 'under the cloake of religion' (pp. 363–4). The biblical episode also shows that patient forbearance in such cases is wasted: David was unwilling to believe any evil of his son, but men 'grounded and setled in evill' will not repay benefits received (p. 364). God will foil their plans because 'whome the Lord hath set up he will maintaine and defende' (p. 364).

So we see that it is in this preliminary discussion of the text's context that Sandys's political theme emerges. This is a very significant feature of this sermon: it was conventional for the advice that the preacher wished his hearers to take home with

[37] T. E. Hartley (ed.), *Proceedings in the Parliaments of Elizabeth I*, vol. 1: *1558–1581* (Leicester: Leicester University Press, 1981), pp. 276–9, p. 278. On similar rhetoric regarding Mary, see Patrick Collinson, *The English Captivity of Mary Queen of Scots* (Sheffield: Sheffield History Pamphlets, 1987), pp. 4–8.

[38] On the preaching rota for St Paul's, see Bodleian Library MS Rawl.D. 399, f. 294[r], or W. Sparrow Simpson, *Registrum Statutorum et Consuetudinum Ecclesiae Cathedralis Sancti Pauli Londiniensis* (1873), Book II, item XIX. The lord mayor and aldermen would not have been present at the sermon on Whitsunday; they would have been at the Newchurchyard sermon endowed by Lord Mayor Thomas Rowe in 1569. This may have made Sandys more willing to make such a politically risky sermon on that day.

[39] This is the text for Francis White's 1618 Spittle sermon, as summarized in Daniel Featley's *The Spouse Her Precious Borders*, in *Clavis Mystica* (1636), *STC*[2] 10730, pp. 439–44.

them, his 'application', to rest on the precepts he revealed from his 'explication' of the text; the preliminary discussion of the text's context merely prepared for the 'explication'. In Sandys's sermon, a long prefatory discussion of Absalom's rebellion precedes the 'explication', which concerns thanksgiving to God, and the application, which is an exhortation to thankfulness. The dangers posed by over-merciful monarchs and their treasonous relations are structurally separate from the primary elements of the sermon, and so the politically resonant points arise as part of the 'background information' for the text, and might be viewed as a digression. Sandys reminds his hearers that what he has described in the initial section of the sermon is no more that the 'occasion the Prophet uttereth these words which I have chosen to speake of at this time' (p. 366). Because this is not formally and structurally part of Sandys's exposition, Sandys is not, strictly speaking, preaching to his congregation about what should be done about Mary; he is merely exhorting them to give thanks to God for their political and religious safety. But the background of the text is, nonetheless, being drawn to their attention in a very pointed way: the hearers are left to draw their own conclusions about the dangers that England might still face if the Queen were as soft-hearted as David.

It would be naïve to say that the early modern authorities could not exert control over Paul's Cross. Yet it would be equally naïve to say that they could exercise a high level of control consistently, week in, week out; or that they behaved with unanimity of purpose with respect to Paul's Cross (a level of agreement that is not evident in any other arena of politics at this time). When necessary, the authorities, secular and ecclesiastic, worked together to make Paul's Cross an effective site for the promulgation of an agreed version of controversial events. At other times, their different aims became manifest as they struggled with each other for the power to control who spoke, and what was said, at Paul's Cross.

PREACHERS AND HEARERS

It was far easier to dictate who preached at Paul's Cross than it was to control what they said there, as Edwin Sandys himself discovered not long after his subversive sermon on Mary and the 'maine treason'. The years 1572 and 1573 saw several sermons delivered at Paul's Cross by senior churchmen on the subject of the *Admonition to Parliament* and the puritan movement more generally. But the other side of this controversy also found a platform for their views at this pulpit, to the evident embarrassment of Sandys, who reported the matter to William Cecil and the Earl of Leicester. In his letter, Sandys insists that he made every effort to establish the conformable credentials of the preachers, but could not, he writes 'know their hartes, and these tymes haue altered opinions'. Richard Crick (then chaplain to the bishop of Norwich but a future leader in the East Anglian presbyterian movement) had been commended 'for learninge and sobrietie' and so appointed to the Cross, but when in the pulpit 'spitefully inveighed against the ecclesiastical pollicie now by lawe established, confirminge Mr *Cartwrightes* booke, as the true platforme of the syncere and Apostolicall churche'. The preacher was 'conveighed away' before Sandys' men caught up with him. Sandys tried to redeem the situation with the appointment of Arthur Wake of Christchurch in Oxford, who had 'made a good sermon' the year before, and so was appointed again. Sandys's chancellor and the archdeacon of Essex both 'conferred' with Wake before the sermon 'and required [him] to have consideracon of these trobled times, . . . that he would speake nothing that should turne to sedicon.' Despite these warnings, Wake's 'whole sermon was consumed in raylinge against this present state, and affirminge to be good whatsoever Mr Cartwright in writinge hath sett downe' and Wake had fled back to Oxford before Sandys could do anything about it. Sandys insists that he has 'dealt so carefully as I canne to keep such fanaticall spirites from the *crosse*' but the 'poison of sedicon' has 'so suddenlie changed these waveringe myndes that it is hard to tell whome a man may trust'.[40] With reference to this letter, Paul Seaver makes the following comment:

The sermon was a problematic tool of government and a potent weapon for 'fanatical spirits' precisely because of its unpredictability; there was no way of assessing a sermon's ill effects until the word had been spoken and the damage done.[41]

Every sermon had the potential to surprise the authorities because, as an oration, it could not be judged in advance. The bishop and his officials had to rely on the preacher's reputation for conformity and the effect of the stern talk from the bishop's representative, usually his chaplain.[42] The bishop himself might speak to the preacher when the need arose, as we see in this anecdote of Joseph Mede's relating to 22 September 1622, the week after John Donne preached on the *Directions for Preachers*. The preacher failed to turn up the day before the sermon, and so was sent for on the Sunday morning:

The preacher came & having made his excuse, the Bishop begain to give him good counsell, That he should take heed that he spake nothing which might be distastfull or unfitt for the present times &c. Then askes him what his text was who told him Galat. 1. v 6.7.8 *I marvaile that you are so soone remooued from him that called you into the grace of Christ vnto another Gospell. &c 7. But there are some that trouble you & would prevert the Gospell of Christ. v. 8. But thou we* &c &c. Whenat the Bishop struck his hand upon his brest swearing that

---

[40] BL MS Lansdowne 17, f. 43, ff. 96^{r-v}. This letter is printed in John Strype, *The Life and Acts of the most Reverend Father in God, John Whitgift*, 3 vols (Oxford, 1822), vol. 3, pp. 31–5. The man who reported Crick's sermon was William Gravet, who claims that Crick had confuted Gravet's defence of the Church's ceremonies, delivered the previous Sunday at Paul's Cross: Inner Temple MS Petyt MS 538, vol. 47, ff. 476^r–478^v. The bishop's reliance on people like Gravet to inform him of such contentious sermons demonstrates yet more forcefully the difficulty of controlling the pulpit.

[41] Paul Seaver, *The Puritan Lectureships: The Politics of Religions Dissent, 1560–1662* (Palo Alto, CA: Stanford University Press, 1970), pp. 59–60.

[42] Sandys's letter implies that having both men confer with Arthur Wake constituted more rigorous scrutiny than was usual. Later letters of appointment to preach at Paul's Cross instruct the preacher to report to the bishop's chaplain at London house before the sermon: *The Works of Archbishop Laud* (Oxford, 1860), vol. 7, p. 47; Bodleian Library MS Rawlinson D. 399, f. 155^r. (This letter was wrongly assigned to Laud: The letter is signed 'Guil. London', so it is either from Laud or Juxon, and 29 November was a Sunday in 1629, 1635, and 1640. But the chaplain mentioned is Dr [Thomas] Wykes, who was chaplain to Juxon.); City of London, Guildhall Library MS 36,711. I would like to thank Richard Webster for referring me to this manuscript.

that text was not allowable for these times. . . . Then the Bishop asked him if he could not change it. He answered No well sayd the Bishop Look to thy selfe, for if you speakest any thing that shall not please I vow to break thy neck & thy back too. The Preacher answered he had nothing to speak but what he would stand to & so was dismissed being sermon time. Yet by & by one of the Bishop's chapleins comes after him & offers to preach for him. But he refused. So taking a litle time to meditate, at length comes forth & makes a preface relating the summe of the former passages as an excuse if he weare not so ready as he should have bin. &c. which much displeased the Bishop; Yet the whole Sermon contained nothing but in generall a discourse of the damnable condition of those who should forsake the faith they had received &c. Onely he concluded That they might expect some application but he was not ambitious of lying in prison & so ended.[43]

The bishop could do little more than threaten: he could guess what kind of interpretation the text would invite, but the preacher might offer nothing but a general 'discourse of the damnable condition of those who should forsake the faith'. The bishop's only other option was to find another preacher, the chaplain who volunteered in this case being the most likely candidate. On this occasion, the bishop appears to have been present at the sermon, and so witnessed the preacher recount their meeting 'which much displeased' him, but at least he knew that nothing seditious had been said. On other occasions, when the bishop was not present and with no written copy of what was said available for examination, the bishop relied on the reports of other witnesses, particularly the members of the political and social elite. The preacher might also be required to write out a copy of what he had said, and swear to the fidelity of that copy as a record of what he said.

Among the most frequent to complain about Paul's Cross sermons in Elizabeth's reign were the lord mayor and aldermen, perhaps because they attended the sermons most regularly, perhaps because the preachers saw them as a target for admonition (they were the governors of the city whose moral failings the preachers addressed). In September 1581, the Corporation wrote to Bishop Aylmer complaining that his chaplain, Lawrence Deios, had 'publiquely defamed us to our faces' in a sermon at Paul's Cross 'in the audience of persons of all partes of this Realme', saying 'to this effect that if the appointing of preachers were comitted to us we wold appointe preachers such as shold defend usury the familie of love and puritanisme as they call it'. Aylmer replies that on hearing 'what construction was made of his wordes' he spoke with Deios and 'some other that were learned being then his hearers' and they said that 'there could be no such meaning gathered owt of any thing that proceeded from him'. Deios's point was merely the 'inconveniences' that would arise if the people had the right to choose their own pastors, 'as in this Citie the people being divided into many sectes and factions', they would choose ministers according to their own inclinations 'and so great tumultes might arise'.[44] And there the matter ended. On another occasion, the Corporation took their complaint to the royal government, not the bishop. Among the Salisbury

---

[43] British Library MS Harley 389, f. 233ʳ, 28 September 1622.
[44] City of London, London Metropolitan Archive, Remembrancia, vol. I, ff. 114ʳ⁻ᵛ, 117ᵛ–118ʳ.

manuscripts is 'A true coppy of a speech uttered at Paules Crosse the 13 of March 1602 by Richard Stock minister, whereat the right honourable the Lord Maior and some of the Aldermen of the citty were offended' sent to Secretary of State Robert Cecil.[45] And one can see why they were offended: Stock exhorts the aldermen to take a fairer proportion of the tax burden of the city on themselves, arguing that the Fifteenths in particular were disproportionately onerous on the poor. He says that every year he hears 'an exceeding outcry and pittifull complaining of the poorer sort, that they are much oppressed of the rich of thys citty'. He is persuaded that 'hardly a man of the Bench or of the Common Counsell, which hath not heard by their collectors at one tyme or other of the lamentable complaintes, the teares and sighs of the poore in most parish'. We hear no more of this matter, but Stock was called to preach at Paul's Cross again in 1606, and that sermon was printed, so once again the Corporation's complaint had little effect.[46]

But there were occasions when a preacher was made to retract accusations made against the Corporation. On 6 March 1586, George Closse 'unjustlie charged the Lord Mayor of the Cittie of London with matters of injustice in a certaine cause by him then repeated before the auditorie' at Paul's Cross. The Corporation complained to High Commission, and Closse was ordered 'in the same place publiquelie to confesse, notifie and acknowledge unto the auditorie his indiscreet and lewd manner of proceeding, and openlie to ask pardon of the Lord Maiour for the same'.[47] The retraction was scheduled for Palm Sunday (27 March), and the auditory was alerted to this the Sunday beforehand, and so 'sundrie rumors and great diversities of reports of the matter' spread in the city, so that 'at the daie and place prefixed was gathered such an assemblie and concourse of people, as by estimation had not been seene there'. Six preachers had been appointed 'to heare the sermon, and to certifie how he discharged his designement'. Closse 'made report of the whole cause as it passed before the maior, alleging sundrie reasons divine and humane, which had mooved him in his former sermon to deal so particularlie'. This explanation satisfied the six preachers, and Closse's case was dismissed by High Commission.[48] But the lord mayor and alderman were not satisfied with an explanation where they seem to have expected an apology and took the matter to the Privy Council, who ordered that 'for the better knowledge of the truthe', the Commissioners should 'call before them not onlie Closse, but some of the best sorte of other persones that were present at his second sermon, and can testifie of his proceedings'. This time, the Commissioners agreed with the lord mayor and aldermen about Closse's second sermon, and reported this to the Privy Council. On 17 July, they ordered that 'some grave and learned person be appointed in his sermon at the Crosse to declare unto the people (the said Closse

[45] HMC, *Salisbury*, vol. 12, p. 672. The manuscript is vol. 92, item 24 of the Salisbury papers, British Library Microfilm M485/18.
[46] Richard Stock, *A Sermon preached at Paules Crosse, the Second of November, 1606* (1609) *STC²* 23276.
[47] *APC, 1586–7*, p. 60.
[48] *Holinshed's Chronicles of England, Scotland and Ireland*, ed. Sir Henry Ellis, 6 vols (London, 1807–8), vol. 6, pp. 888–91.

being present) his said misdemeanours, both in his first and second sermons'. Closse 'should not be suffred to speak publicklie him self, but onlie to stande by'. He was also to be suspended from preaching for a year and was never to be called to Paul's Cross again.[49] John Everard got free of a similarly difficult situation by making an unqualified apology: having criticized the Court of Orphans in a sermon of 11 January 1618, he was censured by the bishop of London. His apology to the lord mayor and aldermen said that he was 'advised . . . by some of approved wisdome and gravity' of the injustice of his accusations, and he now realized that there was a lack of 'discretion and modestye' in his criticizing 'magistrates before a popular Auditorye, apt rather to insult over the errors of others then to amende their owne'. Everard ends his fulsome apology by promising to be 'ready whether privately or publiquely to do them all becoming right'.[50]

The relationship between the preachers at Paul's Cross and the Corporation was not always as fraught as these examples suggest; indeed, printed sermons demonstrate a strong desire on the part of preachers to cultivate the good will of the men in charge of many city livings and other sources of clerical income in the city. There were occasions when preachers' castigation of governmental failures were only too welcome by the City Fathers, and that was when they addressed the subject of London's new commercial theatres. Paul's Cross is famously the place from which stage plays were condemned as corrupting, immoral, and a provocation to divine wrath (although references to the theatres are rarer than modern studies of the subject suggest).[51] In 1577, Thomas White famously argued that, as the 'cause of plague is sin . . . and the cause of sinne are playes: therefore the cause of plagues are playes'; John Stockwood claimed that playgoing on a Sunday, even after church services, was an abuse of the Sabbath, 'which is cause sufficient to stay them'; in 1607, William Crashaw complained particularly of *The Puritaine*, but also of the 'continuall profaning of the Sabbath' in the country. (Plays were forbidden on Sundays by royal proclamation in 1603.[52]) Robert Bolton described

---

[49] *APC, 1586–7*, p. 188.

[50] Public Records Office, State Papers Domestic, 14/95/61.

[51] In addition to those sermons quoted above, only the following references to theatres have been found in Paul's Cross sermons: John Walsall claimed that 'vaine plaiers have had about this citie of London farre greater audience, then true preachers': *A Sermon preached at Pauls Crosse* (1578), *STC²* 24995, sig. E6ᵛ. We have only a note from a sermon by Thomas Spark, 29 April 1579, where he said that theatres were 'the nest of the Divel, and sinke of all sinne': [Anthony Munday], *A Second and Third Blast of Retrait from Plaies and Theaters* (1580), *STC²* 21677, sig. A2ᵛ. Francis Marbury described theatres as 'antisabbatarie': [Marburie], *A Sermon preached at Paules Cross the 13. of June. 1602* (1602), *STC²* 17307, sig. D6ᵛ. Gabriel Price complained of 'Ribaldrie, as in Playes and the like, committed to the presse': *The Laver of the Heart* (1616), *STC²* 20306, p. 78. Samuel Ward encouraged preachers to tell 'players, and jesters, and rimers, and all that rablement' that 'though thou suffer them to personate thee upon their Stages . . . thou wilt owe it them, till they come upon the great Stage before God': *Balme from Gilead* (1617) *STC²* 25035, p. 85. Stephen Denison would have 'the profane stageplayer forsake his unlawfull youth-polluting trade': *The New Creature* (1619), *STC²* 6607, p. 44. John Boys, always one willing to champion unpopular causes, lists 'many new play-houses' among the 'glorious buildings erected about and in this honourable Citie, to the great ornament of our Country': *An Exposition of the Last Psalme* (1615), *STC²* 3464, p. 21.

[52] G. E. Bentley, 'Sunday Performances in the London Theatres', in *The Jacobean and Caroline Stage*, 7 vols (Oxford: Clarendon Press, 1968), vol. 7, p. 10.

the theatres as corrupters of the young, and the same argument was used by Thomas Sutton in 1612. Also in 1612, Robert Milles wondered how anyone would take seriously the claim that plays were edifying and 'compare the idle and scurrile invention of an illiterate bricklayer [Ben Jonson] to the holy, pure, and powerful word of God'. In the same vein, John White complained in 1615 that 'the stages now in this citty, wo is me that I should live to see it, tosse the Scripture phrase as commonly, as they do their Tobacco in their bawdy houses.'[53]

The Corporation of London was famously willing to see the theatres closed, as the preachers exhorted, but they were prevented by the support for the players at court. This did not mean that the preachers' castigations angered the lord mayor and alderman, who listened to criticism that they were powerless to address: rather, it provided them with an additional argument for their resistance to the royal government on this matter. The arguments used in the sermons (provoking God's judgement, the profanation of the Sabbath, the corruption of the youth, blasphemy) are those that the Corporation used when addressing this subject with the Privy Council, and the fact that public preachers exclaimed against them on this matter became part of the argument they used. This is most obvious from the letter sent by Lord Mayor Edward Osborne to the Privy Council, having been prompted by the latter to make better provision for archery practice in the city. The lord mayor asks the Council to bear in mind how far archery and other 'good arts' are decayed by 'unlawfull spectacles as barebaiting, unchast enterludes'. He goes on to say that 'these thinges are objected to us, both in open sermons at Paules cross and else where in the hearing of such as repaire from all partes to our shame and greif when we cannot remedie it'. The Corporation's 'travails' to amend these things 'shall yet be vaine and to no effect without your honorable help and assistance', and a plea for action in the areas outside the city's jurisdiction ends the letter.[54]

Peter Lake has aptly described the anti-theatrical pamphlets and sermons as being designed to 'create a popular push, from both the preachers and perhaps more broadly "the godly" of London, for the regulation of the theatre':

This was an autonomous 'third force', a sort of nascent or notional 'public' and/or 'godly' opinion, called into being, at least in part, by the London authorities and their agents in the press and the pulpit; a third force to which those same authorities could appeal in order both to legitimate and to strengthen their case against the theatre to the Council and court . . . [There was] a public campaign through the press and the pulpit to create a climate

---

[53] Thomas White, *A Sermo[n] preached at Pawles Crosse on the Sunday the Thirde of November 1577* (1578), *STC*[2] 25406, p. 47. John Stockwood *A Very Fruiteful Sermon Preched at Paules Crosse* (1579), *STC*[2] 23285, p. 25; Stockwood repeated this argument in another sermon the following year: *Sermon Preached at Paules Crosse on Bartholomew Day* ([1578]), *STC*[2] 23284, p. 24. William Crashaw, *The Sermon preached at the Crosse, Feb. xiiii.1607* (1608), *STC*[2] 6027, pp. 170–1. Robert Bolton, *A Discourse about the State of True Happinesse* (1611), *STC*[2] 3228, pp. 73–4. Thomas Sutton, 'England's Summons', in *England's First and Second Summons* (1616), *STC*[2] 23502, p. 27. Robert Milles, *Abrahams Suite for Sodome* (1612), *STC*[2] 17924, sig. D6ᵛ. John White, *Two sermons, the Former delivered at Paul's Cross* (1615), *STC*[2] 25392, p. 81.

[54] LMA, Remembrancia, vol. I, ff. 264ʳ⁻ᵛ. The letter is reprinted in E. K. Chambers, *The Elizabethan Stage*, 4 vols (Oxford: Oxford University Press, 1923), vol. 4, p. 295.

of opinion against the theatre to which the city authorities could appeal in their continuing efforts to get the Privy Council and court to act.[55]

On the subject of stage plays, then, the men at Paul's Cross were not just preaching to the choir; their denunciations were providing the lord mayor and aldermen with the material they needed to carry on this dispute with their more powerful neighbours in Westminster. If the Corporation's campaign against the theatres died away after 1603, when playing on Sundays was forbidden and the major theatre companies were given royal patronage, the pulpit at Paul's Cross continued to provide them with ammunition should they choose to take the cause up again, until at least the 1620s.[56] That preachers' complaints against the stage disappear after this date suggests that it was no longer something the increasingly court-oriented Corporation wished to hear.[57]

However complex the relationship between the Paul's Cross preachers and the London government, the Corporation was not the only target for preachers willing to take political risks. On 25 May 1606, Roger Parker preached an 'invective oration' against the House of Commons at Paul's Cross, 'very seditious and slanderous'. So the next day, those MPs who were present 'were appointed to goe up together into the Committee Chamber, and to Collect and set downe the offences Speeches', following which the House decided to send a sergeant to arrest Parker (Parker was warned and got away in time), and also to write a letter informing the Lord Chamberlain of Parker's behaviour, as Parker was due to preach at court the following Tuesday.[58] In 1619, Francis Bacon, then Lord Chancellor, had a 'Mr Shingleton of Oxford' committed for 'declaiming against his court, and ridiculing his Latinities' as well as 'glancing (they say) somewhat scandalously at him and his Catamites as he called them' in a sermon at Paul's Cross.[59] Other preachers offended even greater men, inadvertently or not: in 1607, Edward Robinson made an abject plea to the Privy Council for their help in gaining his release from prison following his 'ignorance and simplicity in taxing the nation

[55] Peter Lake with Michael Questier, *The Antichrist's Lewd Hat: Protestants, Papists and Players in Post-Reformation England* (New Haven: Yale University Press, 2002), pp. 497–8.

[56] Margot Heinemann, *Puritanism and Theatre: Thomas Middleton and Opposition Drama under the Early Stuarts* (Cambridge: Cambridge University Press, 1980), p. 33. For a thorough examination of the negotiations between Corporation and the Lord Chamberlain Henry Carey regarding the regulation of theatres in the city, see Andrew Gurr, 'Henry Carey's Peculiar Letter', *Shakespeare Quarterly*, 56(1) (2005), 51–75.

[57] On the changing political and religious temper of the London government from the 1620s to 1630s, see Valerie Pearl, *London and the Outbreak of the Puritan Revolution: City Government and National Politics, 1625–43* (Oxford: Oxford University Press, 1961), pp. 91–4.

[58] *The Parliamentary Diary of Robert Bowyer, 1606–1607*, ed. David Harris Willson (Minneapolis: University of Minnesota Press, 1931), pp. 179–80; HMC, *Salisbury*, vol. 17, pp. 223–4; vol. 18, p. 146. On the basis of the MPs' complaint (Parker's breach of the convention that proceedings in parliament were not reported outside the house), see David Colclough, *Freedom of Speech in Early Stuart England* (Cambridge: Cambridge University Press, 2005), pp. 140–1.

[59] *The Letters of John Chamberlain*, ed. Norman Egbert McClure, 2 vols (Philadelphia: American Philosophical Society, 1939), vol. 2, p. 243. The *Register of Sermons* assumes that this is Isaac Singleton, then a Canon of St Paul's. It may have been Isaac Singleton, who preached a sermon on the Gowrie Conspiracy in St Mary's, Oxford, in 1615 and signs the printed copy as Bishop John King's Chaplain: *The Downfall of Shebna* (1615), STC^2 22574.

of the Scots in a sermon at Paul's Cross the 7th of June', which had 'given just occasion of offence to his Majesty', something one imagines might have occurred to Robinson before he spoke.[60] John Drope was called into question for his complaints about the King's 'unjust impositions' in a sermon preached on 5 April 1617.[61]

When action was taken against a preacher for something said at Paul's Cross, we see the degree to which the authorities were reliant on reports from auditors to substantiate complaints. Judgments on the validity of the complaints then rested on the ways in which the preacher's words were interpreted, or misconstrued. In 1577, the French Ambassador complained to the Privy Council about a sermon by John Foxe in which Foxe reportedly said that French Protestants were within their rights to take arms against their king. The ambassador sent a 'schedule' of the sermon to the Privy Council, and the Council ordered the bishop of London to 'call the said Foxe before him and some others that were presente therat whom he shall thinck good'. Foxe wrote an explanation to the Council, explaining that it was all a misunderstanding of a piece of wit (so the hearers found it, he says): the French Protestants do not take arms against 'imperial law' but rather according to it, to make the King of France a 'full and perfect king over them', which the Pope's claim to supremacy denies.[62] Roger Parker, who so offended the House of Commons in 1606, was lucky that the King decided to judge the aptness of the MPs' interpretation of his sermon The King informed the House that he had heard Parker's side of the story, 'That the Dr denied some thing, and other speeches he cuppleth with words of mitigation'.[63] In both cases, the preacher's 'words of mitigation' were accepted as sufficient explanation.

As sermons involved the interpretation and application of a scriptural text, their encroachment on 'matters of state' often depended on the ways in which the text was 'applied'. Preachers did not need to refer to political controversy overtly but could be seen to allude to them through biblical analogies, as Edwin Sandys did when preaching on Mary, Queen of Scots. This could lead some preachers to stumble inadvertently onto subjects with controversial ramifications. In 1599, after an incident that had brought the Queen's wrath down on him, Richard Bancroft insisted to Sir Robert Cecil that it was impossible to control what was said at Paul's Cross:

You know, Sir, how impossible it is for me or for any man living to prevent such escapes. When I write unto them that are to supply that place, I charge them in my letters to intermeddle with nothing but with matters of faith, reformation of manners, or with the

[60] HMC, *Salisbury*, vol. 19, p. 458.
[61] *CSPD, 1611–18*, p. 461.
[62] *APC, 1575–77*, p. 294; British Library Harleian MS 417, f. 131ʳ.
[63] *Parliamentary Diary of Robert Bowyer, 1606–1607*, p. 181. There was a similar episode involving a court sermon: John Scott, a Scottish preacher, 'spake and glaunct at matters somewhat suspiciously' in a court sermon of 13 May 1613. Although the Privy Council questioned him and ordered him to preach a clarification in the same place the King countermanded their order, saying 'he heard the sermon himself, and was able to judge and yf he had found cause wold have referred him over to the counsaile himself': *Letters of John Chamberlain*, vol. 1, pp. 453–4.

common adversary. And if they overshot themselves otherwise, I neither have nor will be wanting to call them to account for it, and to proceed against them in such sort as by law I may.[64]

This incident had obviously surprised everyone, involving as it did not some 'fanatical spirit' but Dr John Richardson, a future vice-chancellor of Cambridge University. He was a figure that the authorities thought they could rely on, for (as Bancroft's chancellor, Dr Edward Stanhope wrote), 'he was never of a turbulent spirit'.[65] He had preached at Paul's Cross on 23 November 1599 and the complaint must have followed swiftly: he was put under house arrest and made to deliver the 'capita' of his sermon, which Bancroft had received by 6 December.[66] He was examined by High Commission on 15 December 1599. Establishing what Richardson had said rested on his account of his sermon, as neither Bancroft nor his chancellor were present at the sermon and so were reliant on witnesses' reports, which Richardson claimed 'misconstrued and miscollected' what he had said.[67] The crux of the matter was his reference to the Herodians, the Herodians being usually interpreted as a sect who accused Jesus of being disloyal to the secular powers. Richardson's insistence that he was not 'advised or instructed by anie person' about the section 'touching the Herodians' suggests that the Commissioners' concern was that Richardson had been encouraged to mention the Herodians by Essex's supporters, as an analogy to the claim made by them that the Cecil faction discredited the loyal Essex with the Queen.[68] Richardson was allowed to return to his cure for the Christmas holidays but was ordered to appear again on the first day of the next term and was forbidden to preach anywhere except in his cure and ordered to 'abstaine in all his sermons from intermedling in any matter of estate'. Richardson may well have stumbled into political controversy unawares: when Bancroft sent the 'capita' of the sermon to Cecil, he was unsure whether the latter would need to question Richardson personally, but seemed to think not. 'Certainly, the man hath more learning than discretion,' he commented, 'as, if you speak with him you will soon perceive'.[69]

Whoever reported Richardson's sermon to the bishop had interpreted it as referring to the Earl of Essex, and this fact points to another difficulty the authorities faced in using Paul's Cross for 'propaganda' purposes: the political effectiveness of a sermon depended on the hearers correctly interpreting the preachers' words, and accepting them. The auditory at Paul's Cross may have received

---

[64] HMC, *Salisbury*, vol. 9, p. 407. The letter is dated 4 December 1599.
[65] *CSPD, 1598–1601*, p. 365. For this incident in the context of the Essex rebellion, see Arnold Hunt, 'Tuning the Pulpits: The Religious Context of the Essex Revolt', in Lori Anne Ferrell and Peter McCullough (eds), *The English Sermon Revised: Religion, Literature and History, 1600–1750* (Manchester: Manchester University Press, 2000), pp. 86–114, pp. 91–2.
[66] HMC, *Salisbury*, vol. 9, p. 409.
[67] *CSPD, 1598–1601*, p. 365; Lambeth Palace Library MS 2004, f. 9^r. The examination provides the exact date of the sermon.
[68] Lambeth Palace Library MS 2004, ff. 9–10; Hunt, 'Tuning the Pulpits', p. 91.
[69] HMC, *Salisbury*, vol. 9, p. 409.

political propaganda passively on some occasions; at other times, they did not. The auditory's violent response to Dr Bourne's sermon of 1553 was unprecedented, but the fact that they made clear their dislike of the preacher's message was less unusual. The royal government took concerted action against the effects of Philip Stubbs's pamphlet *The Discoverie of a Gaping Gulf* on 27 September 1579, when a proclamation was issued denouncing it, a letter was sent to the London Corporation demanding the calling in of all copies of the work, and the Bishop of London and Dean of St Paul's met with the London clergy to warn them against 'meddling' in state matters.[70] A sermon, probably at Paul's Cross and possibly on this day, was also part of the campaign (its argument, if our report is correct, followed that of the proclamation very closely), and its preacher was 'instructed' on what to say by Bishop Aylmer of London and Sir Christopher Hatton.[71] According to Aylmer's report of the sermon (which he attended), those instructions were 'with such earnestness advisedly uttered, that it hath much stayed the heady . . . and somewhat quenched the sparks of murmuring, misliking, and miscontruing of matters of State, wherewith the seditious libeller had kindled many of the busier sort'. Aylmer's letter suggests that he had taken pains to 'gather the people's and the preachers' humours' on this subject, but he could not report an unqualified success:

I have understood since the sermon, that as the people well liked of the commendation attributed to her Majesty with the great hope of her continuance, so, to say plainly, they utterly bent their brows at the sharp and bitter speeches which he gave against the author of the book; of whom they conceive and report that he is one that feareth God, dearly loveth her majesty, entered into this course being carried with suspicion and jealousy of her person and safety.[72]

That the sympathy of the hearers was a vital consideration in the approach Paul's Cross preachers took to sensitive or controversial subjects is best demonstrated with reference to preaching after the Earl of Essex's rebellion. Paul's Cross was the site at which Essex had hoped to gather a crowd of supporters for his march on the court. Later, it was also instrumental in the government's plans to reconcile the confused

---

[70] Paul L. Hughes and James F. Larkin (eds), *Tudor Royal Proclamations* (New Haven: Yale University Press, 1969), vol. 2, pp. 445–9; W. H. Overall and H. C. Overall (eds), *Analytical Index to the Series of Records known as the Remembrancia* (1878), p. 29; John Strype, *The Life and Acts of John Aylmer*, (Oxford, 1821), pp. 40–2. For a fuller discussion of Stubbs' pamphlet and public controversies, see Natalie Mears, 'Council, Public Debate, and Queenship: John Stubbs's *The Discoverie of a Gaping Gulf*, 1579', *Historical Journal*, 44 (2001), 629–50.

[71] Aylmer's letter describing the sermon is reproduced in *Memoirs of the Life and Times of Sir Christopher Hatton, K.G.*, ed. Sir Harris Nicolas (1847), pp. 132–4. I would like to thank Dr Arnold Hunt for this reference. Aylmer does not mention Paul's Cross by name, but he says that 'your [i.e. Hatton's] travail and mine with the preacher hath taken good effect; and the instructions which you ministered unto him were . . . profitably remembered'. The auditory is described as a public one, and the only pulpit where the preacher was likely to be briefed by such important figures is Paul's Cross. Aylmer's letter to Hatton is dated 28 September, which was a Monday; the sermon might have been preached before the proclamation, but this is unlikely if we remember that the other element of this campaign can be dated to 27 September. Aylmer says that he was at the sermon, and we know that he was in London on 27 September to meet the London clergy (which happened at 1 o'clock according to Strype, by which time a Paul's Cross sermon would have finished).

[72] Ibid. p. 133.

citizenry to the treason charges brought against the Earl and the likelihood of his execution, especially when it was unclear to the authorities how far sympathy for the Earl extended.[73] The campaign against the Earl showed no more than a degree of coordination, however, and the authorities initially miscalculated Londoners' sympathy; this forced them to change tactics abruptly.[74]

The initial instructions given to London preachers for the Sunday after the rebellion presented it as something long in the planning, that Essex had made a treaty with the Earl of Tyrone when in Ireland as part of his plot, that he was hypocritical in religion, gaining the sympathies of puritans by assiduously attending sermons while promising Roman Catholics (his closest associates being of that religion) toleration. These instructions probably came from Robert Cecil, as the same emphasis on religion and hypocrisy are in the speech he had delivered in the Star Chamber the day before.[75] Cecil was certainly in touch with Bishop Bancroft of London about instructing preachers for that day: the man appointed to Paul's Cross was not to his liking and he asked Bancroft to find another 'more apt for that service'. Bancroft duly appointed John Hayward, Rector of St Mary Woolchurch, 'a man greatly followed in the city' and one who had prayed for the Earl in his illness the previous year.[76] Having delivered these instructions to him and the other ministers on the morning of 14 February, however, Bancroft was informed that the lord mayor had 'determined that none but women shall go to church'; thinking the material he had delivered to the preachers 'unfit to be imparted to women', he asked Cecil if it might be best for the preachers to be 'silent in the matters that I delivered to them this morning'. The sermons went ahead despite this hitch, because on 15 February, Bancroft reported to Cecil that 'the preacher at St Paul's Cross this day hath discharged his duty exceedingly well, and delivered to the people the whole matter of the arch traitor, according to the instructions you were acquainted with'.[77] The campaign was continued for the next four weeks, but the instructions changed, because it became clear that it was not as successful as Bancroft had initially thought.[78] The news-writer Vincent Hussey reported that the preachers at Paul's Cross and elsewhere had been ordered to deliver the 'same matters' about the Earl's treason with the Irish and religious hypocrisy as had been reported by Cecil and others in the Star Chamber but that 'from malice or desire to

---

[73] This is clear from the proclamations of 9 February and 15 February 1601: Hughes and Larkin (eds), *Tudor Royal Proclamations*, vol. 3, pp. 230–3. On the chain of events on the day of the rebellion, see Paul E. J. Hammer, 'Shakespeare's *Richard II*, the Play of 7 February 1601, and the Essex Rising', *Shakespeare Quarterly*, 59 (2008), 1–35, pp. 14–15. On Essex's misunderstanding of his support in the city, see Mervyn James, 'At a Crossroads of the Political Culture: The Essex Revolt, 1601', in *Society, Politics and Culture: Studies in Early Modern England* (Cambridge: Cambridge University Press, 1986), pp. 416–65, pp. 448–53.

[74] On the different instructions delivered to preachers, and their impact, see Hunt, 'Tuning the Pulpits', pp. 97–103.

[75] *CSPD, 1598–1601*, pp. 553–4, 565–8.

[76] HMC, *Salisbury*, vol. 12, p. 201; Hunt, 'Tuning the Pulpits', p. 100. John Hayward is listed as rector of St Mary's Woolchurch since 1593 by Richard Newcourt, *Repertorium Ecclesiasticum Parochiale Londinense* (1708), vol. 1, p. 460.

[77] HMC, *Salisbury*, vol. 11, pp. 52, 55.

[78] Ibid. vol. 11, p. 76; vol. 12, p. 201.

please' they 'amplified it beyond all probability'.[79] A year later, Bancroft reported to Cecil that John Hayward, the preacher from the Sunday after the rebellion, had suffered professionally because of that sermon and had been treated as 'a dissembling time-server' since then.[80]

New instructions were delivered by Cecil to William Barlow before his sermon on the Earl's execution, and it marks an obvious change in approach. The instructions are less directive about what was to be said, leaving things 'to be carried and applied as you like' but they signify to Barlow the Council's wish that he emphasize that a bloodless coup was unlikely (as the earls themselves confessed), and that murder so close to the Queen would have been a 'horror' to her. He was instructed to tell his hearers of the Earl's early impenitence during his trial, and his contempt and distrust for the citizens, made clear in his stated intention of using the Tower as a 'bridle' for the city.[81] Barlow followed these instructions carefully: he makes no mention of plots with the Earl of Tyrone or the King of Spain in his sermon; nor is there any suggestion of religious hypocrisy on the Earl's part.[82] His avoidance of polemical exaggeration (so different to the preaching immediately after the rebellion) suggests a concern to convince the London public of the fairness of the proceedings against the Earl, and to reconcile them to the Earl's fate. Even the biblical text used in the sermon avoids comparisons with disreputable biblical characters, being rather an abstract statement that allows Barlow to concentrate on the religious implications of political disobedience.

Barlow took Matthew 21:22 ('Give unto Caesar the things of Caesar') as his text, and extrapolates from the arrangement of the words in the text (Caesar preceding God) that 'hee which denieth his dutie to the visible God, his prince and Soveraign, cannot performe his dutie to the God invisible' (sig. B3ʳ). He quickly dispatches the explication of the biblical text by describing the 'things' that are Caesar's, and the list includes the subject's obedience and prayers as well as taxes. To deal fully with all the points that this text raises would, Barlow says, take days rather than hours, and so he will 'shut them with an use fitting our present purpose'. This leads him into the 'application' of his text: if these lessons had been heeded by 'some of late, neither had her maiestie been so disquieted, nor the realme thus scandalized' (sig. B7ʳ). This makes the Earl of Essex an example of the disastrous consequences of neglecting scriptural precepts on obedience, precepts agreed by all except treasonous Catholics.

Before embarking on his application of the text to the Earl, however, Barlow attempts to capture the good will of the hearers by testifying to his good faith as a preacher. This is necessary, he says, because of the negative reactions of hearers to the sermons preached the Sunday after the rebellion: the preachers were

---

[79] *CSPD, 1598–1601*, pp. 565–8, 582.
[80] HMC, *Salisbury*, vol. 11, pp. 55; vol. 12, pp. 201.
[81] *CSPD, 1598–1601*, p. 598.
[82] William Barlow, *A Sermon preached at Paules Crosse, on Martii I, 1600* (1601), STC² 1454. These accusations were also dropped from the formal charges brought against the Earl at his arraignment, as John Chamberlain rather cynically remembers: Chamberlain, *Letters of John Chamberlain*, vol. 1, p. 120.

'commanded by authority' to 'descrie the nature and uglinesse of the rebellion', but they are now treated as '*time servers & men pleasers*' (sig. B7ᵛ). Barlow cites Scripture and the Fathers to condemn those who misuse the pulpit to serve men before God; he insists that he cannot be accused of 'time-serving' in his condemnation of the Earl because four years earlier he preached a thanksgiving sermon from Paul's Cross on the success of the Cadiz raid (sigs B7–8ᵛ).[83] But Barlow is bound by the same duty of obedience that he has found within his biblical text, and so, having been appointed to attend on the Earl at his execution, 'I thought my selfe bound in conscience, both to God, her Majestie, and the state, within as shorte time as might bee, to declare unto you, what myselfe in his case know, and what is fit for you to heare' (sig. Cʳ). He promises to relate nothing except what 'these eares of mine have heard from his owne mouth, in that two houres conference with him before his death, and these eyes of mine seene under his owne hand, and subscribed with his name', having requested to see the written confession 'that I might speake nothing whereof I have not by those two meanes certayne knowledge' (sig. Cʳ). Barlow follows this *captatio benevolentia* with an elaborate justification of speaking ill of the Earl after his death. Men's 'faulles and faultes should not be reulcerated nor revived after death' (sig. Cᵛ), but the nature of the Earl's fault made it 'infectious' (sig. C2ʳ), and so 'the remainder and contagion of his offence' must be called to mind, though not 'triumphing and insulting at it'.

The details of the plot are reported from the Earl's confession, with its ramifications driven home by Barlow as the Privy Council instructed: surprising the Queen in her chamber would necessarily have led to bloodshed, to the Queen's great danger; the co-conspirators were Catholic or suspected Catholics. Despite the Earl's protestations that no danger to the Queen's life was planned, how could such a thing be guaranteed, with Catholic co-conspirators (sigs. D3ᵛ–4ʳ)? Barlow also follows the Council's advice in alienating the city's support for the Earl by telling of the plans of the Earl to subjugate the city because, Barlow says, 'he accompted your love at the best to be but vanitie' (sig. D6ᵛ). All things considered (and the thirteen salient points made in the sermon are given again in a summary list in the printed version, sigs D8ᵛ–Eʳ), Barlow asks his hearers to 'judge you with what safetie to the Queenes person; with what peace to the land; with what hope of the Gospels continuance; could this man have lived, if he had been remitted' (sig. Eʳ). Having shown the justification of the Earl's execution, Barlow has applied his text to the 'present purpose', as he said he would; but he ends with a general exhortation that applies his text to the hearers also. The religious and political duty of obedience belonging to every subject is reinforced in the sermon's concluding paragraph:

What now remains? But to conclude with my text, *Give unto Caesar the things of Caesar*, our most gracious Soveraigne, I meane: honour her, obey her, fear her, but above all pray for her,

---

[83] Elizabeth had attempted to restrict celebrations of the Cadiz raid in London, so Barlow's argument that his sermon proves his former support of the Earl probably carried some weight: Paul E. J. Hammer, *The Polarisation of English Politics: The Political Career of Robert Devereux, 2nd Earl of Essex, 1585–1597* (Cambridge: Cambridge University Press, 1999), pp. 253–4.

that shee being the light of this land may shine among us as long as the two great lights of heaven, the Sonne and the Moone endureth. (sigs. E^r–v)

Barlow's sermon is constructed as a lesson in obedience, not as a government statement on the Earl's crimes (which it also was). The earlier, and unsuccessful, attempt to use the pulpit in a blatant attempt to discredit Essex had backfired: the hearers did not accept the veracity of the charges made against him, and consequently considered the preachers who delivered them mere 'time-servers and men pleasers'. The change of tactic evident in Barlow's very different approach to the Earl's execution was more successful: the account of the Earl's prayer at his death appended to the printed sermon circulated in manuscript independently of the sermon, suggesting a wide readership that found the most salient parts of the sermon worth recording.[84]

THE SPANISH MATCH AND LAUDIAN CENSORSHIP

This chapter has attempted to show that Paul's Cross was not the propaganda arm of the Elizabethan and Jacobean royal governments, unambiguously and consistently delivering the 'official line' to the London populace. On occasions when royal, ecclesiastical, and civic authorities worked together, it was a very effective public relations machine: spring and early summer 1559, and spring 1601 (the Earl of Essex rebellion and its aftermath) are two good examples of this. When disagreements existed between the authorities, or between the governors and governed, those disagreements were as likely to be aired at Paul's Cross as anywhere else: it was so effective a medium for addressing the city and the nation that it was very rarely neglected by those 'making public pitches' (in Lake and Pincus's term) on issues disputed within the political nation, from the fate of Mary, Queen of Scots, to the scriptural warrant for presbyterianism. Given the pulpit's effectiveness, we can safely assume that those with authority over Paul's Cross did not consider its unpredictability 'a good thing', but any wish they might have had to make Paul's Cross doctrinally or politically univocal fell foul of the fact that they could never be sure of what the preacher would say until it was too late. They could have changed this (and indeed it was changed later), but the system for controlling the Paul's Cross sermons remained unaltered until the 1620s, which suggests that the disadvantages of greater regulation were thought to outweigh the risks of 'indiscreet' preaching. The Paul's Cross sermons were primarily about the uncontroversial duties of a Christian subject (love of God and attendance at church services, charity to others, obedience to the authorities): our interest in the exceptions may lead us to lose sight of that fact. All of those preachers who stood within the broad category of the 'conformable' (moderate puritans, conformist Calvinists, and avant-garde conformists) were eligible to preach there, and most delivered unexceptionable orations

---

[84] Bodleian Library MS Rawl. D. 719, item 2; Lambeth Palace Library 931, vol. 3, item 62.

that vindicated the 'light touch' regulation practiced by the bishops of London.[85] Paul's Cross was a medium available to the royal, civic, and ecclesiastical authorities when they needed to address the city; otherwise, they left it to the bishop and his chaplains to administer, and only stepped in when the need arose. Although the earlier part of this chapter has shown that they sometimes responded too late, or too ineptly, the subsequent history of the Cross suggests there was some wisdom in this benign neglect.

The ecclesiastical and royal authorities began to take a different approach to Paul's Cross in the 1620s, initially because of the controversy over the Spanish Match and the strengthening of pulpit restrictions to which it gave rise. Criticism of the Spanish Match from London's most public pulpits began almost as soon as the plans to marry Prince Charles to the Spanish Infanta were known: Dr Samuel Page preached one of the Easter Spital sermons in 1617 and was 'taken up for speaking against the Spanish match'.[86] Public disquiet about the Spanish Match became inextricably linked with the other great cause of the time: the Palatinate. In 1619, James's son-in-law Frederick V, Elector Palatinate, accepted the crown of Bohemia in order to prevent Catholic Hapsburg's encroachment on the Protestant Bohemia. He did so without his father-in-law's support, but James was out of step with public feeling in England on this subject, as preaching at Paul's Cross testifies. Lewis Bayly prayed for the King of Bohemia at Paul's Cross in a sermon immediately after Christmas 1619 and was 'rebuked for his forwardnes'.[87] Frederick lost first the Kingdom of Bohemia at the Battle of White Mountain (8 November 1620), and by the end of 1622 the Palatinate itself; from 1621, James's daughter Elizabeth and her children were living as exiles in Holland. For many people in England, including Prince Charles, the return of these lands to their Protestant rulers was a point of honour and a religious duty. But James was unwilling to contribute militarily towards the fight against the Hapsburgs, preferring instead to use the marriage negotiations for Charles as a bargaining tool to make the Spanish Hapsburgs convince their Austrian cousins to return the Palatinate.[88] The link between these two policies may not have been clear to James's subjects, who saw only that the King was doing nothing to help his daughter Elizabeth and her family being ousted from their home in the Palatinate while negotiating for a Catholic bride for his heir.

The vocal opposition to the Spanish Match, from the pulpit and press, created further difficulties for the King. Not only did they intrude on the *arcana imperii*, but they made negotiations with the Spanish more difficult, as they made clear that

---

[85] On the terms scholars use to describe religious affiliations of this period, see 'Introduction', in Peter Lake and Michael Questier (eds), *Conformity and Orthodoxy in the English Church, c. 1560–1660* (Woodbridge: Boydell Press, 2000), pp. ix–xx.

[86] *Letters of John Chamberlain*, vol. 2, p. 74. This is probably Samuel Page, vicar of St. Nicholas, Deptford.

[87] *Letters and Documents Illustrating the Relations between England and Germany at the Commencement of the Thirty Years' War*, ed. S. R. Gardiner (1868), pp. 133–4.

[88] Thomas Cogswell, *The Blessed Revolution: English Politics and the Coming of War, 1621–1624* (Cambridge: Cambridge University Press, 1989), pp. 32–4. On popular feeling for the recovery of the Palatinate, see pp. 20–31; on Charles's concern for the recovery of the Palatinate, see pp. 58–61.

the King's promises about religious toleration for the princess and her entourage would be unpopular at best. Efforts to control the pulpits increased in severity as the crisis deepened. In December 1620, James sent orders to the bishops to forbid preachers dealing with 'matters of state' in their sermons, but these were widely ignored or flouted: the Sunday after this order was given, 'a young fellow' preached at Paul's Cross and spoke 'very freely in generall' on the subject. On 25 February of the following year, John Everard ('Dr Never-out') denounced the cruelty of the Spanish 'in all places where they come' and was imprisoned in the Gatehouse.[89] And these attempts to silence the pulpits on this subject only added fuel to the rumours of a Spanish and popish plot against England.[90] James did what he could to disseminate a more positive message: Tom Cogswell notes that in the 'final rancorous address to the 1621 parliament' James advised MPs to be thankful for the peace they enjoyed when their neighbours suffered the miseries of war. 'The keynote having been struck', Cogswell says, and it was taken up by several of preachers at Paul's Cross who 'elaborated on the blessings of peace and horrors of war'.[91] But whatever good effect these exhortations about the blessings of peace may have had, they were offset by continued preaching on anti-Spanish themes from the same pulpit throughout 1622. On 25 August 1622, John Claydon used a story about Spanish sheep bringing 'murrain' into England in a scarcely veiled criticism of the marriage plans, and was imprisoned. Less than two weeks later, Richard Sheldon (a convert from Catholicism) preached what was in effect a recantation sermon with spectacularly bad timing: the vehement criticisms of Catholicism usual in such a sermon proved embarrassing for the King. Claydon was imprisoned, albeit briefly; Sheldon was 'only checked' for what he said.[92] The episode with Sheldon demonstrated the government's difficulty: preachers had been forbidden to preach on the Match or on 'matters of state'. But anti-Catholicism had become a 'matter of state'; to ban that subject from public sermons required more far-reaching measures than those put in place before.

On 4 August 1622, James promulgated a series of *Directions concerning Preaching and Preachers* through Archbishop Abbot.[93] These 'Directions' marked a sea change in the royal government's approach to the pulpits. Unlike other 'directions' given to preachers at politically sensitive times, these did not detail what the preachers were to say (as had happened after the Essex rebellion), but restricted

---

[89] *Letters of John Chamberlain*, vol. 2, pp. 331, 350.

[90] Thomas Scott, the author of *Vox Populi, or Newes from Spayne* ([London?] 1620), presents the silencing of preachers by the Star Chamber as part of the plot by Gondomar to quell resistance to Spanish plans to overthrow England: reprinted in *Somers Collection of Tracts*, 2nd edn., rev. by Walter Scott (1809), vol. 2, pp. 508–24, p. 520.

[91] Cogswell, *The Blessed Revolution*, pp. 27–8. The sermons that took up James's 'keynote' are Samuel Buggs, *Davids Strait* (1622), *STC²* 4022; Daniel Donne, *A Sub-poena from the Star-Chamber of Heaven* (1622), *STC²* 7021; Robert Harris, *Gods Goodness and Mercy* (1622), *STC²* 12831; and Samuel Purchas, *The King's Towre* (1622), *STC²* 20502.

[92] *Register of Sermons*, p. 121, British Library MS Harl. 389, f. 228ᵛ.

[93] *The Kings Majesties Letter to the Lords Grace of Canterbury, touching Preaching and Preachers*, *STC²* 14379.5. The *Directions* are reprinted in *Documentary Annals of the Reformed Church of England*, ed. Edward Cardwell (Oxford, 1839), vol. 2, pp. 146–51.

all discussion of political, and of several religious and doctrinal, subjects to certain ranks of preachers and pulpits. There was nothing to say that these restrictions would be temporary, and not all seemed particularly relevant to the crisis of 1622. The first direction seems the most formidable and far-reaching, as it seems to prevent preaching on anything other than basically catechetical subjects. It forbids any preacher 'under the degree and calling of a Bishop, or Deane of a Cathedrall or Collegiate Church' to preach on any 'discourse or Common-place . . . which shall not be comprehended and warranted, in essence, substance and effect, or naturall inference, within some one of the Articles of Religion set forth 1562', and even those permitted to preach on other subjects were to do so only on 'Kings dayes, and set festivals'. The second direction had the potential to ban many sermons, as it forbade preaching on Sunday afternoons except on 'some part of the Catechisme'. The third direction forbids any preacher, under a bishop or dean, from preaching to the public on the 'deepe points' of 'Predestination, Election, Reprobation; of the universalitie, Efficacie, Resistibility or Irresistibility of Gods grace'. Those allowed to handle these themes were to do so only 'by way of use and application, rather than by way of positive doctrine, as beeing fitter for the Schooles and Universities, then for simple auditories'. The fourth article most clearly relates to the politics of 1622, and placed a complete ban on all the clergy 'of what title or denomination so ever' from discussing the 'Power, Prerogative, Jurisdiction, Authoritie, or Duty of Soveraigne Princes; or otherwise meddle with these matters of State', except according to the example laid out in the Homily of Obedience. The fifth article also relates primarily to the tense situation during the negotiations with Spain. No preacher 'without invitation from the Text' is to 'fall into biter invectives, and undecent rayling speeches against the persons of either Papist or Puritanes', but when occasion arises they may 'free both the Doctrine and discipline of the Church of *England*, from the aspersion of either Adversarie'. The *Directions* also specified that parish lecturers were to be licensed.

   The effect of these directions depended very much on the way they were interpreted by the clergy and on their implementation. Crucially, the interpretation of these *Directions* delivered at Paul's Cross was by John Donne in a sermon of 15 September 1622.[94] In that sermon, Donne presents his hearers with the justification for the *Directions* that had been formulated by Archbishop Abbot (the powerful friend of the 'godly') and that was circulated in the printed letter ostensibly revealing the King's reasons for the *Directions*.[95] Archbishop Abbot's

---

[94] *The Sermons of John Donne*, ed. E. M. Simpson and G. R. Potter, 10 vols (Berkeley, CA: University of California Press, 1953–62), vol. 4, pp. 178–209. The fullest treatment of this sermon and its political context is Jeanne Shami, *John Donne and Conformity in Crisis in the late Jacobean Pulpit* (Cambridge: D. S. Brewer, 2003).

[95] On Archbishop Abbot see Kenneth Fincham, 'Prelacy and Politics: Archbishop Abbot's Defence of Protestant Orthodoxy', *Historical Research*, 61 (1988). The 'reasons' for the *Directions* were published separately (from the copy of the Archbishop's letter sent to the Bishop of Oxford, *STC* 33), and along with the *Directions* (from the copy sent to the Bishop of Norwich, *STC* 15379.5). Abbot did not write the *Directions* themselves and their author is unknown, although Peter Heylyn says that Laud appeared 'to have a hand' in drawing them up: *Cyprianus Anglicus* (1668), Wing H1699, p. 97.

interpretation of the *Directions* minimizes the restrictions they place on preaching, in terms both of the subjects allowed in sermons and on the allowance for Sunday afternoon sermons on the catechism.[96] It also put a decidedly pastoral emphasis on the King's actions. Abbot's letter says that the King, dismayed that there should be so many defecting to '*Poperie and Anabaptistrie*', reasoned that the cause was the '*lightnes, affectednes, and unprofitablenesse*' of recent preaching, which, '*soaring up in points of divinitie*', is '*too high for the capacities of the people*'. In order to prevent these defections from the Church of England, the practice of preaching is to be reformed in accordance with the methods used in the early stages of the Reformation, as these were successful in '*driving out the one, and kept out* the *other from poisoning and infecting the people of this Kingdome*'. The doctrines that prevented England slipping into either error were those contained in the Thirty-nine Articles, the catechisms, and the Homilies, and so these documents are presented by Abbot as defining the doctrines appropriate for public teaching. They are not examples to be slavishly copied, but they demonstrate '*the whole scope of this doctrine*', which is '*the proper subject of all sound and edifying Preaching*'. Although Abbot presents his letter as the King's own thoughts on the matter, he does not claim to be using the King's words. But this is exactly what John Donne does in his sermon at Paul's Cross: he attributes Abbot's words to the King as direct quotations:

But when men doe neither, neither Teach, nor Preach, but (as his *Majestie* observes the manner to bee) *To soare in poynts too deepe, To muster up their owne Reading, to display their owne wit, or Ignorance in medling with Civill matters*, or (as his *Majestie* addes) *in rude and undecent reviling of persons;* . . . His *Majesty* therefore cals us to look, *Quid primum*, what was first in the whole Church? And againe, *Quid primum* when we received the Reformation in this *Kingdom*, by what meanes, (as his *Majestie* expresseth it) *Papistry was driven out, and Puritanisme kept out.*[97]

Donne's use of Abbot's interpretation of the *Directions* increases the standing of that interpretation as the official one. Through Abbot's letter and Donne's sermon, therefore, the public, including other members of the clergy, were told that the *Directions* were intended to increase the pastoral effectiveness of preaching. In so doing, Abbot and Donne provide an explanation other than political expediency for the *Directions*. They also attempt to quell anxiety about restrictions being placed on the subjects that could be addressed by preachers: Donne follows Abbot in arguing that the Homilies, Articles, and catechisms provide the subject matter around which the preacher could base his sermon, and that these models include 'the whole scope' of divinity.

If the interpretation of the *Directions* promulgated from Paul's Cross was designed to minimize their impact, was their implementation also minimal, especially after the crisis years of 1622–4? The regulations regarding lecturers and

---

[96] Whether this meant that catechetical sermons were allowed, or whether they were to be replaced with examining children by question and answer was unclear at this time: Ian Green, *The Christian's ABC: Catechisms and Catechizing in England c. 1530–1740* (Oxford: Clarendon Press, 1996), pp. 106–7.

[97] *The Sermons of John Donne*, ed. E. M. Simpson and G. R. Potter, 10 vols (Berkeley, CA: University of California Press, 1953–62) vol. 4, p. 202.

catechism do not appear to have been implemented. Restrictions on preaching against Roman Catholicism disappeared after the war began in 1624.[98] But the restriction on preaching on predestination was to have a longer history. The *Directions* of 1622 specified that the 'deep points' of predestination were not to be discussed in public pulpits and by junior clerics. Sermons dealing with these topics were not to be treated as theological lectures: those handling these themes were to do so only 'by way of use and application, rather than by way of positive doctrine'. The emphasis here on the 'deepe points' of predestination is crucial, as it was possible that the more pastoral aspects of this doctrine (the comfort of assurance of faith, for example) might be excluded from the ban. If interpreted in this way, this direction would have little real impact on Paul's Cross sermons, as preachers generally restricted their comments to Calvinist fundamentals (that justification is a free gift of God, based on faith and not works, and effected by the imputed merits of Christ; that those justified had been elected by God; that they are sanctified throughout life and glorified in the life to come). The emphasis is almost invariably pastoral rather than speculative, mostly leading to exhortations to repentance or to perseverance in godliness.[99] But the controversy between Calvinists and Arminians had also found an airing at Paul's Cross,[100] most famously (and thoroughly) by Humphrey Sydenham, whose *Jacob and Esau* was preached on 4 March 1622 and presented a schematic account of supralapsarian predestination in order to refute Arminianism.[101]

That was to be the last systematic presentation of predestination at Paul's Cross, but preachers did continue to mention elements of the doctrine within pastoral contexts in the years after the 1622 *Directions*. In many cases, the preachers referred only to such uncontroversial elements of the doctrine that nothing they said would provoke contradiction from Reformed theologians. For example, Thomas Myriell includes among 'Christian's comforts' given by God 'our predestination to life',

---

[98] The restriction on political and anti-papist preaching was enforced in the period between the promulgation of the *Directions* and the war, but not thereafter, as John Donne makes clear in a sermon preached at St Paul's of 21 May 1626, where he states that sermons 'supplanting, and subverting' Catholic error were now in use again having been silenced during James's laudable attempts to bring peace to Europe: *Sermons of John Donne*, vol. 7, pp. 166–7. The *Directions* did not prevent preachers from 'railing' against Catholics in Paul's Cross sermons: a Mr Wilson was questioned for a sermon of 30 March 1623: *Register of Sermons*, p. 12. Paul Seaver reveals that the Direction relating to the licensing of lecturers was not enforced in the 1620s: *The Puritan Lectureships*, pp. 230–1. Ian Green notes that the order for catechizing in the *Directions* was ambiguous and its implication softened by Archbishop Abbot, so that the impact of the *Directions* was not as directly restrictive as at first appears (*The Christian's ABC*, pp. 106–7).

[99] There were, of course, exceptions. Predominantly doctrinal sermons on predestination were preached at Paul's Cross, the most notable being George Downame's *A Treatise on John 8.36 concerning Christian Liberty* (1609), *STC²* 7124; Miles Mosse, *Justifying and Saving Faith* (Cambridge, 1614), *STC²* 18209; Samuel Gardiner, *The Foundation of the Faythful* (1611), *STC²* 11577; and Nathanael Delaune [Delawne], *The Christians Tryumph* (1617), *STC²* 6550.5.

[100] Stephen Denison, *The New Creature* (1619), *STC²* 6607, p.15; Thomas Bedford, *The Sinne unto Death* (1621), *STC²* 1788, p. 23; Griffith Williams, *The Delight of the Saints*, in *The Best Religion* (1636), *STC²* 25718, p. 423. The sermon was preached in December 1621: *Register of Sermons*, p. 119.

[101] Humphrey Sydenham, *Jacob and Esau: Election. Reprobation. Opened and Discussed by way of Sermon at Pauls Crosse* (1626), *STC²* 23567.

something even Catholic theologians would have agreed with; John Gee, a convert from Catholicism, numbers among the true doctrines rejected by the present Church of Rome 'that we are *justified freely by grace*'.[102] Others mention (but it is no more than that) some of the points that Calvinists and Arminians disputed; there are two examples from 1624 from sermons by Robert Vase and Robert Bedingfield. Vase told his hearers that 'there is evermore an habite of grace, and seed of God' in the soul of the 'faithful member of Christ' and this 'is at all times stirring' and restrains the elect from the most grievous sins; in the same vein, Bedingfield told his hearers that 'sinne is not so in the Elect, as it is in the reprobate', because the elect sin 'by compulsion' rather than with full consent. Both preachers may be referring to the disputed point on whether the elect can fall from grace *totaliter* after justification: Calvinists (and it seems we can number Vase and Bedingfield among them) said no, Arminians said yes.[103] On Palm Sunday 1626, John Gumbleden put a decidedly Calvinist gloss on another much disputed point: limited atonement. Christ was given to save all, by which is meant all those who believed. Within the week, Thomas Aylesbury contradicted him when he preached the Good Friday Passion sermon and declared, 'were every Starre a world, here is plenteous redemption for them all; of great extent, which reacheth unto all'.[104] It seems that the 1622 *Directions* did not prevent disputed doctrines being mentioned at Paul's Cross, but systematic accounts of predestination in 'doctrinal' sermons did stop.

Our sample of printed sermons from Paul's Cross diminishes markedly in the late 1620s, making any comparison to the earlier period more tenuous. But if the sermons we have are representative, then it does not appear that Charles I's declaration of 1626 altered the situation very much. The Declaration did not specify preaching on predestination, as the 1622 *Directions* did; it simply warned clergymen not to 'raise any doubts, or publish, or maintain any new inventions, or opinions concerning religion, then such as are clearly grounded, and warranted by the Doctrine and Discipline of the Church of England, heretofore published'. But coming in the middle of the controversy over Richard Montague's writings, its implications were clear. Both sides of the argument held different views about what counted as the 'new invention' in the theology of grace.[105] Within a year of this Declaration, two preachers at Paul's Cross made passing reference to what they no

---

[102] Thomas Myriell, *The Christians Comfort* (1623), *STC²* 18321, p. 10; John Gee, *Hold Fast* (1624), *STC²* 11705. p. 27.

[103] Robert Vase, *Jonah's Contestation about his Gourd* (1625), *STC²* 24594, pp. 46–7; Robert Bedingfield, *A Sermon preached at Pauls Crosse* (Oxford, 1625), *STC²* 1792, p.18.

[104] John Gumbleden, *Gods Great Mercy to Mankinde* (Oxford, 1628), *STC²* 12514, p. 14; Thomas Aylesbury [Ailesbury], *The Passion Sermon at Pauls-Crosse* (1626), *STC²* 999, p. 2. There is an extensive literature on the disputes between Calvinists and Arminians within the English Church, but on the points raise here, most pertinent is Peter Lake, 'Calvinism and the English Church, 1570–1635', *Past and Present*, 114 (1987), 32–76, and Nicholas Tyacke, *Anti-Calvinists: The Rise of English Arminianism, c.1590–1640* (Oxford: Clarendon Press, 1987), pp. 29–33.

[105] *Stuart Royal Proclamations*, vol. 2, ed. James F Larkin (Oxford: Clarendon Press, 1983), pp. 90–3, p. 92. On publications against Montague and action against him in the 1626 parliament, see Tyacke, *Anti-Calvinists*, pp. 147–57.

doubt considered the Church of England's position. Matthew Brookes declared that 'a regenerate mans estate is perpetuall, he shall neither finally, nor totally fall from this Rock [i.e. faith in Christ]'. Robert Sanderson was more circumspect. In a lengthy discussion of the difference between the grace that restrains us (elect and reprobate) from sins and the 'renewing' grace of sanctification given only to the elect, he says: 'renewing Grace holdeth out unto the end, more or less, and never leaveth us *wholy* destitute'.[106]

Sometime between June 1628 and January 1629, Charles made another, more explicit declaration, which was affixed to a new edition of the Thirty-nine Articles. This demanded that every preacher take the articles in 'the literal and grammatical sense' and not 'put his own sense or comment to be the meaning of the article', and this extended to both public preachers and those in the universities. The declaration was widely seen to be aimed at Calvinists, and was used in that way.[107] At Paul's Cross, there was a discernible shift in the tone and content of the sermons. Predestination was rarely mentioned, in a controversial or in a pastoral context, and this was coupled with a considerable increase in preaching against heresy and schism, and a tendency to use the term 'solifidian' negatively.[108] Controversial points were dealt with emphatically on one occasion,[109] and that was by John Donne in his last sermon at Paul's Cross on 22 November 1629. Donne roundly condemned the 'over-pure dispisers of others', and goes on to describe these as:

men that will abridge, and contract the large mercies of God in Christ, and elude, and frustrate, in a great part, the generall promises of God. Men that are loth, that God should speak so loud, as to say, *He would have all men saved,* And loth that Christ should spread his armes, or shed his bloud in such a compasse, as might fall upon *all.* Men that think no sinne can hurt them, because they are *elect,* and that every sin makes every other man a *Reprobate.*[110]

The last sentence could be interpreted as asserting that the justified man can fall from grace *totaliter*, but it is not sufficiently explicit as it stands to make this certain. The rest of the passage denies limited atonement, and so suggests some kind of

---

[106] Matthew Brookes, *The House of God* (1627), *STC²* 3836, p. 34. Brookes's phrase echoes very closely the title of William Prynne's anti-Montague tract, *The Perpetuitie of a Regenerate Man's Estate*, on which see Tyacke, *Anti-Calvinists*, pp. 156–7. Robert Sanderson, *A Sermon preached at St. Paul's Crosse, Aprill. 15*, in *Two Sermons preached at Paules-Crosse* (1628), *STC²* 21708.5, p. 126. Stephen Denison denounced Arminians as 'mystical wolves' diverting people from true religion in an appendix to his 1626 sermon *The White Wolfe* (1627), *STC²* 6608.3, but the appendix was not part of the sermon as it was preached (p. 37).

[107] Edward Cardwell (ed.), *Documentary Annals of the Reformed Church of England*, 2 vols (Oxford, 1839), vol. 2, pp. 169–73.

[108] Thomas Drant, preaching in 1636, tells his hearers that 'we preach not Solifidianisme': *The Divine Lanthorne* (1637), *STC²* 7164, p. 45, and Oliver Whitbie, preaching the following year, contrasts an active faith with a 'lasie Solifidian *credite*': *Londons Returne* (1637), *STC²* 25371, p. 11.

[109] There was one other reasonably lengthy treatment of predestination, on the subject of Christ's sacrifice being 'sufficient' to save all but 'efficient' only for the elect, in a Spital sermon preached in Paul's in 1637 by John Lynch, but Lynch's distinction is one all parties would have agreed with: *Pascha Christianum*, in John Squire and John Lynch, *Three sermons: Two of them appointed for the Spittle* (1637), *STC²* 23120, pp. 67–8.

[110] *The Sermons of John Donne*, ed. Potter and Simpson, vol. 9, p. 119.

universalist doctrine. But universal atonement was one of the most difficult questions for English Calvinist theologians, as some members of the English delegation at Dort disagreed with the Synod's majority on this subject, and sought a compromise position in Samuel Ward's formulation of 'hypothetical universalism'.[111] It cannot therefore be argued that the statement we find in this sermon is sufficient to prove that Donne was 'Arminian', but it does suggest that the prohibition on preaching on predestination was unequally applied.

Using the 'Register of Sermons' appended to MacLure's 1958 monograph on *The Paul's Cross Sermons*, Nicholas Tyacke surveyed the 'doctrinal tenor' of the Paul's Cross sermons and concluded that 'Calvinist sermons ceased to be printed after July 1628, the same year and very month in which William Laud was translated to the bishopric of London'.[112] The larger sample of sermons now available to us does not contradict this finding: points of doctrine disputed between Calvinists and Arminians were almost never addressed at Paul's Cross after 1628 and when they were, it was not to endorse the Canons of the Synod of Dort. This finding matches research done on Laudian press censorship by Anthony Milton and on Laud's treatment of the London clergy after his elevation to that see in 1628: greater latitude was given to anti-Calvinist and anti-puritan writers and clergymen, and the overall effect was to give an advantage to Laudian preachers and ministers.[113] Anthony Milton also points out that, while attempts to use censorship against religious opponents was nothing new, in the 1630s the Laudians had gained such dominance in the Church that their efforts to do so were markedly more successful:

> Government religious policy was now unidirectional ... Censorship and restrictions were clearly not new to the 1630s, but the hegemony of Laudian opinion clearly was.[114]

This 'unidirectional' religious policy extended to all the authorities with a part to play in Paul's Cross: ecclesiastical, civil, and royal. It had been the lack of such a 'unidirectional' policy between those authorities that had made Paul's Cross a volatile medium in the past.

This was not the only reason why William Laud managed to achieve such formidable control over Paul's Cross. An anecdote of Joseph Mede's was quoted earlier, in which a preacher was called before Bishop Montaigne of London in 1622 and told that the very text he proposed to preach on was 'not allowable for these times'. Another point of interest in this anecdote is that it begins by explaining that the Bishop initially sent, not for the preacher but 'for the copie of his Sermon'.[115]

---

[111] See Lake, 'Calvinism and the English Church', pp. 56–60. On hypothetical universalism, see Jonathan D. Moore, *English Hypothetical Universalism: John Preston and the Softening of Reformed Theology* (Grand Rapids, MI: Eerdmans, 2007).

[112] Tyacke, *Anti-Calvinists*, pp. 248–65, p. 249.

[113] Anthony Milton, 'Licensing, Censorship, and Religious Orthodoxy in Early Stuart England', *Historical Journal* 41 (1998), 625–51; David R. Como, 'Predestination and Political Conflict in Laud's London', *Historical Journal* 46 (2003), 263–94.

[114] Milton, 'Licensing, Censorship, and Religious Orthodoxy', p. 642.

[115] British Library MS Harl. 389 f. 233ʳ.

This is the first reference we have to such a demand being made of a preacher, and references to preachers supplying copies of their sermons after complaints, or of witnesses providing notes, suggests that it was not normal practice before 1622. Bishop Montaigne does not appear to have made this demand of preachers on all occasions after 1622: when 'Mr Wilson' preached 'words full of evill interpretation' against Catholics at Paul's Cross on 30 March 1623, Montaigne wrote to the Privy Council that he had 'called for his sermon' after the event.[116] But in November 1627, it was reported to Joseph Mede that the bishops were prohibiting speakers from discussing the Duke of Buckingham's disastrous expedition to the Île de Ré, and that 'an Oxford man, who that day preached at the cross, had his sermon perused and castrated before he came there'.[117] It was during Laud's time as bishop of London that preachers were routinely required to submit a copy of their sermons in advance. Three letters appointing Paul's Cross preachers are extant from after 1628 (one dated 1633, and two by Bishop Juxon, one dated November 1628 and one from 1638); all three specify that the preacher should bring a copy of the sermon to the bishop's chaplain in London house before the sermon.[118] Seeing a copy of the sermon in advance meant much more stringent controls on what was said in the pulpit: the authorities could 'castrate' the sermon before the preacher spoke, rather than demand an apology after the event. Thomas Cogswell has written that in the late 1620s, as in the years between 1622–3 'the pulpit . . . became something the government feared rather than exploited',[119] and this gave rise to 'tight episcopal controls on publication and preaching'. In the case of Paul's Cross, this fear, and the control to which it gave rise, continued until the Civil War. It is interesting to note that the requirement on preachers to submit a copy of their sermon in advance was to lapse in 1642, when the bishops no longer controlled appointments.[120]

Laud and Juxon's letters of appointment also say that both sermon and prayer should not take more than one and a half hours, which is less than the two hours previously allowed. This may seem like a small point, but it does suggest a desire to lessen the impact of the Paul's Cross sermons. The same policy is evident after the sermons were moved into the choir of the cathedral in 1634. Laud wrote to the heads of the Oxford colleges in 1639 informing them that 'Oxford men who come to preach at Paul's do not so frequently use the prayer which the canon of the Church requires before their sermons, either in matter or form, as the Cambridge

[116] PRO, State Papers, Domestic, 14/142/22.
[117] Thomas Birch (ed.), *The Court and Times of Charles I* (1848), vol. 1, p. 295.
[118] Laud, *Works*, (Oxford, 1857), vol. 7, p. 47; Bodleian Library MS Rawl. D. 399, f. 155^r; City of London, Guildhall Manuscript 36, 711. The letter of appointment nearest in date that is extant was sent by Richard Bancroft in 1601. It merely exhorts the preacher to 'avoid all domestic controversies, and discover to the auditory the absurdities and falsehood of Popery': HMC, *10th Report, Abergavenny, etc.*, part VI, p. 127.
[119] Thomas Cogswell, 'The Politics of Propaganda: Charles I and the People in the 1620s', *Journal of British Studies* 29 (1990), 187–215.
[120] Mr Frane of Pembroke Hall, Cambridge, preached 'in the forenoon at Paul's' (so this was a 'Paul's Cross' sermon), and was 'sent for, as a delinquent' by the House of Commons on 16 May 1642. He was required to bring a copy of his sermon with him: *House of Commons Journal*, vol. 2, p. 572.

men do'.[121] The Paul's Cross sermons had never been part of a liturgical service, and so the rules governing sermons within the context of the liturgy never really applied: Laud's letter implies a wish to 'normalise' this sermon series within the context of the liturgy, presumably so that it would not act as an example to those who resisted his drive against 'sermon-centred piety'.

Laud and his supporters had no love for the Paul's Cross sermons. In January 1625, Laud, then Bishop of St David's asked John Cosin to preach the rehearsal sermon, the high point of the year at Paul's Cross. Richard Montague dissuaded Cosin from doing so: 'You cannot hold against the faction: strong, fierce, potent, especially there', he wrote. If Laud 'and such' were preaching the Spital sermons, then 'repeate you' (that is, 'repeat' their sermons in the rehearsal sermon), but otherwise not. Montague himself had 'never come att the Crosse. I never will. It should do no good but my body harme, my reputation hazard, my cause hurt. For the City, you know, *furioso more calvinisat*'.[122] Writing five years later, Thomas Gataker took a very different view; he reported to Samuel Ward of Cambridge that 'for the points of Arminianisme publiqely preached, it is commonly bruited that few come up either at Court or Crosse, but that touch upon them'.[123] Montague thought he would not find a sympathetic auditory at Paul's Cross; Gataker thought (probably rightly) that his opponents were the only ones appointed to the Cross. In an increasingly divided church, one party had the power to appoint the preachers but no interest in the future of the series. The other felt that the doctrine delivered there was wrong. It is hardly surprising that the role played by the Paul's Cross sermons in Caroline politics diminished markedly in the 1630s. Laud exercised an unprecedented control over the Paul's Cross sermons, but he had little wish to see the series continue in the form it had taken since the Reformation; it was for these reasons that the series diminished.

---

[121] Laud, *Works*, (Oxford, 1857), vol. 5, p. 248.

[122] Richard Montague to John Cosin, 17th Jan 1624/5, in *The Correspondance of John Cosin*, ed. George Ornsby (Durham, 1869), vol. 1, p. 47.

[123] Bodleian Library MS Tanner 71, f. 68.

4

Controlling the Pulpit

One of the conclusions of the previous chapter is that the effective use of Paul's Cross as a site for the dissemination of 'propaganda' required far more than the mere censorship of the sermons delivered there. The Laudian authorities' attempt at thorough monitoring of sermons prior to delivery cost this pulpit at least part of its auditory, making it a far less effective medium for reaching the London public. Control of Paul's Cross necessitated a careful consideration of the likely response of auditors to the government-sponsored messages delivered from that pulpit, as happened in the wake of the Essex rebellion. The necessity of attending to the auditory's response is no less true of the other uses to which the pulpit cross was put throughout this period, many of which were designed to publicize punitive actions by the ecclesiastical or secular authorities against heterodox ideas (through book burnings and recantations) and social and sexual mores (through the performances of public penance). The churchyard of St Paul's Cathedral stood in an open space that was subject to frequent traffic, and so was well situated for such displays of government power. But historians are increasingly aware of the difficulties involved in such displays: their meanings could be contested by those groups that the displays were intended to discredit.[1] Early modern governments had to ensure that the 'official' interpretation of punitive events like book burnings, recantations, and penances gained acceptance, and this required them to make an assessment of the auditors' likely response.

The auditors were not passive recipients of sermons, and on occasion they demonstrated that the pulpit was not simply a one-way medium between governors and governed. The riot during Dr Gilbert Bourne's sermon of 13 August 1553, when Bourne was pulled from the pulpit and had a dagger thrown at him, was almost unprecedented in the violence with which the auditors made clear their disagreement with the preacher's praise of the Marian hierarchy. The next most dramatic instance dates from the following year. On 10 June 1554, a gun was shot

---

[1] Two articles by Peter Lake and Michael Questier have demonstrated this most clearly: 'Agency, Appropriation and Rhetoric under the Gallows: Puritans, Romanists and the State in Early Modern England', *Past and Present*, 153 (1996), 64–107; 'Puritans, Papists and the "Public Sphere" in Early Modern England: The Edmund Campion affair in Context', *Journal of Modern History*, 72 (2000), 587–627. A great deal of work has been done on the allied topic of the representations of state power on the Renaissance stage, the most influential statements on which are Stephen Greenblatt's 'Invisible Bullets: Renaissance Authority and its Subversion', in Jonathan Dollimore and Alan Sinfield (eds), *Political Shakespeare: Essays in Cultural Materialism* (Ithaca: Cornell University Press, 1985), pp. 18–47, and Leonard Tennenhouse, *Power on Display: the Politics of Shakespeare's Genres* (London: Methuen, 1986).

at Dr Henry Pendleton while he preached at Paul's Cross.[2] Less violent, if equally immediate responses to preachers' sermons were not uncommon. William Alley complained in 1565 that 'certayne chattering choghes' had thrown 'certayne rayling billes' into the pulpit when he preached at Paul's Cross in 1560.[3] There is no evidence of this sort of thing happening in the Jacobean period, perhaps due to the changes made to the physical space (the 'sermon houses' and the building of Hurlebutt's wall around the ambulatory), which 'contained' the audience more than before. Subsequent references to negative comments on Paul's Cross sermons are described as coming from 'reports' after the sermon or from subsequent sermons from the Cross itself. Although such 'reports' are extant from Thomas Bilson's 1597 sermon on Christ's descent into hell, that sermon is also notable for a more bizarre incident reported by Sir John Harington. A 'sodaine and causeles feare' was raised in the audience, 'by the frawd or folly of some one auditor', and:

this fear so incrediblie possest not only the whole multitude, but the Lord Mayor and other Lords present, that they verilie beleeved that Pauls church was at that instant falling downe; whereat such a tumult was raised, as not only disturbed their devotion and attention, but did indeed put some of the gravest, wisest, and noblest of that assemblie into evident hazard of their lyves.[4]

We have no indication of what could have caused the 'sodaine fear', but Harington's report emphasizes that it was started deliberately, and was somehow connected to Bilson's theme (Satan, 'that new all this to be trew, ... and wisht that none of the auditory would believe it', is blamed). Bilson's doctrine was unwelcome to many in the city, including some radical puritans and semi-separatists who were quick to respond in print. This sermon stirred up a simmering controversy, as the publication history of the sermon (discussed in Chapter 2) makes clear; perhaps some in the auditory provoked a panic to cut Bilson off in the middle of his oration.

A more usual means by which the auditors made their thoughts known from Paul's Cross was through the pinning up of libels on, or near, the pulpit. But Paul's Cross was not the most obvious place to pin up a libel in London, and it lay very near to Paul's Walk, one of the places in the city most remarked upon for the distribution of libels, whether in written or oral form.[5] The positioning of libels was designed to create maximum publicity (without endangering the secrecy of their writer) but also with an eye towards the appropriateness of the place for the message delivered.[6] The choice of the pulpit suggests that the libeller was making a deliberate statement in publishing his message from Paul's Cross.

---

[2] *Register of Sermons* p. 36; John Stow, *Annales, or A General Chronicle of England. Begun by John Stow, continued ... by Edward Howes, Gent.* (1631 [1632]), *STC²* 23340, p. 624.

[3] William Alley, *Ptochomuseion: The Poore Mans Library* ([1565]), *STC²* 374, vol. 2, f. 137ʳ.

[4] Sir John Harington, *Nugae Antiquae*, ed. Henry Harington, 2 vols (1804), vol. 2, p. 104.

[5] Alastair Bellany, *The Politics of Court Scandal in Early Modern England: News Culture and the Overbury Affair, 1603–1660* (Cambridge: Cambridge University Press, 2002), pp. 80–3; Adam Fox, 'Rumour, News and Popular Political Opinion in Elizabethan and Early Stuart England', *Historical Journal*, 40 (1997), 597–620, pp. 603–4.

[6] Pauline Croft, 'Libels, Popular Literacy and Public Opinion in Early Modern England', *Historical Research*, 68 (1995), 266–85, pp. 271–2.

The libels associated with Paul's Cross do not deal with the great scandals that generated most verse libels in this period: the death of Robert Cecil, the Essex 'nullity' case and the Overbury trials, and the assassination of George Villiers, Duke of Buckingham. But libelling was also a part of 'local political and popular culture'.[7] The following example highlights the extent to which Paul's Cross was seen as a civic venue, one connected with the London citizenry and its government. The lord mayor and aldermen were the target of a libel by Thomas Millington, grocer, in August 1580. Millington 'did uppon Sonday laste past exhibit a libell to the preacher at Pawles Crosse against the Magistrates of this cittye'. It is unclear from this account whether Millington made any attempt to hide his identity as the author (or at least the distributor) of the libel, which would make him highly unusual. He may have handed it to the preacher privately only for the preacher to betray his identity, but this assumes that the preacher could then identify him; it may be that he handed the libel to the preacher in full view of the auditory. If so, this was a gesture of defiance towards the Corporation for which he was committed to Newgate.[8]

Religion was the other obvious subject for a libel exhibited at Paul's Cross. In 1607, Catholic activists succeeded in making an audacious gesture by throwing a libel into the lord mayor's pew, on a Sunday (presumably before, rather than during, the sermon). It feigned 'her late majesty to be in hell tormented by many devils, which caused his Majesty to waver in opinion, with other fictions not fit to be inserted'.[9] News about Paul's Cross sermons feature not infrequently in Catholic polemic,[10] signal of the attention paid to this pulpit as a litmus test for attitudes to Catholicism within the English Church. This libel symbolically returns control of Paul's Cross as a medium of communication to the Catholics, their exclusion from which had been lamented since the 1560s and the 'Challenge' controversy.

In 1629, two more overtly political libels were found, according to Laud's annotation on them, 'at Paul's Cross' on the Sunday before Whitsunday: One castigated the King for losing the love of his subjects and his failure to work with parliament, and the second blamed him for the fiasco at La Rochelle. The religious basis for this assertion may explain why Paul's Cross was chosen for the libel: the King is accused of countenancing idolatry at court, for which God may take away his kingdom, and the death of the King's first child is presented as a punishment from God for his bad stewardship of the kingdom.[11] This inflammatory material was not displayed for all to read, but was tightly sealed (it had 'three seals and a large

---

[7] Bellany, *The Politics of Court Scandal*, pp. 100–1. For a more extensive treatment of this subject, see Adam Fox, 'Ballads, Libels and Popular Ridicule in Jacobean England', *Past and Present*, 145 (1994), 48–83.

[8] City of London, London Metropolitan Archive, Repertory of the Court of Aldermen 20, ff. 104ᵛ (6 September 1580).

[9] Letter from John More to William Trumbull, 5 March 1607: HMC, *Downshire*, vol. 2, p. 22.

[10] Oswald Tesimond said that one of the things that convinced Roman Catholics of James's hatred of them was a sermon by the Bishop of London of 5 August 1605, in which he claimed the King had made a protestation before God of his loyalty to the Church of England: *The Gunpowder Plot: The Narrative of Oswald Tesimond alias Greenway*, ed. Francis Edwards, S.J. (Chatham: Folio Society, 1973), p. 45.

[11] *CSPD, 1628–29*, pp. 550–1, The incident was reported on 17 May 1629.

superscription to the King) and was left lying around in the seating area near the pulpit. When the 'youth' who picked it up was heard to say that it was for the King, the paper was taken from him by 'an old man that belongs to the Cross' (probably the verger of St Paul's who cleaned the pulpit) and submitted to Laud.[12] This is quite a curious case: the libel was sealed and addressed to the King, as if the writer intended it to be a private communication and not an 'open' letter to be circulated; but it was left in a public place where members of the political elite regularly gathered, as if the writer calculated that this was the best way for the document to come to the King's attention. This document does not easily fit with our definition of a libel, a scurrilous or defamatory piece of writing intended to ridicule someone publicly.[13] Rather, it is a 'dehortation' addressed to the King, a castigation of his sins, and a warning of the need to mend his ways; in so doing, the document performed the same function towards the King as the preachers of 'Jeremiads' performed at Paul's Cross. This may explain why the writer considered Paul's Cross the most appropriate place to leave it.

Laud was also the target of libels, not at Paul's Cross but elsewhere in the Cathedral precinct. In 1629, barely six weeks before the libel addressed to the King was found in the pulpit at Paul's Cross, two libels, one addressed to Laud and one addressed to Lord Treasurer Richard Weston, were found in the yard of the dean's house, at the south-east end of the precinct. The one addressed to Laud accused him of being 'the fountain of all wickedness' and warned him to 'repent thee of thy monstrous sins'.[14] On 25 August 1637, a libel was 'fastened to the north gate of S. Paul's', the door closest to the pulpit cross; it said that 'the Government of the Church of England is a candle in the snuff, going out in a stench'. The position of this libel, which complains so explicitly about Laud's religious policy, is suggestive: the door into the Cross Yard was the most prominent spot available, as the pulpit had most probably been pulled down by then.[15]

THE PROSCRIPTION OF HETERODOXY

It was not just the Cross Yard, to the north of the cathedral, that was used for demonstrations of state power; the area of the churchyard in front of the great west

---

[12] *CSPD, 1628–29*, p. 552, 19 May 1629.

[13] For definitions of 'libels' see Alistair Bellany, '"Railinge Rymes and Vaunting Verse": Libellous Politics in Early Stuart England, 1603–1628', in Kevin Sharpe and Peter Lake (eds), *Culture and Politics in Early Stuart England* (London: Macmillan, 1994), pp. 285–371, p. 286.

[14] *The Diary of the Life of Archbishop Laud*, in *Works*, ed. James Bliss (Oxford, 1847–60), vol. 3 (1853), p. 210. The entry is for 29 March 1629. On these libels, see David Como, 'Predestination and Political Conflict in Laud's London', *Historical Journal*, 46 (2003), 263–94, 275–8.

[15] *Diary of Archbishop Laud*, p. 229. Another libel, from two days earlier, was 'found by the watch on the south gate of S. Paul's' and said that 'the devil had let that house to me &c'. Laud was not the target of many of the verse libels surviving in manuscript collections: Alistair Bellany and Andrew McRae (eds), *Early Stuart Libels: An Edition of the Poems from Manuscript Sources*, Early Modern Textual Studies, Texts Series I (2005), available at http://purl.oclc.org/emls/texts/libels/R0. He was, however, the subject of many 'seditious grumblings and libellous ballads' from the 1630s, references to which have survived in the State papers: Fox, 'Rumour, News and Popular Political Opinion', p. 618, and n. 43.

door of the cathedral (near the bishop's palace) was used for the most punitive displays: mutilations and executions. Henry Machyn reports that on 25 December 1551, a pillory was set up in the churchyard 'agaynst the byshope place' for a man who caused a 'fray' in the church; his ear was nailed to the post, and then cut off.[16] On 8 August 1570, John Felton was executed for nailing a copy of the bull *Regnans in Excelsis* (which declared Queen Elizabeth excommunicated) to the door of the bishop's palace. His sentence was initially to have been carried out at Tyburn, but was transferred to St Paul's precinct because that was the scene of his offence.[17] On 20 February 1592, Thomas Pormort, a Roman Catholic priest, was executed for treason 'in Paules Churchyarde, on the West end towards Ludgate'.[18] More notoriously, four of the Gunpowder plotters (Sir Everard Digby, Robert Winter, John Grant, and Thomas Bates) were hanged, drawn, and quartered in the Churchyard outside the bishop's palace on 30 January 1606; on 3 May, Henry Garnet S.J. suffered the same fate there.[19]

Although the objections of Sir Arthur Gorges to the use of this space ('under the eaves of the most famous church of our kingdom' and 'the place of happy memory' where Elizabeth had celebrated the defeat of the Armada) for these executions was ignored,[20] it does remind us of his contemporaries' keen sense of the associations that the physical spaces in the city held, and how that affected the meanings attributed to events staged within it. St Paul's Churchyard was not used for the execution of ordinary criminals, and nor was it the usual place for the execution of Catholics. The royal government's consistent denial that Catholics suffered for their faith (being hanged, drawn, and quartered for treason, usually at Tyburn, rather than burned for heresy) might appear a little compromised by holding the execution of Catholics within an ecclesiastical space (the cathedral precinct). But the precinct was an open space capable of holding a large crowd and was right in the heart of the city: it facilitated a larger number of spectators than other sites. So the choice of this place for these executions must have been one that was carefully weighed. With the exception of Pormort (the details of whose trial might explain his execution here),[21] those executed at St Paul's were more evidently guilty of acts

---

[16] *The Diary of Henry Machyn, Citizen and Merchant-taylor of London, from A.D. 1550 to A.D. 1563*, ed. John Gough Nichols (1848), p. 273.

[17] Julian Lock, 'Felton, John (*d.*1570)', *Oxford Dictionary of National Biography* (Oxford: Oxford University Press, 2004), online edn., Jan 2008 <http://www.oxforddnb.com/view/article/9272>, accessed 22 August 2008; Stow, *Annales*, (1631 [1632] STC² 23340) p. 667.

[18] Stow, *Annales*, (1631 [1632]) p. 764.

[19] W. M. Mathews, *A History of St Paul's Cathedral* (London: Phoenix House, 1957), p. 154; Antonia Fraser, *The Gunpowder Plot: Terror and Faith in 1605* (1996; repr. London: Arrow Books, 1999), pp. 229, 264.

[20] Sir Arthur Gorges to the Earl of Salisbury, 29 January 1606, HMC, *Salisbury*, vol. 18, pp. 36–7.

[21] Some of the details of Pormort's case might help to explain why Paul's Churchyard was chosen for this execution. He took as his alias 'John Whitgift', as Whitgift had been master of Trinity College, Cambridge, when Pormort studied there. When on trial Pormort alleged that during his torture, Richard Topcliffe had offered to free him if he would claim to be the archbishop's godson or illegitimate son, and that Topcliffe claimed to have fondled the Queen's body. These accusations must have circulated widely enough for the authorities to have considered a public retraction necessary, because on the day of his execution Pormort was forced to stand on the ladder of the gallows for two hours while Topcliffe tried to extract a recantation from him. If the choice of Paul's Churchyard was

against the state; it was harder for supporters to claim that the real reason for the executions were the men's Catholic beliefs. Felton's displaying of the papal bull made him guilty of denying the Queen's right to rule; the Gunpowder Plotters were guilty of conspiring to kill the King; and Garnet was tried for being complicit in that plot. The use of the cathedral precinct for these executions implies that in these cases, which lent themselves less easily to Catholic appropriation as martyrdoms, the government took the risk of using this convenient, albeit quasi-religious space. But it was a risk, and one that they did not always calculate correctly: in the case of Garnet, soon hailed as a Catholic martyr, they seem to have got it wrong.

To the north-east of the great west door lay the Cross Yard where Paul's Cross stood; it was not used for executions, but the open space around the pulpit was frequently used for emphatic, if less gory, displays of government power through the burning of books. As with executions, however, the incidents of book burning are less examples of a repressive government with unlimited power over the means of controlling public opinion than of a regime that had to make tactical decisions about the degree to which and the means by which it made public its opposition to heterodox or 'seditious' writings. As David Cressy has written:

The public rituals of censorship formed part of the communications repertoire of the early modern state. The banning and burning of books involved dialogue and discourse, speaker and audience, spectacle and spectators in the making and transmission of meaning. Investigation of this process reveals how the authorities deployed the didactic and communicative media at their disposal, and how subjects and citizens could subvert the proceedings to impose meanings and interpretations of their own.[22]

Book burnings at Paul's Cross were not unknown in the early years of the Reformation, the most famous incident being in 1521, when some of Luther's books were burned there during a sermon by John Fisher, Bishop of Rochester.[23] It is not until 1605, however, that we find the government repeating this practice. Other public sites, including Cheapside Cross, were used on other occasions,[24] and Elizabeth I's policy was rather in favour of what Cressy calls 'low-key disposal of forbidden texts in the kitchens at Stationers Hall or in the residence of the bishop of London'.[25]

---

made in order to give maximum publicity to the retraction of these accusations, the policy backfired. Richard Rex, 'Portmort, Thomas (*c.*1560–1592)', *Oxford Dictionary of National Biography* (Oxford: Oxford University Press, 2004), online edn., Jan 2008 <http://www.oxforddnb.com/view/article/53526>, accessed 22 August 2008.

[22] David Cressy, 'Book Burning in Tudor and Stuart England', *Sixteenth Century Journal*, 26(2) (2005), 359–74, p. 361.

[23] Fisher again preached when books were burned in 1526. See Cecilia A. Hutt (ed.), *English Works of John Fisher, Bishop of Rochester. Sermons and Other Writings 1520–1535* (Oxford: Oxford University Press, 2002), pp. 48–56. In 1546, Tyndale's New Testament and Coverdale's Bible and other heretical works were burned: *Register of Sermons*, p. 27.

[24] John Foxe records the burning of Protestant books belonging to the London merchant Thomas Sommers at Cheapside in 1530: *Actes and Monuments* (1583 edn.), Book 8, p. 1207, *Foxe's Book of Martyrs Variorum Edition Online*, Humanities Research Institute, University of Sheffield, available at http://www.hrionline.shef.ac.uk/foxe/, accessed 22 August 2008.

[25] Cressy, 'Book Burning', p. 364.

James was more ready to have books destroyed in public, and Paul's Churchyard, by now the unrivalled centre of the book trade, was an obvious venue.[26] On nine occasions during his reign, James' government (through proclamation, or orders of High Commission or the Privy Council) had books burned somewhere in St Paul's Churchyard; on four of these occasions, we know the event to have happened at Paul's Cross and to have been accompanied by a sermon. But the aim was not necessarily to have the books, and the opinions they contained, rendered inaccessible: the Catholic books burned in 1605 and 1620 were already prohibited;[27] other works (such as the writings of David Pareus and Conrad Vorstius) were also printed on the Continent, and widely available there, as John Chamberlain points out in the case of Pareus: 'I know not what goode yt can do to burne a few bookes here when they are current all Christendome over'. But Chamberlain also notes the occasion for James's order that the books be burned: 'for that Knight (who preached that scandalous sermon at Oxford) took his authoritie from his writings'.[28] It was the Oxford sermon by John Knight of April 1622, in which Pareus was invoked as an authority on the right of inferior magistrates to take arms, that caused the Privy Council to act against Pareus's books.[29] The purpose was not to destroy all record of Pareus's thought, but to make an emphatic statement that they were considered 'seditious, scandalous, and contrary to the Scriptures' so that preachers and other writers would not repeat Knight's mistake.[30] As Cyndia Susan Clegg writes, 'when James burned books, he did so not to control public access to the ideas censored writers expressed, but to attract attention to how distant their ideas were from his own'.[31] The same motive applied to others: Sir Edwin Sandys's survey of religion in continental Europe, *A Relation of the State of Religion*, was published in June 1605 but was ordered to be burned in Paul's Churchyard by High Commission on 5 November that year. John Chamberlain's report of the matter says that this was 'not without his [Sandys's] owne consent as is saide', and Cyndia Susan Clegg has suggested that Sandys's political ambitions for the 1605 parliament (he was taking an increasingly lead role in the Commons) may have forced him to distance himself from the moderate attitude he had taken toward Catholics in his own book. If he did not ask High Commission for the

---

[26] Book burnings do not seem to have been carried out at the west end of the cathedral except on the occasions when they were burned in the ovens of Stationers' Hall. As the Stationers moved their hall from within the precinct to a site off Ludgate Hill in 1611, the 'Cross Yard' would have been the most obvious public place to carry out book burnings. I am grateful to Dr Ian Gadd for his advice on this matter.

[27] *The Letters of John Chamberlain*, ed. Norman Egbert McClure, 2 vols (Philadelphia: American Philosophical Society, 1939), vol. 1, p. 202; vol. 2, p. 313.

[28] Ibid. vol. 2, pp. 439.

[29] *The History of the University of Oxford*, vol. IV: *Seventeenth-Century Oxford*, ed. Nicholas Tyacke (Oxford: Oxford University Press, 1997), p. 583.

[30] *APC, 1621–1623*, p. 234.

[31] Cyndia Susan Clegg, *Press Censorship in Jacobean England* (Cambridge: Cambridge University Press, 2001), p. 89.

order, he must have spread the rumour that he had done so, in order to avoid a reputation for political miscalculation.[32]

The decision to have some books publicly burned was not the only element in James's strategy for publicizing his and his government's prohibition of certain opinions. An equally important consideration was how much information the audience were given about the books and the reasons for their destruction: only four of the nine instances of book burning in James's reign were accompanied by a sermon in which the errors contained in the books were detailed. Throwing copies of books on a fire without an explanatory sermon provided the audience with a spectacle, but it limited their exposure to the books' contents, a useful consideration if the purpose of the exercise was to dissuade those present from reading books with which they were unfamiliar. For example, there were complex diplomatic and theological issues behind James's order to burn Conrad Vorstius's books 'as well in *Paules* Church-yard, as in both the Universities of this Kingdome' in early 1612. (Vorstius had been accused of holding Socinian views, and Martin Becanus, a Catholic contributor to the controversy over the Oath of Allegiance, had coupled James with Vorstius in these opinions.[33]) But the government might well have wished to avoid making the London spectators of the burning any more familiar with anti-Trinitarian ideas than they already were: in his *Declaration* of 1612, James explained that he considered it timely to have Vorstius's works burned because 'this gangrene had not only taken hold amongst our nearest neighbours; so as *non solum peries proximus iam ardebat*: not onely the next house was on fire, but did also begin to creep into the bowels of Our owne Kingdom'.[34] Within months of the book burning at Paul's Cross, Bartholomew Legate and Edward Wightman were burned at the stake for heresy (Legate in London, Wightman in Lichfield), and Ian Atherton and David Como have posited that both men belonged to an emerging anti-Trinitarian group within pre-existing puritan circles.[35] The burning of Vorstius's works signalled the regime's intolerance of anti-Trinitarian ideas to anyone already familiar with Vorstius's reputation or writings, but the lack of a sermon to accompany this event effectively denied to other spectators any information on the position that Vorstius held. This reflects one of the key considerations in preaching against heterodoxy: to avoid presenting to the hearers errors about which they would otherwise have remained ignorant. In his popular preaching

---

[32] *Letters of John Chamberlain*, vol. 1, p. 214. Cyndia Susan Clegg argues that Sandys did seek the High Commission order for the book's destruction (*Press Censorship in Jacobean England*, pp. 118–23); Theodore Rabb argues that Sandys merely spread the rumour that he had done so in order to 'save face': 'Sandys, Sir Edwin (1561–1629)', *Oxford Dictionary of National Biography* (Oxford: Oxford University Press, 2004), online edn., Jan 2008 <http://www.oxforddnb.com/view/article/24650>, accessed 22 August 2008.

[33] James I of England, *His Majesties Declaration Concerning his Proceedings with the States Generall of the United Provinces of the Low Countreys, in the cause of D. Conradus Vorstius* (1612), *STC*[2] 9233, p. 16; Frederick Shriver, 'Orthodoxy and Diplomacy: James I and the Vorstius Affair', *English Historical Review*, 85 (1970), 449–74, pp. 450–8.

[34] James I, *His Majesties Declaration . . . in the cause of D. Conrad Vorstius*, p. 16.

[35] Ian Atherton and David Como, 'The Burning of Edward Wightman: Puritanism, Prelacy and the Politics of Heresy in Early Modern England', *English Historical Review*, 120 (2005), 1215–50.

manual *The Faithful Shepherd*, Richard Bernard warns that the religious controversies discussed in sermons should be 'such a one, as at that time is abroad, or forthwith, is like to come forth, and also dangerous to the Church', and that it 'bee necessary to bee mentioned and confuted before that Auditorie'.[36] Vorstius's errors might have begun to 'creep into the bowels' of James's kingdom, but a detailed confutation of them would have been counter-productive in so public a forum as Paul's Cross.

Where a sermon did accompany the burning of books, we see the government making the same calculations about the effect of the overall event on spectators and auditors. A sermon made very clear to the auditory at Paul's Cross exactly what was objectionable about the book that was being destroyed. In 1609, a sermon accompanied the burning of the scurrilous *Prurit-anus,* produced in St Omer.[37] The book was arranged as questions answered by scriptural quotations; the combined questions and answers implying scriptural warrant for the claims that Henry VIII was Anne Boleyn's father, that Elizabeth had several illegitimate children, and that James was a foreigner from a barbarous country. Such opinions may not have been 'abroad' in England, and so might have gone without refutation in a sermon; simply burning the book would show the government's disapproval. But the irreverent use of the Bible in this pamphlet made it an easy target for anti-Catholic propaganda, so it is not surprising that the authorities seized the opportunity that the publication of *Prurit-anus* offered. Books by Francisco Suárez were burned at Paul's Cross on 25 November 1613 after a sermon in which 'divers positions of Jesuites (especially Suárez the Spaniard) were read and discussed at Paules Crosse, very derogatory to the authoritie of Princes'.[38] The sermon here was clearly targeted at particular positions of Suárez (those 'very derogatory to the authoritie of Princes'), and not to his works as a whole, some of which was quoted freely by preachers and theologians. The purpose of the sermon was to confute Suárez's claims about temporal government, but no doubt it also served to alert his readers in England to the specific elements of his writings that were to be rejected. The burning of David Pareus's books on 23 June 1622 was also motivated by the government's concern to prohibit all forms of resistance theory. In this case, there was clear evidence that Pareus's errors were 'abroad, or forthwith', as they had been the basis on which John Knight preached the rights of inferior magistrates at Oxford in 1622. The government's concern to make as forceful a statement as possible in this case is clear from the choice of time (the first Sunday of the new law term), and the choice of preacher (George Montaigne, Bishop of London).

[36] Richard Bernard, *The Faithful Shepherd* (1621 edn), *STC²* 1941, pp. 288–9. Bernard also warns that 'old, dead, and by-past heresies, out of all mens memories' should not be raised in sermons, as 'this were but to keepe in minde, what were better buried in oblivion' (p. 287).

[37] *CSP, Venetian*, vol. 11: *1607–1610*, pp. 313–14, 319–20. Robert Johnson reminded his hearers of the 'base pasquils, and most idle assertions contrived without wit, without art, without discretion, without judgement, without the feare of God, without respect to his ordinance' that 'here in this place were of late fired, and burned before your eies' in his sermon preached on 3 September 1609: *Davids Teacher* (1609), *STC²* 14694, sigs E2ʳ⁻ᵛ.

[38] *Letters of John Chamberlain*, vol. 1, p. 488.

Unfortunately, Montaigne failed to live up to the occasion: Chamberlain reports that there 'was a great assemblie but a small auditorie, for his voice was so low that I thinke scant a third part was within hearing'.[39]

The last occasion on which books were burned at Paul's Cross came at the very end of James's reign, on 13 February 1625, and indicates the degree to which the royal government made a calculated risk in ordering the public destruction of books. The book in question was not written by a foreign divine, nor did it address such overtly political topics as resistance theory. *God's Holy Minde Touching Matters Morall, which Himselfe uttered in Tenne Words, or Tenne Commandements*, was a work of 'practical divinity' offering moral precepts derived from the Ten Commandments in the 'question and answer' format favoured by catechetical writers. The writer was Edward Elton, a puritan minister in good standing within the Church of England, having served twenty years as rector of Bermondsey; he had died the year before the book was burned, a fact significant to the censoring of the text. Daniel Featley, the licenser responsible for *God's Holy Minde*, stated in his own defence that he had only 'perused' the first fifty-two pages when he heard of the author's death. Featley says that 'after his decease I left of intermeddling in such a worke', because he could no longer get the author's consent for the changes he thought necessary, but the book subsequently 'tooke the libertie to flie out of the Presse without licence'.[40] Featley tells us that the preacher at Paul's Cross gave several reasons for the book's destruction, but Featley only mentions one of them (the denial of the sacrament to the dying); Elton was also guilty of quite extreme sabbatarian ideas (listing in great detail the activities that cannot be done on the Sabbath and denying the Church's right to designate holy days), and of opposing marriage with papists, something that might have been read in the context of the French Match, the negotiations for which were well advanced by February 1625.[41] Elton clearly held many of the opinions associated with radical puritanism that James particularly disliked, and the combination of these with the tense situation during the negotiations for the French Match (recusancy laws having been suspended in December 1624 in preparation for the marriage) probably explains the decision to make such a public example of Elton's book. But the London public, and the auditory at Paul's Cross, obviously contained some people who agreed with Elton, or who thought that this censorship of a 'godly' writer gave an advantage to the

---

[39] Ibid. vol. 2, pp. 442–3.

[40] Daniel Featley, *Cygnio Cantio* (1629), *STC²* 10731, pp. 4–5. On Featley's 'benign censorship' of texts, see Anthony Milton, 'Licensing, Censorship, and Religious Orthodoxy in Early Stuart England', *Historical Journal*, 41(3) (1998), 625–61, pp. 628–31; Arnold Hunt, 'Licensing and Religious Censorship in Early Modern England', in Andrew Hadfield (ed.), *Literature and Censorship in Renaissance England* (London: Palgrave Macmillan, 2001), pp. 127–46.

[41] Featley, *Cygnio Cantio*, p. 7; Edward Elton, *Gods Holy Mind touching Matters Morall* (1625), *STC²* 7619, pp. 33–4, 106–8, 110–12, 119. Anthony Milton references a manuscript copy of what may be the proclamation ordering the burning of Elton's books, in which eight errors, including sabbatarianism, 'potentially sectarian positions regarding the sacraments', and opposition to marriage with Catholics are listed: 'Licensing, Censorship and Religious Orthodoxy in Early Stuart England', p. 629, n. 9.

ever-watchful papists. Featley describes an 'embleme and Motto' invented by 'the wits of the Citie' to describe the burning of Elton's books as follows:

Saint *Paul's* Crosse is drawne at large, and a number of men, partly running away that they might not see such a spectacle, partly weeping, and wiping their eies to see a booke so full (as they conceived) of heavenly zeale and holy fire, sacrificed in earthly and unhallowed flames: their Motto was,

> *Ardebant sancti sceleratis ignibus ignes,*
> *Et mista est flammae profana piae.*
>
> [Their holy fires burned in sinful fires
> And profane flame was mixed with pious flame.]

In the middest of the *area* there is described a huge pile of bookes burning, and on the one side the Author casting his bookes into the fire, with this Motto:

> *Sancte (nec invideo) sine me liber ibis in ignem.*
>
> [Holy book, go into the fire without me, nor do I envy you.]

And on the other side a Popish shaveling Priest answering him with this motto in the next verse:

> *Hei mihi quod domino non licet ire tuo.*
>
> [Woe is me that it is not allowed for you to go with your master.][42]

Whatever the particular errors in Elton's works that that preacher at Paul's Cross denounced 'by authoritie', the perception of the event in London, if Featley's account is to be trusted, was that a work of 'heavenly zeale' was being destroyed. The 'emblem', as Cyndia Susan Clegg writes, 'recalls woodcuts of Marian book-burnings in Foxe's Book of Martyrs', and its suggestion that papists were biding their time until they could start burning Protestants again echoed popular unrest about the dangers of leniency towards Catholics, the opposite message to the one that the government wished to promote in 1625. There was a risk involved with burning a book by a conscientious, albeit undeniably puritan, English minister, particularly when the work concerned was designed as an exercise in religious instruction, not 'controversial divinity' or polemic. It appears that the government miscalculated the risk on this occasion. There were no further incidents of book burning in the Cross Yard for the remaining nine years that the sermons were preached there. The Caroline government concentrated on pre-publication censorship to a greater degree, and 'when it went after the few books that slipped through the licensing system, it did so thoroughly, convincingly, and with style', writes David Cressy, the most famous example being the burning of William Prynne's *Histrio-Mastix*. But that book was burned by the public hangman in front of the pillory where Prynne was mutilated, and the pillory stood in nearby Cheapside.[43]

---

[42] Featley, *Cyngio Cantio*, pp. 5–6. Translations from the Latin taken from Clegg, *Press Censorship in Jacobean England*, pp. 87–8.
[43] Cressy, 'Book Burning in Tudor and Stuart England', pp. 369–70.

THE PERFORMANCE OF ORTHODOXY

A more regular spectacle at Paul's Cross was provided by the performance of penance by those guilty of misconduct or religious heterodoxy. The punishment assigned to those guilty of their first offence was to confess their errors in a recantation, and sometimes also to carry a faggot of wood to signify the penalty they would suffer should they relapse. Extensive use was made of Paul's Cross to discredit traditional Catholicism in the early years of the Reformation: the public confessions of Elizabeth Barton, the 'Holy Maid of Kent', and her associates were made from there, and it was the site chosen for the destruction of the Rood of Boxley and the exposure of the Blood of Hales.[44] Those who had fallen foul of Henry's Six Articles were forced to make public recantations, and leading Reformers such as Edward Crome (on three occasions in all), Thomas Becon, Robert Wisdom, and Nicholas Shaxton all did so at Paul's Cross.[45] The pattern continued under Edward VI: the Catholic cleric Richard Smith recanted his views at Paul's Cross. In Mary's reign, married priests did penance; so did Elizabeth Croft, the woman guilty of the hoax 'through the which the pople of the whole Citie were wonderfullie molested'. (Croft gave a strange whistle through the wall, and her companions interpreted 'what the spirit said' in a seditious manner.)[46]

The appearance of recanting heretics did not stop with Elizabeth's accession. Four Dutch Anabaptists 'bore faggots' at Paul's Cross in 1575, and five members of the Family of Love recanted their beliefs there in the same year.[47] In 1585, the Protestant minister John Hilton had penance imposed upon him after he abjured anti-Trinitarian heresies in convocation. He was ordered to 'attend at *Pauls* crosse upon the Preacher, Sunday next all the time of the Sermon, and there penitently stand before the preacher, with a faggot on his shoulders'.[48] It is noteworthy, however, that these cases all involve those guilty of Protestant error: the aim of 'conforming' the population to the new settlement of religion was better effected by the campaign of preaching against Catholic priests and teachings that dominated Paul's Cross until the 1570s. Thereafter, clerical converts were encouraged to

---

[44] *Register of Sermons*, pp. 18, 21. On the sermons concerning the 'Holy Maid of Kent' and the 'Blood of Hales', see Ethan H. Shagan, *Popular Politics and the English Reformation* (Cambridge: Cambridge University Press, 2003), pp. 62–3, 81–5, 170–2.

[45] *Register of Sermons*, pp. 24, 25, 27; On Edward Crome, see Susan Wabuda, 'Equivocation and Recantation during the English Reformation: The "Subtle Shadows" of Dr Edward Crome', *Journal of Ecclesiastical History*, 44 (1993), 224–42.

[46] *Register of Sermons*, pp. 28, 36, 37; Stow, *Annales* (1631[1632]), p. 624. Stow also reports that a cat, tonsured, dressed in vestments with its front paws tied together with a 'singing cake' between them being hung from Cheapside Cross in April 1554. The bishop had it cut down and 'shewed at Paules Cross by the Preacher D. Pendleton' (*Annales* (1631[1632]), p. 623).

[47] *Register of Sermons*, pp. 55–6. The 'form of the recantation' made by the Dutch Anabaptists is given in Stow, *Annales*, (1631[1632]) p. 679. Christopher Vittels, another member of the Family of Love, may have done penance at Paul's Cross for Arian heresies in 1559: Christopher Marsh, *The Family of Love in English Society, 1550–1630* (Cambridge: Cambridge University Press, 1994), p. 75.

[48] Thomas Fuller, *The Church History of Britain* (1655), Wing F 2416, Cent. XVI, Book IX, pp. 174–5. See also *Records on Convocation*, ed. Gerald Bray, 20 vols (Canterbury, 1509–1603), vol. 7, p. 507.

preach recantation sermons but ordinary Catholics who conformed were not made to recant their Catholicism. Inter-Protestant conflict continued to be aired from Paul's Cross: in 1627, in what turned out to be only the mid-point in a long-running dispute between the ordained minister Stephen Denison and the radical lay preacher John Etherington, Denison preached a lengthy and bitter sermon against Etherington as the latter stood by the pulpit doing penance as the leader of the 'Hetheringtonian' sect.[49]

The most significant recantations were those that were incorporated into a sermon by the penitent himself. Recantation sermons by Catholic priests were not a feature of Elizabeth's reign until the hardening of confessional lines after the launch of the Jesuit mission to England and the response to this by parliament in 1581. The success of the Catholic mission, and particularly the steadfastness of the first group of missionaries, was a blow for the Protestant authorities, and not surprisingly they made every effort to encourage the conversion and recantation of Catholic priests where they thought there was any possibility of it happening.[50] One of the first group of clerical converts from Catholicism, Lawrence Caddey, delivered a declaration against the Pope and Catholicism from Paul's Cross in late 1582 or early 1583. On 1 December 1588, William Tedder recanted his Catholic beliefs; a week later Anthony Tyrrell did the same. In 1593, Thomas Clarke recanted at Paul's Cross after a sermon delivered by 'Mr Buckeridge' (possibly John Buckeridge, later Bishop of Ely).

The 'motives' for conversion provided by these recantation sermons was an important part of their propaganda effect. All provided some kind of denunciation of Catholic doctrine, but not all were particularly detailed, and much of what they said had been heard already at Paul's Cross many times. But more significant was the validation of Protestant doctrine they provided: the converts described their experience as the work of God's grace converting them (in the strict sense) from sinfulness to repentance. This spiritual renewing then caused their turning away from doctrinal (Catholic) error to the truth of the Protestant Church of England.[51] The speaker's personal experience was offered as proof, bypassing the need to engage in intricate and confusing theological explanations. This made the recantation sermon far more persuasive to a greater number of auditors than the traditional anti-Catholic confutation sermons. Thomas Clarke's epistle to his recantation

---

[49] Peter Lake, *The Boxmaker's Revenge: 'Orthodoxy', 'Heterodoxy' and the Politics of the Parish in Early Stuart London* (Manchester: Manchester University Press, 2001), pp. 2–11.

[50] Michael Questier, 'English Clerical Converts to Protestantism, 1580–1596', *Recusant History*, 20 (1991), 455–77, pp. 456–9.

[51] In his study of clerical conversion, Michael Questier (*Conversion, Politics and Religion in England, 1580–1625* (Cambridge: Cambridge University Press, 1996), pp. 58–70) shows how converts described their experience in terms of a spiritual conversion, with the denominational change being represented only as an outward effect of an inward change. Catholics and Protestants differ in their teaching on the nature of conversion (Catholics claiming that the will cooperates with God's grace, whereas Protestants consider man's faculties passive in the process). Converts narrate their experience within the doctrinal framework appropriate to their new affiliation. Converts to Protestantism expressed their conversion in terms taken from 'the theology of the Puritan evangelical wing of the Church of England', the group that was more adamant about maintaining the division between the Church of England and Catholicism.

sermon demonstrates this priority. When delivering it he omitted 'some things which were thought necessary by divers to have bene spoken of, as Transubstantiation, Indulgences, service in an knowen tongue, & such like'. These doctrinal issues were not the primary purpose of his sermon, which was 'to confesse & acknowledge my fault, and generally to renounce and abjure all those false opinions which I once held'.[52] The refutation of Catholicism, therefore, derives from these men's experience of it as a sinful state from which the grace of God called them. They mirrored in their individual experiences the Church's process of reformation and so simultaneously justified the continued divisions in the Church and assured their hearers that they all stood on the right side of that divide.

Whatever the advantages of having former Catholic priests denounce their fellows, staging a public recantation was a risky strategy because it offered a platform to men whose religious allegiances might still be unstable. Of those who recanted at Paul's Cross, two of the five from Queen Elizabeth's reign fell short of expectations.[53] Robert Persons reported that 'the heretics' were 'determined to make capital' out of Laurence Caddey's renunciation of Catholicism in 1583, and so 'it was ordered that the preacher who was to preach on the following feast at the most celebrated pulpit in London, namely, at St. Paul's Cross, should take him with him to declare publicly the things they should suggest against the Pope and the Roman religion'. 'Being a very coarse-looking fellow', Persons continues, 'he did this with such a bad grace that they were ashamed of him'.[54] Whether this report of Caddey's performance at Paul's Cross is true, Caddy did embarrass the English authorities in a far more serious way in February 1583 when he returned to the Continent and the Catholic faith in the company of another lapsed convert, John Nichols.[55]

Worse again was the behaviour of Anthony Tyrrell. Tyrrell was arrested in July 1586; while in prison, he converted and gave Burghley evidence (not all of it reliable) about the Babington plot and agreed to spy on his fellow prisoners. One of those he implicated in the plot was a friend and fellow-cleric, John Ballard, who was executed later that year. Tyrrell repented his change of allegiance after his release from prison in March 1587, and left England for the Continent. But he returned to England shortly after and was arrested again. He was again persuaded to recant his Catholicism at Paul's Cross and was given pen and paper to prepare this

---

[52] Thomas Clarke, *The Recantation ... made at Paules Crosse* (1593), *STC²* 5366, sig. A3ᵛ.

[53] A third, Thomas Clarke, apparently reverted to Catholicism in 1610, but this does not appear to have been widely known: Questier, 'English Clerical Converts', p. 470.

[54] J. H. Pollen, S.J. (ed.), 'Memoirs of Fr Persons S.J., 1581–84 (contd)', *Catholic Record Society, Miscellanea* 4 (1907), 9.

[55] 'The satisfaction of Laurence Caddey, touching his frailties, and fall from the Catholike Church, at his retorne into England', printed in [William Allen] *A True Report of the late Apprehension and Imprisonment of John Nichols Minister* (Rhemes, 1583), ARCR 13. Nichols (or Nicholls) had been a Church of England curate (at Withycombe, Somerset) before his conversion to Catholicism: Michael Mullett, 'Nicholls, John (1555–1584?)', *Oxford Dictionary of National Biography* (Oxford: Oxford University Press, 2004), online edn, Jan 2008 <http://www.oxforddnb.com/view/article/20112>, accessed 15 December 2009. He recanted before the other clerical prisoners in the Tower in 1581: *A Declaration of the Recantation of J. Nichols* (1581), *STC²* 18533.

recantation.[56] According to Robert Persons, it was the political implications of Tyrrell's actions (his renunciation in 1587 of the evidence that he had gave about the Babington plot) that lay behind the Protestant authorities' wish for him to make such a public recantation.[57] But the plan backfired badly. Before the sermon, Tyrrell underwent another change of heart, and instead of writing a recantation of Catholicism, he prepared a renunciation of Protestantism and another repudiation of his testimony on the Babington plot. He used the paper that he had been given for his recantation to write copies of a statement of his renewed adherence to Catholicism; this statement was released to the auditory by Tyrrell, who was pulled from the pulpit as soon as his intentions became clear. A copy fell into the hands of two Catholics, who sent it to Persons. He gives us this description:

But in the main space, all was in marvellous hurly and burly at Paul's Cross, where the people had heard three sermons in one hour, all contrary one to the other; the first of the preacher in praise and credit of Tyrrell; the second of Tyrrell himself in derogation of the preacher; the third of Justice Young threatening death to those that should believe Tyrrell. But the concourse of people was so unruly as Tyrrell was carried away on men's shoulders to the goal of Newgate, by St Nicholas' shambles in Newgate market, the Protestants crying out vengeance upon him, and he weeping bitterly and knocking his breast, and affirming that he had done nothing that day but upon mere force and compulsion of his conscience.[58]

The story does not end here: in late 1588, Tyrrell converted to Protestantism, and was again called to Paul's Cross to explain his motives and recant his former beliefs. This time, he did as he had promised; the sermon was printed,[59] Tyrrell was pardoned and rewarded with the rectory of Dengie in Essex. Tyrrell's first performance at Paul's Cross demonstrates what a risky strategy it was for the English authorities to allow lapsed Catholic clerics access to this pulpit; the fact that they gave Tyrell a second chance to deliver the correct message from Paul's Cross indicates that such recantations of Catholicism were nonetheless considered powerful weapons in the propaganda war against the Catholic mission.

But recantations were not the only use that could be made of converting clerics, nor necessarily the best. In July 1602, William Atkinson, a Catholic priest who was acting as a spy among the Catholic prisoners of Newgate, wrote to Sir Robert Cecil

---

[56] Peter Holmes, 'Tyrrell, Anthony (1552–1615)', *Oxford Dictionary of National Biography* (Oxford: Oxford University Press, 2004), online edn., Jan 2008 <http://www.oxforddnb.com/view/article/27950>, accessed 16 July 2009; Christopher Devlin, 'An Unwilling Apostate: The Case of Anthony Tyrrell', *The Month*, n.s., 6 (1951), 346–58. Tyrrell's case is an extremely complex one. As Questier shows, he was no 'worldly subservient ex-priest', having undergone many hardships in his time as a missionary. Genuine religious doubt, a feeling of conflicting loyalties prompted by the Armada, and a possible belief that temporary cooperation with the Protestant authorities was permissible if it enabled future missionary actions might explain his behaviour ('English Clerical Converts', pp. 462–7).

[57] 'The Fall of Anthony Tyrrell', ed. John Morris, S.J., in *The Troubles of our Catholic Forefathers, related by themselves*, 2nd ser. (1875), pp. 487–8. This text is Robert Persons's edition of a narrative written by Tyrrell in 1587 repenting his lapse from Catholicism. Persons was preparing it for the press, but Tyrrell's subsequent action rendered it useless as propaganda.

[58] 'Fall of Anthony Tyrrell', ed. Morris, pp. 496–7.

[59] William Tedder and Anthony Tyrrell, *The Recantations as they were severally pronounced by W. Tedder and A. Tyrrell* (1588), *STC*[2] 23859.

protesting the sincerity of his conversion despite 'some oversight' in the information he had provided. Atkinson promised to do whatever Cecil demanded to show his good faith, including 'a public recantation at Paul's Cross, at what day your Honour shall vouchsafe'.[60] There is no record of Atkinson preaching at Paul's Cross, but he continued to act as a spy for the English government among the English recusant community well into the reign of James I.[61] If Atkinson made a public testimony of his rejection of Catholicism at Paul's Cross, he would have been of little use to the government as a spy: they had to choose which purpose (propaganda or intelligence) he best served.

Although the number of Catholic clerical converts diminished in James I's reign, the policy of demanding public recantations was no less important.[62] Archbishop Abbot made a deliberate policy of recruiting former Catholic priests for anti-Catholic propaganda, often rewarding them financially for their willingness to cooperate with the regime. A notable example of this is John Gee, curate at Newton in the parish of Winwick, Lancashire, where he had been a crypto-Catholic for some of the time. Gee preached at Paul's Cross on 31 October 1624; although this was not a formal recantation sermon, Gee admitted to having been a Catholic and talked of his miraculous escape from the 'Fatal Vespers' at the residence of the French ambassador in Blackfriars on 26 October 1623.[63] There was only one formal recantation sermon by a Catholic cleric in James's reign, but it was a very newsworthy event for two reasons: the preacher had been a minister in the Church of England before he joined the Society of Jesus, and he had taken part in Catholic anti-Protestant polemic before his return to the Church of England.

Theophilus Higgons had converted to Catholicism while serving as rector of Garford, Yorkshire, around 1609. This was made very public by the pamphlets he produced during and after his conversion. He reports that a conference with Catholics led him to question Protestant teaching on Purgatory, prayers for the dead, and the nature and authority of the visible Church.[64] Wavering, though not yet converted, he published a small tract called *A Briefe Consideration of Mans Iniquitie* (1608), in which he denied the efficacy of human merits and the distinction between mortal and venial

---

[60] HMC, *Salisbury*, vol. 12, pp. 235–6. On Atkinson, see Godfret Anstruther, *The Seminary Priests: A Dictionary of the Secular Clergy of England and Wales, 1558–1850* (Ware: St Edmund's College, 1969–77), p. 13. Atkinson had been imprisoned at least twice since he first arrived in England in 1595.

[61] Michael C. Questier, *Catholicism and Community in Early Modern England: Politics, Aristocratic Patronage and Religion, c. 1550–1640* (Cambridge: Cambridge University Press, 2006), p. 285, and nn. 177, 356.

[62] Michael Questier estimates that fifty seminarians converted to Protestantism in the second half of Elizabeth's reign, but only seventeen did so in James I's reign (although this figure does not include Protestant ministers who converted and then reverted to the Church of England): 'The Phenomenon of Conversion: Change of Religion to and from Catholicism in England, 1580–1625', D.Phil. thesis, University of Sussex, 1991, p. 169. On the use of such converts by the Jacobean authorities, see Questier, 'John Gee, Archbishop Abbot, and the Use of Converts from Rome in Jacobean Anti-Catholicism', *Recusant History*, 24 (1993), 347–60.

[63] John Gee, *Hold Fast* (1624) *STC*² 11705; Questier, 'John Gee, Archbishop Abbot', pp. 347–50.

[64] Antony Charles Ryan, 'Higgons, Theophilus (1578–1659), *Oxford Dictionary of National Biography* (Oxford: Oxford University Press, 2004), online edn., Jan 2008 <http://oxforddnb.com/view/article/13241>, accessed 17 July 2009; Theophilus Higgons, *A Sermon preached at Pauls Crosse the Third of March, 1610* (1611), *STC*² 13455.7, pp. 43–4.

sins. Later, he explains that this tract was set out to see whether Catholics could answer his doubts.[65] Whether he was answered or not, he probably left England later that year, as 1609 saw the publication of a tract giving his 'motive' for conversion. Following an attack in Sir Edward Hoby's *A Letter to Mr. T.H.,* he wrote an *Apology* defending himself.[66] Considerable efforts were made to return Higgons to the Church of England, by Sir Edward Hoby and others, but Higgons spent two years in training at Douai and St Omer before returning to England.[67] In his Paul's Cross sermon, he insisted that he returned to England as a mission priest. While in England, he reverted to Protestantism, under the spiritual direction of Thomas Morton, then Dean of Winchester. As a sign of his 'hearty reunion' with the Church of England, he publicly recanted his Catholic beliefs at Paul's Cross on 3 March 1611. The sermon attracted a great deal of publicity: William Trumbull received three letters that made mention of it. Sir William Browne reported to Trumbull that lords of the Council, the nobility, 'divers bishops', and an auditory so large 'the like audience was never seen in the place' heard it delivered.[68] The sermon was printed and went through three editions in the year of its delivery, something that few sermons achieved. Higgons was rewarded with a benefice (the rectory of Hunton near Maidstone, Kent) for his public confession, and he remained there. In this case, the strategy of having Higgons make a public recantation of Catholicism was a success.

Richard Sheldon, who converted to Protestantism in 1612, also provided anti-Catholic propaganda for the English government. He wrote in favour of the Oath of Allegiance, but also complained about the 'Semi-Brownists or fiery Precisianists' who 'reprove' converts like himself whose preaching is 'firme and zealous for the maintenance of those articles (Christian and Apostolicall) Canons (Goodly and Godly) to which they have subscribed'.[69] Sheldon's one appearance at Paul's Cross was not a success, however: growing more virulently anti-Catholic as time passed, Sheldon preached at Paul's Cross on 1 September 1622 and in his sermon showed the Roman Catholic Church to be the 'beast' of the Book of Revelations. Such designations of the Catholic Church (as Antichrist, Babylon, or 'the beast') were common in early recantation sermons, as they showed conversion as a move from spiritual blindness into the 'true church'. But such identifications of the Church of Rome as 'antichristian' were increasingly unpopular, and this sermon was seen as

---

[65] Theophilus Higgons, *A Briefe Consideration of Mans Iniquitie* (1608), *STC²* 13453; *The Apology of Theophilus Higgons lately Minister* (Roan, 1609), ARCR 432, p. 25.

[66] *The First Motive of T.H. . . . to Suspect the Integrity of his Religion* ([Douai], 1609), ARCR 433; Sir Edward Hoby, *Letter to Mr T.H. late Minister, now Fugitive* (1609), *STC²* 13541; Higgons, *Apology* (Roan, 1609), ARCR 432.

[67] Richard Etkins (a fellow chaplain to Bishop Ravis with Higgons) travelled to Douai to try and convince Higgons to come home. In February 1609, Sir Edward Hoby wrote to Salisbury asking him to enquire of 'one Fitzjames, latelie come over' for information, because Hoby thought that Higgons could be reclaimed (Questier, 'The Phenomenon of Conversion', p. 114, and Questier, *Conversion, Politics and Religion in England, 1580–1625* (1996), p. 60 n 98).

[68] Sir William Browne to Trumbull; William Devick told Trumbull that there was 'an infinite number of people' at Higgons' sermon: HMC, *Marquess of Downshire*, vol. 3, pp. 28–33.

[69] Elizabeth Allen, 'Sheldon, Richard (1570?–1651?), *Oxford Dictionary of National Biography* (Oxford: Oxford University Press, 2004), online edn., Jan 2008 <http://www.oxforddnb.com/view/article/25307>, accessed 17 July 2009; Richard Sheldon, *A Survey of the Miracles of the Church of Rome* (1616), *STC²* 22399, sigs 2¶ᵛ⁻ʳ.

'railing' against Catholics in a way that the recently promulgated *Directions for Preachers* had forbidden. Sheldon was reprimand for his sermon, and it was not printed until 1625.[70]

Subsequent attempts to use recantation sermons for propaganda purposes also fell foul of inter-Protestants disputes. Richard Carpenter was ordained a Catholic priest in 1635 and came to England, only to convert to Protestantism and preach a recantation sermon 'at Paules'. He later reported that before he preached, he received instructions from Juxon's chaplain Samuel Baker. Baker told him 'not to speake much against the Church of Rome, because I was bred up by them, only to put in some litle against them, to sattisfy the common people', but that he was to say one cause for his conversion was 'the sight of the orders & ceremonies in the Church of England, a thing which never entred into my heart, till hee put it in'. After the sermon, Carpenter asked for it to be printed 'as all had ben in that kinde', but Baker refused 'because now the Church of Rome and we were in a faire and quiet way, and it was not fit to multiply controversies'. When Carpenter presented his 'solid reasons' for conversion in subsequent sermons, Laud heard of it and rebuked Carpenter. Carpenter's motives for leaving the Catholic Church clearly did not match the new understanding of Catholicism (as a defective church that nonetheless retained the essence of Christian doctrine) being promoted by the Laudians. His 'testimony' as a convert was of little use to them, and this was reflected in Carpenter's reward for his recantation: he was given a benefice, but in a centre of Catholic recusancy (at Poling in Sussex, four miles from Arundel Castle), where his parishioners 'made a jeast boath of Religion and mee'.[71]

The last recantation sermon that we can claim to be a 'Paul's Cross' event reflects the very different religious politics of the date on which it was preached. Thomas Gage's *The Tyranny of Satan, Discovered by the Teares of a Converted Sinner* was preached on 28 August 1642, six days after the King raised the royal standard at Nottingham. The Paul's Cross sermons were moving from the control of the bishop and his chaplains to the Corporation. (The exact moment of transition is not clear, but the printed sermon, published in October, carries a dedication to the puritan and parliamentarian Lord Mayor Isaac Penington.[72]) Gage returned to the theme familiar from the Elizabethan recantation sermons: the Church of Rome is Babylon, and Gage was 'almost 40 years thus

---

[70] Richard Sheldon, *A Sermon preached at Paules Crosse Laying open the Beast, and its Marke* (1625), *STC²* 22395.

[71] Richard Carpenter, 'Complaint against Mr Baker', 1640: Centre For Kentish Studies, MS CKS–U350/Q5. Carpenter made the same charges in a letter to Sir Edward Dering, possibly dated to 1635: Centre for Kentish Studies MS CKS–U350/C2/53. William E. Burns, 'Carpenter, Richard (1604/5–1670?)', *Oxford Dictionary of National Biography* (Oxford: Oxford University Press, 2004), online edn., Jan 2008 <http://www.oxforddnb.com/view/article/4739>, accessed 15 July 2009. On the changing interpretations of the Church of Rome within the Church of England, see Anthony Milton, *Catholic and Reformed: The Roman and Protestant Churches in English Protestant Thought 1600–1640* (Cambridge: Cambridge University Press, 1995).

[72] The copy of the sermon purchased by George Thomason bears the date 'Octo.3d'. The Court of Aldermen started formal proceedings to take control of the sermons two days later, on 30 August 1642: LMA, Rep. 56, f. 8ᵛ.

blinded . . . in confusion and slavery' until he was rescued by 'the mercies of God, like stars in a winter night shining most comfortably into my cold and frozen soule'. Gage is therefore an example to others never to despair of God's mercy, who can rescue the sinner 'when deepest you are in sin, and according to mans judgement, hardest to be brought out of it'.[73] The Church of Rome is once again the sinful state from which God calls the sinner; change of religion is the outward manifestation of inward conversion. The history of recantation sermons at Paul's Cross suggests that their successful use depended on this very straightforwardly anti-Catholic theme. The softening of attitudes to the Church of Rome of the 1620s and 1630s confused this message and made the recantation sermon of dubious value for the religious and secular authorities.

PENANCE AND HIGH COMMISSION

The recantation of heresy by clerics and laymen was one form of public penance. More common were the 'shaming' punishments assigned by the ecclesiastical authorities for those guilty of sexual misconduct or, in the case of the clergy, for scandalous professional failings. Public penances were often demanded by the church courts, usually at a diocesan level, but the stipulation that penance should be performed at Paul's Cross was rather unusual, being reserved for particularly notable, and scandalous, cases. This was because the purpose of penance was supposedly remedial: once the sinner had made satisfaction for his or her fault, they were forgiven and rehabilitated into the Christian community of their parish. But penance also served as a deterrent: most penances were performed in the offending party's parish church, with the penitent standing prominently and their fault(s) publicized to all their neighbours. In a society where one's 'credit' and reputation could have a direct bearing on one's ability to do business, this was no light matter, and so church courts sometimes offered lesser, less public alternatives to penitents. Conversely, for more serious cases, or in cases where the sexual misconduct was considered scandalous, a more public site for the penance was demanded, sometimes the local market place.[74] Demanding that someone perform their penance at Paul's Cross, one of the most public places in the kingdom, was to maximize the sentence.

While we cannot be sure which courts demanded the penances at Paul's Cross for those guilty of heresy,[75] most of those who did penance at Paul's Cross for

[73] Thomas Gage, *The Tyranny of Satan* (1642), Wing G116, p. 24. On Gage, see Allen D. Boyer, 'Gage, Thomas (1603?–1656)', *Oxford Dictionary of National Biography* (Oxford: Oxford University Press, 2004), online edn., Jan 2008 <http://oxforddnb.com/view/article/10274>, accessed 17 July 2009.

[74] Martin Ingram, *Church Courts, Sex and Marriage in England, 1570–1640* (Cambridge: Cambridge University Press, 1987), pp. 54–5, 249, 336–7.

[75] Heresy cases were dealt with sometimes by bishop's courts, sometimes by the Court of High Commission, and sometimes by ad hoc ecclesiastical commissions set up for a particular case: Roland G. Usher. *The Rise and Fall of the High Commission*, with introduction by Philip Tyler (1913; Oxford University Press, 1968), pp. 42–3.

sexual misconduct were ordered to appear there by High Commission, the prerogative court dealing with ecclesiastical matters.[76] High Commission had powers to fine and imprison that the other church courts did not have, and so bishops sometimes transferred difficult cases from their diocesan courts to High Commission. As with other church courts, many High Commission cases involved matrimonial disputes, sexual misconduct, and clerical disobedience.[77] The ministers who did penance at Paul's Cross were made to atone in public not just for what they had done, but for the scandal they had brought upon their profession. For example, on Sunday 30 June 1627, an unnamed minister did penance at Paul's Cross for having married 'without licence or asking the banes, in a Chappell where he had neither cure nor charge', Sir Charles Howard, son of the Earl of Nottingham, and Arbella Smith, the daughter of Edward Smith of Middle Temple, a lawyer. The seriousness of the cleric's crime is demonstrated not only by the demand for public penance at the Cross, but by his suspension from the ministry for three years.[78] The records for High Commission cases that are extant (from October 1631 to June 1632) show that penance at Paul's Cross was often considered as a punishment for serious clerical misconduct, although the protracted nature of the cases makes it hard to discern how often it happened. Mr Viccars, minister at Stamford in Lincolnshire, was accused of keeping conventicles and making statements from the pulpit that were divisive and bordering on the heretical (that not hearing two sermons on a Sunday was a great sin and liable to lead to the sin against the Holy Ghost, for example). Two of those hearing the case (Sir Nathaniel Brent and the Bishop of London) suggested sentences that included public penance at Stamford and Paul's Cross. It is not clear that Viccars accepted the confession tendered to him, and so it is not certain that the penance was performed. In June 1632, John Etsall, an associate of the antinomian John Eaton, was accused of writing in favour of Eaton. Sir Nathaniel Brent again suggested that the sentence should include a public confession at Paul's Cross, but we do not know how the case concluded and whether the penance was performed.[79]

As with other 'performances' of state power, the success of public penance for the regime depended on the event following the expected pattern, and in many cases this might not be taken for granted. As with recantations of heresy, it was vital that the penitent played the part assigned to them, standing 'penitently' by the preacher

[76] Stow reports that Brocas (see below) had been 'convicted before the High Commissioners' (*Annales*, (1631[1632]), p. 1005); Sir Robert Howard was cited before the High Commission: H. M. Chichester, 'Howard, Sir Robert (1584/5–1653), rev. Sean Kelsey, *Oxford Dictionary of National Biography* (Oxford: Oxford University Press, 2004), online edn., Jan 2008 <http://www.oxforddnb.com/view/article/13934>, accessed 15 August 2008. The anonymous parishioner of St Swithin's who did penance at Paul's Cross and in his parish church did so by order of the High Commission in 1629: Richard Cooke, *A White Sheete, or A Warning for Whoremongers* (1629), *STC*² 5676, p. 4; in 1631, Sir Giles Allington was sentenced by the High Commission: *CSPD, 1631–3*, p. 41.

[77] Usher, *Rise and Fall of the High Commission*, pp. 99–100, 154–5.

[78] British Library MS Harl. 390, f. 276ᵛ. The letter is reprinted in Thomas Birch, *The Court and Times of Charles I* (1848), vol. 1, p. 249.

[79] S. R. Gardiner, *Reports of Cases in the Court of Star Chamber and High Commission*, (Camden Society, ns, 39, 1886), pp. 221, 238, 273–4, 319.

throughout the sermon. This did not always happen: in 1547, a Colchester farmer was made to repeat his penance at Paul's Cross for his denial of Christ's descent into Hell: on the first occasion, he had left his cap on, and this was taken as a token of insincerity.[80] More dramatic was the case of John Blackal, who did penance at Paul's Cross on 6 August 1571. Blackal had served as a minister for twelve years even though he was 'never lawfully called, nor made by any bishop'; four days after his penance at Paul's Cross, he was set in the pillory at Cheapside for having forged a commission from the archbishop of Canterbury. Blackal was a bigamist with four wives and was said to have 'runne, from countrie to countrie, from town to town, leading about with him naughty women', including one called 'greene Apron'. But he did not play the penitent at Paul's Cross; instead, he denounced the man who preached the sermon with 'many foule and sclaunderous reports'. That preacher, John Northbrooke, is our only source for Blackal's crimes and punishment; he preached the sermon because it was he who denounced Blackal. But his account of Blackal's penance suggests that Northbrooke's own position was not unassailable. Northbrooke describes himself as one who had converted from his evil ways, and could claim no more than that he was not 'altogether as wicked, as he [Blackal] declared', and innocent 'for the most part' of the accusations Blackal had made. Blackal's accusations were plausible enough for Northbrooke to be called before High Commission himself. By then Blackal had escaped prison and could not be called as a witness, and so he 'left the infamie to mee, bihinde him'. Northbrooke's publication of this account, in a dedication to Bishop Gilbert Berkeley (the man who ordained him) of a catechetical work, is an attempt to undo the damage that Blackal had done when he appeared at Paul's Cross. Northbrooke hopes to satisfy those 'fickle heades, and unstable people, which knowe mee not in person' when they 'reade this my litle treatise of my faith'.[81] Such public performances were reported outside of London, and their propaganda effect for Roman Catholics needs to be considered too. In the 'Apologie of T. F. in defence of himself and other Catholics', written in 1599, the fact that 'Eaton the preacher did penance' at Paul's Cross and in the pillory at Cheapside 'for lying with his daughter' is reported as evidence of the Church of England's lax morals.[82]

The use of Paul's Cross as a site for penance was by no means confined to the clergy, but laypeople who appeared there were involved in cases that were either

---

[80] *Register of Sermons*, p. 30.

[81] John Northbrooke, *Spiritus est Vicarius Christi in Terra* (1571), *STC²* 18663, sigs Bᵛ–B3ʳ. In the dedication, Northbrooke describes Berkeley as the man who ordained him but he does not mention the fact that Berkeley was also his diocesan and the patron of his living: 'Johannes Northbrooke (CCEd Person ID 59111)', *The Clergymen of the Church of England Database 1540–1835*, available at http://www.theclergydatabase.org.uk, accessed 20 July 2009. Northbrooke does not mention his benefice (Walton-in-Gordano in Somerset) at all, describing himself only as a 'minister and preacher of the word of God' on the title page and signing the epistle dedicatory from Redcliffe in Bristol. He had only been made rector there the previous October, and may well have wanted to retain some distance between his parish and the events at Paul's Cross.

[82] *A Defence of the Catholyke cause … Written by T[thomas] F[itzherbert] With an apology, or defence, of his innocency* ([Antwerp], 1602), ARCR 279, sig. Nᵛ. No other source on this incident has been found to corroborate the story or to identify 'Eaton'.

notorious or considered particularly scandalous. On 15 August 1574, Agnes Briggs (or Bridges) and Rachel Pinder (aged twenty and twelve) did penance for pretending to be possessed by the devil. Their case had evidently stirred a lot of interest, as Stow reports that they had 'marveilously deluded many people, both men and women, but also divers such persons as otherwise seemed to be of good wit and understanding'.[83] Pamphlets describing Pinder's exorcism had already been published, and this appeared to have spurred Archbishop Parker into investigating the case further, the Archbishop being convinced that such possession were effectively impossible.[84] He was probably also keen to avoid awarding the puritan ministers involved the honours of defeating Satan.[85] The public humiliation that the girls suffered (they 'acknowledged their hypocriticall counterfeiting with penitent behaviour', according to Stow) was the penalty for getting caught in the crossfire of ecclesiastical factions, but it delivered Parker an effective 'public relations' victory.

Other cases were handled less well: on 27 January 1612, Mary Firth, the infamous 'Moll Cutpurse' or 'Roaring girl', appeared before the bishop of London's Consistory Court, accused of having appeared 'in Powles church' on Christmas night 'with her peticoate tucked up about her in the fashion of a man . . . to the great scandal of divers persons who understood the same & to the disgrace of all womanhood'. The bishop remanded her to Bridewell until this charge and an accusation that she had been acting as a bawd were investigated further.[86] The lesser charge (cross-dressing) appears to have been upheld, as Firth did penance at Paul's Cross on 9 February. Paul's Cross was probably considered the appropriate place for this penance, as the offence she committed happened in St Paul's Cathedral. Firth was also 'a notorious bagage', and public punishment for her scandalous behaviour was doubtless deemed appropriate. But the much-quoted description of the event by John Chamberlain makes evident why public penances were difficult events to stage:

and this last Sonday Mall Cut-purse, a notorious bagage (that used to go in mans apparell and challenged the feild of divers gallants) was brought to the same place, where she wept bitterly and seemed very penitent, but yt is since doubted she was maudelin druncke, beeing discovered to have tipled of three quartes of sacke before she came to her penaunce: she had the daintiest preacher or ghostly father that ever I saw in pulpit, one Ratcliffe of Brazen Nose in Oxford, a likelier man to have led the revells in some ynne of court then to be where he was, but the best is he did extreem badly, and so wearied the audience that the best part went away, and the rest taried rather to heare Mall Cutpurse then him.[87]

---

[83] Stow, *Annales* (1631[1632]), p. 678.

[84] Philip C. Almond, *Demonic Possession and Exorcism in Early Modern England* (Cambridge: Cambridge University Press, 2004), pp. 58–70.

[85] The tussle within the Church over exorcism and distinguishing the Church of England's practice from that of Roman Catholics is detailed by Thomas Freeman, 'Demons, Deviance and Defiance: John Darrell and the Politics of Exorcism in late Elizabethan England', in Peter Lake and Michael Questier (eds), *Conformity and Orthodoxy in the English Church, c. 1560–1660* (Woodbridge: Boydell Press, 2000), pp. 34–63.

[86] P. A. Mulholland provides a transcription from the Consistory of London Correction Book in 'The Dating of *The Roaring Girl*', *Review of English Studies* ns, 28 (1977), 18–31, pp. 30–1. (Standard abbreviations expanded and superscriptions lowered silently.)

[87] *Letters of John Chamberlain*, vol. 1, p. 334.

The wrong preacher was chosen (a young, unbeneficed man who lacked gravity), and Firth, drunk before the sermon began, did not adopt the penitential demeanour necessary for the spectacle to carry the meaning intended by the authorities.

Some cases involving laypeople were not necessarily 'scandalous' in the sense that they were already the subject of gossip, but they involved particularly flagrant breaches of sexual morality for which the harshest sentence available (appearing in the most public place in the kingdom) seemed appropriate. The High Commissioners might also be sure that the spectators agreed with the preacher about the severity of the crime and the need for exemplary punishment. On 13 March 1586, a man did penance at Paul's Cross for an adultery whose circumstances were particularly serious. The man had 'unlawfullie used' a maid in his household for five years, and she had borne him at least one child. The mother was found guilty of murdering the children and executed at Tyburn 'the last sessions next before the publication hereof by the preacher'. The preacher informed his hearers that the man had been acquitted of complicity in the murder but said 'is it not likelie that he can be excuseable from privitie in the offense', as he must have known the girl was pregnant. Although the penitent had 'escaped the like execution as his fellow offendor had suffered', he was 'certeine to hang in hell fier' if he did not heartily repent. The penitent was indeed lucky that the law 'released him from the gallows'.[88] In the 1580s, infanticide was being defined through case law, and there was a trend towards presuming the guilt of the mother in cases where illegitimate babies delivered secretly died shortly after birth. Accomplices were sometimes also indicted for murder. The trend towards increased indictments and convictions for infanticide has been linked to the fear of 'bastardy' and the growing social regulation of the poor.[89] It is unlikely that the man who appeared at Paul's Cross so soon after his lover had been hanged would have elicited much sympathy from the audience at Paul's Cross.

A man guilty of a very similar crime did penance at Paul's Cross in 1629. Richard Cooke, the incumbent of St Swithin's, preached when the man did penance there and he tells us that penance had also been done at Paul's Cross.[90] The penitent was a parishioner of St Swithin's parish in London and had an affair with one of his maid-servants over a period of two years. The preacher tells us that the young woman had died, but we do not know how: the man had promised to make restitution to those he had wronged when he appeared at Paul's Cross, but the preacher asks 'What satisfaction can you ever make to that servant of yours, who by your base and beastly fornications with her, came to a shamefull and untimely death?'.[91] In both these cases, the High Commission demanded the severest penance of men guilty of abusing their

---

[88] *Holinshed's Chronicles of England, Scotland and Ireland*, ed. Henry Ellis, 6 vols (London, 1807–8), vol. 6, p. 889.

[89] Peter C. Hoffer and N. E. H. Hull, *Murdering Mothers: Infanticide in England and New England 1558–1803* (New York: New York University Press, 1981), pp. 6–19, 98–104. This trend ultimately gave rise to the 1624 Infanticide act, in which the concealment of the birth of an illegitimate child could be treated as evidence for its murder.

[90] Richard Cooke, *A White Sheete, or A Warning for Whoremongers* (1629), *STC*[2] 5676, pp. 32–3.

[91] Cooke, *A White Sheete*, pp. 34–5.

position as masters of a household and whose victims (though described as 'whores' and 'strumpets') paid far higher penalties than their employers.

What is perhaps more striking for our history of Paul's Cross was the readiness of High Commission to demand the same penalty from members of the ruling class. In the same letter in which Chamberlain recounts Moll Firth's performance, he tells of another penance, 'the other weeke', of 'a younge mignon of Sir Pexall Brockas ... whom he had entertained and abused since she was twelve yeares old'. We know very little of this case, except that Sir Pexall Brocas also did penance at Paul's Cross on 24 October 1613,[92] and that this attracted quite a bit of attention. An entry on it was included in the 1632 edition of Stow's *Annales*, detailing how the knight 'did open penance at Paules Crosse. He stoode in a white sheete, and held a stick in his hand, having been formerly convicted before the high Commissioners for secret, and notorious adulteries with divers women'.[93] William Trumbull, Ambassador to the Netherlands, received two letters mentioning the event, and one, from Sir John Throckmorton, indicates why the occasion was considered newsworthy: it was, Throckmorton says, 'a just and acceptable example. It were to be wished upon such persons the like punishment were more frequently executed. Then should not our Church government undergo so many great scandals'.[94]

Where most church courts turned a blind eye to the sexual misdemeanours of the social elite, High Commission did tackle such cases.[95] But demanding that members of the elite stand in front of the crowd at Paul's Cross in a white sheet was an assertive move, an 'acceptable example', as Throckmorton's letter to Trumbull puts it, designed to show the power of High Commission. Sir Pexall Brocas' case was not one that invited sympathy, and this may have been one of the factors (along with the severity of his crime) that encouraged the Commissioners to demand such a public punishment. In 1618, public penance was performed by a member of the aristocracy, and this too was a serious case unlikely to have evoked public sympathy. Lady Anne Markham was the wife of Sir Griffin Markham, a Catholic exiled since 1604 for his central role in the 'Bye' plot. Some time after her husband's exile (when he was known to be alive) Lady Markham married one of her servants bigamously, and this became common knowledge. She was made to pay a fine and perform penance, with her 'husband' at Paul's Cross, and this was reported in newsletters with no sign that there was any sympathy for the lady. Indeed, George Carew remarked to Sir Thomas Row that 'the wonder is that either of them escaped death, to which they were liable by a recent statute', bigamy having been made a felony by an act of 1604.[96]

[92] Sir Pexall Broccas had an estate at Steventon in Hampshire but 'lived chiefly in London': *Victoria Country History, Hampshire*, vol. 4, p. 172.
[93] Stow, *Annales* (1631[1632]), p. 1005.
[94] HMC, *Downshire*, vol. 4, p. 235, 242.
[95] Ingram, *Church Courts, Sex and Marriage*, p. 186.
[96] *CSPD, 1611–18*, 516. See also HMC, *Downshire*, vol. 6, p. 338. Ingram, *Church Courts, Sex and Marriage*, pp. 149–50. Markham probably evaded the felony because the act made an exemption of those whose spouses had been 'beyond the seas' for seven years (which Griffin Markham was, although he was known to be alive).

High Commission was a powerful institution, but it did not stand apart from the factional politics of early modern England, and its use of Paul's Cross for public penance might have been motivated by politics as much as by the will to bring notorious sinners to heel. On 17 March 1625, Sir Robert Howard was excommunicated by High Commission for refusing to answer questions regarding his relationship with Frances, Viscountess Purbeck, and this sentence was pronounced publicly from Paul's Cross, the only such incident on record. The reasons for this very public shaming of Howard become clear when we consider the parties involved in this case. The Viscountess was the sister-in-law of the Duke of Buckingham, and she had secretly given birth to a son in October 1624 who was widely reputed to be Howard's, not her husband's. Although her husband, John Villiers, seems to have been willing to accept the situation,[97] his brother was not: Buckingham agitated energetically between January and March 1625 to have his sister-in-law's adultery proved and a divorce for his brother secured.[98] He was doubtless prompted by the speed with which the news of his sister-in-law's predicament spread: by 12 February 1625, John Chamberlain, writing to Dudley Carleton in The Hague, assumed that the latter had 'heard of the Lady Purbecke and her faire yssue, which busines hath exercised this whole town now a good while'.[99] Buckingham took the advice of two of his clients, Attorney General Sir Thomas Coventry and Solicitor General Sir Robert Heath, that the matter should be pursued in the Court of High Commission: it could meet at once, not having to wait for the law term to begin, and once that Court had found the Lady Purbeck guilty of adultery, a divorce could be obtained in the secular courts.[100] Both parties duly appeared before High Commission on 5 March, at which time Lady Purbeck took the oath and answered her interrogators 'wittilie, and cunningly' but Sir Robert Howard refused to take the oath *ex officio* and answer questions.[101] He was imprisoned for two days, but released on claiming parliamentary privilege. He was called before the Commission again on 17 March, where he produced evidence for his claim to parliamentary privilege, but this was rejected. Again he refused to take the Oath and so was pronounced contumacious, and excommunicated.[102]

When Sir Robert Howard's rejected claim to parliamentary privilege in this matter was debated in the 1626 parliament, all the witnesses questioned agreed that the Commissioners who viewed Howard's proof and rejected it were John Williams,

---

[97] Buckingham insisted that his brother be kept away from Lady Purbeck in case she would 'draw from him something to his disadvantage' (*CSPD, 1623–1625*, pp. 476–7; see also pp. 471–2, 474).

[98] *The Diary of Archbishop Laud*, p. 156; *CSPD, 1623–1625*, pp. 463, 471–2, 474. Buckingham also considered having Lady Purbeck accused of using sorcery on him and his brother, but was advised that this charge was unlikely to be proven: *CSPD, 1623–25*, pp. 476–7; *The Court of King James the first*, 2 vols (1839), vol. 2, p. 377; *Letters of John Chamberlain*, vol. 2, p. 601.

[99] *Letters of John Chamberlain*, vol. 2, p. 599.

[100] *CSPD, 1623–1625*, pp. 478–9; *Court of King James the First*, vol. 2, pp. 376–7.

[101] *Cabala, sive Scrinia Sacra, Mysteries of State and Government* (1654), Wing C184, pp. 103–4.

[102] *Proceedings in Parliament, 1626*, vol. 2: *House of Commons*, ed. William B Bidwell and Maija Jannson (New Haven: Yale University Press, 1992), pp. 327–8.

Lord Keeper and Bishop of Lincoln, and Henry Montagu, Earl of Manchester and Lord President of the Council, both clients of Buckingham.[103] Williams had been keeping Buckingham briefed on the proceedings, writing three detailed letters to him about it.[104] The case was evidently highly politicized: Sir Henry Martyn, a civil lawyer present on the Commission, told the House of Commons that 'he had not seen so great an appearance in the High Commission as was when Sir Robert Howard's business was handled, but cannot tell who of them can thither to serve turns, but thinks some of them were brought'. When pressed, he said he did not know who came 'to serve turns', but that the 'assembly was extraordinary'.[105]

The unprecedented order that Howard's excommunication be denounced from Paul's Cross was most probably calculated to please Buckingham by embarrassing Howard. It may also have been intended to counteract the public sympathy for Howard and the Lady Purbeck: John Williams admitted that the 'major part' of the Commission's auditors were 'the Hee and Shee good fellowes of the town', who 'extreamly commended' Howard for his 'closenesse and secrecie'. 'Though he refused to be a Confessor', Williams quips, 'yet he is sure to die a Martyr, and most of the Ladies in town will offer at his shryne'.[106] John Chamberlain thought that the Lady Purbeck 'hath a hard taske' and reported that a servant of the Archbishop of Canterbury 'was committed, for speaking in her behalf, and how hardly she was used to one of her adverse proctors'.[107] The use of Paul's Cross to shame Sir Robert Howard was not lost on MPs either: in their debate of 1626, one suggested that those who had misinformed the Commission on Howard's right to parliamentary privilege be made to 'declare their errors' at Paul's Cross, 'where he was publicly disgraced'.[108]

The harsh treatment of Howard and Viscountess Purbeck can be explained by the embarrassment they caused the Duke of Buckingham, but this more aggressive treatment of the gentry and aristocracy by High Commission was a trend that would continue in Charles I's reign, as would the increasing unpopularity of the court.[109] Just as Sir Robert Howard used his parliamentary privilege to evade High Commission's proceedings, the last case of public penance at Paul's Cross that we know of also involves a show of strength by the Commission against members of the social elite who sought to use other courts to circumvent its authority. On 12 May 1631 High Commission fined Sir Giles Allington, who had taken as his second wife Dorothy Dalton, the daughter of his half-sister. Dalton's father was

---

[103] *Proceedings in Parliament, 1626*, vol. 3, pp. 104, 141, 142, 144, 148.Williams's rejection of Howard's claim to privilege may have been owing to the fact that the sitting of parliament for which the privilege was claimed had been prorogued *Proceedings in Parliament, 1626*, vol. 2, p. 327 n.6.
[104] *Cabala*, pp. 103–7.
[105] *Proceedings in Parliament, 1626*, vol. 3, pp. 102, 100.
[106] *Cabala*, p. 104.
[107] *Letters of John Chamberlain*, vol. 2, pp. 607–8.
[108] *Proceedings in Parliament, 1626*, vol. 2, p. 333.
[109] Susan Doran and Christopher Durston, *Princes, Pastors and People: The Church and Religion in England, 1500–1700* (Routledge, 2003), pp. 195–6. Usher, *The Rise and Fall of the High Commission*, pp. 316–34.

also fined, and the couple were ordered to do penance at Paul's Cross.[110] This verdict was the end of a more protracted case: Allington had appealed his case to the Court of Common Pleas, and the judge issued a prohibition, a writ forbidding the church courts from dealing with the matter until after a hearing on the proper jurisdiction of the case. The use of these writs to prevent cases being heard by High Commission had become commonplace after the 1580s, leading to a serious clash between Chief Justice Coke and the Church hierarchy, especially Archbishop Bancroft, in 1609 and 1610. Thereafter, prohibitions had been sought less often because the government's support for High Commission meant the writ was unlikely to halt the proceedings completely.[111] This is what happened in Allington's case: between the writ being issued and the hearing about whether the Commission should proceed, Laud made clear his determination to have High Commission's power asserted. Joseph Mede (ordinarily no friend of William Laud's) writes that:

The Bishop of London [Laud] shewed himselfe a man of spirit & courage For between the time of the tendering of the Rules from the Common pleas & the day of the censure and that as some say at the Counsell table, he spake in his manner. If this Prohibition (quoth he) had taken place, I hope my Lo: Grace of Canterbury would have ex communicated throughout his Province all the judges who should have a hand therein. For mine owne part, I will assure you, if he would not, I would have done it in my Diocesse, & my selfe in person denounced it both in Pauls Church & other churches of the same against the author of so enormous a scandal to our Church & religion. I know not what you will think of it in the Countrey, but we say here It was spoken like a Bishop indeed.[112]

Mede the cleric was evidently pleased with Laud's assertiveness, but his letter suggests that he was unsure about how his secular correspondent (Sir Martin Stutevile) would see things ('I know not what you will think of it in the Countrey'); Mede clearly saw this case as an assertion of episcopal power: he begins the letter by noting that Allington had been 'stript of all protection of the Common law', and ends by saying that Laud had 'spoken like a Bishop indeed'. The Commission's show of strength extended beyond the sentence pronounced: Mede includes a marginal note saying that it was thought unlikely that the penance would be commuted. (Having said that, we have no definite source to say that the couple did appear at Paul's Cross.)

Allington and Howard were clearly guilty of the breaches of church law with which they were charged, but the nature of the crimes is noticeably different to that of Sir Pexall Brocas: there is no suggestion that their relationships were not consensual (not an altogether anachronistic consideration for this period), or that they were without the support of their peers. Sir Giles Allington's father-in-law was fined because it was he who procured the licence for the marriage, suggesting that neither family saw anything wrong with it. Sir Robert Howard was evidently committing

---

[110] *CSPD, 1631–3*, p. 41.
[111] Usher, *The Rise and Fall of the High Commission*, pp. 159–63, 180–201, 321–2.
[112] British Library MS Harl. 390, f. 550ʳ.

adultery, but the conduct of his lover's family over her marriage to John Villiers in 1617 had not been forgotten: Frances was the daughter of Sir Edward Coke, and his insistence on the match with Villiers despite Frances's objections had been the subject of much gossip.[113] These two cases did not come to Paul's Cross because they were particularly heinous, but they were scandalous in that they were much spoken of and involved prominent people. Their prosecution was designed to make a point. As J. P. Kenyon writes:

With the power to fine and imprison it [High Commission] reduced many recalcitrant spouses to order, and the successful prosecution of Sir Giles Allington for incest and Viscountess Purbeck for adultery showed that the wealthy and the well born could no longer order their private lives as they wished, irrespective of the laws of God and the Church. It was not a welcome discovery.[114]

The resentment of the 'wealthy and the well born' was a contributing factor to the abolition of the Court of High Commission by parliament in 1641. The effects of this resentment on Paul's Cross are harder to gauge, but it does seem that the Caroline High Commission was readier to use Paul's Cross to bring the 'wealthy and the well born' to heel than had previously been the case, and that may well have led to a dislike of the sermon series itself, as the fact that the fines from High Commission cases often went to fund the rebuilding of the cathedral turned many members of the social elite against that project. If the regime (bishops, king, and Privy Counsellors) had to judge the effects of public spectacles carefully, it seems that they were increasingly miscalculating the risks.

---

[113] Frances' mother, Lady Hatton, also objected to the match, which was designed to help Coke recover the King's favour. The political imperatives of the match forced both women to comply in the end: *Letters of John Chamberlain*, vol. 2, pp. 88–9, 91–2, 100.

[114] J. P. Kenyon, *The Stuart Constitution: Documents and Commentary*, 2nd edn. (Cambridge: Cambridge University Press, 1986), p. 160.

5

The Monarch and Paul's Cross: Preaching on Political Anniversaries

Book burnings, public penances, and recantations at Paul's Cross were means of displaying the authority of the government, particularly the royal government, to the London public; it has been argued that these events required careful orchestration if they were to achieve what the regime expected of them. The most documented events at Paul's Cross, however, involved more positive displays of monarchy: visits of the ruler to hear a sermon there. Although Elizabeth, James, and Charles each attended Paul's Cross only once each in their reign, the arrangements made for these occasions reveal something of the different approaches to 'public relations' of all three monarchs, and more particularly of the role that Paul's Cross played in their attempts to project a positive public image of royal power.

Elizabeth attended a sermon at Paul's Cross in the culmination of the week-long (but rather delayed) celebrations of the defeat of the Armada that took place between 17 November (her Accession Day) and 24 November 1588. The Accession Day fell on a Sunday, and there was a sermon at Paul's Cross by Bishop Thomas Cooper of Winchester that gave thanks for the defeat of the Armada. Stow tells us that the Queen had been expected to attend this sermon but her appearance was postponed. In the meantime, the 19th of November of that year had been declared a public holiday across Elizabeth's realms, and at Paul's Cross there was another sermon giving thanks for the defeat of the Armada.[1] That Sunday (24 November), the Queen processed to St Paul's Cathedral from Somerset House in a display that must have been very remarkable. Stow tells us that she travelled in a 'chariot-throne, made with foure pillars, behind to have a Canopie, on the toppe whereof was made a Crowne Imperiall, and two lowers pillars before, whereon stood a Lyon and a Dragon, supporters of the Armes of Englande, drawne by two white horses'. She was accompanied by the Privy Council, the French Ambassador, the Judges, and indeed most of her court, in an elaborate procession.[2] But Paul's

---

[1] David Cressy, *Bonfires and Bells: National Memory and the Protestant Calendar in Elizabethan and Stuart England* (London: Wiedenfeld and Nicolson, 1989), pp. 118–19; John Stow, *Annales, or a Generall Chronicle of England* (1631 [1632]), *STC*² 23340, pp. 750–1.

[2] Stow, *Annales*, (1631 [1632]), p. 750. A plan of the procession was included in John Strype's edition of Stow's *Survey of London* (1720), Book III, ch. 8, p. 171 (available online through the Stuart London Project, Humanities Research Institute, University of Sheffield, http://hrionline.ac.uk/strype).

Cross was only one venue in this elaborate event that began with the Queen being greeted by the Lord Mayor and aldermen at Aldgate, and by the Bishop of London and Dean of St Paul's 'and other of the Clergie, to the number of more than fifty, all in rich coapes' at the great west door of the cathedral. In the cathedral, the Queen heard the litany sung in the choir before moving through the north transept and into the sermon house. We know nothing of the sermon except that it was preached by John Piers, Bishop of Salisbury. After the sermon, the Queen dined in the bishop's palace and processed home 'with great light of torches' to Somerset House that evening. The Queen's attendance at the sermon does seem to have been an important part of the event, because 'an excellent dyttie of the queen's cominge to Paul's Cross' was produced and entered for publication within days of the event (though it is now lost).[3] But it was the ostentatious pageantry of the event (the Queen in her chariot-throne, the cathedral clergy in their copes), rather than anything said in the sermon, that was thought most notable about the event. Paul's Cross was a convenient venue for the culmination of the procession, no doubt because it was more public and accommodated more people than the cathedral choir. It can be argued that the site, not the pulpit, was most significant to a Queen who knew the value of personal appearances in the city but who had no great taste for preaching.

Her successor was different in both respects, and his appearance at Paul's Cross was very much more focused on the sermon delivered on that occasion. The political climate at the time of James's visit (26 March 1620) was also rather different, and less favourable to the King. Nonetheless, James made elaborate preparations for his visit, even ensuring that the tobacco house and tippling house near the west gate of the cathedral were demolished beforehand.[4] This was a mark of his aim in the visit, which was centred on the cathedral and the sermon delivered on the day. Considerable uncertainty, and therefore gossip, surrounded the reasons for his visit, given the growing unease over the situation in the Palatinate and over the Spanish Match. Sir Francis Nethersole reported to Dudley Carleton that the 'Catholics say that the King's approaching visit to St Paul's is to hear the Bishop of London preach on the Spanish Match; the Protestants that he goes to exhort the people to contribute for the King of Bohemia, who will be publicly prayed for; the truth being that it is to advance contributions towards the re-building of St Paul's'.[5] Like his predecessor's, James's procession was met at the city's boundary (Temple Bar) by the Lord Mayor, Recorder, and aldermen of London; the 'several companies of London in their severall places, in their Liveries and Banners gave their attendance all the way to Paules', according to Stow's *Annales*. But the procession was marred by a row over precedent between the

---

[3] John Nichols, *The Progresses and Public Processions of Queen Elizabeth*, 3 vols (1823), vol. 2, p. 544.
[4] *Acts of the Privy Council, 1619–1621*, p. 165.
[5] *CSPD, 1619–23*, p. 132, Sir Francis Nethersole to [Carleton], 21 March 1620. See also, pp. 131, 133.

younger sons of earls and knights who were Privy Councillors.[6] Where Elizabeth had attended only a litany sung in the choir, James heard evening prayer 'performed with Organs, Cornets and Sagbots' before going to the sermon house.[7] John King, considered among the most eloquent preachers of the day and Bishop of London, preached for the King. The subject of his sermon and even the biblical text on that he preached had been chosen by James, and the sermon was published in print rapidly on the King's instructions.[8] It was a polished performance, skilfully weaving arguments for the renovation of the cathedral with reassertions of the blessings the English Church (and its people) received through their pious and wise king. Like Elizabeth, James was entertained with a banquet at the bishop's palace, but we do not hear of any evening torchlight procession. The lasting impression of the event was that made by the printed copy of John King's eloquent sermon.

Elizabeth I's visit showed an understanding of the uses of public spectacle; James I's visit demonstrates an equally astute sense of the impact of the printed sermon. Arrangements for Charles I's visit suggest that neither consideration was attended to. It seems that the King did not think of his appearance at Paul's Cross as a public event from which a positive image of his reign could be projected, either through public spectacle or printed sermon. Indeed, it appears to have been arranged so as to avoid publicity altogether. The King came to St Paul's by coach, early (about 8am) on the morning of Sunday, 30 May 1630, ostensibly in thanksgiving for the birth of Prince Charles the previous day. He was accompanied by 'the great Lords of his Councell', but we do not hear of a procession, or of the monarch being met at the city boundary by the Corporation. Proceedings in the church were much the same as for James's visit: the bishop, chapter, and choir of the cathedral met the king at the great west door; service was sung in the choir before the King went to the 'sermon house' for the Paul's Cross sermon. But unlike James's visit, no particular arrangements were made for the sermon. All we know is that it was preached by 'a Suffolke man' (where both Elizabeth and James were addressed by a bishop) and that his text was Judges 14:18 ('If ye had not plowed with my heifer, ye had not found out my riddle'), which is not a text with any obvious connection to the celebration of a royal birth.[9] These facts suggest that the person appointed for that Sunday in the usual way simply took his turn. After the sermon the King 'returned to S. James', apparently without dining with the bishop as Elizabeth and James had

[6] Stow, *Annales*, (1631 [1632]), p. 1033; *CSPD, 1619–23*, pp. 133, 135. The order that the procession should have taken is recorded in Lambeth Palace Library, Porteus Papers 17, f. 140. I would like to thank Professor Stephen Taylor for this reference.

[7] Stow, *Annales* (1631 [1632]), p. 1033. Dugdale reports that James heard only an anthem: *The History of St Pauls Cathedral in London* (1658), Wing D 2482, p. 135. Stow's account offers more detail and is to be preferred.

[8] 'The truth is, my text was not taken but given me, though not by a voyce from heaven, as that of St. Austins *Tolle lege, Tolle lege*; yet by a voyce from earth, that is next to heaven': John King, *A Sermon at Paules Crosse, on Behalfe of Paules Church, March 26. 1620. By the B. of London. Both preached and published by his Majesties Commandement* (1620), STC² 14982, pp. 32–3.

[9] *Diary of John Rous, 1625–1642*, ed. Mary Anne Everett Green (London, 1856), p. 53. This text is Samson's response when he discovers that his Philistine wife has revealed the solution to his riddle to her people. It is, therefore, an inauspicious text for a sermon before Charles I and would not have been chosen for a royal visit.

done, and John Stow tells us that the King's 'intent of coming thither was not knowne to any, untill that morning early', which effectively denied the Corporation and the Bishop the chance to offer the King the hospitality that they had showed his predecessors.[10]

Charles kept his visit private, which might have suited the ostensible aim of giving thanks for the birth of the prince but which wrong-footed those who considered it their duty to entertain him. It also militated against Charles's other purpose in going to St Paul's, which was to restart James's halted renovation of the cathedral; in this regard, the visit must be viewed as a failure, as it did not generate the interest in the project that James's visit had. Even Dugdale's *History of St Paul's* (1658) mentions James's visit to St Paul's, but not Charles's. An opportunity to publicize, and to explain, a project that the King wished to see realized was flittered away by Charles's desire to avoid the London crowd and his suspicion of the printing press.[11]

These three royal visits reveal much about Elizabeth, James, and Charles I's attitudes to Paul's Cross and the sermons delivered there. What is most revealing, I would argue, is that only James I showed an interest in the sermon itself, and only the sermon delivered before him survives in print. Elizabeth was a consummate manipulator of her 'royal image',[12] but the pulpit was not a medium she attended to with much care. I have argued elsewhere that James I was a more skilful manipulator of his 'royal image' than has been supposed: although he did not relish the public spectacles that Elizabeth managed so well, he understood how the pulpits and the printing press could be used to explain his policies (and projects like the rebuilding of St Paul's) to those outside elite courtly circles. Indeed, pulpits and the printing press allowed James to project a positive image of his rule more effectively across his three kingdoms than could personal appearances in the metropolis. James had a keen interest in sermons and considered himself a good judge of their quality. He does appear to have understood very well how to provide preachers with the guidance they needed in presenting his personal past and his policies to the English public. James's 'royal image' was transmitted effectively by

---

[10] Stow, *Annales*, (1631 [1632]), p. 1045.

[11] The only printed source on Charles's visit other that Stow's *Annales* is the brief mention in *Hopton's Concordancy*, where it is reported that Prince Charles was born on May 29 and 'the next day being Sunday, the king with the Lords of the Councell came to Paules and heard a sermon at the crosse': *Hopton's Concordancy enlarged, containing a briefe and more perfect account of the years of our Lord God thank any other heretofore published* (1635), *STC*[2] 13781, sig. Q3[r]. On Charles's dislike of public appearances, see Malcolm Smuts, *Court Culture and the Origins of a Royalist Tradition in Early Stuart England* (Philadelphia: University of Pennsylvania Press, 1987), pp. 200–1 n. 62, p. 212. Kevin Sharpe rightly points out that where 'James I had a sharp sense of the word as the medium for the projection of his kingship . . . Charles was preoccupied with visual representation': *The Personal Rule of Charles I* (New Haven: Yale University Press, 1992), p. 181; on Charles' style of kingship in general, see also pp. 179–98, 209–21, and Conrad Russell, *The Causes of the English Civil War* (Oxford: Clarendon Press, 1990), Ch. 8, 'The Man Charles Stuart'.

[12] Much has been published on this subject, but the most pertinent to the argument made here are Natalie Mears, *Queenship and Political Discourse in the Elizabethan Realms* (Cambridge: Cambridge University Press, 2005), pp. 217–56; A. N. McLaren, *Political Culture in the Reign of Elizabeth I: Queen and Commonwealth, 1558–1585* (Cambridge: Cambridge University Press, 1999), pp. 12–45.

preachers who studied the printed statements made by the King on such crucial topics as the Gowrie Conspiracy, Gunpowder Plot, and the Oath of Allegiance. In this respect, James was a more prominent figure to the auditory at Paul's Cross than his predecessor (although her memory was very much alive in Jacobean sermons) or his successor.[13] What follows will not rehearse that argument; it will continue to argue that the presentation of the monarch (in terms of their personal qualities and as divinely ordained ruler) was a task frequently undertaken in sermons, and particularly in sermons preached on political anniversaries (the anniversary of the monarch's accession, of the Gowrie and the Gunpowder plots). But it will concentrate on how the preachers approached the composition of these sermons.

THE ROYAL IMAGE AND THE PREACHER'S DUTY

The preacher standing at Paul's Cross had a primary obligation to God and the Church; however much Paul's Cross was used by political factions and ecclesiastical rivals, the sermons' purpose was to explain to the hearers their duty to God and man. Contemporaries kept a sharp eye out for preachers who strayed too far towards overtly partisan positions in political controversy; we have seen that the public responded negatively to preaching on the Essex revolt when the preachers made implausible allegations against the Earl, and that William Barlow had to defend himself from charges of 'time-serving' when preaching on Essex's execution. We should not be surprised by the number of ministers who were willing to deliver a message of political and social obedience: unity and obedience were highly valued virtues and the preachers appointed to Paul's Cross were taken to be 'conformable' clergymen. But we should not expect these men to deliver political propaganda, as if that too was part of their duty. Even praising the monarch for his or her wisdom and virtue needed to be incorporated within the primary duty to deliver the message of 'law and gospel' from the pulpit. The surest way to demonstrate this fact is by examining the sermons preached on political anniversaries delivered at Paul's Cross.

These sermons were an innovative feature of Paul's Cross after the Reformation, developing slowly under Elizabeth, peaking in frequency and prestige under James, and dying away under Charles I. They were additions to the usual series of Sunday sermons, taking place on the day of the anniversary concerned (rather than the nearest Sunday), and they became an important part of the civic ceremonial associated with Paul's Cross. Many of the sermons preached after the 1590s were printed. It will be argued here that the success of the political anniversary sermons at Paul's Cross owed much to the ways in which the preachers handled their themes. Conventions for preaching on political anniversaries developed over the course of Elizabeth's reign, and those conventions are characterized by a resolute

---

[13] Mary Morrissey, 'Presenting James VI and I to the Public: Preaching on Political Anniversaries at Paul's Cross', in Ralph Houlbrooke (ed.), *James VI and I: Ideas, Authority, and Government* (Aldershot: Ashgate, 2006), pp. 107–21.

separation of secular politics from the duties ordained by the Scriptures: to thank God for good government and to obey the monarch. It was axiomatic that the role of any preacher was to explain to his auditory how the Scripture he had chosen helped them to understand their duties to God and man. He preached a message 'fit for the hearers'. The preachers at Paul's Cross had to find a way of preaching about the monarch while still addressing the sermon's teachings to a popular audience. As a result, the conventions on preaching on political anniversaries that developed at Paul's Cross meant that the sermons gave at least as much attention to the relationship between God and his English Church as they gave to its Supreme Governor.

The blessings of peace and Protestantism that Elizabeth's accession brought to England were integral to the public image of the regime from the early days of the Queen's reign.[14] But Elizabeth did not pay consistent attention to sermons as a form of public representation. Although she took care to be seen at sermons, appearing regularly at the 'preaching place' at Whitehall, she considered her physical presence, not any account of her in the sermon itself, to be the attraction.[15] Elizabeth did pay careful attention to the use of religion in promoting the duty of obedience and loyalty to the monarch through the use of liturgies and 'forms of prayers' on occasions such as her recovery from illness (in 1562 and again in 1568), the defeat of rebellion (1570), and the discovery of assassination plots (1585). These prayer services were drawn up by the bishops under the order of the Privy Council and copies of them were printed for parishes to purchase. Many had a wide circulation through the bishops' apparitors and sumners.[16] None of these events became annual celebrations, however: it was the anniversary of the Queen's accession that established itself as the occasion for political anniversary sermons and other forms of celebration. Marking the anniversary of the Queen's accession began quite early, with reports of bell-ringing in celebration of 17 November from as early as 1567.[17] It was not an official public holiday, giving people the day off work, yet celebrations of the accession were widespread and popular. David Cressy observes that 'it is difficult to discover what combination of official prompting and local enthusiasm gave birth to the developing national observance'.[18] By 1576, with the publication of Grindal's *A Forme of Prayer with Thanksgiving, to be used every year, the 17th of*

---

[14] A good example of this is the *Allegory of the Tudor Accession*, probably dating from 1572, in which Elizabeth stands with Peace and Plenty beside her Reforming brother and father and opposite her Catholic sister. See Margaret Aston, *The King's Bedpost: Reformation and Iconography in a Tudor Group Portrait* (Cambridge: Cambridge University Press, 1993), pp. 128–30.

[15] See Peter McCullough, *Sermons at Court: Politics and Religion in Elizabethan and Jacobean Preaching* (Cambridge: Cambridge University Press, 1998), pp. 42–9, p. 48.

[16] William Keatinge Clay, *Liturgies and Occasional Forms of Prayer set forth in the Reign of Queen Elizabeth* (Cambridge, 1847); Mears, *Queenship and Political Discourse*, pp. 165–6.

[17] J. E. Neale, 'November 17th', in *Essays in Elizabethan History* (London: Jonathan Cape, 1958), p. 10; Cressy, *Bonfires and Bells*, pp. 52–3. Natalie Mears notes that as early as 1564, the parish of St Peter Westcheap marked the Accession Day. But she argues that the occasion was probably 'conceived as admonitory, rather than celebratory', in view of Elizabeth's failure to instigate further reform of the Church in the eyes of her more 'godly' subjects (*Queenship and Political Discourse*, pp. 232–3); on the popularity of the Accession Day, see pp. 250–2.

[18] Cressy, *Bonfires and Bells*, pp. 53, 56.

November, it can certainly be claimed that there was 'national observance' of the Accession Day.[19] We do not know if sermons on the accession were as widespread as the ringing of bells, but they do seem to have been a part of this observance from quite early on. The earliest example from Paul's Cross is John Jewel's sermon on Joshua 6:1–3 preached on the Accession Day in 1567, but this fact is referred to only at the end of the sermon and is not advertised on the title page.[20] We do not hear of an Accession Day sermon being preached at Paul's Cross again until 1581, but by then it had become an annual event, with records for five sermons from that decade surviving.[21]

This was the first significant aberration from the pattern of weekly Sunday sermons (apart from the unimpeachably orthodox Good Friday Passion sermon), and so it demonstrates the hold that 17 November had taken on the popular imagination. But the principle of annual celebratory sermons was not extended to other events. Most notably, the thanksgiving day after the defeat of the Armada (19 November 1588) was not repeated annually, and commemorating the Armada's defeat seems to have been bundled in with the Accession Day celebrations two days earlier.[22] The Elizabethan authorities responded to public sentiment on the accession and channelled the relief over the Armada into acceptable public displays of loyalty. Through sermons, they ensured that an appropriate interpretation of these events was remembered and associated with useful political lessons: loyalty and obedience. But the Accession Day sermon was not instituted in a coordinated way from the centre.

Nor were the Accession Day sermons uncontroversial in their earlier years. Catholic polemicists claimed that it was idolatry to make a fallible, sinful mortal the focus of religious celebrations, particularly when the veneration of the Virgin Mary was discouraged; Elizabeth's Accession Day also replaced a saint recognized in the calendar (St Hugh of Lincoln).[23] These were the charges responded to by Thomas Holland in the defence of Accession Day celebrations that he appended to the second edition of his Paul's Cross Accession Day sermon of

---

[19] Keatinge Clay, *Liturgies and Occasional Forms of Prayer,* pp. 548–61.

[20] *Certaine Sermons preached before the Queenes Majestie, and at Paules Crosse* (1583), *STC²* 14596, sigs. A^r–D6^v. On sig. D5^v, Jewel says 'even upon this day, I say, the xvii of this moneth, God sent his handmaide, and delivered us'. For Paul's Cross as the most likely venue for this sermon, see Chapter 3.

[21] It is likely that sermons from the 1570s have been lost. Edwin Sandys probably preached on the accession when he was bishop of London, as he took the custom to York when he became archbishop: *Sermons made by the most Reverende Father in God, Edwin, Archbishop of York* (1585), *STC²* 21713, sermons 3 and 4. For sermons from the 1580s, see *Register of Sermons,* pp. 61, 62, 66. Two sermons were printed: John Whitgift's of 1583 and Thomas White's of 1589: [John Whitgift], *A Most Godly and Learned Sermon* (1589), *STC²* 25432; Thomas White, *A Sermon preached at Paules Crosse the 17. of November An. 1589* (1589), *STC²* 25407.

[22] Cressy, *Bonfires and Bells,* pp. 118–24.

[23] Roy Strong observes that the celebration of the accession may have been an adaptation of the Catholic celebrations of St Hugh of Lincoln. A seventeenth-century anecdote recorded that bell-ringing on the Accession Day began from the Catholic stronghold of Lincoln College in 1570, and covertly celebrating St. Hugh rather than the queen ('The Popular Celebration of the Accession Day of Queen Elizabeth I', *Journal of the Warburg and Courtauld Institutes,* 21 (1958), 86–103, p. 87).

1599.[24] Some puritans objected to the praise of the Queen within a sermon. In 1581, Richard Rich (whom Patrick Collinson has described as 'a member of a family famous in three generations for its godly religion and politics') was questioned before High Commission for saying that treating the Accession Day as a holy day with sermons and prayers would make the Queen 'a god'. Rich and his fellow disputant Robert Wright were imprisoned and petitioned for release in June 1582, arguing that 'the Bishop of London was not opposed to their release if the Queen's displeasure could be appeased'.[25] This seems to be the sort of complaint that John Whitgift responded to in his Paul's Cross Accession Day sermon of 1583:

> Likewise thos fantasticall spirits are likewise here reprooved, which dissalow and mislike this manner of yerelie celebrating this day . . . as though wee did it superstitiouslie, or dedicated the day unto her, as to some Sainct, whereas in deede wee do but our duetie, and that which is most lawfull for us to doe.[26]

This aspect of the Accession Day sermon did, however, present a problem for preachers. Encomiastic rhetoric was problematic because of its associations with Catholic preaching on the saints; the praise of living, sinful Christians was even harder to accommodate to an ideal of preaching centred on the explication of Scripture. This explains why preachers on the Accession Day consistently deny that their sermons are to be understood as 'panegyrics' in the normal sense. Only two sermons from this period use the word 'panegyric' in their title, and in both the meaning of the term is modified. In his *Panegyris D. Elizabethae* of 1599, Thomas Holland argues that Accession Day sermons do not flatter the monarch, but that they teach subjects the duty of obedience. In *An Holy Panegyrick*, preached in 1613, Joseph Hall says that the religious obligation to 'celebrate the blessing of a king' (rather than to celebrate the king himself) is paramount throughout.[27] In 1608, Richard Crakanthorpe remarks that 'it is not my meaning, nor is it fit, to make a panegyricall Oration in this place at large'.[28] This did not mean that no human being could be praised from the pulpit: exemplary figures, particularly from the Bible, could be discussed within exhortations to virtue, but not in order to praise them. Particular individuals could be commemorated within sermons, according to the preaching theorists, provided the presentation of their virtues was designed to edify the hearers,

---

[24] *The Apologie or Defence of the Church and Common-wealth of England for their Annual Celebrations of Q. Elizabeths Coronation day the 17. Of November*, in *Panegyris D Elizabethae*, (Oxford, 1601), *STC²* 13597, esp. sigs H^r–H4^v. The first edition of this sermon is *STC²* 13596.5, [[H] -e paneguris] *D. Elizabetha* (Oxford, 1600).

[25] HMC, 8th report, *Manuscripts of the Duke of Manchester*, vol. 2, p. 27, no. 120; Patrick Collinson, 'Elizabethan and Jacobean Puritanism as Forms of Popular Religious Culture', in Christopher Durston and Jacqueline Eales (eds), *The Culture of English Puritanism, 1560–1700* (London: Macmillan, 1996), pp. 32–57, p. 47.

[26] [Whitgift], *A Most Godly and Learned Sermon*, sig. B7^r.

[27] Thomas Holland, *Panegyris D. Elizabethae* (Oxford, 1601), *STC²* 13597, sigs I2^v–I3^r, P3^v. Joseph Hall, *An Holy Panegyrick. A Sermon preached at Pauls Crosse* (1613), *STC²* 12673, p. 2. John Howson repeats many of the same points in his Oxford Accession Day sermon of 1602: *A Sermon preached at St Maries Oxford* (1602), *STC²* 13884, sigs C^v–C4^v.

[28] Richard Crakanthorpe, *A Sermon at the Solemnizing of the Happie Inauguration or our Most Gracious and Religious Soveraigne King James* (1609), *STC²* 5979, sig. B4^r.

not simply to celebrate those named. Those whose actions provided examples of virtue for the hearers, or those whose lives were in other ways demonstrable of God's providence, might be described in order to rouse the hearers to imitation or to thanksgiving. Hyperius of Marburg included encomia in the 'instructive' type of sermon as means of exhorting the hearers to follow the virtue exemplified in biblical figures:

> To the kind *instructive* doe appertaine al those thinges in especially which the *Rhetoricians* have placed in the kinde *deliberative.* . . . Further, those thinges that be peculiar to the kinde *demonstrative*, and *encomiastical*, shal be reduced to this forme. For when it falleth out that there is praised in the ecclesiastical assembly either some person, as Abraham, Job; or in deede, as the invincible fortitude and constancy of the Machabees in confession of the truth: or any thing els, as bountifulnesse towardes the poore, hospitality, concorde, Prophesye, fasting, Prayer: no manne doubteth these thinges therfore chiefely to bee done, to the entent the hearers might be provoked either to the imitation of the lyke in their common trade of life, or truly to praise and magnifye God, which would have such notable thinges accomplished of his chosen.[29]

In practice, this meant that the Queen's virtues could be described in detail, but only if the preacher's reason for doing so was to remind his hearers to give thanks to God who 'would have such notable things accomplished by his chosen'. Preachers could therefore extol the Queen's record as monarch as a means of exhorting their hearers to give thanks to God for the peace, religious freedom, and plenty they enjoyed. In this way, preachers could avoid the accusation that they were using the office of preaching to praise a sinful mortal. This is the approach that Thomas Holland took in his defence of Accession Day celebrations. Arguing from 1 Timothy 2:1–2 ('I exhort you therefore, that first of all, supplications, prayers, intercessions, and giving of thanks, be made for all men; For kings, and for all that are in authority; that we may lead a quiet and peaceable life in all godliness and honesty') Holland presents the theme of the Accession Day sermon as follows:

> The exposition of Scripture chosen by the Minister that day is such as is set to perswade the auditory to due obedience to her Majesty and to be thankfull to God for her Majesties happy and flourishing regiment these 43 yeeres: and to excite them to pray unto God long to continue her Grace amongst us (if it be his blessed will) & to deliver her Highnesse from all malice of her enemies.[30]

John Whitgift's sermon asserted that the purpose of the Accession Day sermon was 'to give God thankes for the great and wonderfull benefits, which we enjoy thorough his goodnes by the minsterie of her Majestie, whome it pleased him as this day five and twentie yeares to place in the Throne of this Kingdome, and to praie unto him for her long life and prosperitie'.[31] We see here a convention for the preaching of political anniversary sermons that reconciles the celebration of such

---

[29] Hyperius (Andreas Gerardus), *De Formandis Concionibus Sacris* (1553), trans. John Ludham, *The Practis of Preaching* (1577), *STC²* 11758, ff. 150ᵛ–151ʳ.
[30] Holland, *Panegyris D. Elizabethae*, sig. I2ᵛ.
[31] [Whitgift], *A Most Godly and Learned Sermon*, sig. B7ʳ.

occasions with the religious duties of the auditors through the idea of thanksgiving for good government. Thomas White puts it succinctly in his 1589 Accession Day sermon: the 'duty of the day' is 'exhortation to Thanksgiving'.[32]

This strategy was certainly made easier by the currency of the providential Protestant reading of English history that we now associate most strongly with John Foxe. This gave a particularly prominent place to Elizabeth's accession.[33] By this reading, '17 November represented more than the Accession Day of a monarch. Rather, it signified the turning point in England's religious history, a providential divide between the nightmare of popery and the promise of the development of God's true church', as David Cressy puts it.[34] This was the interpretation of Elizabeth's succession promoted by Grindal in his liturgy for the Accession Day. The first reading of this service was a choice of the story of good King Jehosaphat (2 Chronicles 17–20), 'the history of King Hezekiah' (2 Kings 18–20), or 'the sum of the history of King Josia' (2 Kings 22–23).[35] The second reading drew its conclusion from the previous presentation of godly monarchs: it was Romans 13. The psalms (21, 85, 124, and 100) are psalms of deliverance. The prayer with which the service ends offers thanksgiving for the blessing of 'liberty both of bodies and minds' from 'war and oppression, both of bodies by tyranny and of conscience by superstition, restoring peace and true religion' and asks that the Queen may 'long and many years reign over us' as a means to continuing 'the great blessings, which thou has by her thy minister poured upon us'.[36] This understanding of the accession was promulgated yet more widely by the preachers at Paul's Cross. Its usefulness to them lay in the way that it linked biblical texts (the good kings of the Old Testament, the psalms on Israel's deliverance from its enemies) to the occasion (the monarch's accession). The crucial element of this method was the creation of an analogy between the events narrated in Old Testament with recent English history. In Elizabethan and Jacobean sermons, Elizabeth's accession was compared to God's restoration of true religion under Hezekiah and Josiah; her virtues as a monarch were compared to those of Israel's leaders and heroes through whom God had previously carried out his providential plan. Through the analogy, God's continuous care for the church was asserted.

---

[32] White, *A Sermon preached at Paules Crosse*, p. 49.

[33] Patrick Collinson, *The Birthpangs of Protestant England: Religious and Cultural Change in the Sixteenth and Seventeenth centuries* (London: Macmillan, 1988), pp. 12–14; John King, 'Fiction and Fact in Foxe's *Book of Martyrs*', in David Loades (ed.), *John Foxe and the English Reformation* (Ashgate: Scholar Press, 1997), pp. 26–31. For an important qualification to this reading of Elizabeth's accession, see Thomas S. Freeman, 'Providence and Prescription: The Account of Elizabeth in Foxe's "Book of Martyrs"', in Susan Doran and Thomas S. Freeman (eds), *The Myth of Elizabeth* (London: Palgrave Macmillan, 2003), pp. 27–55.

[34] Cressy, *Bonfires and Bells*, pp. 53–6, esp. 53. See also Neale, 'November 17th', pp. 9–20; Strong, 'The Popular Celebration of the Accession Day of Queen Elizabeth'.

[35] On Elizabeth as the reforming, iconoclastic King Hezekiah, see Aston, *The King's Bedpost*, pp. 113–27.

[36] Keatinge Clay, *Liturgies and Occasional Forms of Prayer*, pp. 548–61.

This is evident in John Duport's Accession Day sermon of 1590. His text was Psalm 118:24 ('This is the day that the Lord hath made; let us rejoice and be glad therein'), and he explains his choice of text as follows:

and therefore having duly considred what might be most fitte for me to speake in the eares of this greate people, I confesse I could find nothing so sutable every way, either in regarde of the time that we celebrate, or of the great mercies that wee have received at Gods hands, or of the measure of thankfulnes that we are bound to render to his Majesty for the same, then to say to you as this people doth here, This is the day, &c. For touching the greatest blessing that ever God bestowed on this land, if you aske when it was, I answeare, This is the day &c. if what it was, I answere, it was the coronation of her excellent Majesty, wherwith the L. hath made this a famous and an honorable day to al posterity: if what we must render for the same, I answere, we must rejoice, we must be glad: so that the summe of all I can say unto you, is the same that this people saith here, This is the day &c.[37]

'This people' with whom Duport and his hearers are compared are the Israelites, and the occasion being celebrated in Psalm 118 is David's accession to the throne after his defeat of Saul. The Geneva Bible's gloss on this verse informs the reader that this is the day 'wherein God hath showed chiefly his mercy by appointing me [i.e. David] king and delivering his Church'. This text is, Duport says, 'so sutable every way' to the celebration of Elizabeth's accession: like David, Elizabeth has been appointed monarch and through that accession, God has delivered his church. As the people of Israel were delivered from tyranny by David, so the people of God's church in England were delivered from popery by Elizabeth's coming to power. The same text was used by John Howson in an Accession Day sermon preached at St Mary's, Oxford, in 1602, and he introduces it as follows:

This Psalme is a Psalme of thanksgiving, which *David* song unto God, when hee was first invested into his kingdome, and translated the Arke of the Lord from the house of *Obed Edom, 2. King. 6.* with melody and musicke and great festivitie; in which he not only exhorteth *all men* in a generalitie to praise God, & in specialitie both *Jewes* and *Gentiles*, such as were after the spirit borne of the seed of *Abraham*, and detested Idolatrie as *Abraham* did: but actually bringeth in himself, *ver* 17, the people in this verse, and the Priests in the 26. verse, glorifying God for these great blessings.[38]

The use of analogies between the Queen and biblical figures became an established part of Accession Day sermons at Paul's Cross. Thomas Holland's Accession Day sermon of 1599 involved an elaborate presentation of the Queen of Sheba as she was praised by Christ in Matthew 12:42 ('The Queene of the south shall rise in judgment with this generation, and shall condemne it: for shee came from the utmost partes of the earth, to heare the wisdome of Salomon: and, beholde, a greater than Salomon is heere'). As printed, the sermon ends rather abruptly after discussing the presentation of the Queen of Sheba (her piety, wisdom, and

---

[37] John Duport, *A Sermon preached at Paules Crosse on the 17. day of November 1590* (1591), *STC²* 7365.5, sig. A3ᵛ. Duport's sermon is the most 'panegyrical' of those extant from Paul's Cross, as it deals mostly with a description of the Queen's personal and political virtues.

[38] John Howson, *A Sermon preached at St Maries Oxford* (1602), *STC²* 13884, sig. Aʳ.

authority) in the text but it does not mention Elizabeth or her Accession Day. Yet in the preface to the sermon, Holland says that the fitness of the text to 'the time, place and persons' arising from 'the mutual resemblance, by way of comparison, in the two persons then spoken of' (Elizabeth and the Queen of Sheba) is 'evidently declared'.[39] It is probable that the more detailed presentation of the analogy between the two queens was shortened in order to make more room for Holland's defence of Accession Day celebrations.

Not all Accession Day sermons used such analogies between biblical history and England's recent past to explain the significance of the Queen's accession. Another approach was to use a prescriptive text (just as the 1576 liturgy used Romans 13 as a reading). John Whitgift's 1583 sermon does this; Whitgift's chosen text was Titus 3:1–2 ('Put them in mind to be subject to principalities and powers, to obey magistrates, to be ready to every good work. To speak evil of no man, to be no brawlers, but gentle, shewing all meekness unto all men'). This enabled him to incorporate a discussion of the Queen's accession, and his hearers' duties to their Queen, through the doctrine of obedience found in the text. Prescriptive texts like these lent themselves to discussions of the duties of loyalty and obedience, which were certainly much repeated in Accession Day sermons. It was harder to use them to demonstrate the hearers' duty to give thanks to God for the accession, but that duty was the means by which preachers could justify a celebratory tone in Accession Day sermons. In short, prescriptive texts tended to produce less appealing sermons. This may explain why Whitgift's 1583 sermon was not published until 1589, when it served as part of the bishops' campaign against Martin Marprelate.

JAMES AND THE PROTESTANT CALENDAR

The Accession Day sermons that began in the late 1560s had become a well-established annual event at Paul's Cross by James I's accession. The two decades that followed saw a great increase in the preaching of political anniversary sermons, and the reasons for this expansion can be found in James's character and style of government. Lori Anne Ferrell writes of James I that he was 'unique in his obsessive attention to the task of literary self-promotion and description, a characteristic reflecting his unenviable position as a foreign king in England'. 'Given his talent for writing, his knowledge of theology, and his love of religious debate', Ferrell argues, 'it is not surprising that James I turned to his bishops and court preachers for assistance in this task of governing by polemic. Sermons, not masques, were the major organs of political self-expression at the Jacobean court.'[40] Peter McCullough has demonstrated the extent to which James expanded on the arrangements for court preaching that were in place on his succession. Where Elizabeth had been content to keep to preaching at court to the Lenten 'season', with three sermons a

---

[39] Holland, *Panegyris D. Elizabethae*, sigs a2ᵛ, bʳ⁻ᵛ.

[40] Lori Anne Ferrell, *Government by Polemic: James I, the King's Preachers and the Rhetorics of Conformity, 1603–1625* (Palo Alto, CA: Stanford University Press, 1998), p. 10.

week in the seven weeks of Lent, James had preaching in court all year round and made the sermon the central point of Sunday observations in the Chapels royal. James enjoyed sermons, and was a confident judge of preaching.

When he came to the throne of England, James retained the custom of celebrating the Accession Day (now 24 March) but he innovated by making other political anniversaries more formally fixed points in the calendar. On 12 July 1603, a letter was sent from the Privy Council to the bishops asking them to make the arrangements for the annual observation of 5 August (the anniversary of the Gowrie Conspiracy) as a public holiday with a liturgy, and the anniversary was duly commemorated on 5 August 1603 in London, not much more than a week after James's coronation.[41] Sermons were a conspicuous part of commemorations of the Gowrie Conspiracy in England, probably because of the lead James took in this regard: he heard a sermon every Tuesday as well as on the anniversary of the event. We have an almost unbroken record of court sermons on the Gowrie Conspiracy between 1603 and 1625, eight of them preached by the most famous of court preachers, Lancelot Andrewes.[42] The example of the court quickly spread to Paul's Cross, with the first sermon that we know of being preached in 1605 (by Richard Vaughan, Bishop of London).[43] The commemoration of the Gowrie Conspiracy with anniversary sermons as well as a public liturgy established the pattern that would be followed in 1605. Among the first actions of the parliament after the discovery of the Gunpowder Plot was to legislate for annual 'morning prayer, preaching, or other service of God' to '*give* unto almighty God *thanks* for this most happy deliverance'.[44] Annual sermons at Paul's Cross, at court, and elsewhere became a fixed part of the anniversary celebrations of 5 November. It was a particularly popular subject for preaching at Paul's Cross, and we have records of Paul's Cross sermons from 1607, 1608, 1613, 1614, 1617, and 1622.

By 1605, there were three points in the year, almost evenly spaced (24 March, 5 August, and 5 November) when the auditors at Paul's Cross heard recent political events (the King's accession, and the defeats of the Gowrie Conspiracy and of the Gunpowder Plot) rehearsed as part of the Protestant, providential narrative of English history. The opening episode of that narrative, Elizabeth I coming to the throne to settle the Church, was not neglected.[45] This appears to have been

---

[41] 'The Council's Letter to the Archbishop of Canterbury about celebrating the 5th of August yearly', in *Documentary Annals of the Reformed Church of England*, ed. Edward Cardwell, 2 vols (Oxford, 1839), vol. 2, p. 40. Interestingly, unlike the Accession Day or the anniversary of the Gunpowder Plot, 5 August was celebrated with 'cessation from work and labour' (p. 42). The Scottish Parliament had made 5 August a 'day of thanksgiving' with freedom from labour in 1600.

[42] There are records of a 1603 court sermon on Gowrie by Archbishop Tobie Matthew and of sermons for ten subsequent years, eight of them by Lancelot Andrewes: Peter McCullough, 'A Calendar of Sermons Preached at Court during the Reigns of Elizabeth I and James I', disk accompanying *Sermons at Court*.

[43] See *Register of Sermons*, p. 85, and *The Gunpowder Plot: The Narrative of Oswald Tesimond alias Greenway*, ed. Francis Edwards, S.J. (Chatham: Folio Society, 1973), p. 45.

[44] *Statutes of the Realm*, vol. 4(ii), pp. 1067–8.

[45] On the commemoration of Elizabeth's reign in Jacobean England, see Alexandra Walsham, '"A Very Deborah?":The Myth of Elizabeth as a Providential Monarch', in Susan Doran and Thomas S. Freeman (eds), *The Myth of Elizabeth* (London: Palgrave Macmillan, 2003), pp. 143–68, pp. 157–62.

expected by the auditory: John Chamberlain reports that John Donne's Accession Day sermon of 1617 was 'exceedingly well liked generally, the rather for that he did Quene Elizabeth great right, and held himself close to the text without flattering the time too much'.[46] In the last Accession Day sermon of James's reign, that for 24 March 1625, Barten Holyday told his hearers that God had 'advanced' the memory and 'the victory of that Queene, which perpetually conquered her enemies, and her sexe'.[47] No less providential than Elizabeth's succession was God's provision of a successor to her. The anxiety of that time is memorably conjured up by John Donne in his Accession Day sermon of 1617:

And when every one of you in the City were running up and down like Ants with their eggs bigger then themselves, every man with his bags, to seek where to hide them safely, Almighty God shed down his *Spirit of Unity,* and recollecting, and reposedness, and acquiescence upon you all. In the death of that Queen, unmatchable, inimitable in her sex; ... in her death we were all under one common flood, and depth of tears.... God took pleasure, and found a savor of rest, in our peaceful chearfulness, and in our joyful and confident apprehension of blessed days in his Government, whom he had prepared at first, and preserved so often for us.[48]

James had united the kingdoms of England and Scotland and had produced a male heir, and so he had secured the peace and true religion that he inherited. His reign was easily incorporated into the narrative of God protecting England by securing stable government for it. Joseph Hall's *An Holy Panegyrick* (preached on the Accession Day in 1613) uses a prescriptive text from the historical books (1 Samuel 12:24–5, 'Therefore fear you the Lord, and serve him in truth with all your hearts, and consider how great things he hath done for you. But if ye do wickedly, ye shall perish, both ye and your king.') This allowed him to press home the religious duty of political obedience while using the example of Israel's history to remind his hearers that good and bad kings are sent from God.[49] Preachers were also keen to add James's own favoured self-description to the narrative of God's dealings with England. In 1609, Richard Crakanthorpe took a text on the Queen of Sheba (2 Chronicles 9:5–9, 'And she said to the king, it was a true word which I heard in my own land of thy sayings, and of thy wisdom ... Then she gave the king six score talents of gold, and of sweet odours exceeding much, and precious stones'), but his purpose was not to flatter Elizabeth, as Thomas Holland had done. The analogy that Crakanthorpe offered was biblical Solomon and 'England's Solomon', 'whose wise rule is a blessing and whose people are fortunate in their king', as the Queen says in the text. The comparison between England's kings and David and Solomon was to be used of King Charles too: William Laud's Accession Day

---

[46] *The Letters of John Chamberlain,* ed. Norman Egbert McClure, 2 vols (Philadelphia: American Philosophical Society, 1939), vol. 2, p. 67.

[47] Barten Holyday, *A Sermon preached at Pauls Crosse, March the 24. 1624* (1626), *STC²* 13616, pp. 39–40.

[48] *The Sermons of John Donne,* eds G. R. Potter and E. Simpson, 10 vols (Berkeley: University of California Press, 1953–62), vol. 1, p. 217.

[49] Joseph Hall, *An Holy Panegyrick* (1613), *STC²* 12673.

sermon of 1631 used a text from the Psalms (Psalm 72:1, 'Give the king thy judgments, O God, and thy righteousness unto the king's son') for a sermon that used a comparison between David and Solomon to emphasize the blessing of a secure succession, particularly now that Henrietta Maria had given birth to an heir.[50]

The main elements for an Accession Day sermon changed little over our period: God's care for the English had been demonstrated to them, and so the hearers were exhorted to do the duties that this continued care demanded, which were to give thanks to God and be obedient to the monarch.[51] The providential pattern of recent history was demonstrated through a comparison with God's care for the Israelites, and particularly their kings. This was a very flexible method of structuring a political sermon: it allowed the preacher to press home the analogy with as many or as few points of comparison as he wished. For example, John Rawlinson begins his sermon by stressing the difference between James and King Saul: it was the people's rejoicing in their king that was the point of comparison he wished to make.[52] It was argued in Chapter 2 that the strength of a sermon's argument rested on the links that the preacher created between his biblical text (analysed in the 'explication') and the 'application' of the text to his hearers' 'life and manners'. The former gave weight and authority to the latter. The strength of the links between biblical text and recent history varies considerably in political anniversary sermons. One reason for this is the preachers' wariness that they might be accused of 'wresting' Scripture to flatter the sovereign if the comparison with biblical patri- archs was too strained. For example, when arguing for the similarities between James and Solomon as king, the fulcrum of his sermon, Richard Crakanthorpe is at pains to limit the comparison: James is wiser than any king England or Europe has ever seen, but he is not wiser than the king that God himself called wisest:

It is not my purpose to make any parallel to *Salomon*, of whom God himselfe hath saide, that none should be like unto him: nor take uppon me to set forth unto you, any portraiture of that wisedom, which no *Zeuxes* nor *Apelles* can otherwise expresse, ... Yet with all loyall submission, let mee this much say, and say much lesse then I do conceive: Neither can this present age, nor al the Chronicles (I say) not of great *Britaine* onely, but of all *Europe*, present unto us a King, indued with such admirable gifts of learning, Judgement, and memory; adored with so many princely and Heroicall Vertues, Justice, Clemency, and Wisedome; especially, with that Divine and Heavenly wisedome, which is the Fountaine

---

[50]   Richard Crakanthorpe, *A Sermon at the Solemnizing of the Happie Inauguration* (1609), *STC*[2] 5979; William Laud, *A Commemoration of King Charles his Inauguration* (1625), Wing L579.

[51]   Joseph Hall describes the 'tribute of loyaltie and thankfulnesse' owed on the Accession Day: *An Holy Panegyrick*, p. 2. John Rawlinson says that his text argues for thanksgiving 'for having a king', and for having 'such a king': *Vivat Rex* (1619), *STC*[2] 20777, pp. 29–30. Richard Crakanthorpe mentions 'some few' of the blessings England receives by James' reign 'to stirr us up to magnifie and blesse Gods glorious name' and to 'to love and honour that Sacred Majesty whom God hath chosen to be his royal instrument, whereby so many and great blessings are derived unto us': *A Sermon at the Solemnizing of the Happie Inauguration*, sig. B4[r]. John Donne exhorts his hearers to 'sacrifice our humble thanks to God' for James' accession: *A Sermon preached at Pauls Cross*, in *The Sermons of John Donne*, vol. 1, p. 219.

[52]   Rawlinson, *Vivat Rex*, p. 2.

and foundation of all the rest; with Religion, Piety, Zeale and constant Magnanimity to professe, maintaine, and uphold the truth of God, and of his Gospell.[53]

This needs to be stressed: preachers on political anniversaries had to retain the distinctness of the two subjects that they were comparing: biblical history and contemporary politics are kept separate even while particular points of analogy were argued. For this reason, many of these sermons make a clear structural separation between biblical history and the political anniversary, and this separation is retained even as the argument creates analogies between the two. The historical context of the scriptural text is first described; the events celebrated on the occasion of the sermon are then introduced, and an analogy between the two is created.

The message of political anniversary sermons was always much the same. Whether preaching on the accession, the Gowrie Conspiracy, or the Gunpowder Plot, preachers reminded their auditors that God had blessed England with good government, and that the appropriate response to such blessings is thanksgiving to God and obedience to the monarch. There are, nonetheless, marked differences in the ways in which the Gowrie Conspiracy and the Gunpowder Plot were handled by preachers at Paul's Cross. For many of the sermons on the Gowrie Conspiracy, for example, the creation of analogies between biblical events and the sermons' topic themes (already seen in Accession Day sermons) was extended further, with the separation of biblical and recent history being maintained with particular care.[54] The peculiar nature of the Gowrie conspiracy provides a possible explanation for the very rigid separation of biblical and contemporary history that was such a marked feature of these sermons.

The Gowrie Conspiracy caused unease in Scotland as well as England, because there were no witnesses to the whole episode except the King, and because the story he told was rather odd (that John Ruthven, Earl of Gowrie, and his brother Alexander conspired to assassinate the King by luring him away from his entourage into a room where they had placed an armed man). Yet James lost no time in making this story public. Within hours of the conspiracy, James wrote an account of it to his Privy Council; George Nicolson, an English agent in Edinburgh, sent a report to Cecil the day after the event.[55] Sermons were delivered giving thanks for the King's deliverance, including one at the market cross in Edinburgh with the King in attendance.[56] Within a month, the King's account of the events of 5 August, with all the available testimonies against the Gowries appended, was published: by

---

[53] Crakanthorpe, *A Sermon at the Solemnizing of the Happie Inauguration*, sigs B2^{r-v}.

[54] This seems to be a particular feature of Paul's Cross sermons on this event. Unfortunately, too few sermons from pulpits other than the court survive to enable us to make a comparison, and the court sermons are not representative of the venue, eight of the ten extant being by Andrewes, who was no passive follower of convention in his preaching.

[55] The fullest account of these events is to be found in W. F. Arbuckle, 'The Gowrie Conspiracy', *Scottish Historical Review*, 36 (1957), 1–27, 89–110. *CSP Scotland*, vol. XIII, part 2, pp. 678–80.

[56] Arbuckle, 'The Gowrie Conspiracy', pp. 13–14; The refusal of five Edinburgh ministers to preach on the King's escape threatened to undermine the King's presentation of the events. Alan MacDonald has revealed that these ministers were in the minority, and that the form of thanksgiving was agreed by the synod on 3 September without anyone objecting: *The Jacobean Kirk, 1567–1625: Sovereignty, Polity and Liturgy* (Aldershot: Ashgate, 1998), pp. 93–4.

11 September, an English version of this narrative was entered in the Stationers' Register. Printed in Scotland as *Gowreis Conspiracie: A Discourse of the Unnatural and Vyle Conspiracie Attempted against the Kings Majesties Person at Sanct Johnstown upon Twysday the 5 of August 1600*, the King's narrative was printed in England twice in 1600 (with the title *The Earle of Gowries Conspiracy against the Kings Majestie of Scotland*) and there were four more editions in 1603.[57]

It was this reading of the Gowrie Conspiracy that provided Paul's Cross preachers with the details of the plot on which they drew for recounting the Gowrie Conspiracy and interpreting it for an English audience. All of the extant Paul's Cross sermons on the conspiracy take much the same approach, offering a fairly extensive retelling of events and taking the King's *Gowries Conspiracie* as their source. Sometimes rather minor details are submitted to minute interpretation, showing that *Gowries Conspiracie* was read with some care. For example, John Milward in *Jacobs Great Day of Trouble*, preached in 1607, seizes on several small points in the narrative, including the fact that Alexander Ruthven put his hat back on when he had the King imprisoned. Milward spells out the significance of the gesture:

Secondly, in him I observe the proud and scornful heart of a Traytor, that when he had closed and locked in his Soveraign in a straight roome, so unmindfull was he of Majestie, he changed his former faire words into foule deeds, clapt on his hatte, swearing and staring in the face of his king; menacing and threatning him, now with hands, and words, and bands, whom not long since he solicited with all duety and meditation, to have beene one of his Majesties chamber.[58]

At first reading, then, it would seem that the English preachers on the Gowrie Conspiracy experienced none of the unease about this strange tale that some of their Scottish colleagues had shown. A more careful examination of the sermons suggests that the texts do betray some unease with the story that the King told.[59] Although the preachers repeat the story within the sermons, they invariably keep it at arms' length from their biblical text, by keeping the points of analogy between their biblical text and the events of the Gowrie Conspiracy as few as possible. Often, the only point of comparison is that 'the lord's anointed' was in danger. To keep their biblical and contemporary themes separate in this way, preachers usually dealt with them sequentially, expounding the biblical paradigm first, in the 'explication' of their biblical text. The 'application' of the sermon then recounted the events of the Gowrie Conspiracy, and the two events are connected through the

---

[57] David Calderwood says that the narrative was printed a month later: *The History of the Kirk of Scotland*, ed. Thomas Thomson, 8 vols (Edinburgh: Wodrow Society, 1842–9), vol. 6 (1845), p. 45. The Scottish edition is *STC²* 21465.5; the English editions are *STC²* 21466–21467.5. A Latin translation was printed in Edinburgh in 1601, *STC²* 21468.

[58] John Milward, *Jacobs Great Day of Trouble and Deliverance* (1610), *STC²* 17942, sig. F4ᵛ.

[59] The (probably apocryphal) story of Lancelot Andrewes kneeling before the King and asking him to confirm the truth of his narrative does imply that there was some unease about the story in England. Andrewes preached on the Gowrie Conspiracy eight times, so he must have found a way to reconcile any uncertainty over the story (if he felt there were any) with his conscience: Kenneth Fincham, *Prelate as Pastor: The Episcopate of James I* (Oxford: Clarendon Press, 1990), p. 49; Ferrell, *Government by Polemic*, p. 193.

figure of the endangered king. In the exhortation that followed, the hearers were encouraged to praise God for his care of the King, and therefore the kingdom. For example, in *Jacobs Great Day of Trouble*, on Jeremiah 30:7 ('Alas, for this day is great, none hath beene like it, it is the time of Jacob's trouble: Yet shall he be delivered from it'), John Milward spends the first half of his sermon discussing the afflictions of God's people (the Israelites and now the Christian Church), the reasons for the suffering, and the uses of affliction. He then applies his text by showing the sufferings of England's own 'Jacob' (Jacobus) and by drawing comparisons between the courage and virtue of both Jacobs. Similarly, Barten Holyday's sermon from 1623 discusses his text (Psalm 18:48–9, 'Thou hast delivered mee from the violent man. Therefore will I give thanks unto thee O Lord among the Heathen; and sing praises unto thy name') as a psalm of praise, where David describes God's strength in protecting his people and delivering the king from his enemies. The story of this psalm, of David's deliverance from Saul, is, he says, analogous to the events of the Gowrie Conspiracy, and he retells the story to highlight the similarity.[60]

These sermons practice a rigid separation of the biblical text from its 'application' to the Gowrie Conspiracy, and they deliberately limit the points of comparison to the figure of the endangered King. Even when recounting the events of 5 August 1600, the preachers keep the King's narrative structurally separate from their recapitulations of biblical deliverances. This does not mean that they refused to endorse the King's account of the conspiracy, but it does suggest that they did not endeavour to find a pattern of links between the events of the Gowrie Conspiracy and other providential deliverances. It is also worth noting that these sermons rarely extend the scope of their discussion beyond the figure of the king himself. Samuel Purchas describes how his text refers to God's blessing on David and 'his seed forever', but explicitly rejects the more general thrust of the latter part of the biblical verse, restricting its reference to 'this king'.[61] The danger that the Gowrie Conspiracy represented is therefore restricted to the king; his danger affects the hearers only insofar as it threatened to take away the future king of England. This may explain why the sermons fail to generate the same tone of celebration found in other accession or Gunpowder Plot sermons even when they make use of many of the same themes and techniques. Despite the 'grand style rhetoric' and the vividness with which preachers recreate the events of that day, the threat that James faced remained rather remote to the Paul's Cross auditors.

The Gunpowder Plot did threaten very immediate danger to at least some of the auditors at Paul's Cross, and preaching on that event is not surprisingly vehement and vivid, but the sermons are far less homogenous than those on the Gowrie Conspiracy. This is inspite of the fact that Paul's Cross Gunpowder Plot sermons

[60] Barten Holyday, *A Sermon preached at Pauls Crosse, August the 5. 1623* (1626), *STC²* 13615, p. 18.
[61] Samuel Purchas, *The Kings Towre and Triumphant Arch of London.* (1623), *STC²* 20502, sigs A6ʳ⁻ᵛ.

were strongly influenced by two texts that quickly established conventions for preaching on the subject: the King's speech to parliament of 9 November 1605, and William Barlow's sermon delivered at Paul's Cross the following day.[62] Barlow, who had already done sterling work for the authorities at Paul's Cross after the Earl of Essex's execution, had been appointed to preach that Sunday but was obliged to write a new sermon in haste following the discovery of the plot. We are told this in the dedicatory epistle, which also reveals that he used the King's speech in Parliament of the previous day as his briefing on the events of the plot and that 'divers circumstances' were also 'imparted' to him the night before by the Earl of Salisbury.[63] Barlow's sermon therefore engages in what Lori Anne Ferrell has called 'a reciprocal act of ventriloquism', as the King's speech itself borrows 'the forms and language' of a sermon, 'from his opening citation of Psalm 145: 9 . . . through his utilization of homiletic-style text divisions'.[64]

Most preachers at Paul's Cross followed James I's and Barlow's lead, taking their texts from the Book of Psalms (rather than the historical books of the Old Testament favoured for Accession Day and Gowrie Conspiracy sermons). The texts used are mostly associated with mercy (and deliverance), thanksgiving, and celebration. These were themes common to political anniversary sermons, but they were also themes prominent in James's speech to parliament. There he made himself a particular example of God's mercy, having been subject to 'dayly tempest of innumerable dangers . . . not onely ever since my birth, but even as I may justly say, before my birth: and while yet in my mother's belly'. Barlow took up James's point about being preserved by God, and made it the basis for a comparison with King David, the writer of the psalms.[65] But such comparisons are not so a prominent feature of preaching on the Gunpowder Plot as they are of sermons on other political anniversaries, and subsequent preachers on this event did not structure their sermons around the sustained examination of such analogies, as they did for Accession Day or Gowrie Conspiracy sermons. Perhaps the creation of such comparisons were unnecessary in this case, the details of the intended plot and its potential consequences being proof enough that God had saved England from destruction. Preachers concentrated instead on the Plot as one in a sequence, a pattern of providential deliverances of England or of its rulers. Martin Fotherby (preaching in 1607) and Robert Tynley (preaching in 1608) told their hearers that God had saved the English from attack by water in 1588, and again from fire in 1605. John Boys, in his sermon for 1613, listed Elizabeth's survival of Mary's reign and the putting down of the Northern rebellion as earlier examples of God saving

---

[62] 'Speech to parliament of 9 November 1605', in *King James VI and I, Political Writings*, ed. Johann P. Sommerville (Cambridge: Cambridge University Press, 1994), pp. 147–58; William Barlow, *The Sermon preached at Paules Crosse, the Tenth day of November* (1606), STC² 1455, sig. D4ᵛ.

[63] William Barlow, *The Sermon preached at Paules Crosse, the Tenth day of November* (1606), STC² 1455, sigs A3ᵛ–A4ʳ.

[64] Ferrell. *Government by Polemic*, p. 74.

[65] 'Speech to parliament of 9 November 1605', in *Political Writings*, p. 152; Barlow, *The Sermon preached at Paules Crosse, the Tenth day of November*, sig. D4ᵛ.

Protestant England from Catholic cruelty and rebellion.[66] In all Gunpowder Plot sermons, the auditors were encouraged to give thanks for the failure of a plot that would have led to deaths among their own number, political unrest throughout the country, and the threat of foreign invasion, and the preachers painted lurid pictures of the death and chaos that might have resulted had God not prevented the plotters.[67]

What is most characteristic of these sermons is their trenchant anti-Catholicism, and here we see the preachers depart to greater or lesser degrees from the example given by the King in his speech to parliament. James's speech goes to great lengths to distinguish those guilty of the plot from those among the Catholic community who remain loyal to the government, a distinction he sought to make a political reality with the Oath of Allegiance. James insisted that some English Catholics 'may yet remaine good and faithfull Subjects' and are not to be blamed for the plot; nor were Catholic monarchs, with whom James intends to stay on good terms. This is a distinction that William Barlow and his fellow preachers at Paul's Cross did not make. Barlow gives considerable space to his description of the 'inhumane crueltie', indeed 'hyperdiabolicall divelishnes' of the plotters; he later tells his hearers that the 'Romanists' make 'this practise of murthering princes . . . an *Axiom* of *Theologie*'.[68] Barlow used more heated language than James, but he placed the blame squarely on Catholic doctrine rather than James's recusant subjects. His lead was not followed by others. Martin Fotherby warned his hearers to be watchful 'not onely of our secret Papists, but also of our open Recusants too', whose rejoicing on the 5 November is the 'cruel joy which wicked *Esau* had; that (yet for all this) they hope, that *The time of mourning will one day fall uppon us*'. The next year, Robert Tynley insisted that 'this Religion falsly termed Catholike, utterly perverteth the lawfull subjection of people to their Soveraignes', but he also recites other foiled plots ('*Tichbourne, Parry, Squier, Walpoole*' to show that continued danger of treason that English Catholics (and especially Jesuits) represent.[69] Most emphatic is William Goodwin's sermon for 1614:

write, what shall I write! write this religion a religion of treason, and a religion of Conspiracy. Write! what shall I write! write this religion a religion of blood, and a religion of Massacre, write! what shall I write, write this religion a religion of forswearing and a religion of perjury, write! what shall I write! write this religion a religion of lying and a religion of equivocation,

---

[66] Martin Fotherby, *The Third Sermon*, in *Foure Sermons lately preached* (1608), *STC²* 11206, pp. 80–1; Robert Tynley, *Two Learned Sermons* (1609), *STC²* 24472, p. 26; John Boys, *An Exposition of the Last Psalme* (1613), *STC²* 3464, pp. 17–18.

[67] For example, see Barlow, *The Sermon preached at Paules Crosse, the Tenth day of November*, sigs C2ᵛ–C4ᵛ; William Goodwin, 'A Sermon Preached at Pauls Cross the 5° of November 1614. by Doctor Goodwyn then Vice Chancellor of Oxford', Dr Williams Library MS 12.10, ff. 7ʳ–16ʳ, f. 12ʳ; Boys, *An Exposition of the Last Psalme* (1613), pp. 18–19.

[68] Barlow, *The Sermon preached at Paules Crosse, the Tenth day of November*, sigs. C2ᵛ, E3ʳ. It should be pointed out that he goes on to say that '*Knox* and *Buchanan* . . . come very neare to the same dangerous position' (sig. E3v). On this aspect of Barlow's sermons, see Ferrell, *Government by Polemic* (1613), pp. 77–81.

[69] Fotherby, *The Third Sermon*, p. 77; Tynley, *Two Learned Sermons*, p. 11.

150				The Monarch and Paul's Cross

[. . .] I do them no wrong, for it is not the villany of a few men, but the impiety of their
villany. It is a small matter to find men that carry bloody minds, but it was never heard of
among Turks, nor Jews, nor Cithians, nor barbarians, it was never heard of I say that religion
should set on and animate men to villany, and then defend the lawfulness of it.[70]

    Lori Anne Ferrell has noted how the choice of preacher and the latitude given
preachers for anti-popery in their sermons depended on the King's policy, being
rather muted between 1605–8, until the pope's response to the oath was known,
and then more pronounced as part of the campaign to encourage Catholics to take
the oath nonetheless it cooled down thereafter, as evidenced by Andrewes's near
monopoly on Gowrie sermons at court. She has also analysed with great care the
way that preachers like Barlow picked up and extended the denunciation of
puritanism contained in James's speech.[71] Ferrell is clearly right to see James's
choice of preachers as indicative of his policy, and undoubtedly the 'king's preachers' at Paul's Cross and at court followed the general direction of the king's policy
(although taken on its own, Paul's Cross provides too small a sample for this to be
apparent, with only five sermons being printed and another one extant in manuscript). It might also be suggested, however, that this anti-Catholic rhetoric was not
really designed to prove the wickedness of Catholic doctrine and the nefariousness
of papists generally: the probable impact of the Plot, had it succeeded, gave as much
proof of this as the hearers could ask. Rather, the anti-Catholic rhetoric in
Gunpowder Plot sermons functions as the premise for arguments on other elements
of Jacobean religious politics.

    What is most surprising about the Gunpowder Plot sermons at Paul's Cross is
how heterogeneous they are. Exhortations to thanksgiving, reassertions of God's
providential care for England, and, most emphatically, denunciations of Catholicism are the only characteristics that these sermons share with each other and with
other political anniversary sermons. This is inspite of the clear lead that the King's
speech and Barlow's sermon offered to preachers. The Paul's Cross Gunpowder
Plot sermons do use the same argumentative method (creating analogies with Old
Testament figures) as other political anniversary sermons, but they sometimes
digress so far from their main theme of thanksgiving that they might almost fit
into other sermon genres. For example, the unprinted 1614 sermon by William
Goodwin (then Vice-Chancellor of Oxford) is one of the very few Gunpowder Plot
sermons that does not take a text from the Book of Psalms. His text is Ezekiel 24:2
('Son of man, write thee the name of the day, even of this same day: the king of
Babilon set himselfe against Jerusalem this same day'), a text that invites commemoration but also warns of a present danger. Goodwin reminds his hearers of the
original context: Ezekiel and Daniel were sent 'to comfort and minister consolation'
(f. 7ʳ) to the exiled Israelites, their exile being God's punishment for their sins.
England has received 'as great and miraculous and wonderfull a preservation, as ever

[70] Goodwin, 'A Sermon Preached at Pauls Cross', Dr. Williams Library MS 12.10, f. 15ʳ.
[71] Ferrell, *Government by Polemic*, pp. 86–104, 69–81. James pronounces himself convinced that
some papists, 'especially our forefathers', may be saved and that he thinks it 'crueltie of Puritanes
worthy of fire, that will admit no salvation to any Papists': *Political Writings*, p. 152.

the Israelites had in the red sea, in the wilderness, among the enemies' (f. 10ᵛ). This comparison between England and Israel (both favoured by God, both ungrateful, both threatened with punishment) is the basis of the Paul's Cross 'Jeremiad' or 'national warning sermon', a sermon of exhortation that uses the example of Israel to rouse the English auditors out of their religious complacency. In this sermon, we see an exhortation to thankfulness (characteristic of the political anniversary sermon) being superimposed on a national warning sermon.

A similar, though less overt, mixing of sermon genres can be found in the Gunpowder Plot sermons of Martin Fotherby, Robert Tynley, and John Boys. Tynley's sermon shows its generic mix on the title page: in the sermon 'are examined divers passages of that lewde English libell, written by a Prophane Fugitive, against the Apologie for the Oath of Allegeance'. The libel in question is Robert Persons, *The Judgment of a Catholicke English-man* of 1608.[72] Tynley's sermon belongs to the 'confutational' genre, in which the hearers are warned against false doctrine and its teachers. The confutational sermon concentrated on presenting Catholic activists as deceitful, and did so by exposing lies and errors in their work. This demonstrates that they are unreliable guides on Christian doctrine. (This will be described in greater detail in Chapter 6.) The Gunpowder Plot commemorated in this sermon is one of the pieces of evidence (along with the practice of equivocation and the Marian persecutions) for the duplicity and cruelty of the Catholic Church and its defenders. Having reminded his hearers of the evils of popery, Tynley can make his contradiction of Person's text relatively swift. What is almost forgotten, however, is the usual purpose of the political anniversary sermon. Two pages before the end of the printed sermon, Tynley reminds himself and his hearers that 'there remaine yet two points unhandled: the one, of the deliverance of the Church from her enemies: the other, of the duetie of praise & thanksgiving to be performed for this deliverance'.[73] Tynley manages to handle both points, although rather briefly.

John Boys and Martin Fotherby divert from the theme of commemoration and thanksgiving to engage in inter-Protestant disputes. The second edition of John Boys's *An Exposition of the Last Psalme* (1615) advertises that it includes a 'Short Apologie for our Holy Daies in the Church of England'.[74] Boys' text (Psalm 150, 'O praise God in his holiness, etc') provides him with an argument for the Church's holy days and their liturgies. The wickedness of the Gunpowder Plot is taken as read, and becomes the basis for an argument defending 5 November as a holy day. Boys acknowledges that his sermon pulls in two directions: he writes that 'were

---

[72] The full title and running title make clearer the identification with the 'Catholike letter' referred to by Tynley: *The Judgment of a Catholicke English-man, living in Banishment for his Religion, Written to his Private Friend in England, Concerninge a late Booke set forth, and entituled; Triplici Nodo, Triplex Cuneus, or An Apologie for the Oath of Allegiance* (St. Omar, 1608), ARCR 628. The running title is 'A letter of a Catholicke touching the new Oath of Allegiance'.

[73] Robert Tynley, *Two Learned Sermons* (1609) STC² 24472, p. 26.

[74] This is STC² 3465. The title page says that the sermon is being 'joyned to the Festivals as a Short Apologie for our Holy Daies in the Church of England', the 'Festivals' being Boys' *An Exposition of the Festival Epistles and Gospels used in our English Liturgie. Together with the Reason why the Church did Chuse the Same* (1613), STC² 3462.

I not (according to the text and the time) foreward to prosecute the gunpowder men' he would 'take up the bucklers against idle *Novelists* utterly condemning the *festivals of holy Saints* established in our Church by good order of law'. But Boys is not particularly 'foreward' in prosecuting the gunpowder men, and spends more time defending the commemoration of 5 November.[75] Martin Fotherby is also concerned to defend the established Church from enemies within. His text is Psalm 81:1–5 ('Sing joyfully to God our strength', etc.), and Fotherby opens his sermon by treating his sermon as a call to 'jubilation', which word he interprets in minute detail. The Gunpowder Plot is one occasion for such fulsome rejoicing, and the Church is right to commemorate such deliverances with 'jubilation'. Fotherby's interpretation has shown 'jubilation' to mean 'the Ecclesiasticall psalmodie and musicke of the church, . . . *In Hymnes, and Psalmes, and Spirituall songs*'. Fotherby's sermon has become an argument in favour of church music: giving thanks for deliverance from the Gunpowder Plot need not be argued, and serves instead as the premise for a defence of 'hymnes, and psalms, and spiritual songs' against the 'uncleane and filthie birds' who call for an unneeded further reformation and by whose 'jarring sounds, as it were by the yelling of Mewes, and the scritching of Owles, the holy musicke of our church is greatly disturbed'.[76]

We can argue, therefore, that the denunciation of the plotters and the commemoration of the Plot is not the preacher's real aim in these sermons: that is taken for granted. Because he can assume that his hearers share his conviction that the Gunpowder Plot was unprecedentedly wicked, the preacher can use that assumption as the basis for an argument on something else, such as a defence of the English Church and its liturgies. 'Anti-popery' is the glue that sticks these sermons together, and when anti-popery became a politically sensitive subject, the Gunpowder Plot sermon began to suffer a decline. It required all the skill that John Donne had mastered to preach the Paul's Cross Gunpowder Plot sermon in the year of the 1622 *Directions for Preachers* and its prohibition of 'railing against' Catholics. He succeeded in that sermon by maintaining a stark distinction between James's Catholic subjects and the Catholic Church's treasonous resistance theory, a distinction that we last saw in James's speech to parliament in 1605. Notwithstanding the skill and care taken with its composition, this sermon was not printed immediately after its delivery (although Donne seems to have planned for print publication).[77] No Gunpowder Plot sermon from Paul's Cross was printed in the remainder of James's reign. There was, however, a marked increase in the

[75] Boys, *Exposition of the Late Psalme*, *STC²* 3464, pp. 12–15.

[76] Fotherby, *The Third Sermon*, in *Foure Sermons* (1608) pp. 69, 84–5.

[77] On this complex and subtle sermon, see Jeanne Shami, *John Donne and Conformity in Crisis in the Late Jacobean Pulpit* (Cambridge: D. S. Brewer, 2003), esp. pp. 130–2. The existence of a presentation copy of this sermon in the Royal Manuscripts of the British Museum (discovered by Shami) demonstrates that Donne had expected the King to authorize the publication of the sermon, which did not happen. The sermon was first printed in the *Fifty Sermons* of 1649: see the introduction to Jeanne Shami, *John Donne's 1622 Gunpowder Plot Sermon: A Parallel-text Edition* (Pittsburgh: Duquesne University Press, 1996). My 'John Donne as a Conventional Paul's Cross Preacher' (in David Colclough (ed.), *Professional Donne* (Cambridge: D. S. Brewer, 2003), pp. 159–78) also considers this sermon.

publication of Gowrie Conspiracy sermons from Paul's Cross. Only one of the sermons extant was printed before 1622 (Milward's *Jacob's Great Day of Trouble and Deliverance* from 1607, printed in 1610). Thereafter, the sermons for 5 August 1622, 1623, and 1624 were printed within a year of being preached.[78] This cluster of publications suggests that the Gowrie Conspiracy had become a more attractive, because less politically sensitive, subject on which to preach. The preacher made the same exhortations to thanksgiving and could make use of the same vehement rhetoric to do so, but as anti-popery was not part of his theme, he would not be found guilty of 'railing' against Roman Catholics.

CAROLINE NEGLECT

The disappearance of printed Gunpowder Plot sermons from Paul's Cross continued after Charles I's accession: we know of only one Gunpowder Plot sermon preached at Paul's Cross after Donne's sermon of 1622 and it was not printed. That sermon was preached on 5 November 1631 by Joseph Naylor, then a Fellow of Sidney Sussex College, Cambridge, and later Archdeacon of Northumberland and chaplain to Bishop Thomas Morton.[79] Naylor's sermon has all of the characteristics of the political anniversary sermon. The text (Psalm 124:5–7) was chosen by Naylor as one 'sutable & correspondent to the nature of the day, wherein you have brieflie but expreslie sett forth the livelie Images & representations of all these 3: *Danger: Deliverance: Gratulation*' (f.4ʳ). Naylor emphasizes the many examples of providential deliverances that England can boast. He tells his hearers:

if the Scriptures were silent of examples for our purpose (which yet nothwithstanding are vocall & plentifull almost in everie page) yet it was but our reflectinge upon our owne *Chronicles* & in them upon a paire of our latest Governour that never to be parallelld *Paragon Queene* & our late deceased *Pacificall* King. And in their lives may we runn & read, the livinge *Characters* & pregnant testimonies of *Gods powerful Providence*. (f. 28ʳ)

Most characteristic of sermons on the Gunpowder Plot is the virulence of the anti-Catholic language: God delivered them from 'those *Snares of Hell, that Master-peece of Satan*, that *Beelzebub of Treasons*' (f. 6ʳ). The plotters were 'a generation of vipers: so drunken & intoxicate with the verie dregges of the cupp of *Babilon*: so full of *Romish Jesuiticall* poison' that they could plan such a terrible act (f. 25ᵛ).

[78] Samuel Purchas, *The Kings Towre* (1623), *STC²* 20502, preached in 1622; Barten Holyday, *A Sermon preached at Pauls Crosse* (1626), *STC²* 13615, preached in 1623; Thomas Adams, *The Temple. A Sermon preached at Pauls Crosse the fifth of August 1624* (1624), *STC²* 129.

[79] The sermon is St Paul's Cathedral Library MS 52.D60.01, 'Dr Joseph Naylor at Pauls Crosse on the 5 November'. On f. 47ᵛ, Nailor says that the Plot happened 'this day 26 yeares nowe gone', making 5 November 1631 the date of the sermon's delivery. On Naylor, see Venn, *Alumni Cantabrigienses*, 10 vols (Cambridge: Cambridge University Press, 1922–58) and William Hutchinson, *The History and Antiquities of the County Palatine of Durham*, 2 vols (Durham, 1823), vol. 2, p. 227.

There is nothing unusual about this sermon in itself; the only unusual thing is that a young clergymen looking for a benefice (Naylor would become Rector of Howick in 1632) would choose not to publish a Paul's Cross sermon preached on a prestigious occasion. David Cressy has shown that commemoration of 5 November 'began to lose its unifying character' in Charles's reign. Puritan preachers 'used 5 November as an occasion to emphasize the dangers of creeping popery and the necessity of further reformation;...the Caroline regime sought to muffle the commemoration'. Naylor was no puritan (indeed he criticized the '*Puritanicall New-England Sectaries*' in the sermon, f. 40ʳ), but his brand of anti-popery was unwelcome, on this occasion in particular. But there is a similar decline in the records for other political anniversary sermons after 1625, which points to a new attitude to Paul's Cross and not just to 5 November. We know of three, possibly four, political anniversary sermons from Paul's Cross that were published in Charles's reign: the Accession Day sermons of 1631, 1639, 1640, and 1642.[80] The concentration of sermons around the years of the Bishops' Wars and the outbreak of the English Civil War merits our attention.

It was not that the Caroline authorities discouraged commemoration of the king's accession: the canons of 1640 were the first that ordered 'all manner of persons within the church of England' to 'celebrate and keep the morning of the said day in coming diligently and reverently unto their parish church or chapel at the time of prayer'.[81] But the Laudian clergy were more prescriptive than their Elizabethan predecessors about how the accession was to be celebrated: the people were to go to their parish churches and hear the liturgy established for the purpose (although the canons did allow for a sermon as part of the service). Stand-alone sermons like those at Paul's Cross did not fit into the pattern approved by the hierarchy, and so were neglected. The tradition of having an extra sermon on the day of political anniversaries was one that Laud and Juxon (bishops of London and appointers to Paul's Cross) were not obliged to maintain, and it is possible that they did not demand that preachers be appointed for 27 March and 5 November if those dates did not fall on a Sunday. Of the three extant Caroline accession sermons, two were preached in a year on which 27 March fell on a Sunday. (Henry King's 1640 sermon is the exception.) Alternatively, it may be that the sermons were preached (Joseph Naylor preached his Gunpowder Plot sermon on a Saturday), but

---

[80] Henry Valentine's *God Save the King* (1639), *STC*² 24575, was preached '*in St Paul's Church the 27th of March 1639*'. By this date, the outdoor pulpit at Paul's Cross was no longer in use and Accession Day sermons would have been preached in the cathedral choir in the morning. The printed copy of Valentine's sermon does not say that it was 'appointed for the Cross', as is the case with other 'Paul's Cross' sermons preached between 1634 and 1643. Valentine's sermon may have been preached as part of the cathedral's own sermon provision, although their sermons were usually in the afternoon and we have no records of Accession Day sermons being preached regularly in the cathedral. Valentine had no known connection to the cathedral. For these reasons, it seems likely, but is not certain, that this sermon was part of the Paul's Cross series.

[81] 'Constitutions and Canons Ecclesiastical, ... M.DC.XL', in Edward Cardwell (ed.), *Synodalia, A Collection of Articles of Religion, Canons, and Proceedings of Convocation in the Province of Canterbury, from the year 1547 to the year 1717*, 2 vols (Oxford, 1842), vol. 1, pp. 392–3.

that the preacher was discouraged from having the sermons printed.[82] This neglect of Paul's Cross sermons on political anniversaries lost the regime a valuable forum from which to convince the London population of its good intentions.

It was not until 1638, with the outbreak of the Bishops' Wars, that the royal authorities seem to have remembered the potential of political anniversary sermons for encouraging loyalty and obedience to the regime. By then it seems that Caroline preachers had forgotten the conventions that had been established in the previous reigns for preaching on these occasions. Although we must work with a small sample of sermons, it can be shown that the Caroline political anniversary sermons delivered at Paul's Cross (or, after 1634, in the cathedral choir) fail to set the correct exhortatory tone. They do not deliver a message of shared thanksgiving to their hearers, a message of thanksgiving within which prescriptions to political obedience might be made without 'wresting' Scripture. It is noteworthy that in two of these three sermons, we also see a drift away from the method of constructing political sermons that dominated the Cross in James's reign. In the Accession Day sermons of 1631, by William Laud, and of 1642, by Richard Gardiner,[83] the 'explication' of the biblical text is not kept structurally separate from the 'application' of the sermon's teachings to its hearers. This makes the points of comparison between biblical history and contemporary politics less clear, and muddles the hearers' sense of how biblical examples and recent history were being linked. (Those links, it must be remembered, were the best proof of the preacher's argument in any sermon.)

William Laud's Accession Day of 1631 was preached on Psalm 72:1 ('Give the King thy Judgements O God, And thy Righteousnesse unto the Kings son'), but the text was 'explicated' in a way that excluded his hearers. The text is said to be a prayer by King David for himself and Solomon, and so the auditory are made to overhear a conversation between God and king. Laud does address himself to his hearers, but in doing so, he uses the second person, as if the lessons of the biblical text did not apply to him:

And here it is fit for you a little to take a view of your own happinesse, and to blesse God for it: for you live under a King, that keepes his Lawes in his life. (13)

Previous Paul's Cross preachers on political anniversaries invariably used the first person plural: all were obliged to thank God for the benefits of good government.

---

[82] There is some evidence that the sermons were preached, but it is difficult to interpret. The City Cash Books, which are extant for 1633 and later, record annual payments to preachers who delivered sermons at Paul's Cross, and the number of preachers paid varies between fifty-four and fifty-six. Assuming that there were fifty-one sermons on Sundays (excluding Easter Sunday), and one sermon on Good Friday, that still leaves payment for two or more 'extra' sermons each year. But the records do not detail when the preachers being paid had delivered their sermons (so we can't be sure whether the 'extra' sermons include an Accession Day sermon), and we have no records for the period before Laud was bishop of London with which we might compare these figures: City of London, London Metropolitan Archive, City Cash Book 1, ff. 143^r, 238^r; City Cash Book 2, ff. 45^v, 135^v, 212^v; City Cash Book 3, ff. 47^v, 141^v; City Cash Book 4, ff. 45^v, 141^v.

[83] Laud, *A Commemoration of King Charles his Inauguration* (1645) Wing L.579. The royal coat of arms is printed on the verso of the first leaf, suggesting the sermon was printed by order of the royalists. Richard Gardiner, *A Sermon appointed for Saint Pauls Crosse* (1642), Wing G231.

Near the final exhortation of his sermon, Laud states that he will not 'break out into any large panegyricks, and praises, no, not of a gracious King'. Rather, he has 'come hether to preach a kind of Gospel to you, even glad tidings, that God in the mercies of Christ (whose the Gospel is) hath given you a wise, and just, and religious King' (p. 30). Yet Laud has preached a panegyric: he has made the praise of the King the main purpose of his oration, rather than the God-given mercy that such a king represents for his hearers.

Henry King's more successful Accession Day sermon of 1640 also praises the King far more than it pronounces the traditional themes of obedience and thanksgiving. The hearers' duties of obedience and thanksgiving are dispatched in about a page (pp. 38–40), and the remainder of the sermon's 'application' of its biblical text concerns the King, whose virtues are described in great detail. King justifies this by citing the extraordinary virtues of Charles, which he has observed personally (pp. 56–8), and begins by acknowledging that 'this is no place to give Titles to Men, but to give Honour to God' (p. 56). But he has, nonetheless, forgotten to direct his message to his hearers and instead shown how his biblical text relates to a monarch who is not in the auditory. In effect, both Laud and King preach *at* their hearers about the king, rather than preaching *to* them on the religious duties of obedience and thankfulness for a stable regime. It is worth noting that both sermons assume an auditory unwilling to hear praises of the king. In King's case, where the Bishops' Wars made talk of peace and unity difficult,[84] this might be expected. In Laud's case, however, it seems to be more a matter of rhetorical tone-deafness. He begins his sermon by saying that 'the Age is so bad, they will not indure a good King to be commended for danger of flattery, I hope I shall offend none by praying for the King' (p. 4), an unmistakable insult to the hearers that would hardly capture their good will.

The extent to which Caroline preachers on the accession at Paul's Cross had lost the ability to communicate with their hearers is evident from the sermon delivered there by Richard Gardiner on 27 March 1642, barely three weeks since the passing of the Militia Ordinance. By the time the sermon was preached, Charles I was in York. According to S. R. Gardiner, 28 March, the day when the Parliament voted to imprison some of the Kentish petitioners, was the moment 'if any one moment can be selected as that in which the Civil War became inevitable'.[85] Richard Gardiner was a Royalist and a Laudian,[86] and he was

---

[84] King refers to the 'cement which combined' England and Scotland as 'now grown loose' and that 'distance appeares to make them look like two againe' and he prays that God may 'in his good time close the rupture, and as our Gracious Soveraigne hath by all meanes endeavoured their re-uniting . . . so in the returne to their obedience unto him, they may be rendred one with us againe': *A Sermon preached at St Pauls March 27 1640* (1640), *STC²* 14970, p. 44.

[85] Michael Braddick, *God's Fury, England's Fire: A New History of the English Civil Wars* (London: Allen Lane, 2008), p. 210; S. R. Gardiner, *History of England from the Accession of James I to the Outbreak of the Civil War, 1603–1642*, 10 vols (1883–4; repr. New York: AMS Press, 1965), vol. 10, pp. 178–82, p. 182.

[86] Gardiner dedicated this and another sermon (preached on Act Sunday in Oxford, 1622), to his patron Edward Sackville, Earl of Dorset, a Royalist who had stopped attending the House of Lords earlier in March. Gardiner also dedicated a Latin sermon preached in Oxford in 1631 to Laud: Richard Gardiner, *A Sermon preached at St Maries on Oxford on Act Sunday last in the After-noone 1622* (1622), *STC²* 11568; idem, *Concio ad Clerum habita in Templo Beatae Mariae Oxon* (1631), *STC²* 11560. His

speaking before a deeply divided Corporation: the Common Council elections of December 1641 had transferred power from the conservative aldermen, many of them Royalists, to their more radical opponents, but this shift in power would not be complete until 11 July 1642 when Lord Mayor Richard Gurney was impeached.[87] The task facing Gardiner that day was certainly not easy, but in carrying it out, he failed to observe the conventions that had worked so well in the past.

The text of the sermon is 1 Timothy 2:1–2 ('I exhort therefore that first of all supplications, prayers, intercessions, and giving of thankes be made for all men: For Kings and for all that are in authority, that we may leade a quiet and peaceable life, in all godlinesse, and honesty'). This text had been the basis on which Thomas Holland had built his defence of Accession Day celebrations in *Panegyris D. Elizabethae* (1601); John Whitgift made a digression on the same subject with the same text in his Paul's Cross Accession Day sermon of 1583, and it was the text used by John White in his Accession Day sermon of 1615.[88] Gardiner returns to an established proof-text for preaching on the accession, but he does not take from it the overarching structure of exhortation to obedience and thanksgiving that we find in those earlier sermons. His sermon picks up different topics with his handling of each section of the biblical text, and the overall impression this creates is of a disjointed oration whose themes could not be incorporated into a coherent 'explication' of the biblical text.

Gardiner's text asks for 'prayers and supplications' but he loses sight of this once he has passed the section on 'prayers for all men', and instead deals with issues of obedience, resistance, and mutual obligations in the commonwealth. Gardiner is different to all other Paul's Cross preachers that we know of in that he chooses to discuss the monarch's duties to his subjects: he details both the king's 'duty' and his 'dues' (p. 17). Among these duties are the defence of religion and of the fundamental laws of the kingdom, which, Gardiner pointedly remarks, 'his majesty declares he doth, and will doe' (p. 16). There is slippage here between Gardiner's use of 'king' as an abstract political notion and as referring to Charles I. What began as abstract doctrine on the reasons for praying for the king (the benefits of monarchical government) drifts into a consideration of Charles I's understanding of the constitution. Something similar happens when Gardiner discusses taxation (another subject usually absent from these sermons). The king, he says, has a duty to safeguard the people, and the people in return 'should yeeld all subsidiary helpes that tend to the advancement of the honour, and glory of the King' (p. 17). If the king's own funds fall short of what is needed for the public good and his own

livings were sequestered during the war: Newton E. Key, 'Gardiner, Richard (1590/91–1670)', *Oxford Dictionary of National Biography* (Oxford: Oxford University Press, 2004), online edn., Jan. 2008 <http://www.oxforddnb.com/view/article/10360>, accessed 13 May 2008.

[87] Valerie Pearl, *London and the Outbreak of the Puritan Revolution: City Government and National Politics, 1625–43* (Oxford: Oxford University Press, 1961), pp. 132–57.

[88] Holland, *Panegyris D. Elizabethae*, sigs a3ʳ, I3ʳ; [Whitgift], *A Most Godly and Learned Sermon*, sigs B6ʳ–B7ᵛ; John White, *A Sermon preached at Paules Crosse upon the foure and twentieth of March, 1615* in *Two sermons* (1615), *STC²* 25392.

dignity 'it is naturall that supply be adminstred to him from inferiour members' (p. 18). Again, Gardiner makes an appeal to the good will of the hearers:

And now let me entreate that none impose a meaning farre wide from my drift. It was never in my heart, or tongue, any way to infringe the proper rights, liberties, and proprieties of the people: I move only for a voluntary, free aide, or assistance. It were a great disservice to the King to inflame his Prerogative to the evacuation of the Subjects *Right*; both must be kept entire to keepe up the King, and Kingdome. (p. 18)

Gardiner needs that good will because he has moved from discussing theories of monarch to a definite engagement with current political disputes (pp. 18–19).

In all this, Gardiner is (and a preacher should not be) a 'long way from his text'[89]: his discussion of Charles's actions as king is meant to form part of a discussion of the nature and benefits of monarchy, which in turn is meant to explain why the biblical text encourages prayers for kings. Gardiner's discussion of Charles's record has no place in the 'explication' of that biblical text; it should belong to the 'application' of the scriptural text to present problems. In short, Gardiner is not maintaining a clear distinction between his interpretation of the biblical text and his 'application' of that text to the political problems of his day. Consequently, the sermon has drifted into political controversy, and has failed to integrate the praise of the king within the framework of thanksgiving for his reign that Jacobean preachers had perfected.

It is only when Gardiner returns to his text to discuss the words 'a quiet and peaceable life' that he begins to refer his arguments directly to his hearers. He tells them that political disunity is the enemy of peace, and that 'domestical foes' of two sorts, the papists and the 'new fangled *Sectaries*', threaten the peace (pp. 25–6). But then Gardiner digresses unnecessarily onto a very divisive subject. He expresses his wish to 'discharge my whole conscience' about images in churches (p. 30), a topic not invited by his text. Again, there is an appeal for the good will of the hearers, followed by a defence of images (of '*sacred* stories, and some undoubted Saints'), not for '*adoration*' but 'as *Ornaments, or Historicall Commemoratives*' (p. 30). Following the Laudians' campaign of reintroducing images to demonstrate 'the beauty of holiness', Gardiner's ostensibly eirenic gesture would undoubtedly have appeared provocative.[90]

In his final exhortation, the hearers are asked for 'their supplications, prayers, Intercessions, and thanksgivings to magnify the *Almighty*' who has given them 'a renowned *King*, who is an indulgent, & carefull father of the Church, and Commonwealth, a constant, *Exemplary Encourager,* and Advancer of *all godlinesse,*

---

[89] William Chappell said hearers are liable to say 'specially in reproofs . . . *he strayed farre from his Text*': *The Preacher* (1656), Wing C1957, p. 12.

[90] See Margaret Aston, 'Puritans and Iconoclasm, 1560–1660', in Christopher Durston and Jacqueline Eales (eds), *The Culture of English Puritanism, 1560–1700* (London: Macmillan, 1996), pp. 92–121; Kenneth Fincham and Nicholas Tyacke, *Altars Restored: The Changing Face of English Religious Worship, 1547–c.1700* (Oxford: Oxford University Press, 2007); Graham Parry, *The Arts of the Anglican Counter-Reformation: Glory, Laud and Honour* (Woodbridge: Boydell and Brewer, 2006).

and honesty' (p. 34). Even this final exhortation demonstrates the failure of Gardiner's sermon. The praise of the king has overwhelmed the ostensible subject of the sentence (exhortation to pray for the king). In the circumstances, it is not surprising that Gardiner should mount a defence of Charles and his government, but his failure to integrate political and religious themes, to combine a defence of the king's actions with the religious duties enjoined by his biblical text, is revealing of the Laudians' failure to make good use of Paul's Cross. The methods for integrating scriptural precepts and political obligations used by Elizabethan and Jacobean preachers were ignored by these men. The more overtly propagandistic model for political preaching that they adopted was a failure, as shown by the abrupt shifts in tone and argument of Gardiner's sermon, the last such political anniversary sermon from Paul's Cross.

6

Preaching against the Church of Rome:
Anti-Catholicism and Anti-Popery

In the past, Reformation history was preoccupied with arguments about whether Protestantism was naturalized in England 'from above' or 'below', rapidly or slowly, as Christopher Haigh put it. But the work of scholars like Haigh and Eamon Duffy, which has revealed the resilience of traditional religious beliefs and practices, has also required Reformation scholars to take a closer look at the assumptions they make about the means by which the Reformation was effected.[1] Particularly relevant to this study is the challenge that Christopher Haigh has issued to those of us who lazily take for granted sixteenth- and seventeenth-century preachers' assertions about the efficacy of preaching in converting the English to Protestantism. In *English Reformations,* Haigh wrote that Protestant ministers like George Gifford, Arthur Dent, and William Perkins 'seemed to propagate too intellectual and demanding a religion, above the capacities of ordinary people'.[2]

Preachers at Paul's Cross had certain advantages in this respect: the auditory was very mixed, including some who were sufficiently educated to follow abstract doctrine. Some of the ordinary hearers may have already encountered Protestant ideas, which were circulating in London since the early 1520s.[3] Or they may have witnessed some of the events in which Catholicism was discredited, such as the exposure of the Blood of Hales or the Maid of Kent. But none of these things demonstrates that the preachers at Paul's Cross were successful in reconciling their hearers to the Elizabethan Settlement. Any attempt to measure that success would appear doomed to failure, because of our inability to judge, at this distance in time, what the auditors believed. A second problem is one of definition: if we could

---

[1] Christopher Haigh, 'The Recent Historiography of the English Reformation', *Historical Journal,* 25 (1982), 995–1007. See, in particular, Haigh, *English Reformations: Religion, Politics and Society under the Tudors* (Oxford: Clarendon Press, 1993); Eamon Duffy, *The Stripping of the Altars: Traditional Religion in England, c.1400–c.1580* (New Haven: Yale University Press, 1992).

[2] Haigh, *English Reformations,* p. 283. See also Haigh, *The Plain Man's Pathways to Heaven: Kinds of Christianity in Post-Reformation England, 1570–1640* (Oxford: Oxford University Press, 2007). Andrew Pettegree's account of Reformation preaching across Europe gives a more positive assessment of its effectiveness: *Reformation and the Culture of Persuasion* (Cambridge: Cambridge University Press, 2005), pp. 10–39.

[3] Susan Brigden, *London and the Reformation* (Oxford: Clarendon Press, 1989), pp. 106–18.

discover what the auditors at Paul's Cross believed about God and his Church, we would then need to define whether that was sufficiently 'orthodox' to designate them as 'Protestant' or 'Catholic'.

In what follows, no attempt is made to recover what the auditors at Paul's Cross believed; instead, the discussion will centre on what the preachers assumed about the confessional identities of their auditors, and this is something that can be discovered by examining the ways in which the preachers addressed their auditory. We cannot prove that Paul's Cross preachers were successful in converting the population of London to a body of Christian doctrines that we can define as 'Protestant'. We can, however, gauge something of the religious identity (albeit nothing of the religious beliefs) of the hearers at Paul's Cross by charting changes in the ways that their preachers addressed them. The preachers at Paul's Cross developed flexible methods for preaching on the doctrinal and ecclesiological changes brought in by Elizabeth's first parliament and convocation, and they modulated their preaching to reflect their hearers' acceptance of those changes. While we cannot discover whether the auditors at Paul's Cross were 'Protestant' or 'Catholic', we can say whether the preachers addressed them as a group that accepted the term 'Protestant' as a description of their confessional allegiances. Where preachers in the 1560s spoke to their auditors as people sympathetic to traditional devotional practices, after the 1580s they addressed their hearers as people who consider themselves Protestants, and Catholics (foreign or domestic) are assumed to be absent. I argue that the target of anti-Catholic preaching, and its purpose, changes between 1560 and 1630, and in that change we see a reflection of the perceived religious loyalties of the population that the preachers at Paul's Cross addressed.

The sermon genre used at Paul's Cross to make doctrinal differences intelligible to a lay audience was called the 'confutational' sermon, and the Paul's Cross confutational sermons now extant provide a coherent sample for examining the changes in tone and target of anti-Catholic preaching over the period 1560–1630. The confutational sermon was not designed to teach doctrine, but to warn against heresy. As delivered at Paul's Cross, it was used to convince the hearers that the Catholic clergy were unreliable spiritual guides, and this was demonstrated by their espousal of false doctrine for self-interested reasons. Consequently, preachers chose arguments that made the differences between the English and the Roman Catholic Churches clearest (rather than necessarily most fundamental). A close examination of anti-Catholic sermons demonstrates that the Paul's Cross preachers knew their audience, and changed the form of their anti-Catholic arguments to suit the changing beliefs and allegiances of their hearers. We must not look only at what the preachers say about Catholicism per se, but rather at how they position their hearers with respect to Catholicism: as misguided followers, as potential backsliders, or as stalwart opponents.

THE 'CHALLENGE' CONTROVERSY AND THE CONFUTATIONAL SERMON

It is no exaggeration to say that one sermon dominated anti-Catholic preaching at Paul's Cross in the first decade of Elizabeth's reign, and that was John Jewel's 'Challenge' sermon, first delivered on 26 November 1559 and again on 31 March 1560.[4] Many of the arguments from the 'Challenge' sermon were used by Jewel in his *Apologia Ecclesiae Anglicanae* of 1562, and not surprisingly the two controversies became enmeshed when Thomas Harding responded to both of these works. Sermons by Jewel and Alexander Nowell (who joined in the controversy on the *Apologia*) against Harding meant that the debate returned to Paul's Cross until at least 1566.

A. C. Southern called this 'the great controversy', an appellation well deserved when one considers how long the debate ran, how many writers were involved, and the stature of many of those contributors on both sides.[5] And yet many scholars have taken a negative view of the 'Challenge', judging its methods unlikely to succeed with lay readers.[6] Scholars of an older generation were particularly uneasy about the *ad hominem* arguments used by both sides, and sometimes declared the 'winner' of the debate on the basis of anachronistic assumptions about 'gentleman-ly' behaviour in debate.[7]

These standards are not just anachronistic, but inappropriate because they mistake the audience of these works. The sermons and books produced in this controversy were not aimed at professional theologians who could judge the relative

---

[4] John Jewel, *The Copie of a Sermon Pronounced by the Byshop of Salisburie at Paules Crosse*, part 2 of *The True Copies of the Letters betwene the Reverend Father in God John Bisshop of Sarum and D. Cole* ([1560]), *STC²* 14612.

[5] A. C. Southern counts sixty-four exchanges in the controversy: *English Recusant Prose, 1559–1582* (London: Sands, 1950), pp. 60–6.

[6] Christopher Haigh describes the 'Challenge' controversy as 'an interminable literary wrangle' (*English Reformations*, p. 254). Gary W. Jenkins describes Jewel's *Replie* as a 'tedious and pedantic reponse' to Harding's 'almost equally tedious and pedantic' work: *John Jewel and the English National Church: The Dilemma of an Erastian Reformer* (Aldershot: Ashgate, 2006), p. 73. Some scholars have been more positive: Michael Questier's sees Jewel's 'challenge' as being a successful polemical strategy at first, but argues that the subsequent exchanges with Harding made it impossible to repeat this success: *Conversion, Politics and Religion in England, 1580–1625* (Cambridge: Cambridge University Press, 1996), pp. 15–20. W. J. Torrance Kirby views the 'Challenge' sermon as having 'remarkable significance' for the formation of religious identity, and the subsequent controversy as 'one of the epic confrontations of the English Reformation', not least because it 'weaved together' disputes over the sacraments with those over the supremacy: 'The Public Sermon: Paul's Cross and the Culture of Persuasion in England, 1534–1570', *Renaissance and Reformation / Renaissance et Réforme*, 31(1) (2008), 3–29, pp. 14–22.

[7] For example, W. M. Southgate asserts that 'in the heat of controversy Harding was not as level-headed as Jewel' and that Jewel's 'raised eyebrow was far more effective than Harding's bludgeoning': *John Jewel and the Problem of Doctrinal Authority* (Cambridge, MA: Harvard University Press, 1962), pp. 87–8. John E. Booty offers a better sense of what was at stake for Harding and Jewel than the nineteenth-century scholars he quotes, but he continues the tradition of seeing Jewel as more 'restrained' than Harding: *John Jewel as Apologist of the Church of England* (London: SPCK, 1963), pp. 62–81, 124–5. Gary W. Jenkins is the only writer on the 'Challenge' to criticize Jewel (as being 'less interested in argument and more interested in scoring rhetorical points' than his Catholic respondents): *John Jewel and the English National Church*, pp. 73–85, p. 74, pp. 123–49.

merits of the Patristic sources cited on both sides. The contributors to the 'Challenge' controversy must be seen as addressing each other only in a formal sense: the real audience was the English laity, as readers and hearer at Paul's Cross, and it was their conviction that both sides strove to gain. The 'Challenge' sermon, and the texts to which it gave rise, were designed to convince the hearers to accept Elizabeth's settlement and abandon Catholic practices. It is a sermon whose primary aim is the conformity of its hearers to the new Church.

That the 'Challenge' was intended to counter the laity's continued adherence to the Mass becomes clearer when we examine the sermon as a whole. Introducing his text (1 Corinthians 11:23, 'I have recyved of the lord, that thing whiche I also have delivered unto you: that is, that the Lord Jesus in the nyghte that he was betrayed, tooke breade, etc'), Jewel suggests a parallel with recent English history. St Paul admonishes the Corinthians for the errors that they had allowed to creep into the celebration of the Eucharist and offers advice on preventing such corruptions: 'he calleth them back, to the first originall, and to the institution of Christe from when they were fallen' (sig. A3^v). This advice is now pertinent to the English people because the Holy Communion has been restored to the same order that was delivered by Christ and practised 'for the space of fyve or sixe hundred yeares, throughout all the whole Catholick church of Christ without exception' (sig. A7^v). Nonetheless, some people still 'unadvisedly, and wilfully runne headlong to the Masse: of a good zeale (I hope) but not accordyng unto knowledge' (sigs A7^v–A8^r). Jewel says he will explain why the Mass has been forsaken, and why those who 'delite in it' are misled.

Jewel begins by discussing the fact that holy things can be abused. The sacrament can be abused, for example, in being used to 'purge' oneself of a scandalous accusation. Jewel then describes other practices that he labels as abuses but which Catholics did not consider corrupt, such as adoration of the host. Jewel emphasizes the threat of idolatry involved in Catholic devotions to the consecrated elements of the Eucharist, a threat unknown to the laypeople piously attending the Mass (sigs C6^v–C8^r). But Jewel's purpose is not to explain debates over Eucharist theology here, because only the Catholic position is discussed in detail. The effect of his one-sided description of Catholic practices is to make one group of clerics (the Catholics) appear to offer complex arguments for dangerous teachings; the others seem to assert a simple truth. Where the Catholics wrest Scripture, the Protestants 'brynge you nothynge but Gods holy worde, which is a sure rocke to builde upon, and will never flete, or shrynke' (sig. E2^v). The comparison, therefore, is not between doctrines: it is between teachers of doctrine. And only one group of teachers is said to bring 'Gods holy worde' to the people.

It is from this comparison of Catholic and Protestant teachers that the 'challenge' is launched. The printed copy reports the version delivered on 31 March 1560, the third time the sermon had been preached, the second time at the Cross.[8] It contains

---

[8] The sermon was delivered at court before the Queen and Privy Council at Whitehall in the outdoor 'Preaching Place' on 17 March 1560. This was the third Sunday in Lent, the season in which court sermons were most regular. The 'Preaching Place' was a more open venue than the Chapel Royal, facilitating greater numbers of non-elite hearers: Peter McCullough, *Sermons at Court: Politics and*

Jewel's repetition of the initial challenge and his augmentation of it from fifteen to twenty-seven articles. It also gives a sense of the original 'challenge' being much talked of, and the impact it must have made by its apparent confidence and deceptive scope:

I remember, I layed out then here before you, a number of thynges that are nowe in controversie, whereunto our adversaryes wyll not yelde. And I sayde, perhappes boldlye, as it myghte then seeme to summe man. But as I my selfe, and the learned of our adversaries themselves do wel know, sincerely and truly, that none of all them, that thys daye stande agaynste us, are hable, or shall ever be able to prove agaynst us, any one of all those pointes, eyther by the scriptures, or by example of the primitive Church, or by the olde doctrours, or by the auncyent general councelles. (sigs F5ᵛ–F6ʳ)

Jewel might well be confident: the strength of this challenge lay in the exactness with which the articles were defined: all were the product of medieval scholastic theology or medieval devotional habits. For example, Jewel did not ask for proof of the real presence of Christ in the Eucharist, as he tells Henry Cole, because 'sum colour or shadow of the doctours' might be produced by the Catholic side.[9] Instead, he demanded Patristic statements that Christ's body is 'substantially, corporally, carnally, or naturally' present in the host and that only the 'accidents' of bread and wine persist after the consecration. Terms such as 'accidents' do not pre-date the elaboration of Eucharistic theology in the years leading up to the Fourth Lateran Council (1215). As the 'challenge' demanded explicit statements from the first six hundred years, Jewel could rest assured that he would not be forced to recant.

Jewel goes on to tell his hearers that the Catholic clergy (now ranked against the hearers as 'our adversaries') had over-awed the laity in the past by claiming the authority of the Church Fathers for their practices, 'an easie mater it was so to doe, specially before them, that lacke either leysure, or judgment to examine their proufes' (sig. G2ᵛ). Jewel is now challenging them to produce the evidence of antiquity of which they had boasted. Of course, the hearers are not really being asked to examine the proofs: they still lack the 'leysure, or judgment to examine' them. Jewel's argument is about the reliability of the teachers of doctrine. And the proof of his trustworthiness is apparent in the audacity of his challenge.

Here a distinction must be made between the various forms of debate that harboured under the umbrella term 'controversial divinity'. The use of the word 'controversial' to describe the interdenominational disputes at this period evidently places them in the tradition of scholarly disputation and argument *in utramque partem*.[10] Anti-Catholic preaching at Paul's Cross was something different,

---

Religion in Elizabethan and Jacobean Preaching (Cambridge: Cambridge University Press, 1998), pp. 42–9; On Jewel's delivery of the 'Challenge' at court, see p. 94. McCullough notes that this was the first court sermon to be printed.

[9] Jewel, *The True Copies of the Letters*, sigs A7ʳ⁻ᵛ.

[10] *Controversiae* were used as a grammar school exercise (arguing *pro* and *contra* on any issue) in preparation for the serious use of rhetoric in public life and scholarly debate: see Quentin Skinner, *Reason and Rhetoric in the Philosophy of Hobbes* (Cambridge: Cambridge University Press, 1996),

however, because it was addressed to a lay audience untrained in the theological details of the questions at issue. Preaching theorists described this rather as the 'confutation' or 'redargution' of doctrinal errors.[11] Richard Bernard put it most succinctly when he described the confutational sermon as one in which 'the doctrine is used to confute and overthrow an error or heresie'.[12] When Humphrey Sydenham preached against Arminian views of predestination, he drew a distinction between a 'debate' and the confutational sermon: 'the time and place suggest me rather to resolve than debate; and convince, than dispute an errour'.[13]

Preaching theorists lavished detail on the ways that errors can be confuted effectively: by presenting positive proof from theological principles, from Scripture, from the writings of the Fathers, and by demonstrating the weakness of the opponent's arguments.[14] But presenting detailed arguments on doctrinal matters could be counterproductive, given the lay auditory of these sermons. If the preacher failed to persuade his hearers, he would worsen the situation by hardening the hearer's conviction of the error.[15] Another strategy was to attack the character, or *ethos*, of the opposition. Aristotle wrote that the speaker's *ethos* was one of the three forms of persuasion (along with emotional appeals and dialectical arguments) available to the orator. The *Rhetorica ad Herennium* added to this the observation that the destruction of the opponent's *ethos* can also be effective in persuading one's hearers.[16] This was important for confutational preaching because it allowed a preacher to destroy an opponent's case without discussing it in detail: if an opponent is shown to speak lies, then he is not on the side of truth. Such ethical attacks were allowed by Hyperius of Marburg in a confutational situation, for which he cited the precedent of Jesus's denunciation of the Pharisees:

Indeed he may touch the persons, sometimes also sharpely, after which sorte we see the Pharisees to be handeled of Christ: but he must in no wise pretermitte gravitie, whereunto it behoveth a godly zeale to be joyned, and that (as the Apostles speaketh) according to knowledge; finally thorough love he ought to avoyde all offence givinge.[17]

---

pp. 27–8, 29–30. On the philosophical lineage of *controversiae*, see Michael J. Buckley, S.J., 'Philosophical Method in Cicero', *Journal of the History of Philosophy*, 8 (1970), 143–54.

[11] William Perkins, *The Art of Prophecying*, in *Works*, 3 vols (1616–18), *STC²* 19651, vol. 2, p. 668; John Wilkins, *Ecclesiastes* (1646), Wing W 2188, pp. 15–17; Matthew Sutcliffe, *De Recta Studii Theologici Ratione* (1602), *STC²* 23459, pp. 75–6; Anon., *Officium Concionatoris* (1655), Wing O157, p. 31.

[12] Richard Bernard, *The Faithfull Shepherd* (1607; 1621 edn), *STC²* 1941, p. 274.

[13] Humphrey Sydenham, *Jacob and Esau. Election. Reprobation Opened and Discussed* (1626), *STC²* 23567, p. 5.

[14] For example, see Hyperius [Andreas Gerardus], *De Formandis Concionibus Sacris*, trans. John Ludham, *The Practis of Preaching* (1577), *STC²* 11758, ff. 146ʳ–148ᵛ; Bernard, *The Faithfull Shepherd*, pp. 275–6; Sutcliffe, *De Recta Studii Theologici Ratione*, p. 82.

[15] Bernard, *The Faithfull Shepherd*, pp. 283–7.

[16] Aristotle, *The 'Art' of Rhetoric*, trans. John Henry Freese (Loeb Classical Library, 1926; repr. 1994), I.II.3; II.I.5, pp. 16–17, 170–1; *Rhetorica ad Herennium*, trans. Harry Caplin (Loeb Classical Library, 1959; repr. 1989), I.V.8, pp. 14–15. This point is also made by Thomas Wilson in his *The Arte of Rhetorique* (1553), *STC²* 25999, f. 56ᵛ. On *ethos* in Aristotle, see William W. Fortenbaugh, 'Aristotle on Persuasion through Character', *Rhetorica*, 10 (1992), 226–30.

[17] Hyperius, trans. Ludham, *The Practis of Preaching*, f. 149ʳ.

These, then, are the characteristics of the 'confutational' sermon: the preacher attempts to convince his lay hearers of his opponents' errors; he does not debate those errors with his opponents. And he uses whatever means are available to demonstrate the errors in their teachings, but also their untrustworthiness as teachers. The 'Challenge' sermon places the laity as judges between Catholic and Protestant theologians (not as judges of Catholic and Protestant theology) and this address to the laity was to be sustained in the controversy that followed.

The initial response to the 'Challenge' sermon was rapid, coming the day after it was preached at court on 18 March 1560 in a letter by Dr Henry Cole, the Marian Dean of St Paul's.[18] Cole attempted to shift the debate from a public exchange to a scholarly disputation: he asks that Jewel respond 'rather *dialectice*', because the matter 'more requireth learning then wordes' (sig. A2ᵛ). Cole wonders why Jewel has chosen matters of lesser significance (such as the language of the service), rather than the fundamental points at issue (such as the Real Presence). Jewel's answer, of course, is that he chose issues on which the Catholic Church can be shown unambiguously to have departed from the practice of the early Church (sigs A7ʳ⁻ᵛ). Cole's letter and Jewel's answer make clear that both parties know that this is not an exercise aimed at furthering doctrinal debate among professionals; Cole's attempt to turn the 'Challenge' into a professional debate shows that Jewel had found a strong position from which to argue. Neither side gave way, and the correspondence ended.

It was not until 1564 that the great outpouring of books and pamphlets on the 'Challenge' really took off, and this may not be unrelated to the fact that the same year saw Lady Anne Bacon's translation of Jewel's *Apologia* go into print: again, an audience literate in English was given the Protestant side of the Reformation story, and the Catholics, now established in collegiate houses in Louvain, could not afford to leave it unanswered.[19] Four Catholic writers printed responses to the challenge in that year;[20] all were Louvainists and all probably worked in collaboration with each other. By far the fullest, and most important, of these was Thomas Harding's

---

[18] The letters between Jewel and Cole were printed with the 'Challenge' sermon in *The True Copies of the Letters* ([1560]) *STC²* 14612.

[19] The two debates became entangled after 1565, when Harding wrote against the 1564 translation of Jewel's *Apologia*, having written his *Answere* to Jewel's 'Challenge' sermon the previous year: Peter Milward, *Religious Controversies of the Elizabethan Age: A Survey of Printed Sources* (London: Scholar Press, 1978), pp. 4–5. In a letter to Henry Bullinger dated 8 February 1566, Jewel expressed exasperation that his *Replie* to Harding was no sooner published but Harding's *Confutation* of Jewel's *Apologia* appeared: *The Zurich Letters, AD 1558–1579*, ed. Hastings Robinson, 2 vols (Cambridge, 1842–5), vol. 1, pp. 147–8.

[20] John Martiall does not refer to the 'Challenge' specifically, but does confute charges of idolatry made there and elsewhere in his *A Treatyse of the Cross gathred out of the Scriptures, Councelles, and Auncient Fathers of the Primitive Church* (Antwerp, 1564), ARCR 513. Thomas Dorman deals with only four articles in *A Proufe of Certeyne Articles in Religion, denied by M. Juell, sett furth in Defence of the Catholyke Beleef therein* (Antwerp, 1564), ARCR 169. John Rastell's *A Confutation of a Sermon, pronounced by M. Juell, at Paulles Crosse* (Antwerp, 1564), ARCR 671, follows similar lines of argument begun by Cole and Harding.

An Answere to Maister Juelles Chalenge (1564). The *Answere* clearly made an impact, and temporarily shifted the burden of proof back onto Jewel.[21]

Jewel's work on a *Replie* must have begun immediately after the publication of Harding's *Answere*, but Jewel and his colleagues did not wait until it was printed before beginning their counter-offensive against the Louvainists. Alexander Nowell, Dean of St Paul's, preached at Paul's Cross twice that year: firstly, on 30 April 1564, in answer to Harding's *Answere* and again on 19 November, on another of the Louvain answers to Jewel's 'Challenge', Thomas Dorman's *Proufe of Certeyne Articles in Religion, denied by M. Juell* (1564).[22] On 27 May 1565, Jewel preached against Harding's *Answere*, using arguments that would reappear in his *Replie*.[23] Thomas Harding heard of this sermon, and published an open letter to Jewel asking for a full copy of the sermon. Equally importantly, he defends his text against Jewel's allegations and accuses Jewel of misrepresenting him to the auditory at Paul's Cross:

> Thinke you, maister Juell, that whereas in the xxvii. day of Maie last you made a sermon at Paul's Crosse to abuse the eares of the ignorant people with scoffes and devyses against certaine authorities in my book alleaged, for a foreshewe of your booke that now is in printing, that you must not come to a straighter accompt of the mater in the triall and handling of lerned men? . . . Wherefore I require you, if your mynde be in dede to have the truth knowen to the people, and not under your gay rhetorike to abuse them in errour, let me have your whole Sermon, as your selfe will stand to it.[24]

Added to this was another short epistle to the hearer of Jewel's sermon, who 'may in this so stoute Denyall of truthes easely be caried into a wonderous Confusion'. He asks them to 'suspend for a time thy Verdict in the Cause' (p. 58) until Harding had a chance to answer Jewel properly. Jewel, it seems, did not send Harding this copy, but continued his attack on Harding at Paul's Cross, preaching against Harding's *Answere* again on 8 July 1565. As the *Replie* was printed that August, these two sermons preached in advance of its appearance suggest an anxiety on the part of the English bishops to publicize the fact that an answer to Harding was forthcoming, and that it would vindicate Jewel's challenge.

---

[21] Jewel may have been under pressure to respond to Harding's *Answere* as quickly as possible. On 30 January 1565, Jewel wrote to the Earl of Leicester saying that he knew his response to Harding's *Replie* was 'greedily looked for'. He notes that 'the whole rout of the adversaries, and also a great number of the unlearned friends, think the matter so sure of the other side, that it is not possible to make any answer'. Jewel reassures the Earl that he had 'well and particularly considered the whole case before I first began to speak', and he defends his 'slow dealing' in producing an answer because it will be 'larger than I would, and therefore requireth the more leisure', as 'haste and expedition' in this would 'betray the cause': *The Works of John Whitgift*, ed. Revd John Ayre (Cambridge, 1851–3), vol. 3, p. 624. Jewel wrote a similar letter the same day to William Cecil: *The Works of John Jewel*, ed. Revd John Ayre, 4 vols (Cambridge, 1845–50), vol. 4, pp. 1262–3.

[22] *Register of Sermons Preached at Paul's Cross, 1534–1642*, pp. 47–8.

[23] A. C. Southern says this sermon was preached against Harding's *Confutation* of Jewel's *Apologia* (*English Recusant Prose*, p. 63), but Peter Milward follows John Strype in taking it to be primarily a response to the *Replie*: Milward, *Religious Controversies of the Elizabethan Age*, p. 3. The first page of a manuscript copy of this sermon survives in PRO C 24/71. I would like to thank John A. W. Lock for informing me about this manuscript.

[24] John Strype, *Annals of the Reformation*, 4 vols (Oxford, 1824), vol. 1, part II, p. 524.

Harding, meanwhile, continued to get news of Jewel's sermons at Paul's Cross, even though he was not sent a copy of the first Paul's Cross sermon. In *A Briefe Answere* dated 26 July, Harding reports that Jewel claimed to have found ninety-seven errors in the first eighty leaves of Harding's *Answere*.[25] The numbering of these errors in Harding's *Briefe Answere* is the same as that printed in Jewel's *Replie*. This indicates that this claim was made by Jewel in much the same form in both the two sermons and in the *Replie* (though the latter was probably much expanded in detail). We can, therefore, use Jewel's *Replie* to gain an indication of how he continued the 'Challenge' controversy in these two sermons at Paul's Cross during summer 1565. Harding's *Answere* could not be accused of failing to produce citations from the Fathers, so Jewel had to prove that each and every citation was faulty, because it was either irrelevant or misquoted. And there were points when the proof on either side was rather harder to determine. When arguing for the reservation of the host, Harding used the story of St Basil's Mass as recounted in a biography written in the name of Amphilochius of Iconium. Should any deny the verity of this story, Harding had offered as proof the antiquity of the manuscript in which it was found:

For the auctoritie of his treatise, this much I can saye. Be syde that it is set foorth in a booke of certaine holy mens lyves printed in Colen. And besydes very great likelyhode appearing in the treatise its selfe: it is to be sene in the librarie of Saint *Nazarius* in the citie of *Verona* in Italie, written in veleme for three hundred yeres past, bearing the name of *Amphilochius* bishop of *Iconium*.[26]

In the first of his Paul's Cross attacks on the *Answere*, Jewel answered this with considerable relish. The reputation of Basil, the evidence of an ancient manuscript, all of these Jewel seems to grant, only to add:

But I mee selfe have had this unknowen Doctour in my poore Librarie these twentie yeeres and more, written likewise in veleme, as true, as faire, and of as good record in al respectes, as that other of Verona: in deed not under the name of Amphilochius: but no doubtes very auncient, as it may soone appeare. For the same Authour in the same booke hath written also the life of Thomas Becket, who lived at the least seven hundred yeeres after that Amphilochius this writer was dead.[27]

It is, however, a double-edged victory. Jewel reminds his readers that although 'the very names of olde godly Fathers are woorthy of muche honoure', in the past 'many vaine tales have been covered under the name of olde fathers' (*Replie*, p. 82). How can

---

[25] Harding, *A Briefe Answere of Thomas Harding* (Antwerp, [1565]), ARCR 373, sig. A11ʳ.

[26] Thomas Harding, *An Answere to Maister Juelles Chalenge* (Louvain, 1564), ARCR 371, f. 30ʳ.

[27] John Jewel, *A Replie unto Hardinges Answere* (1565), *STC²* 14606, p. 82. Jewel was right to question the authenticity of this *Life* of St Basil, but its status had not been established at the time both men were writing. This *Vita et Miracula Basilii Magni* was printed under the name of Amphilochius of Iconium in 1644; it is still unclear when the *Vita* was written, but it may been in the early eighth century: *Clavis Patrum Graecorum*, ed. Maurice Geerard, vol. II (Turnhout: Brepols, 1974), no. 3253; Raymond Van Dam, *Becoming Christian: The Conversion of Roman Cappadocia* (Philadelphia: University of Pennsylvania Press, 2003), pp. 166–8, 218 n 8.

the laity judge the citations presented by both parties as proofs when they are told that the citations cannot be taken at face value?

There were problems even more intractable than the canon of the Fathers' works. Both sides accused each other of 'wresting' their sources by mistranslation, but textual and printing problems complicated matters. In the *Brief Answere*, Harding defends himself against an accusation of misquotation made in Jewel's Paul's Cross sermon of 8 July 1566. Jewel accused Harding of having 'mangled S Augustine's place. . . . written *speculae* for *specula*, had made S Augustine speake false Latin, and had done I can not tell what'. Harding cites 'sundry Paris printes in folio, and of Lions print in octavo' that use '*speculae* not *specula*': the lay readers or hearers were hardly in a position to compare editions of Augustine's works. But Harding is well aware that this is part of Jewel's confutational strategy: what matters is the impression of unreliability created by the accusation of misquotation, particularly in reporting authorities unavailable to the lay reader:

By this I perceive, whereas M. Juell to impaire my credite in the opinion of the unlerned people, charged me with incongrue speach in the Latine tong, he would if he could, also charge me with incongrue behavioure in Christian life. For that is the marke he shooteth at, to discredit my person, whereas he seeth, he is not able to disprove the doctrine that I defend.[28]

In effect, neither side could give way on any issue: every error or omission is treated as deliberate,[29] because it affords an opportunity to discredit the opponent, and discrediting the opponent is a readier way of convincing the lay audience than proving the point through the increasingly problematic citations from the Fathers. This, then, is the real function of the *ad hominem* arguments that modern scholars find so uncongenial. Both sides were keenly aware of the difficulty, if not impossibility, of winning the debate simply by the Patristic evidence presented. Rather, any convincing or conversion that might be done would be done by convincing the hearers and readers of the greater reliability of one writer over the other.

In August 1565, Jewel's *Replie* to Harding's *Answere* was printed. But the 'challenge' controversy continued to dominate anti-Catholic preaching at Paul's Cross well into 1566, as other preachers took up the subject. We are fortunate indeed to have manuscript notes of almost a complete year of Paul's Cross sermons

---

[28] Harding, *A Briefe Answere*, sigs A10^r–11^r. In his *Replie*, Jewel repeats the accusation of mistranscription and mistranslation that he had made in the sermon as follows: 'M. Hardinge hath notably falsified, bothe S Augustines woordes in the Latine, and also his owne Translation in the Englishe. S Augustines woordes be these, *Communis est nobis omnibus, qui fungimur Episcopatus officio, quamuis ipse in eo praemineas celsiore fastigio, Specula pastoralis:* Which woordes M. Hardinge by wilful depravation hath altered thus, *Celsiore fastigio speculae pastoralis:* And so hath leafte the Adjective *Communis* without a Substantive and the principal Verbe, *Est,* without a Nominative Case: And, to serve his turne, hath caused S. Augustine to speake false Latine. This place of S Augustine may be Englished thus: *The pastoral Watche Tower is common to us al, that beare the office of Bishops: albeit thy preeminence is greater, as fitting in the higher roome.* M. Hardinges translation is thus, *Thou thy selfe hast the preeminence over al, being in the toppe of the pastoral Tower:* Wherein these woordes (Over al) are not founde in S. Augustine, but onely divised at pleasure by M. Hardinge' (*Replie*, p. 250).

[29] For more examples, see Jewel, *Replie*, pp. 182, 240.

in Bodleian MS Tanner 50, giving us a fuller account of preaching at the Cross from May 1565 to November 1566 than we have for any other year in its history. Of the forty-three sermons preached between Jewel's sermon on Harding's *Answere* of 27 May 1565 and the end of 1566, eighteen were confutational sermons, and confutational material featured as digressions in another four.[30] Three of these confutational sermons refer directly to either Harding's *Answere* to Jewel's 'Challenge' or his *Confutation* of Jewel's *Apologia Ecclesiae Anglicanae*.[31]

Preaching on 4 November 1565, Nicholas Robinson of Queen's College, Cambridge, took as his text the parable of the wedding feast (Matthew 22). The first section describes *sola fide* justification through the figure of the wedding: the spouse is the soul, who is acceptable only because 'the vertue of her husband is an amount sufficient for her' (f. 10[r]). The marriage creates the Church, which 'shall continue to the worlds end and what other religion hath risen since is heresye'. Robinson warns his hearers that 'we must not crye out of ceremonies in the church which be of mans invention', which suggests that at least some of his hearers wanted them back. The Catholic clergy who try to scare the laity into accepted ceremonies are compared to the scouts sent into the land of Canaan: their reports nearly induce the Israelites to return to Egypt until Caleb and Joshua convince them that there was nothing to fear. Robinson brings the metaphor home to Paul's Cross:

even so now a dayes do certen which willfully runne into other countreyes and their do lyve at less ease then they might at home . . . therby do drive the people agayn into the bondage of Rome, but in haue stept the Bishope of Salisbury and Mr Nowell whom I may well terme Calibe and Jushua, and haue showed the weaknes of their foundation, etc. (f. 10[v])

Thomas Bickley, chaplain to the archbishop of Canterbury, preaching on 2 December 1565 on Matthew 21:1–2, also took occasion to preach against Harding. As summarized in the Tanner 50 notes, the sermon's main argument concerns Christ's humility and his sovereignty, as seen in the entrance to Jerusalem on an ass, but Bickley takes several opportunities to digress into anti-Catholic confutation. By far the longest digression is on Harding's *Confutation of . . . An Apologie of the Church of England*. Bickley took much the same strategy that Jewel had used in his sermons: denying the reliability of Harding's proof-texts, and by extension the reliability of Harding as a writer and teacher. Harding had denied the evidence for 'Pope Joan' because she is not found in the list of popes drawn up by 'Athanasius the library keper', but Bickley answers that this omission is a deliberate one made by the Catholic historians. In just the same way, 'now a dayes it is

---

[30] A sermon is taken to belong to the confutational genre if its denunciation of heterodoxy (in this case, Roman Catholicism) is structurally integral to it: that is, if the confutation of Catholic error is one of the 'doctrines' identified in the 'division' of the scriptural text, or if confutation is one of the 'applications' of the 'doctrines' so derived. Otherwise, confutational material is treated as a digression.

[31] Thomas Harding, *A Confutation of a Booke Intituled An Apologie of the Church of England* (Antwerp, 1565), ARCR 374. Milward describes this as Harding's 'controversial materpiece': *Religious Controversies of the Elizabethan Age*, p. 5.

knowen well enoughe how in Quene Maries tyme, there was a talke of the Quenes delyvery, processions and bonfyers for the same, but one John Stowe in his cronicle perceavinge this to mak agaynst their vanitie hath left it clean out' (f. 15ᵛ). The point of this digression is not to inform the hearers about papal history, because the passage ends with an apostrophe: 'o mr hardinge will yow never leave your lyenge' (f. 16ʳ). The topic was clearly of greater interest to our note-taker than the main subject of the sermon, the final section of which is dispatched in one sentence.

The sermon delivered the following week also suggests a sustained interest in the 'Challenge' controversy by the Tanner 50 note-taker. Woollock, Superintendent of the Scottish congregation,[32] preached on 9 December 1565 on Romans 15:1. The Tanner 50 notes suggest that the sermon was on the idea of 'edifying', in its literal sense of building up the Church. The means of edifying are good life and doctrine, and the means to good doctrine are the Scriptures. Those that deny the laity access to the Scriptures, as the Catholics do, are not building up the Church (f. 16ᵛ). Harding, who is accused of converting from Protestantism in merely eleven days following Queen Mary's accession, is cited as an example of Catholic perfidy: Woollock knows that Harding was 'an other man once', becuase they were 'bothe in one colledge and the Duke of Suffolk's servants' (f. 17ʳ).[33] Harding's instability in religion is the context in which his writings against Jewel are condemned, with a rehearsal of the central argument of Jewel's 'Challenge':

This Hardinge hath written a booke an aunswer to the Apologye of the Churche of England, and I would wishe every man that redeth it, as he shall aunswer befor god, to read it with an indifferent judgment, for I protest before [sic] it is the vaynest book that ever I read since I was man, and full of nothing ells but scoldinge, such a scold in a house or streat were worthy the Cokinge stoll, and he in ever place almost calleth it our new gospell, your new gospell, herin he condemneth all the old fathers, for we teach non otherwys then as they did, but they are rather to be called new masters, who will giue over god for advantage. For let them haue gayne, a groat for a masse etc then all is well and they be pleased. (f. 17ʳ)

But this interest in the 'Challenge' needs to be set against the growing tedium generated by the to-and-froing of accusations and rebuttals, something demonstrated by the Tanner 50 note-taker's responses to a new episode in one of the polemical exchanges ancillary to the 'Challenge'. Alexander Nowell had joined in the 'Challenge' controversy in 1564 with his two sermons (first against Thomas Harding and then against Thomas Dorman's *A Proufe of Certeyne Articles in Religion, denied by M. Juell*). He followed this with a printed *Reproufe* against

---

[32] I have been unable to identify this preacher.

[33] In 1542, Harding served as chaplain to Henry Grey, then Marquess of Dorset, later Duke of Suffolk, at which time he was taken to be a Protestant by many of his contemporaries. L. E. C. Wooding, 'Harding, Thomas (1516–1572)', *Oxford Dictionary of National Biography* (Oxford: Oxford University Press, 2004, online edn., Jan 2008 <http://www.oxforddnb.com/view/article/12264>, accessed 1 Oct 2009. The 'inconstancy' exhibited by both men (Jewel subscribed before going into exile under Mary; Harding was associated with Protestantism under Edward VI) is a subject both writers use to discredit the other. On this, and the strong similarities between Jewel's and Harding's backgrounds, see Booty, *John Jewel as Apologist*, pp. 62–82.

Dorman in 1565.[34] Dorman responded in December 1565 with a tract entitled *A Disproufe of M. Nowelles Reproufe*, and in the preface he made much of Nowell's failure to answer his whole book (Nowell's *A Reproufe* responded only to Dorman's first article). Dorman also claims that statements made by Nowell in *A Reproufe* prove that Nowell had preached the 1564 Paul's Cross sermon against Harding's *Answere* without reading the *Answere* in full.[35] Nowell responded in a Paul's Cross sermon of 27 January 1566. Extraordinarily, Nowell did not deny Dorman's most damaging suggestion: he told his hearers that Harding's book 'cam not to my hands past iii days befor I preached heer and rather two days then three' and appealed for sympathetic consideration of his motives: 'but alas if I happen to read ther some things that weare to found might I not lawfully geve warning of them seing they were come in all mens hands allmost'.[36] He 'protests' that 'yf then wear non other cause then that I would never speake that'. He also defended his decision not to answer all of Dorman's articles on the grounds that Dorman's argument was the same as Harding's, and so Jewel's *Replie* which was 'redy to come into print' would answer both Catholic writers. Having defended his sermons of 1564, Nowell then turned to refute Dorman's *Disproufe*, promising to 'read first his first booke and then his second' so the hearers could see how certain proofs that Dorman offers in the first are denied in the second (f. 24[r]), but such a detailed comparison of two complex controversial works must have been difficult to follow, if not tedious to hear, and the Tanner 50 note-taker did not bother to copy out any of it. (The notes end with 'these be his words'.) Clearly the note-taker thought that the most memorable (indeed, noteworthy) part of the sermon was Nowell's admission that Dorman was right when he accused Nowell of preaching against a book that he had not finished reading.

The last sermon found in the Tanner 50 manuscript also concerns a point disputed between the Catholic and Protestant writers of the 'Challenge' controversy. Bishop Robert Horne of Winchester responded to a work circulating in manuscript by John Feckenham, Marian Abbot of Westminister, on the Oath of Supremacy. Horne's printed response, *An Answere . . . to a Booke entitled, The Declaration of such Scruples*, was printed in the summer of 1566,[37] and on 10

[34] Dorman, *A Proufe of Certeyne Articles in Religion, Denied by M. Juell* (Antwerp, 1564), ARCR 169; Alexander Nowell, *A Reproufe, written by Alexander Nowell, of a Booke entituled, A Proufe of Certayne Artices in Religion denied by M. Juell* (1565), STC² 18740. Nowell followed this in 1566 with a longer tract, *The Reproufe of M. Dorman his Proufe of Certaine Articles in Religion &c.* (1566), STC² 18742. See Milward, *Religious Controversies of the Elizabethan Age*, pp. 7–8.

[35] Thomas Dorman, *A Disproufe of M. Nowelles Reproufe* (Antwerp, 1565), ARCR 168, sigs *[r]–*2[r]. Nowell's *Reproufe* said that Dorman's and Harding's arguments on the pope's supremacy were so similar that one response (John Jewel's) would suffice. Dorman responded by saying that only someone who had not read both books could claim they were similar, and so Nowell must have 'uttred his malice at Powles Crosse' before reading Harding's *Answere* (sig. *[v]).

[36] Bodl. MS Tanner 50, Sermon notes from St Paul's Cross, ff. 23[v]–24[r].

[37] Robert Horne, *An Answeare made by Rob. Horne, Bishoppe of Wynchester, to a Booke entituled The Declaration of suche Scruples, and Staies of Conscience touching the Othe of Supremacy, as M. John Fekenham, by writinge did deliver unto the L. Bishop of Winchester, with his Resolution made thereunto* (1566), STC² 13818. Horne's epistle is dated 25 February 1565, i.e. 1566, and he tells the reader that Feckenham's tract began circulating 'an whole yeere' previously, and that he acquired a copy in April (sigs *2[r–v]). Feckenham's tract is not extant, except insofar as Horne reproduces it within his answer. Feckenham had been in the custody of Horne from 1563 to 1565: C. S. Knighton, 'Feckenham, John

November 1566 Horne rehearsed his arguments before the auditory at Paul's Cross. His text was Revelations 2:12–13 ('And to the Angel of the Church in Pergamos write these things sayth he which hath the sharpe sworde with two edges: I know thy workes, and where thou dwellest even whear Satans seat is, and that thou holdest fast thy name, and has not denyed my fayth, even in those days when Antipus my faythfull martyr was slayen amonge yow, where Sodom dwelleth') and he used his text to mount a defence of the queen's supremacy. He begins by explaining that the figure who 'hath the sharp sword with two edges' is Christ, and from this identification Horne delivers a lengthy account of the doctrine of the two swords, temporal and spiritual power, both of which only Christ wields. It is the papists who contravene this teaching, as it is the pope who seeks to exercise temporal power while claiming spiritual authority. The queen's supremacy does not offend the doctrine of the two swords because the Queen does not preach (ff. 121^r–123^v).

This part of the sermon is conducted in a measured way, with no *ad hominem* remarks. But Horne leaves this argument aside for a time when he considers the words 'thou dwellest even wher Satans seat is' from his text. 'Satan's seat' is the Church of Rome, and this anti-Catholic theme is directed at his hearers:

If I thought heer wear no Romanists, or at least should not understand of it, I would say nothinge of it, but because I know ther be, I will show by demonstration how it is the seat of Satan, I will speake of it not for Romes sake, for our sake. (f. 125^v)

In proving that the Church of Rome is the 'seat of Satan', Horne departs from many previous preachers, and from the tradition of the 'Challenge' controversy, by attacking the Catholic Church as an institution, rather than attacking its corrupt clergy. The Catholics admit, Horne tells his hearers, that 'ther wear many bishops which haue had their souls and bodyes to the devell, ther wear many heretics, yea many wicked men, . . . but some will say admit the persons are not good but ill, will yow therfor condemne the Sea' (f. 125^v). Horne insists to those Catholics still attending Paul's Cross that he does 'condemne the Sea', that there was more wrong with the Catholic Church than its faulty members. The papacy's abuse of the two swords is one demonstration of a systematic fault in the institution, and through it Horne brings the two parts of his sermon together. To hammer home the point, and to assist those who could not follow the argument about the supremacy and the two swords, Horne concludes by arguing that 'wher truth is persecuted, vice and synne mayntayned, is the Sea of Satan, this is in Rome, and therefore it is the Sea of Satan' (f. 125^v). Horne's attack on all Catholics, not just Catholic teachers and clerics, is indicative of a change emerging in the way preachers addressed the auditory at Paul's Cross: the preachers increasingly assume that any adherents to Catholicism among their hearers are in a minority.

(c.1510–1584)', *Oxford Dictionary of National Biography* (Oxford: Oxford University Press, 2004, online edn., Jan 2008 <http://www.oxforddnb.com/view/article/9246>, accessed 14 October 2009.

'MAIMED PROTESTANTS', RECUSANTS, AND THE EMERGENCE OF ANTI-POPERY

By the end of 1566, references to the 'Challenge' controversy were infrequent in Paul's Cross sermons. There was one final sermon at Paul's Cross that closed the subject, and that was by Jewel on 15 June 1567, in response to Thomas Stapleton's *A Returne of Untruthes* (1566).[38] Paul's Cross would not be used in a campaign of anti-Catholic preaching on this scale again. The number of sermons whose sole purpose was anti-Catholic confutation diminished rapidly after 1567. For the rest of Elizabeth's reign, our records provide only about one sermon a year primarily devoted to the confutation of Catholic doctrine and polemic. This may be partly an effect of our evidence, as we have fewer records of sermons for those years than we have from Tanner 50 for 1565–6; it may also reflect the declining urgency of confutational preaching. The Paul's Cross preachers increasingly assumed that most of their hearers had at least conformed to the Protestant Church. By the late 1570s, preachers at Paul's Cross were addressing an auditory for whom traditional Catholicism was barely a memory. But Tridentine Catholics may have been part of their auditory at Paul's Cross nonetheless. Catholic polemics suggest that the Paul's Cross sermons were attended by some Catholics, and that anti-Catholic material in some sermons was reported abroad (as we saw that Harding gained reports of Jewel's sermon on his *Answere*).[39] The Church authorities may have demanded attendance at Paul's Cross sermons by those whose religious loyalties were suspect: in 1581, the recusant Thomas Paget wrote to Francis Walsingham, asking to be excused from attending a Paul's Cross sermon. The previous year, Paget had fourteen weeks of instruction in Protestantism from the dean of Windsor, a punishment for his arranging a sermon by Edmund Campion S. J. Attending Paul's Cross was probably meant to reinforce the dean's instruction.[40] Although conversion was not unknown among convinced Catholics and Protestants, Paget is a very different type of Catholic to the confused and pliable

---

[38] Thomas Stapleton, *A Returne of Untruthes upon M. Jewelles Replie* (Antwerp, 1566), ARCR 732. It is possible that another response to Harding was preached after this date. In 1582, Herbert Westfailing, Vice-Chancellor of Oxford, printed a Paul's Cross sermon that refutes Harding's arguments on the Eucharist and mentions Harding's *A Detection of Sundrie Foule Errours* of 1568. But the sermon is not dated, and Westfaling's epistle suggests that there was some delay between the sermon being preached and printed: Herbert Westfaling, 'Two Sermons touching the Supper of the Lorde', in *A Treatise of Reformation in Religion* (1582), *STC²* 25285.

[39] Catholics continued to report what was said at Paul's Cross. In July 1615, Humphrey Clesby of Morpeth was reported to have spoken 'of a sermon preached against popery at Paul's Cross, [and] said there would soon be a redress of their oppressions': *CSPD, 1611–1618*, p. 301. A Catholic pamphlet of 1635 takes the form of a dialogue between an imprisoned Catholic priest and a 'precisian' Protestant minister who has preached at Paul's Cross and a report of whose sermon has reached the Catholic: N.N., *Maria Triumphans* (Saint Omer, 1635), ARCR 563, sigs. A5ʳ, A6ʳ.

[40] *CSPD, 1581–90*, p. 1. On Paget, see Peter Holmes, 'Paget, Thomas, fourth Baron Paget (c.1544–1590)', *Oxford Dictionary of National Biography* (Oxford: Oxford University Press, 2004), online edn., Jan 2008 <http://www.oxforddnb.com/view/article/21118>, accessed 27 October 2009. Paul's Cross was also used in this way for Protestant recusants: In 1594, Christopher Bowman, a goldsmith, is reported to have refused to go to his parish church, 'nor to Paul's Cross, to hear a sermon, seeing that any man, however wicked he may be, is admitted to receive the communion': *CSPD, 1591–4*, p. 324.

traditionalist that Jewel addressed with the 'Challenge' sermon. The sermons of the 1570s and 1580s addressed an audience whose identification with Protestantism was increasingly strong, and whose enemy, the stubborn recusant, was increasingly absent.

The conformity of the London population to the Elizabethan Protestant Church did not mean that the confutation of Catholicism disappeared from preaching at the Cross, as the ecclesiastical authorities still made use of this pulpit in the longer game of conversion. As the number of dedicated confutational sermons declined, anti-Catholic polemic was increasingly used as an element (a warning, a negative example) within sermons of other genres, particularly doctrinal and exhortatory sermons. John Foxe's Passion sermon of 1570 is a good example of this combination of doctrine, exhortation, and confutation.[41] It offers a detailed exposition of *sola fide* justification and includes in its printed version a denunciation of Catholic teaching on the subject.[42] It is, strictly speaking, a doctrinal sermon, being more concerned with the presentation of Protestant doctrine than with the confutation of the Catholic position. Nonetheless, it has as one of its stated aims the conversion of Catholic members of the auditory and readership. In the epistle to the reader, Foxe writes that one of his purposes was to do the papists 'some good'. But it is equally clear that these English Catholics are considered at best a minority of his hearers and readers, compared to those 'afflicted in conscience', who are the principal addressees of this epistle. Foxe wishes to 'remove this disease of ignoraunce' from 'these above rehearsed' (i.e. the Catholics) so that they 'may be reduced into the Kynges hieway of their salvation', but he writes also and 'especially for you that be mournyng in conscience'.[43] This second group, 'whom the terrour of the law to much oppresseth' are distinguished from the Catholics, but they are defined by their doctrinal ignorance: they do not yet fully understand *sola fide* justification. Whether that makes it hard for us to describe them as Protestant, it is clear that Foxe did not consider them Catholic. Foxe addresses his auditory as one that is predominately Protestant-identifying.

In the peroration to his sermon *On Christ Crucified*, Foxe appeals to those who have been 'straungers, unaquaynted, or enemyes unto God' to be reconciled with 'the lyvyng God', and not with 'the Bishop, whom we call Pope of *Rome*, who as I understand of late hath sent hys proctors and messengers to reconcile you to him'

---

[41] This notable sermon was translated into Latin and printed in both languages: John Foxe, *A Sermon of Christ Crucified* (1570), *STC²* 11242.3; *De Christo Crucifixo Concio* (1571), *STC²* 11247.

[42] The confutational aim of the sermon was not lost on its hearers. Notes on this sermon taken by the parson of St Agnes (presumably the parish of St. Anne and St. Agnes) and corrected by Foxe survive in BL Harleian MS 425, ff. 131–3. I would like to thank Tom Freeman for alerting me to this manuscript. The second and third leaves of the notes appear to be in the wrong order. The summary of Foxe's sermon given in these notes retains the confutational material, in effect giving it greater weight because of the summary treatment of the sermon as a whole. For example, the note-taker preserves Foxe's contrast of the Gospel's power to save with the failure of Cardinal Pole's much vaunted message of reconciliation with Rome. Foxe's lengthy meditation on the Passion, which takes up much of the latter half of the sermon as printed, is summarized in three sentences.

[43] Foxe, *A Sermon of Christ Crucified*, sig. A3ᵛ. On this sermon see V. Norskov Olsen, *John Foxe and the Elizabethan Church* (Berkeley, CA: University of California Press, 1973), pp. 116–19.

(pp. 57–8). Foxe's sermon was preached one month after Pius V's promulgation of *Regnans in Excelsis*, and this may be what is referred to here. (*Regnans in Excelsis* was promulgated in March 1570, but did not reach England until the May of that year.[44]) It was undoubtedly the subject of a sermon by Edmund Bunny, Chaplain to Archbishop Grindal, preached on the 10 June 1571, and its consequences were already emerging in this sermon.[45] Bunny confutes the pope's claims to supremacy over temporal rulers, telling his hearers that 'the Romish Bul hath of late lifted up his horne against our gracious Soveraigne, against thys our country, and the estate thereof. But Gods name be praised, this Buls hones are now sawed, he cannot goare us' (sig. H2ʳ). But Bunny also denounces 'the wilfull obstinate papistes whych wyll not once vouchsafe to come to the congregation and heare it' (sig. B2ᵛ). This is the first time a preacher makes mention of the recusant, a Counter-Reformation English Catholic who adopted or persisted in a principled refusal to attend Church of England services. Bunny's sermon is the only one to make explicit mention of *Regnans in Excelsis* in our records of Paul's Cross from that year, and so Bunny is the most senior member of the clergy to respond to the crisis of 1570/1 from Paul's Cross;[46] if any other preachers discussed it, no one considered it worth printing the sermon, and no reporter thought it newsworthy. This is all the more remarkable when we remember that the bill was posted on the door of the Bishop's Palace, within the cathedral precinct, and that the man who posted it was executed on the west side of the cathedral. Two bishops preached at Paul's Cross in 1571: Richard Cox, Bishop of Ely, and John Jewel preached against the puritan campaign against the Prayer Book in the parliament then sitting.[47] This suggests that the bishops did not think that the Northern Rebellion and *Regnans in Excelsis* were likely to spark large-scale defections from the Church in London, but that puritan agitation was finding a ready audience.

There may have been little fear of London reverting to Catholicism, but the refusal of some to conform, even nominally, was still a recurring subject at Paul's Cross. Those who stood back from the Reformation were increasingly spoken of as being absent from the auditory, and their ignorance (which Jewel and Foxe had treated as a condition from which the hearers were to be rescued) was increasingly characterized as a wilful rejection of the preacher's message. Thomas White told his hearers that recusants 'are obstinate stil' but that there were also many 'poysoned

---

[44] Wallace McCaffrey, *Elizabeth I* (London: Edward Arnold, 1993), p. 131.

[45] E.B., *A Sermon preached at Pauls Crosse on Trinity Sunday, 1571* (1576), *STC²* 4183. *STC²* attributes this sermon to Edward Bush, but notes that it is sometimes attributed to Edmund Bunny. The latter seems the more likely attribution given the confutational theme and the discussion of ceremonies and discipline in the Church of England.

[46] Thomas White may be referring to the Northern Rebellion when he gives examples of those who trust in arms and not God; their 'remembraunce is rufullye refeshed, as it were but yesterdaye' in the 'late and lamentable confusions', but this sermon was preached in December 1576: *A Sermon preached at Pawles Crosse on Sunday the ninth of December 1576* (1578), *STC²* 25405, p. 42.

[47] *Register of Sermons*, p. 51. On these sermons, see Chapter 7. Bunny addressed the controversy over vestments too, but he challenges the position for which the bishops were campaigning: the cap, tippet, and surplice are 'the smallest of many matters' but 'they do no small hurt in the Church of God': *A Sermon preached at Pauls Crosse on Trinity Sunday*, sig. F4ᵛ.

Protestants and maymed professours' in England, who think that 'faith justifieth and yet workes doe no harme' or that 'prayer for the dead is charitie'. Inadequate preaching and catechizing is partly to blame, but so are the 'maimed professours' themselves: overly complex sermons are 'leaving them behind, who are content to linger and never to come forwarde'.[48] Preaching in 1578, John Walsall (preacher at Christ Church in Canterbury and former tutor of Anne Bacon's sons[49]) promised his hearers that he would 'joyne battell and incounter with' any Recusants present at his sermon of the same year (sig. D2^r). Walsall evidently assumed they were not, as he denounced the recusant through mimickry: 'In our masse time', he says, 'we lived as we lusted, Priestes were good fellowes, adulterie was borne withall, bread was bigger, ale was stronger, beefe more plentifull, troutes fatter and better . . . We were borne and christened in the Masse time, our forefathers were of that stamp, we wil none of this new doctrine' (sigs D6^v–D7^v). Walsall's 'carnal gospellers' are different only because they 'will bee accounted protestantes' for pragmatic reasons ('by reason of the state and time present') but 'they cherish none, trust none, keepe companie and delight heartely in none, but such as are notorious and knowne Papistes' (sigs E^v–E2^r): these 'Church papists' are also spoken of as figures absent from the auditory at Paul's Cross.[50] Like White's 'maimed professors', Walsall's recusants and Church papists were guilty of a failure to believe the Scriptures, and indicative of that failure was their absence from the auditory at Paul's Cross.

The Paul's Cross preachers assumed that the Catholic community was not attending their sermons, but we have seen that Catholics did report on what happened at Paul's Cross. Perhaps it would be more accurate to say that the preachers did not *address* their sermons to a Catholic community who were now keeping apart from the English Church's services. The Cross was still a public space from which responses to Catholic propaganda might be made, although it never regained the leading role it had played in the 1560s. The focus of Protestant–Catholic polemic was changing and the Paul's Cross sermons were not keeping up, which suggests that the printed text, and not the pulpit, had become the established medium from which to launch religious controversies. Preaching in 1576, Richard Curteys rehearsed Jewel's argument that Catholic writers claim great antiquity for their Church but that their doctrines were no more than four hundred years old.[51] By then, this was a tired argument, and it provoked no response.

---

[48] Thomas White, *A Sermon preached at Pawles Crosse . . . in the Time of the Plague* (1578), *STC*[2] 25406, pp. 29–31.

[49] John Walsall, *A Sermon preached at Pauls Crosse. 5 October, 1578* ([1578]), *STC*[2] 24995, sig. A6^v. See also Virgil B. Heltzel, 'Young Francis Bacon's Tutor', *Modern Language Notes*, 63(9) (1948), 483–8.

[50] Alexandra Walsham, *Church Papists: Catholicism, Conformity and Confessional Polemic in Early Modern England* (Woodbridge: Boydell, 1993).

[51] Richard Curteys, *The First Sermon preached at Paules* Crosse in *Two Sermons preached by the Reverend Father in God the Bishop of Chicester* (1576), *STC*[2] 6140, sig. D2^v. The *Register of Sermons* dates this sermon to 1577 (presumably on the grounds that the 1576 date on the title page meant 1576/7 and the sermon was preached before the year changed on 25 March) but it is more likely to have been preached in March 1576. Peter McCullough dates the second sermon in this volume, preached at court on the third Sunday in Lent, to 25 March 1576. As both sermons are dated to 1576 on the title page, the printer evidently took 1 January as the start of the year.

The new focus of debate was on the definition of the Church, the so-called 'marks of the true Church' by which the Christian could know where to go for instruction and the means of grace. The Magisterial Reformers had defined the true church by the administration of the sacraments and the preaching of the Word, and this was a definition commonly used by English preachers. But it was a definition that left the position of the Church of Rome ambiguous: was its teaching sufficiently corrupt to exclude it from the definition of a 'true Church'?[52] The Catholic argument was based on history, and it had the advantage of avoiding doctrinal definitions by relying on institutional continuity: the marks of the true Church were said to be antiquity, universality, and visibility. The Roman Church had been in continual existence since the Apostles' time, and the succession of popes could prove this; it was a visible institution for all of that time, as the historic record shows, and it is found throughout the world, including the Americas. These arguments found their way into English Catholic polemic through the work variously known as 'Bristow's Motives' or 'Bristow's Demands' or 'Allen's Articles'. First printed in 1574, it was addressed to a lay Catholic, and provided 'motives' for remaining Catholic; in its revised form, it contained *'Demaundes to bee proponed of Catholikes to the Heretickes'*, and among the demands were to prove when the Protestant religion arose and what Church could show fifteen hundred years of continuous history.[53] By the end of the 1570s, these arguments were finding an echo at Paul's Cross, but the sermons that confuted them were doing no more than rehearsing the arguments being made in other Protestant printed sources, and they rarely consider these arguments in great detail. John Stockwood told his hearers on Bartholomew's Day 1578 that the Catholics may 'bragge never so muche of antiquitie, succession, unitie, unversality, or what other glorious or gorgious shew soever they pretende', but Christ has forsaken them, because they 'caste hym off', and then he moves on to another point.[54] John Dyos[55] preached an anti-Catholic confutational sermon on 19 July 1579, less than a month before the arrival of the Duke of Anjou at the English court for what appeared to be the final stages of

---

[52] Paul D. L. Avis, *The Church in the Theology of the Reformers* (London: Marshalls Theological Library, 1981), pp. 1–7, 64–77; Anthony Milton, *Catholic and Reformed: The Roman and Protestant Churches in English Protestant Thought, 1600–1640* (Cambridge: Cambridge University Press, 1995), pp. 270–310.

[53] Richard Bristow, *A Briefe Treatise . . . conteyning Sundry Worthy Motives unto the Catholike faith* (1574), ARCR 67; Richard Bristow, *Demaundes to bee proponed of Catholikes to the Heretikes* (1576), ARCR 69; Milward, *Religious Controversies of the Elizabethan Age*, pp. 39–46. On the adaptation of this text in popular verse form ('I pray thee protestant'), and its wide dissemination, see Alison Shell, *Oral Culture and Catholicism in Early Modern England* (Cambridge: Cambridge University Press, 2007), pp. 95–103. The turn to historical arguments by Catholic apologists is described by Lucy Wooding, *Rethinking Catholicism in Reformation England* (Oxford: Clarendon Press, 2000), pp. 225–47.

[54] John Stockwood, *A Sermon preached at Paules Crosse on Barthelmew day . . . 1578* ([1578]), *STC²* 23284, sig. C2ʳ.

[55] John Dyos, *A Sermon preached at Paules Crosse the 19. of Juli 1579* (1579), *STC²* 7432. Dyos does not name a benefice in his printed sermon, and so he has been difficult to identify. But he may be the John Dias who dealt with Lawrence Caddy, the Catholic priest who converted and delivered a recantation from Paul's Cross: J. H. Pollen, S.J. (ed.), 'Memoirs of Fr Persons S.J., 1581–84 (contd)', *Catholic Record Society, Miscellanea*, 4 (1907), p. 9.

marriage negotiations.[56] Dyos's sermon concerns the nature of the Church, and he begins by defining the Church before offering standard proofs that the Catholic Church is rather the 'Church of Antichriste' (sigs 37^r–43^v).[57] From here, Dyos moves on to more current debates, on the arguments based on the antiquity, universality, and apostolic succession of the Roman Church.

Dyos argues that true antiquity must be measured by the truth of Christ, which is 'from everlasting' and therefore 'more auncient than all customes' (sigs 45^r–46^r). Universality is 'no true note of the Church' either, because the Gospel has never been preached throughout the whole world (sig. 47^r). On the apostolic succession, Dyos argues that it is not institutional or personal succession that matters, but succession of doctrine (sigs 49^{r-v}), because 'they are not alwayes godly that succeede the godly'. From here, Dyos moves on to consider false doctrine as proof that the Roman Church is not a true Church (sig. 62^v), and this brings him back to the central points of Jewel's 'Challenge':

This doctrine that the sacrament of the alter (as they terme it) is the true, naturall, reall, carnall, corporall, and substantiall bodye of Christ, is a dreame of Antichrist the Byshop of Rome, and cannot be proued, neither by holy scripture, nor by auncient fathers. (sigs 64^v–65^r)

It is significant that Dyos spends relatively little time on the most topical subject he raises (the 'marks' of the Church are dealt with quite quickly in the middle of his sermon). Older points, including the repetition of the central argument of Jewel's 'Challenge', are given greater attention near the final exhortation with which the sermon ends. This is not a sermon that will provoke a response from Catholic writers, because there are answers to these arguments already in print. But Dyos may not have aimed at provoking a reply in the way that Jewel had: such responses would be counterproductive if the preacher was addressing his Protestant-identifying auditors, not Catholics whose minds might be changed. Dyos is reciting what had become common arguments, and not necessarily out of a lack of intellectual ambition. There was a real purpose to this repetition of accepted positions: it served to remind his hearers why they were right to identify themselves with the Protestant Church of England.

The year after Dyos's sermon, 1580, marked the beginning of the Jesuit mission and the new anti-Catholic laws passed in response to this by parliament.[58] This new 'popish' threat prompted the Corporation to attempt to weed out Catholic

---

[56] McCaffrey, *Elizabeth I*, pp. 199–200. Anjou arrived on 17 August; Dyos preached his sermon on 19 July. McCaffrey notes that 'as early as March [1579] sermons was preached against the match' (202). Toleration for Catholics may have been feared by Protestants, but it was, according to Patrick Collinson, 'never even a remote danger': *The Elizabethan Puritan Movement* (London: Jonathan Cape, 1967; repr. Oxford: Clarendon, 1990), p. 200. Dyos alludes to this near the end of the sermon: The Catholics are now 'very bold: They are in their ruffe, and looke for a day' (sig. 76^v).

[57] A full exposition of this passage referring it to the papacy was preached by John Dove at Paul's Cross: *A Sermon preached at Pauls Cross the 3. of November 1594. Intreating of the Second Coming of Christ, and the Disclosing of Antichrist* (1594), *STC^2* 7086.5, sigs D3^v–E3^v.

[58] J. E. Neale, *Elizabeth and Her Parliaments, 1559–1581* (London: Jonathan Cape, 1953), pp. 386–92.

sympathizers among their officers: on 12 April 1580, the Court of Aldermen ordered that all of the inferior officers of the Sheriffs' Court were to attend on the Sheriffs every Sunday at the Paul's Cross sermon, and any absences to be reported to the alderman so that the party in question could be dismissed from office. Anyone otherwise expressing 'any thinge in defence of papystrye' was to be reported in the same way.[59] But the response to the Catholic mission found within the sermons delivered from Paul's Cross was as muted as the response to *Regnans in Excelsis*: Edmund Campion's 'brag' and 'Reasons', his trial and execution, all of which dominated Catholic–Protestant polemic in 1580 and 1581, were the subject of only one Paul's Cross sermon that we can identify. It was preached in 1586 and is not extant.[60] In 1580, as in 1570, Paul's Cross was not used by the authorities in a concerted campaign to confute and rebut Catholic propaganda. Instead, it was used to confirm an auditory already sure of the rectitude of their choice of religious allegiance, and to harden the division between England's Protestant and Catholic communities. The association between Catholics and disloyalty that first emerged after *Regnans in Excelsis* became even more prominent in the representation of Catholics at Paul's Cross. Anthony Anderson's sermon, preached on 23 April 1581, is the first extant Paul's Cross sermon that post-dates the new laws against Catholics.[61] Anderson's text is Luke 13:6, the parable of the vineyard, and he makes a simple two-part division on the blessings of God to his 'fig-tree' and a warning against complacency. The dangers posed by the English Catholic community are presented in the starkest terms: 'Let a survey be taken hereof betixt the Papist, and the true Protestant, the one is ready to rebell at every motion, the other alwayes presse to aid aucthoritie, with gods, landes, & life' (sig. D3ᵛ). Although Anderson acknowledges that recusants are a minority (the Gospel has won 'infinite soules in this nation . . . as well in thys Citie, as in the realme abroade', sigs G2ʳ⁻ᵛ), he warns that the Catholic mission could partly reverse this, as 'their private persuasions are great' (sig. E6ʳ).

In this sermon we get the first mention of what John Bossy has described as 'seigneurial Catholicism', the retrenchment of the Catholic community around the estates of nobles and gentlemen able to afford the necessary protection for Catholic worship to take place covertly.[62] Anthony Anderson tells his hearers that the Catholic Recusant is:

---

[59] City of London, London Metropolitan Archive, Corporation of London Rep. 20, ff. 59ᵛ–60ʳ.

[60] Milward, *Religious Controversies of the Elizabethan Age*, pp. 54–64. Abraham Fleming contributed an account of Campion's mission and execution to the continuation of Holinshed's *Chronicles*, and there he cites from a sermon by 'D. Sellar' preached at Paul's Cross on 6 February 1586. The citation repeats an anecdote about Catholics claiming that the Thames miraculously stopped at Campion's death: Raphael Holinshed, *et al*, *The Third Volume of Chronicles* (1586), *STC²* 13569, p. 1329.

[61] Anthony Anderson, *A Sermon Preached at Paules Crosse, the 23. of Aprill . . . 1581* (1581), *STC²* 570. Anderson styles himself as 'Minister of Gods holy Gospel' in his dedicatory epistle, but he had a benefice in Medbourne, Leicestershire, since 1573: Gary W. Jenkins, 'Anderson, Anthony (d. 1593)', *Oxford Dictionary of National Biography* (Oxford: Oxford University Press, 2004), online edn., Jan 2008 <http://www.oxforddnb.com/view/article/467>, accessed 3 November 2009.

[62] John Bossy, 'The Character of Elizabethan Catholicism', *Past and Present*, 21 (1962), 39–59; Bossy, *The English Catholic Community, 1570–1850* (London: Darton, Longman and Todd, 1975), pp. 11–74.

not onley an enimy to God, his religion, and his Majestie in his heart, but he maketh according the valor of his countenance, the Countrie by proportion where he dwelleth very Papisticall with him. If he be a Gentleman, he corrupteth his tenants, and the godly Minister there hath small joy of his labor: but if a Justice of Peace (as too manye such there are) then hee goeth very neere (if not) to corrupt sundrye his fellowe Benchers, yet by the fleshly favor they owe him and through the linkes of bloude or affinite to him, or other their friendes, they are become very sparing of religions fruit, both bearing with his Popery, and all hys, and also, not so dutifull to God, and his Majestie, for the purging of the country of such bitter trees or fruites as they, of faithfulnesse ought, or for their owne persuasion should, were they not made barren by such a bitter Fig tree. (sigs E3ᵛ–E4ʳ)

That a preacher at Paul's Cross would describe a Catholic gentleman as someone whose relations with his own local community undermines the English state shows that the Catholic laity had become as distant from the sympathies of the Paul's Cross preachers as the Catholic clergy had been for John Jewel.

In this, and in many other sermons of the 1570s and 1580s, the Church papist and the recusant are figures set up by the preachers as a means of contrasting zealous Protestantism with sinfulness and error: they are the absent 'other' against which the orthodoxy and loyalty of the Paul's Cross hearers could be emphasized. This is not confutational preaching, designed to convince the hearers of Catholic error, because there is no attempt to present arguments against Catholic practices or doctrines at all. This is 'anti-popery', a rhetorical strategy designed to strengthen the hearers' sense of their separation from 'popery' and to remind them that they stood on the right side of the gaping gulf that separated religion from 'anti-religion'.[63]

Anti-popery became a constant of Paul's Cross preaching; indeed, there is an anti-papistic digression in almost all Paul's Cross sermons from the 1580s onwards, and their content became highly standardized, and for some of the more educated auditors, tediously predictable. John Manningham's diary preserves notes of a sermon probably preached at Paul's Cross in December 1602.[64] Catholic claims about the visible Church occupied much of the sermon, and Manningham dutifully recorded these arguments. But he seems to have been out of sympathy with the preacher's style. He describes him as 'one with a long browne beard, a hanging looke, a gloting eye, and a tossing, learing jeasture', and he says that the sermon was 'a strong continued invective against Papistes and Jesuites. Not a notable villainous practise commmitted but a pope, a cardinall, a bishop or a priest had a hand in it'. And Catholics complained that Paul's Cross was used for invective designed to denigrate them before their Protestant compatriots. In 1592, the Catholic historian and apologist Richard Verstegan reported that a preacher at Paul's Cross 'affirme that it was a more better acte to assist Turks, then Papistes', and in 1612 the Jesuit John Floyd claimed that when 'the persecution is hottest' the Protestant ministers

---

[63] This analysis borrows heavily from Peter Lake, 'Anti-popery: The Structure of a Prejudice', in Richard Cust and Ann Hughes (eds), *Conflict in Early Stuart England: Studies in Religion and Politics, 1603–1642* (London: Longmans, 1989), pp. 72–106.

[64] *The Diary of John Manningham of the Middle Temple, 1602–3*, ed. Robert Parker Sorlein (Hanover, NH: University Press of New England, 1976), pp. 156–7. The sermon was preached 'at Paules' on 19 December.

'seeke to kindle the same fiery impressions of hatred in others, wherewith themselves are inraged' and to do so, conjure up monstrous errors 'to fright poore men
out of their wits, against the faith of their Ancestours'. According to Floyd, these
sermons are essentially polemical instruments in a confessional war.[65]

THE USES OF ANTI-POPERY

Anti-popery was no use for conversion, but conversion was no longer the primary
concern of the Paul's Cross preachers. It was a device for addressing Protestants, as a
means of exhortations to godliness and greater zeal (in opposition to papistic 'anti-
religion'), and as a means by which they could be exhorted to unity despite internal
divisions. The latter was one of the most important uses of anti-popery at Paul's
Cross. It was a particularly valuable strategy for the puritan ministers within the
Church, because anti-popery was a point on which they agreed with the Church
authorities. It was, therefore, a subject they could address without any risk of raising
disputes between members of the English Church.[66]

George Gifford, an Essex minister heavily involved in setting up a covert
presbyterian organization (the *classis* movement) within the English Church in
the 1580s, preached a sermon at Paul's Cross in 1591 on the theme of Church
unity among Protestants and the duty of obedience to the Church authorities by
'private persons'.[67] Separation from Catholics is justified, as they are the 'enemies of
the holie religion', but the English are guilty of disagreements 'even among
brethren, which professe the same holy doctrine and faith of our Lord Jesus
Christ' (sigs A8ᵛ–Bʳ). Unity must be in truth, Gifford then explains, and the
Catholic Church is no more than 'a conspiracy of wicked traitors against Christ'
(sigs B4ʳ–B5ʳ). In 1601, Henoch Clapham, a former separatist, preached two
sermons at Paul's Cross in which he contrasted the Church of England's (correct)
understanding of the Mosaic Law in the New Covenant with the errors of Catholics
and separatists.[68] Francis Marbury, whom Patrick Collinson has described as 'a
Northampton hothead and even suspected of being Martin Marprelate', preached
there in 1602. Marbury had been elected to a lecturership in St Saviour Southwark
in the same year, and the election was made on the condition that Marbury did not
have to read the Prayer Book service, so his conformity was still no more than
partial.[69] His sermon exhorted his hearers to zeal, defining their religion against a

---

[65] Richard Verstegan, *A Declaration of the True Causes of the Great Troubles, presupposed to be
intended against the Realme of England* ([Antwerp, 1592]), ARCR 760, p. 20; John Floyd, S.J., *The
Overthrow of the Protestants Pulpit-Babels* (1612), ARCR 297, p. 9.

[66] On this point see Milton, *Catholic and Reformed*, pp. 31–46.

[67] George Gifford, *A Sermon preached at Pauls Crosse the thirtie day of May, 1591* (1591), *STC²*
11862.3.

[68] Henoch Clapham, *A Description of New Jerusalem* (1601), *STC²* 5336.5; Alexandra Walsham,
'Clapham, Henoch (fl. 1585–1614)', *Oxford Dictionary of National Biography* (Oxford: Oxford
University Press, 2004); online edn., Jan 2008 <http://www.oxforddnb.com/view/article/5431>,
accessed 10 November 2009.

[69] Francis Marbury [Marburie], *A Sermon preached at Paules Cross the 13. of June. 1602* (1602),
STC² 17307; Collinson, *The Elizabethan Puritan Movement*, p. 433; Paul Seaver, *The Puritan*

Catholicism that made its adherents traitors ('When men are lost this way, they are lost to God, and they are lost to their prince: there is not a Papist made, but Queen *Elizabeth* loseth a subject', sig. B5ᵛ) and atheists ('Poperie . . . hath nothing in it to allure anie but hypocrites and those which are in a faire way forwardnesse to degenerate into Atheisme', sig. D4ᵛ).

Another use of 'anti-popery' became more prominent after the Gunpowder Plot, and this was to integrate a warning on the dangers of popery with exhortations to greater zeal and godliness from individuals and communities. On 2 November 1606, Richard Stock preached a 'national warning' sermon on the plague of the previous years, Among the means of preventing further punishments from God was the strict enforcement of the laws against Catholics, who were a threat to the Church by their proselytizing of the weak, and to the state by their treasonous plots. English Catholics are the 'little foxes' who destroy the vines, a reference to Canticles 2:15 and the text on which Thomas Jackson spoke to the same effect in January 1608.[70] The 'Jeremiad', or 'national warning' sermons are primarily sermons of exhortation to godliness on an individual and communal level,[71] and they treated the problem of recusancy and the threat of conversions to Catholicism posed by missionary activity as examples of the community's failure to regulate itself on godly lines. In a 'Jeremiad' targeting 'luckwarmness in religion', Thomas Sutton makes a vehement apostrophe to the judges in the audience, and exhorts them to 'cut off the trayterous heads of Priests and Jesuites, that hinder the peace, to whip and censure our besotted Recusants, that repine at the growth of the Gospell'; if they do not act against 'our hollow-hearted and popish fondlings', they 'more dishonour God by want of zeale, then ever you can honour him by your profession'.[72]

Until the 1620s, anti-popery was a theme very unlikely to lead a preacher into political or doctrinal heterodoxy, which may explain why the bishops were content to allow puritans like Richard Stock, Francis Marbury, and Henoch Clapham take their turns in this pulpit. It may also explain the readiness of preachers to address contentious doctrinal issues under the cover of anti-popery. Three sermons from the first half of James's reign attack Catholic teaching on justification, all three concentrating on the Catholic denial of assurance of election and assertion that the elect may fall from grace *totaliter*, points also in dispute between Calvinists and Arminians. William Sclater's *A Three-Fold Preservative* was the first of these. It was preached in 1609, and the text was Hebrews 6:4–6, on those 'who have partaken of

Lectureships: The Politics of Religious Dissent, 1560–1662 (Palo Alto, CA: Stanford University Press, 1970), p. 145. Marbury's questioning before the Bishop of London in 1578 is recorded in John Udall's *A Parte of a Register* ([Middelburg], 1593), *STC²* 10400, pp. 381–6.

[70] Richard Stock, *A Sermon preached at Paules Crosse, the second of November, 1606* (1609), *STC²* 23276, pp. 15–25, esp. 18; Thomas Jackson, *Londons New-yeeres Gift. Or The Uncouching of the Foxe* (1609), *STC²* 14303.

[71] The earliest 'national warning' sermon to include anti-papist themes was Thomas White, *A Sermon preached at Pawles Crosse on Sunday the thirde of November 1577* (1578), *STC²* 25406. The title page indicates that White's sermon was preached during an outbreak of plague.

[72] Thomas Sutton, *Englands First and Second Summons: Two Sermons preached at Paules Crosse* (1616), *STC²* 23502, pp. 187–9.

the holy ghost' falling away and not being recovered. Sclater begins by saying of his text that 'of late it hath bene wrested to prove, that even cast-awaies may be by faith united unto Christ, truly justified', but only temporarily, and cites Bellarmine in the margin; it has also been used

> with as great confidence, though lesse probability urged to prove, that Gods children *chosen to salvation, called according to his purpose,* may (at least for a time) fall from the state of grace, lose justification not onely *in foro conscienciae,* and in respect of feeling, but even *before God,* lose sanctification, both in respect of *exercise and measure,* as also *the very* habit.

Because of this 'the more diligence is required of us in the unfolding of it'.[73] Samuel Gardiner presents his *The Foundation of the Faithful* (1611) as a refutation of Catholic teaching on predestination; however, he spends almost no time on the Catholic teaching that election arises from God's foresight of human merits and concentrates instead on 'this impossible matter of the seducement of the Elect, Totally and Finally', a position identified with Arminians as well as Catholics.[74] Nathanial Delaune, the son of Huguenot minister William Delaune, preached in 1617 on *The Christians Triyumph, manifested in the Certitude of Salvation.* The sermon deals almost entirely with assurance of faith (that the elect can be certain of salvation in this life) against the Roman Catholic position. Assurance was also a point disputed between Calvinists and Arminians, but Delaune does not name Arminians as opponents at all.[75] Before the Synod of Dort brought these disputes to the attention of the English laity, preachers may have shied away from mentioning such contentious 'school points' in a public pulpit; some also felt compelled to defend the 'Calvinist consensus'. Treating these questions as elements of erroneous Catholic teaching allowed them to do so covertly, while also putting in place an association between Catholicism and any teaching that denied these points.

But it would be naïve to think that all anti-Catholic preaching was designed merely to disguise other concerns. When occasion demanded, Paul's Cross was used by the authorities to respond directly and immediately to Catholic propaganda, and the best example of this is the sermon delivered on 25 November 1621 by Henry King in response to rumours that his father, Bishop John King of London, had made a deathbed conversion to the Catholicism.[76] Not surprisingly, the 'peak' years for anti-Catholic preaching in James I's reign are 1607–11 (during the Oath of Allegiance controversy) and 1620–4 (during unrest over the Spanish Match). But the arguments about Catholic loyalism and resistance theory arising from the Oath of Allegiance were not launched from Paul's Cross: it was the court pulpit and

---

[73] William Sclater, *A Threefold Preservative against Three Dangerous Diseases of these Latter Times* (1610), *STC²* 21847, sigs B^{r–v}.

[74] Samuel Gardiner, *The Foundation of the Faythfull* (1611), *STC²* 11577. The sermon was preached in January 1610/11.

[75] Nathanial Delaune [Delawne], *The Christians Tryumph, Manifested by the Certitude of Salvation* (1617), *STC²* 6550.5.

[76] Henry King, *A Sermon Preached at Pauls Crosse, the 25 of November. 1621* (1621), *STC²* 14969. The claim that John King converted was printed in Richard Broughton, *English Protestants Plea* (Saint Omer, 1621), ARCR 80, p. 19.

the press that took the lead in defending the Oath. Paul's Cross merely reiterated its traditional anti-papistical themes more vehemently and more regularly.[77]

That Paul's Cross was airing old-fashioned anti-popery in James's reign is most evident in the prominence given to the identification of the pope with Antichrist in many of the sermons preached there. The conventions for anti-popery were then built around themes and proof-texts already much in use, the most important of which was Revelations 18:4 ('And I heard another voice from heaven say, Go out of her my people, that ye be not partakers of her sins, and that ye receive not of her plagues').[78] The doctrines conventionally derived from this text provided arguments for the continued separation of the Church of England from the Church of Rome. This was an indirect response to Catholic apologetic and controversial techniques. Michael Questier has shown that:

Protestantism became vulnerable if it did not constantly make a clear enough distinction between itself and Rome. If it did not, Catholic polemicists might argue that the Church of England could not claim to be a Church at all since it was divided against itself: various elements of its thought corresponded to Catholic ideas while others were evident of factious Protestant extremism. Catholic polemic thus constructed a bridge over which 'moderate' Protestants could cross.[79]

Paul's Cross preachers sought to demolish this 'bridge'. Rather than argue about the Church of England's history, they identified the Catholic Church as a false Church by using the identification of the papacy with Babylon and Antichrist (a feature of Protestant polemics since Luther's *Babylonian Captivity* and given even greater currency in England through John Foxe's *Actes and Monuments*).[80] Reading 'Babylon' in Revelations 18:4 as a reference to the papacy provided ready justification for the maintenance of the division between the churches: any reconciliation with Rome would be disastrous for England, because it would cause her to share the plagues foretold. It also assured the hearers that they were promised victory in a conflict that had become a semi-permanent feature of English life. But this tactic and this text was also used by the English separatists, and so preachers found themselves confuting on two fronts.

The first example of this is William Symonds, in *A Heavenly Voyce*, preached in January 1606.[81] Taking Revelations 18:4 as his text, Symonds uses a simple

[77] On the importance of court sermons in particular, see Lori Anne Ferrell, *Government by Polemic: James I, the King's Preachers, and the Rhetorics of Conformity, 1603–1625* (Palo Alto, CA: Stanford University Press, 1998), pp. 89–104.

[78] On the use of Revelations 18:4, see Milton, *Catholic and Reformed*, pp. 100–1, 322–3; on the identification of the papacy with the Antichrist, see pp. 93–110. Michael Questier notes that Revelations 18:4 was often used in Jacobean converts' tracts: 'John Gee, Archbishop Abbot, and the Use of Converts from Rome in Jacobean anti-Catholicism', *Recusant History*, 21 (1993), 347–60, p. 353.

[79] Michael Questier, 'The Phenomenon of Conversion: Change of Religion to and from Catholicism in England, 1580–1625', D.Phil., University of Sussex, 1991, p. 113.

[80] Olsen, *John Foxe and the Elizabethan Church*, pp. 59–74. The identification of the pope with Antichrist had been preached at Paul's Cross several times during Elizabeth's reign, most notably, and at greatest length, in Laurence Deios, *That the Pope is that Antichrist: And An Answer to the Objections of Sectaries* (1590), *STC²* 6475, and Dove, *A Sermon preached at Pauls Crosse the 3. of November 1594 STC²* 7086.5.

[81] William Symonds, *A Heavenly Voyce* (1606), *STC²* 23591.

comparison of the cruelty of Babylon and the Church of Rome to prove the identification. The dangers of contagion and of sharing in the punishments that God will visit on Babylon and her confederates provide reasons for forsaking her (sigs B2ᵛ–B3ʳ). That the voice instructs God's people to 'goe out of her' demonstrates that the godly sometimes live under the government of the ungodly, confuting both the separatists who claim 'it is not possible for *Christians* to live under the government of unchristian Governors' (sig. B3ᵛ) and the Catholics who 'demaund of us where our Church hath been for these thousand yeeres. It was among them, though they were not of it' (sig. B4ʳ).

A year later, William Crashaw preached another sermon on the same theme (but with Jeremiah 51:11 as his text: 'We would have cured Babel, but she would not be healed: let us forsake her, and go every one into his own country: for her judgement is come up into heaven, and lifted up to the clouds').[82] In his sermon, Crashaw justifies the Reformation by using the metaphors of sickness in his text: the true Church sought to help her obstinate enemies, but could not. Separatists from the English Church are merely schismatics: they have not tried to 'heal' the church (p. 34). 'Babel' in the text is 'mystical Babylon', which Crashaw identifies with the Church of Rome (p. 39). The Roman Church had twenty 'wounds', doctrinal errors, and corrupt laws that were apparent at the time of the Reformation and have not been healed since.

Crashaw prided himself on being an anti-Catholic controversialist, and his was the first Paul's Cross sermon since Robert Horne's of 1566 to provoke a response. This may have been because Crashaw was not content to rehearse anti-papistic truisms, and so he sought new proofs that Catholicism was an 'anti-religion'. By the time the sermon was printed, there had been responses by both of Crashaw's targets, the 'papists and the Brownists'.[83] Henry Ainsworth responded to Crashaw for the separatists with a simple and effective argument. He says that Crashaw failed to show any essential difference between the Protestant–Catholic division and the Protestant–separatist one. Where Crashaw argues that the separatists have not sought to heal the English Church, with devastating simplicity Ainsworth uses the same argument against the Church of England: 'I answer, we have sought your healing, even as by your own doctrine the faithful *Jewes* sought the cure of *Babel*: & as your selves have sought the healing of *Rome*'.[84]

The Catholic response was less straightforward, but John Floyd succeeded in putting Crashaw on the defensive in *The Overthrow of the Protestants Pulpit-Babels* of 1612. Crashaw had said that Catholics persist in the twenty errors that he described and he 'spared no cost . . . nor time' (sig. ¶2ᵛ) in proving detailed bibliographical evidence for his accusations. John Floyd responds by contradicting a great many of these individual citations in order to destroy Crashaw's credibility

---

[82] William Crashaw, *The Sermon preached at the Crosse, Feb. xiiii.1607. Justified by the Authour, both against Papist, and Brownist, to be the truth* (1608), *STC²* 6027.

[83] Henry Ainsworth, *Counterpoison* ([Amsterdam], 1608), *STC²* 234; Floyd, *Overthrow of the Protestants Pulpit-Babels*. On this controversy, see Peter Milward, *Religious Controversies of the Jacobean Age: A Survey of Printed Sources* (London: Scholar Press, 1978), pp. 161–3.

[84] Ainsworth, *Counterpoison*, p. 251.

as a guide on controversial divinity. Floyd also accuses Crashaw (not unfairly) of puritanism: he asks whether Crashaw professes 'his owne religion' or 'the Kings' because there was a time when a voice saying '(*Crashaw, Crashaw, go to Geneva*) did ring strongly in his eares'.[85] Floyd's most effective weapon is the witty mockery of Crashaw we see here, which is an effective rebuttal of Crashaw's plodding insistence that every Catholic custom is proof of its antichristian corruption. Floyd even mocks Crashaw's reading of his biblical text, because the comparison does not work: for the analogy to hold, it would be the English Protestants who had been 'led captyve, kept in prison, who *mourne upon the bankes of Babylon*, sighing out *Geneva* psalmes by the *Thames* side' while Catholics 'rule the sterne of the state, live in mirth, joy and joyllity, & doe wonderfully afflict and prosecute the righteous soules of those good *Israelites* that they are weary of their lives' (p. 81).

The fact that William Crashaw's sermon provoked two responses rhetorically more effective than his sermon shows the wisdom of Crashaw's contemporaries in their avoidance of anything other than the well-worn themes of anti-popery. As their sermons were addressed to an overwhelmingly Protestant auditory, there was no need, and indeed possible danger, in trying to break new polemical ground from Paul's Cross. When Thomas Thompson preached on the necessity of separation from the popish Antichrist, he followed the format used by his predecessors in the pulpit.[86] Thompson says the text invites 'lamentation, and exultation', fraternal lamentation for the enthrallment of their recusant fellows, who are exhorted to free themselves from the tyranny of Rome and the treachery of equivocating and deceptive missionary priests (pp. 169–75), and exultation at the blessing England enjoys since becoming free of Rome. England has 'the Word plentifully preached', 'absolute libertie from all forrayne power' and her trade and agriculture have prospered since the Reformation (pp. 186, 192), all of which proves that the Reformation conforms to God's will. This makes the Church of England's continued separation from the Church of Rome vital: 'our departure from the *Romish synagogue*, doe nothing else at all, but what Scripture commandeth, Reason perswadeth, Ancient Fathers preached, and some learned Papists doe allow' (p. 194). This argument necessitates another: the confutation of separatists from the Church of England. Thompson rehearses the argument that separation is only justified by fundamental errors of doctrine; for this reason he says that the 'Schismatical Brownists' are on 'a very shaken, and weak foundation' (p. 209).

Preaching on Revelations 18:4 (and similar texts) offered the Paul's Cross preachers an effective way of enforcing confessional divisions without needing to

---

[85] Floyd, *Overthrow of the Protestants Pulpit-Babels*, pp. 13–14, 58–9. Floyd also claims that the Earl of Salisbury refused to patronize the sermon and that Parliament ordered that the letter dedicating Crashaw's *The Jesuit's Gospel* to them be suppressed. No record of a controversy over either of these dedications can be found, but *STC²* does note that the preliminaries to *The Jesuits Gospel*, including the dedication to the Lower House, have been cancelled in what appears to be a later issue of the work. Floyd's charge may be true, therefore.

[86] Thomas Thompson, *Antichrist Arraigned in a Sermon at Pauls Crosse* (1618), *STC²* 24025. We do not know when the sermon was preached: Thompson's dedicatory epistle states that it was preached 'long time since'. His text was 1 John 2:18–20.

provide proof that Catholics polemicists might answer (as Floyd did Crashaw). But this type of preaching depended on an agreement by members of the auditory, and the English Church, that the identification of the pope with Antichrist had been proven beyond doubt. When this idea was challenged, by conformist writers who treated the Catholic Church merely as a flawed Church (and not the seat of the Antichrist), Paul's Cross preachers of anti-popery found that themes and topics that had been thoroughly conventional and unobjectionable in previous years were so no longer.[87]

This was particularly true of the years 1622–4, when 'railing' against Catholics contravened the *Directions for Preachers*. Richard Sheldon's questioning after he preached his sermon 'laying open the Beast, and his mark' at Paul's Cross within weeks of the *Directions* has already been mentioned. John Gee was another convert from Catholicism who preached on this subject, but he had the good fortune to appear after the 'Blessed Revolution' of English politics on the failure of the 'Spanish Match'. His sermon, of 31 October 1624, had as its text Revelations 3:11 ('Behold, I come quickly, hold fast that thou hast, that no man take thy Crowne'), and the text seems to have been chosen primarily to facilitate a discussion of the reason for Gee's celebrity. Gee had not 'held fast'; he had converted to Catholicism, but he reverted to Protestantism after surviving the 'Fatal Vespers' (when the floor collapsed under mass-goers at the French Ambassador's house in the Blackfriars on 26 October 1623[88]). The sermon is not skilful in its construction, forceful in its argumentation, or elegant in its prose style. Gee was an 'anti-Catholic celebrity', and at Paul's Cross he merely performed his only trick. The most likely reason for Gee's appointment was to make clear that anti-popery was allowed at Paul's Cross again.

But this was not quite a return to the *status quo ante*. The early years of Charles's reign saw a diffusion of the focus of confutational sermons, and an intensification of denunciations of puritans as well as Catholics as enemies of the Church. Where denunciation of Protestants had been limited to separatists who wrongly interpreted the injunction to leave 'Babylon', after the mid-1620s the preachers' ire fell increasingly on all 'disturbers' of the Church's peace. A ready example of this is found in the sermon that Matthew Brookes preached on 30 May 1626.[89] His sermon *'wherein may be seen whom we are to repute hereticks, and schismatics'* took as its text Romans 16:17–18 ('Now I beseech you, brethren, marke them which cause divisions and offences, contrary to the Doctrine which ye have learned, and avoid them. For they that are such, serve not our Lord Jesus Christ, but their own belly, and by good words, and fair speeches, deceive the hearts of the simple'). Brookes re-describes the target of his text's warning ('them which cause divisions and offences') as being 'in the common language of the Church . . . *Heretickes* and *Schismatickes*'.

---

[87] On this, see Milton, *Catholic and Reformed*, pp. 110–72.

[88] John Gee, *Hold Fast* (1624), STC[2] 11705. On John Gee, see Michael Questier, 'John Gee, Archbishop Abbot, and the Use of Converts from Rome', *Recusant History*, 21 (1993). On the 'Fatal Vespers', see Alexandra Walsham, '"The Fatal Vesper": Providentialism and Anti-Popery in Late Jacobean London', *Past and Present*, 144 (1994), 37–87.

[89] Matthew Brookes, *A Sermon preached at Pauls-Crosse, May 30. 1626* (1626), STC[2] 3837.

Having identified the target of St Paul's admonition, Brookes proceeds to define these two groups, creating links between them even as he describes the differences. Both claim to be Christian, but where heretics maintain fundamental errors, schismatics 'break onely the bond of love, whereby wee are tied one to another' (p. 6). Church history demonstrates 'Gods dreadfull judgement' on heretics, of which an example from recent English history is 'the house at Blackfriars' (another reference to the 'Fatal Vespers', p. 7); in this way, Catholics are unobtrusively identified as heretics. The actions that characterize schismatics are detailed in terms that make their identification equally ambiguous: the fates of Corah, Dathan, and Abiram are 'a judgement able to warne all succeeding ages, to take heed how they goe apart from the congregation of the Lord; and more especially those that will separate themselves from our Church, for some few Ceremonies and formalities retained therein' (p. 9).

With these definitions and identifications given, Brookes returns to the biblical text. He now rebundles all causes of 'division' and offences together, as he moves on to the Apostle's injunction to avoid such people. Magistrates in particular are warned to 'admonish the people to take heed of the leaven of Jesuites, Anabaptists, Brownists, and all deviders and offenders whatsoever, and let them marke them to restraine their madnesse' (p. 20). But Brookes's 'deviders and offenders' include many that preachers like Symonds, Crashaw, and Thompson exempted when they preached against 'papists and Brownists'. Brookes conflates all sorts of disagreements with the *status quo* in the English Church into something tantamount to schism:

Againe, this being their aime, wee need not wonder if in this flourishing Church of *England*, and as it were in the noone-tyde of the Gospell, as well the doctrine, as the discipline of the Church, being agreed upon in public convocation, by the learned and religious of this Land, and authorised by law, you have yet many among you, who willingly would (and doe as farre as they dare) alter the form of our publike Church-Service, and Ceremonies: and feigne would innovate something, either in respect of substance or of circumstance, and if you have Sects of *Anabaptists, Brownists, Papists, Familiasts, Catharists*, and those who mislike all things but their own inventions. For what wonder shall I bring if that I tell you, that it is possible there may be covetous men among us? (p. 25)

Here, those who 'would' change the liturgy (who 'feign would innovate something') are thrown together with '*Anabaptists, Brownists, Papists, Familiasts, Catharists*' into one undifferentiated mass of 'covetous' people 'who mislike all things but their own inventions'. Brookes exhorts magistrates to use 'the power of the sword' against those who cause divisions 'contrary to the doctrine that wee have received', but does offer one rather vague sop to conventional attitudes on the relative guilt of Catholics and puritans:

Let mee beseech them [magistrates] to marke those that cause devisions and offences, contrary to that received doctrine. Yet with a just distinction as well of the persons of those that cause devisions and offences (for some are obstinate, and some are tractable) as also of the devisions, and offences by them caused and maintained; (for of those also, some are damnable, some onely dangerous, and to the honour of the Church of God scandalous. (p. 37)

Brookes' sermon is not an anti-Catholic confutational sermon: it does not engage with anti-Catholic apologetics, nor offer reasons (fairly argued or polemical) for maintaining confessional divisions. Neither is it an exercise in 'anti-popery', because it hardly deals with Catholicism as a denomination at all. Despite the title page and the early definitions of heresy and schism, Brookes uses his text to condemn *all* troublers of the church, a group so diverse that only the vagueness of his text ('good works' and 'fair words') allows him to bundle them up like this. The point of conflating all of these 'disturbers' of the church is, of course, to associate the puritan members of the Church of England (and not merely the separatists from that church) with the sorts of threats traditionally laid at the door of Catholic agitators. Insofar as there is 'anti-popery' in this sermon, it is being used as a stick with which to beat Brookes's puritan colleagues/opponents. And this use of anti-popery tells us far less about the representation of Catholicism at Paul's Cross in Charles I's reign than it does about representation of puritanism. That is the subject that we address next.

7

Preaching against the Puritan Movement

Any attempt to describe the ways in which the puritan movement was discussed in the Paul's Cross sermons must begin with the now-extensive literature on the definitions of puritanism, or, to be more exact, on the difficulty of defining this amorphous concept.[1] The origins of the term are undoubtedly polemical, and this makes it not implausible to suggest that it was primarily an insult used by the less 'godly' on their more ostentatiously devout neighbours. The ease with which contemporaries (and modern scholars) could identify the stereotypical 'puritan', however, suggests that there was greater coherence to the idea of a 'puritan' than a purely pejorative use of the term will explain.[2] Elizabethans knew what a puritan looked like when they saw one, and at least one saw the similarity between the godly John Dod and '*Ananaias,* one whom at a play in the Black-Friars she saw scoffed at, for a holy brother of *Amsterdam*'.[3] But this does not mean that 'puritanism' was so coherent an ideology that we can identify a single 'essential' characteristic: puritans were neither necessarily presbyterians nor Parliamentarian. They were all certainly Calvinist, but this was no litmus test because Calvinism was the established theology of the Elizabethan and early Jacobean Church. Puritan ministers may have made more frequent and overt references to predestination (particularly in pastoral contexts) than other ministers did, but the exact extent of this emphasis is impossible to quantify from the sources extant. And so the historiography of English puritanism has left us with two definitions: one too small (the 'movement' that campaigned to bring the English Church in line with

---

[1] Useful summaries of this literature are Margo Todd, *Christian Humanism and the Puritan Social Order* (Cambridge: Cambridge University Press, 1987), pp. 1–14; Christopher Durston and Jacqueline Eales, 'Introduction: The Puritan Ethos, 1640–1700', in Christopher Durston and Jacqueline Eales (eds), *The Culture of English Puritanism, 1560–1700* (London: Macmillan, 1994), pp. 1–31; John Coffey and Paul C. H. Lim, 'Introduction', in John Coffey and Paul C. H. Lim (eds), *The Cambridge Companion to Puritanism* (Cambridge: Cambridge University Press, 2008), pp. 1–15.

[2] Patrick Collinson, *The Puritan Character: Polemics and Polarities in Early Seventeenth-Century English Culture* (Los Angeles: William Andrews Clark Memorial Library, University of California, 1989); Collinson 'Ecclesiastical Vitriol: Religious Satire in the 1590s and the Invention of Puritanism', in John Guy (ed.), *The Reign of Elizabeth I: Court and Culture in the Last Decade* (Cambridge: Cambridge University Press, 1995), pp. 150–70; Peter Lake and Michael Questier, *The Antichrist's Lewd Hat: Protestants, Papists and Players in Post-Reformation England* (New Haven: Yale University Press, 2002), pp. 568–9; Christopher Haigh, 'The Character of an Antipuritan', *Sixteenth Century Journal*, 35 (2004), pp. 671–88.

[3] This anecdote is reported of Joan Drake, who was suffering from a kind of religious melancholy that Dod was seeking to relieve. The episode is quoted by Patrick Collinson, 'Antipuritanism', in Coffey and Lim (eds), *Cambridge Companion to Puritanism*, pp. 19–33, p. 24.

other Reformed Churches, not least in the introduction of presbyterian church government) and one too large (all zealous supporters of the preaching, teaching, and practice of a Reformed Protestantism in England).[4] As the scholar who has most eloquently described both kinds of puritanism, it is not surprising that Patrick Collinson has also coined the phrase that best captures the difficulty of trying to define puritanism alone: the label 'puritan', he has written, 'tells us about the two halves of a stressful relationship. . . . Puritanism and Antipuritanism belong together'.[5]

This chapter follows Professor Collinson's lead, and will attempt to look at the crucial moments of stress in the relationship between the 'super-Protestants who often went by the name of puritans'[6] and their (often no less godly) fellow-ministers who preached from Paul's Cross. Some of those fellow-ministers were bishops, men that the monarch charged with the administration of the Church according to the settlement of 1559. The acceptance of that settlement as final, and the gradual development of positive enthusiasm for its liturgy and ecclesiology, forms the other half of the 'stressful relationship' by which puritan agitation for 'further reformation' must be understood.[7] Over the course of our period, preaching on the matters in dispute between those we call puritans and those we call conformists shows the emergence, and then the hardening, of party lines within the Church of England. Where anti-Catholic preaching began with a sharply drawn division between fraudulent Catholic teachers and trustworthy Protestant preachers, such a stark division is found in anti-puritan preaching at Paul's Cross only after Richard Bancroft's 1589 sermon. By the 1580s, anti-Catholic confutation had descended into thoroughly conventional 'anti-popery', divorced from current polemics. Anti-puritan themes, on the other hand, were responses to particular events, being delivered (during Elizabeth's reign at least) at times of puritan agitation in parliament or press. We can assume from this that preachers only addressed anti-puritan themes when they thought that the hierarchy's position needed to be defended.

This leaves us with several clearly designated episodes: 1565–6, the vestiarian controversy that first brought to the attention of the public the divisions within the newly established Church; 1571–3, the years of dispute over a presbyterian model for the English Church, from Thomas Cartwright's dismissal from Cambridge in December 1570 to the *Admonition to Parliament* of 1572 and the first rounds of the printed controversy between Thomas Cartwright and John Whitgift that followed; and 1589–91, the years that saw uproar over the Marprelate pamphlets (an indirect consequence of Archbishop Whitgift's conformity drive of 1584), which

---

[4] A far more thorough account of the historiography of puritanism is Peter Lake's 'The Historiography of Puritanism', in Coffey and Lim (eds), *Cambridge Companion to Puritanism*, pp. 346–71.

[5] Collinson, 'Antipuritanism', p. 24.

[6] The phrase is Patrick Collinson's: 'Puritanism as Popular Religious Culture', in Durston and Eales (eds), *Culture of English Puritanism*, pp. 32–57, p. 46.

[7] Peter Lake, *Anglicans and Puritans?: Presbyterianism and English Conformist Thought from Whitgift to Hooker* (London: Unwin Hyman, 1988); Judith Maltby, *Prayer Book and People in Elizabethan and Early Stuart England* (Cambridge: Cambridge University Press, 1998).

contributed to the Star Chamber trial that brought the clandestine presbyterian movement to an end.[8] Thereafter, it is more difficult to speak of a puritan 'movement', as the energy and attentions of the godly were diverted into other, less confrontational, channels: the 'practical divinity' that was such a famous feature of English puritanism was hardly something to be denounced from Paul's Cross. Even the Hampton Court conference passed without a campaign from Paul's Cross being conducted by either party. But the ideological fissures within the Church remained and re-emerged in the 1630s.

As with anti-Catholic confutational preaching, we must be aware of the auditory and readership at whom the preachers aimed: from the time of Jewel's 'Challenge', anti-Catholic preaching was addressed to the lay auditory at Paul's Cross, not the Roman Catholic clerical opposition. But there were two targets for anti-puritan preaching: one was an audience of fellow-ministers (who would have to take a position on the issues debated), and the other was the lay auditory (who might support or oppose their ministers). These debates were, at least initially, *in utram-que partem*, with both sides hoping to change the other's mind through pulpit and print media. Richard Bancroft's 1589 sermon breaks this convention, using instead the techniques of 'confutational' preaching familiar from anti-Catholic sermons; in these sermons, we remember, the aim is not to convince an opponent through argument but to warn the hearers, as innocent bystanders in a theological debate, of the dangers posed by the duplicitous opposition. And so the sermons started to address just one audience: the lay conformists, who were given dire warnings of the dangers of puritanism (which were increasingly conflated with separatism or caricatures of anti-monarchical Scottish Presbyterianism). The small group of ministers who appeared at Paul's Cross in Charles I's reign were overwhelming conformist in outlook. They preached peace against the dangers of innovation, and presented their puritan opponents as outsiders from a Church characterized by a narrowing range of opinions.

THE VESTIARIAN CONTROVERSY

We are fortunate indeed to have very complete records of Paul's Cross for the years of the first conformity drive, that by Archbishop Matthew Parker over the wearing of clerical vestments. Most of these records come to us in the form of notes found in Bodleian MS Tanner 50, which details at least thirty-eight Paul's Cross sermons,[9]

---

[8] It was while searching for evidence of the author of the Marprelate tracts and the secret press used to print the tracts that the bishops' pursuivants came across incriminating documents regarding the *classis* movement and a copy of the then secret *Book of Discipline*: Patrick Collinson, *The Elizabethan Puritan Movement* (London: Jonathan Cape, 1967; repr. Oxford: Clarendon, 1990), pp. 403–5.

[9] Foliation and catchwords reveal that there are two breaks in the manuscript, with ff. 40–56 and ff. pp. 87–119 missing; in both cases the end of one sermon and the beginning of another are missing. The unidentified fragments (the two sermons where the beginning is missing) have been discounted. A sermon by Robert Crowley preached on 18 October 1565 'in the Church' is included, as it is not clear whether this was a sermon intended for the cathedral or a Paul's Cross sermon preached there because of the weather.

giving the preachers' names and the dates on which the sermon were delivered. This reveals how widespread opposition to the vestments was among those clergy that the bishop of London relied on to maintain regular preaching at the Cross. There were twenty-five sermons delivered between 25 January 1565 (when the Queen wrote to Parker demanding conformity in clerical dress) and March 1566 (when thirty-seven London ministers were suspended) by preachers we can identify. Of these, eight sermons were delivered by men who had signed the petition against enforcements of vestments that was presented to the Ecclesiastical Commissioners on 20 March 1565.[10] The Paul's Cross preachers listed in the petition were frequent preachers there, including Thomas Cole, James Calfhill, and Thomas Lever, and men of considerable standing in the Church, including Alexander Nowell, Dean of St Paul's.

After the deprivation of London ministers in March 1566, there was a change of personnel at Paul's Cross, with objectors to the surplice who had appeared in 1565 being replaced by more conformist ministers.[11] Those who persisted in their objection to the surplice and were deprived in March 1566 did not re-appear at Paul's Cross that year. Thomas Lever, highly esteemed for his plain and bold sermons, made his last appearance that we know of in October 1566; the following year, he lost his prebend at Durham Cathedral for nonconformity. John Gough, Rector of St Peter's Cornhill and an emerging leader of the London puritan movement, appeared at Paul's Cross on 6 January 1566, was deprived later that year, and as far as we know never appeared at Paul's Cross again. Like Gough, Robert Crowley was an emerging leader of the London puritan movement; he preached at Paul's Cross on 18 October 1565, and was deprived in 1566.[12] But in these early years of Elizabeth's reign, the bishop had to find able, unimpeachably Protestant preachers to fill the rota at Paul's Cross, and to exclude all of those who objected to the vestments in any way would have meant the exclusion of many very able men, including Alexander Nowell, the most frequent preacher in Paul's Cross's history. And Patrick Collinson also notes that for many of those who signed the petition against the enforcement of vestments in March 1565, this was 'the end rather than the beginning of their dissent'.[13] Excluding only those for whom this

---

[10] On the Queen's letter, see Collinson, *Elizabethan Puritan Movement*, pp. 68–74; on the petition of March 1565, see pp. 74–5, and Brett Usher, 'The Deanery of Bocking and the Demise of the Vestiarian Controversy', *Journal of Ecclesiastical History* 52(3) (2001), 434–455, pp. 448–9. A second sermon by Thomas Cole might be added to this number: according to John Stow, Cole preached on 26 January 1564. However, it seems unlikely that this is meant for January 1564/5, as Stow specifies that the date is 'by order of the Kalendar', the yere to be accomptid from newe yers day forward' and that the sermon was preached on a Wednesday, which is the case for 1564 but not 1565: *Three Fifteenth-Century Chronicles, with Historical Memoranda by John Stow, the Antiquary, and Contemporary Notes of Occurrences written by him the Reign of Queen Elizabeth*, ed. James Gairdner (1880), pp. 128–9.

[11] Collinson, *Elizabethan Puritan Movement*, p. 84.

[12] Ben Lowe, 'Lever, Thomas (1521–1577)', *Oxford Dictionary of National Biography* (Oxford: Oxford University Press, 2004), online edn., Jan 2008 <http://www.oxforddnb.com/view/article/16535>, accessed 8 January 2010; Brett Usher, 'Gough, John (1521/2–1572)', Oxford: Oxford University Press, 2004; online edn., Jan 2008 <http://www.oxforddnb.com/view/article/11137>, accessed 8 January 2010; Basil Morgan, 'Crowley, Robert (1517x19–1588)', Oxford University Press, 2004; online edn., Jan 2008 <http://www.oxforddnb.com/view/article/6831>, accessed 8 January 2010; all accessed 8 January 2010.

[13] Collinson, *Elizabethan Puritan Movement*, pp. 84, 75.

was the beginning rather than the end of 'their dissent' had a far less serious impact on the calibre of preachers at the Cross. So we might look again at the preachers who appeared at Paul's Cross in 1565 and 1566, and see whether the 'puritan' wing of the Church was excluded from this pulpit permanently, or temporarily.

Of the twenty-three men who preached at Paul's Cross at the height of the controversy (between 1565 and March 1566), the opinions of four are unknown and twelve had some objection to vestments and ceremonies (eight signed the petition of March 1565, as we have seen; others voted for liturgical reform in the 1563 convocation). But only eight of that twelve persisted in their objections and are later identifiable as 'puritans'. Another seven preachers might best be described as conformists (they were willing to conform or voiced no objection to vestments or ceremonies).[14] John Jewel is included among these conformists because he would preach in defence of vestments in 1571 even though he was never enthusiastic about their use; he appeared at Paul's Cross twice in this period (in May and July) in advance of the publication of his *Replie* to Harding's *Answere*. After the deprivations of March 1566 until November 1566, we have records of seventeen preachers: seven men whose opinions are unknown; six men who made some objection to the vestments but who did not persist in their opposition; and four men who appear to have had no objection to the vestments.[15] That seven of the seventeen Paul's Cross preachers were men that we know so little about (parish clergymen or Oxford fellows) suggests that the bishop's chaplains had to search harder to find preachers to fill the rota, no doubt because several regular preachers were unavailable to them. But this does not mean that there was a complete change in the sort of preacher appearing at Paul's Cross, or in the tenor of the sermons preached there. There is considerably continuity too: three preachers (Alexander Nowell, William Day, and John Bullingham) preached before and after March 1566, and Nowell and Day are numbered among the 'non-persistent objectors'. Although the absence of men like Thomas Lever and Robert Crowley was no doubt a loss, we should not assume that their absence was permanent: our records for the years after 1567 do not allow us to establish when or if the puritans returned, but we have good reason to believe that the impact of Parker's campaign was

---

[14] Two preachers delivered two sermons in this period: Bishop John Jewel and John Bullingham. Both are numbered among the conformists here, along with Edmund Guest, Bishop of Rochester, John Whitgift, John May, George Gardiner, and Nicholas Robinson. John Jewel expressed dislike of the vestments privately, calling them 'theatrical habits' in a letter to Peter Martyr of 1559: *The Works of John Jewel*, ed. Rev. John Ayre, 4 vols (1850), vol. 4 (1850), pp. 1221–4. Those who signed the petition against the surplice were Robert Crowley, Thomas Lever, Thomas Cole, Edmund Freke, John Gough, Alexander Nowell, James Calfhill, and Nicholas Kervile. Freke and Nowell did not continue their opposition thereafter. Four other preachers voiced objections to the vestments, particularly in the 1563 convocation: Thomas Bickley, William Turner, John Oxenbridge, and William Day. Bickley and Day did not object thereafter; Turner was deprived and Oxenbridge would sign the Book of Discipline in 1588.

[15] The six who objected to vestments in the 1565 petition or the 1563 convocation, but not thereafter, are Thomas Becon, Thomas Watts, Alexander Nowell, William Day, Matthew Hutton, and Robert Horne, Bishop of Winchester. The four conformists are John Young, John Bridges, William Overton, and John Bullingham.

short-lived.[16] 1566 was probably not a watershed in the history of Paul's Cross' relationship to puritanism, and we have good reason for thinking that the emerging puritan wing of the Church of England still had access to this most influential pulpit.

We can conclude that both sides in the vestiarian controversy had access to Paul's Cross, even if that access was more limited in 1566 for those who objected to the surplice. We should also note that this was not a controversy on which many explicit statements were made in sermons delivered from the Cross, and those statements that we know of are from those who objected to the surplice. Robert Crowley, preaching on 18 October 1565, sought to correct the impression he had made 'in my last sermon that I preached here' (now lost) which 'was taken and otherwise reported then I ment'. Crowley's point was that sobriety of dress is needed, not uniformity: St Luke wore the clothes of a physician and this was nonetheless appropriate for an Evangelist, since 'the sobryety of apparell of Prests doth not consist in one certen kinde of apparell, for who would thinke that it wear sober apparell for the prophets to use the apparell of the priests of the Ethnickes'.[17] On 1 September 1566, after those who refused to conform had been deprived but while the Queen was away from London on progress, 'Mr Pady, chaplain to the Robert Horne of Winchester',[18] attempted to make anti-Catholic capital from the dispute over vestments and ceremonies. He spoke of the conservative priests who were merely 'counterfettinge protestants', and exhorted the hearers to help ministers and magistrates in driving out such men. Enthusiasm for religious ritual was a sure sign of doctrinal corruption:

Ther is a scisme at this day in the Church of god, not of great and principal matters as god be thanked therfor but of a trifle, but of a small sparke a greater flame may arise that which heerin Satan goeth about to deface, god stoppeth it and turneth it to his glory, and omnia bene. The Ipocrits are mad[e] manifest, . . . the secret Papists they open them selves, they will have crosse and candels and omnia bene, and so the secret enemies are mad[e] now open enemies, when the Quens majestie shall see those hot enemies, I trust god willinge, that when they be rooted out, his scisme allso shalbe rooted out, and omnia bene all thinges shalbe well.[19]

---

[16] The sources make a fully accurate comparison of the preachers at Paul's Cross before and after 1566 impossible, as two of our most important sources end at this time (Machyn's diary in 1563, and the Tanner 50 notes in 1566). Thereafter, we rely on printed copies or notes on individual sermons, which means that we have a less full picture of preaching at Paul's Cross between 1567 and c.1580 (when print publication becomes much more common) that for the years 1558 and 1565. Given the shortage of preachers willing to undertake a Paul's Cross sermon at this time, and in light of their subsequent careers, it seems unlikely that men like Calfhill or Cole were permanently excluded from Paul's Cross: see Usher, 'The Deanery of Bocking and the Demise of the Vestiarian Controversy', pp. 450–4.

[17] Bodleian Library MS Tanner 50, f. 8[v].

[18] The most likely identification for this preacher is David Padye, who was a Prebendary of St Paul's and then of Winchester Cathedral: CCEd Person ID 73169, The Clergymen of the Church of England Database, http://www.theclergydatabase.org.uk/index.html, accessed 18 January 2010.

[19] Bodleian Library MS Tanner 50, ff. 84[v]–85[r]. I take it that Padye is using 'crosses and candels' as a synecdoche for ecclesiastical ceremonies, including the wearing of vestments. He may also be referring once again to the cross (or crucifix; the terms used are inconsistent) and candles notoriously retained in the Queen's chapel.

There was no campaign by conformist preachers explaining the need to enforce the use of clerical vestments. Indeed, the theme for sermons across this two-year period is remarkably consistent: the corruption of the Roman Church, and particularly the pope, and the need for moral reformation by the English in gratitude for the peace and freedom of the Gospel that they now enjoyed. The evidence provided by the notes from Tanner 50 suggests that the 'Challenge' controversy between Jewel and Harding was still of greater significance than the internal debates over clerical vestments.

CHURCH GOVERNMENT AND THE
ADMONITION TO PARLIAMENT

This was to change within a few years. The first airing of the growing divisions between the conforming bishops and their more radical colleagues from Paul's Cross was in 1571. There are several significant differences between this and the vestiarian controversy that point to the growing severity of the dissention. In 1565, everyone agreed that ecclesiastical dress was a 'thing indifferent' about which the English Church was free to make its own arrangements. Enthusiasm for clerical vestments was rare among the bishops, particularly among the Marian exiles: for men like John Jewel and Richard Horne, they were an interim measure, or something to be endured out of obedience. And so initially there was little difference between both sides of the dispute. Many of those who had objected to the vestments were of the same generation and had shared the experience of exile with those who argued for them. The disagreement was primarily about how to balance the necessity of obedience to the ecclesiastical authorities in their prescription of clerical vestments with the inappropriateness of a Reformed clergy using the same vestments that were associated with Catholicism and the rituals of the Roman Catholic liturgy.

By 1571, however, puritans were beginning to see episcopacy itself as the root of the problem. There are many, complex reasons for this: the bishops enforced the rules regarding vestments and liturgical rituals (such as the sign of the cross in baptism), but they were powerless to reform the Church's finances so that pluralities (the holding of more than one position that entailed pastoral responsibility, a 'cure of souls') were abolished and an income sufficient to attract a preaching (which increasingly meant a graduate) clergyman was attached to every parish. The incomes (regardless of the expenses) of bishops, many of them pluralists, meant that the bishops appeared to be the worst examples of the Church's faults, not the source of redress.[20] A generational gap separated the bishops from many of the radical puritan ministers, and the bishops were perceived by some of the younger puritans as men who had compromised their earlier principles for the sake of money and

---

[20] Lake, *Anglicans and Puritans?*, pp. 26–8. On the parlous financial state of the Church in Elizabeth's reign see Christopher Hill, *Economic Problems of the Church from Archbishop Whitgift to the Long Parliament* (Oxford: Clarendon Press, 1956).

worldly honour. An alternative to episcopacy was available in the presbyterian system that had developed in Geneva and whose divine sanction had been argued first by Theodore Beza but more recently had been lectured on in Cambridge by Thomas Cartwright.[21] The young leaders of a now identifiable puritan movement campaigned against the bishops, in press and parliament, not just because the latter were ineffective in 'edifying' the Church, but because their very claim to superiority over other ministers was unscriptural. The Bible did provide a model for Church government, and it did not include bishops.[22]

As a result, there is an increasing difference between the tone adopted by the bishops and that used by their opponents in the disputes of the 1570s: the bishops' sermons tend to adopt a conciliatory tone, minimizing the points at issue and attacking their opponents as 'disturbers' of the Church's peace. The puritans' answers sometimes adopt the tone of inter-confessional confutation, abandoning the fiction of fraternal castigation and denouncing the bishops as enemies of the Gospel. Of course, the bishops had the advantage of ready access to the pulpits of England, which they could use to full advantage. Doubtless, it was easier to adopt a reasonable and forgiving tone from a position of such strength, and adopting such a tone was advantageous to those addressing a lay auditory that might be sympathetic to 'painful' and 'godly' ministers in dispute with their bishop.

That was certainly the case in the two sermons preached while Parliament and Convocation sat in 1571. This parliament was, in the words of J. E. Neale, 'the hinge between the past and the future. Presbyterianism had not yet developed its parliamentary propaganda; but lack of sympathy with the bishops was clear'.[23] In April 1571, MP Richard Strickland instigated a series of bills that would have enacted the entire puritan programme: subscription to the thirty-six more strictly doctrinal of the Thirty-Nine Articles would be compulsory for the laity as well as the clergy; the Prayer Book would be purged of the ceremonies considered objectionable; and ecclesiastical discipline would be based on Cranmer's *Reformatio Legum*, newly edited by John Foxe and reprinted. Although capturing the initiative in the Commons, Strickland's programme had support from neither the Privy Councillors in the parliament nor from the bishops and it contradicted the Queen's express instructions not to discuss such topics.[24] Unsurprisingly, this attempt to legislate for puritan reformation failed.[25] Meanwhile, in the Convocation taking

---

[21] Lake, *Anglicans and Puritans?*, pp. 2–4.

[22] Collinson, *Elizabethan Puritan Movement*, pp. 101–13.

[23] J. E. Neale, *Elizabeth and Her Parliaments, 1558–1581* (London: Jonathan Cape, 1953), p. 181.

[24] Ibid. pp. 188–93. Although he disagrees with Neale's claim that Strickland was part of an organized opposition, a 'puritan choir' in this parliament, or that Sir Thomas Norton was Strickland's ally in all aspects of this campaign, M. A. R. Graves agrees that Strickland's bills thwarted more moderate proposals, including measures supported by the bishops: 'The Management of the Elizabethan House of Commons: The Council's "Men-of-Business"', *Parliamentary History*, 2 (1983), 11–38, esp. pp. 12–24.

[25] The bill demanding clerical subscription to the doctrinal of the Thirty-Nine articles became a statute (Neale, *Elizabeth and her Parliaments, 1558–1581*, pp. 206–7). A bill against simoniacal practices in ecclesiastical livings was the only other measure from Strickland and Norton's programme to be enacted (ibid. p. 217). The bill enforcing the taking of Communion on pain of a hefty fine also made its way through parliament in April, being formally concluded on 25 May but it was then vetoed by the Queen

place at the same time, a series of canons were agreed that demanded, among other things, a review of all preaching licenses and subscription to the Articles by all in receipt of new licenses: the 'chief puritans', including Thomas Lever, Thomas Sampson, John Field, and Edward Dering, were all made to appear at Lambeth.[26]

The appearance of two bishops preaching on the same controversial topic within the same month that Parliament was sitting was no accident.[27] Whether John Jewel and Robert Horne offered their services or were chosen by Archbishop Parker and their fellow bishops is unknown, but the choice of these two to deliver the bishops' first answer to the puritans from Paul's Cross is significant: both had been Marian exiles and 'Coxian' in the Frankfurt troubles. Both had appeared at Paul's Cross more than once. They were men whose sincere attachment to the principles of a Reformed, preaching ministry could not be doubted but whose commitment to the idea of conformity was also well known. The sermons delivered by Jewel and Horne in April 1571 are not extant, except insofar as they are reproduced in the responses to them written by two leading London radicals, William White and Thomas Wilcox.[28]

We do not know the text on which Jewel spoke, but 'in the entrye' of his discussion of current disputes, he cited Jeremiah 23:28 'where it is sayd he that hath my worde let hym speake my word fayhfully, what is the chaffe to the wheate sayeth the Lord' and said words to the effect that as 'we have the wheate, let us not strive for the chaffe'.[29] Secondly, Jewel is said to have claimed that he 'came not to defend those thinges', but he nonetheless offered examples of Apostles undergoing ritual ceremonies (Paul circumcising Timothy in Acts 16; Paul shaving his head as a ritual connected with the Nazarite vow he took, ff. 48ᵛ–49ʳ). He quoted 1 Corinthians 6:13 ('as meate was for the belye, & the body for meate, yet god should destroy them both') to argue that 'apparrell [is] for the backe' and not worth disagreeing over. Jewel reportedly said 'what is white? what is blacke? what is square? what is rounde? etc'; the vestments are 'creatures of god', to be put to use

(pp. 212–16). The proposal for reforming the Prayer Book never went further than the first debate, in which the Commons decided to ask the Queen's permission to take the matter further (p. 200).

[26] John Strype, *The Life and Acts of Matthew Parker*, 3 vols (Oxford, 1821), vol. 2, pp. 57–9, 65–7.

[27] The *Register of Sermons* also lists a sermon by Bishop Richard Cox of Ely, possibly for 15 April, but this reference is problematic. Cox was active in drawing up the 'Canons' of 1571 and would be on Parker's Commission to review preaching licenses in the summer of 1571: Strype, *Life of Matthew Parker*, vol. 2, pp. 60–1, 65–7. This makes a Paul's Cross sermon by him at this time not unlikely. But the source for the *Register's* entry for this sermon cannot be traced, and 15 April 1571 was Easter Sunday, the only Sunday when there was no sermon at Paul's Cross.

[28] 'Certaine griefes justly conceived of B. Jewells sermon, with a brief awnswer to some parte therof, writen by W.W. and drawne into form by T.W.', and 'An awnswer to such Arguments as B. Horne used in his sermon at Paules Crosse upon the 2d Sonday after Easter Anno 1571, to mainteyne the remnants of Antichriste'. Both items are calendared with extensive quotations in *The Seconde Parte of a Register: Being a Calendar of Manuscripts under that Title Intended for Publication by the Puritans about 1593, and now in Dr Williams's Library, London*, ed. Albert Peel, 2 vols (Cambridge: Cambridge University Press, 1915), vol. 1, pp. 79–82. The response to Jewel's sermon is also extant in Bodleian Library MS Selden Supra 44, ff. 48–52.

[29] Bodleian MS Selden Supra 44, f. 48ʳ.

(ff. 50ᵛ–51ᵛ). But this conciliatory approach was matched by a denunciation of those who troubled the Church over such matters. Jewel is reported as saying that 'those which did not content themselves therewith, were wanton and full, and had not the spirite of god', which White and Wilcox note was 'a very hard and severe judgment' (f. 48ᵛ). Later in the sermon he cited 1 Corinthians 3 (presumably verse 4, 'For while one saith, I am of Paul; and another, I am of Apollos, are ye not carnal?') to criticize those 'which are sayde to be sectaries and renters of the church' (in White and Wilcox's words, f. 50ᵛ), but he also offered vehement exhortations to maintain the Church's unity, reportedly saying that he wished to be cast into the sea with Jonah if he was 'the cause of this rent in the Church'.

Robert Horne's sermon of 29 April is harder to reconstruct, as it is not summarized by White and Wilcox in detail, but it does appear to follow Jewel's conciliatory line: he said he would stop what he was doing if it were shown to be unlawful.[30] Horne apparently wished 'those cut off that did trouble us', a harsh statement but one matched by Horne's puritan respondents. When Horne made positive mention of Jewel's recent sermon, Wilcox and White denied the commendation: when 'defendinge Christs Church against the open papist' Jewel 'did well and is much to be commended', but now, being 'an enemy to syncerity and the truth of Christs gospell, he doth evill and is worthy to be reproved'. At this stage of the confrontation between puritans and conformists, the puritans appear more ready to adopt a confutational position, denying fellowship with their opponents and positioning them as 'enemies of the truth'.

A more audacious move was made by the puritan movement in 1572 when they published *An Admonition to Parliament*, 'public polemic in the guise of an address to Parliament' (in Patrick Collinson's phrase).[31] The *Admonition* charged MPs in the upcoming parliament to put right all that was wrong with the Church, and the wrongs they listed include episcopal government and a liturgy based around set prayer rather than preaching. This brought the bishops back to Paul's Cross, and on 27 July 1572, Thomas Cooper, Bishop of Lincoln, preached a sermon in response to the *Admonition* just a month after it was printed. The argument of his sermon is known to us only through the response made to it by a supporter of the *Admonition*, probably Job Throckmorton.[32]

Throckmorton does not tell us what scriptural text Cooper used, and he organizes his response to Cooper around five points that may not reflect the structure of the original sermon: Cooper's 'maintaining of an ignorant & unlearned ministerie'; his 'magnifying' of the Prayer Book; his defence of 'the ungodly titles,

[30] 'An awnswer to such Arguments as B. Horne used in his sermon at Paules Crosse upon the 2d Sonday after Easter Anno 1571, to mainteyne the remnants of Antichriste', in *The Seconde Parte of a Register*, ed. Peel, vol. 1, pp. 81–2, esp. 81.

[31] Collinson, *Elizabethan Puritan Movement*, p. 118.

[32] This is Inner Temple Library, Petyt MS 538, vol. 47, ff. 459–62. It is discussed in Leland H. Carlson, *Martin Marprelate, Gentleman: Master Job Throckmorton Laid Open in his Colors* (San Marino, CA: Huntington Library, 1981), pp. 314–19. On Throckmorton, see Patrick Collinson, 'Throckmorton, Job (1545–1601)', *Oxford Dictionary of National Biography* (Oxford: Oxford University Press, 2004); online edn., Jan 2008 <http://www.oxforddnb.com/view/article/27391m>, accessed 2 February 2010.

and unjust Lordship of Bishopps'; his 'depraving' of presbyterianism ('the governement which Christ hath left to his Church'); and lastly his wresting of Scripture in
the process (f. 459ʳ). Cooper's was evidently a more hard-hitting sermon than those
by Jewel and Horne. He accused the 'good men' who wrote the admonition of
being 'about to hinder the course of the gospell, and to gape for your lyvinges'
(f. 459ʳ).[33] On the substantive issues regarding episcopacy and presbyterianism
(which are treated near the end of Throckmorton's response and so presumably
came in the latter half of Cooper's sermon), Throckmorton has little to say by way
of counterargument beyond a basic denial. Cooper is accused of having tried 'to
prove these antichristian titles, Archbishop, lord bishop . . . etc. in ministers of the
gospell lawfull' (f. 460ʳ). Where Cooper argued that 'the externall forme of
government in the church' appertained 'to order', Throckmorton accuses him of
having 'judged it an error' to 'have them don according to the prescript of Gods
word' (f. 460ʳ). Cooper evidently ended his sermon with a ringing denunciation of
those who campaigned against the bishops. In doing so, Throckmorton says that he
'joynd as it were in one yoke, papists, & jealous gospellers, wishing severe punishments by lawe to be appointed for them', which caused some to think 'you spake
rather of choler than charitie' (f. 460ʳ).

The response of Throckmorton, like those of White and Wilcox, circulated in
manuscript among the 'godly', but it was not publicly available in the way that the
bishops' sermons of 1571 and 1572 were, and this may partly explain the hard-
hitting language of these two tracts. But puritan ministers who were not immediately involved with the *Admonition* were not barred from Paul's Cross: Laurence
Humphrey, till then a leading puritan but one who did not support the *Admonition*, preached there in 1572 and his appointment was probably for the prestigious
Rehearsal Sermon. If so, one of the sermons he 'rehearsed' would have been the
Good Friday Passion Sermon of Laurence Chaderton, a man whose presbyterian
beliefs would not emerge until the 1580s.[34] The case *for* presbyterianism was not
promulgated at Paul's Cross, and in this sense the puritan movement had less access
to Paul's Cross that was the case during the vestiarian controversy. Indeed, on
the two occasions when preachers did pronounce praise for Cartwright and presbyterianism, it was treated by all concerned as a lapse in the bishop's control over
the pulpit. The first preacher, Richard Crick, was 'conveighed away' before the

---

[33] The same accusation was made at Paul's Cross by John Young, later bishop of Rochester, in
1573: [William Whittingham], *A Brief Discours off the Troubles begonne at Franckfort* ([Heidelberg],
1574), *STC²* 25442, sig. A2ᵛ; *Register of Sermons*, p. 54.

[34] Thomas Drant says that his sermon was commended by 'that learned man Doctour
Humfrey . . . at Paules crosse': *A Fruitfull and Necessary Sermon* (1572), *STC²* 7166, sig. A2ᵛ. Drant's
was the Spital sermon for the Tuesday of Easter week that year, and praise of the Spital preachers was
conventional in the Rehearsal sermon at Paul's Cross. On Humphrey, see Thomas S. Freeman,
'Humphrey, Laurence (1525x7–1589)', *Oxford Dictionary of National Biography* (Oxford: Oxford
University Press, 2004); online edn., Jan 2008 <http://www.oxforddnb.com/view/article/14156>,
accessed 4 February 2010. For Chaderton's Passion Sermon, see London Metropolitan Archive,
Repertory of the Court of Aldermen 17, f. 297ʳ. On Chaderton, see Patrick Collinson, 'Chaderton,
Laurence (1536?–1640)', *Oxford Dictionary of National Biography* (Oxford: Oxford University Press,
2004); online edn., Jan 2008 <http://www.oxforddnb.com/view/article/5010>, accessed 4 February
2010.

bishop's men could arrest him; the second, Arthur Wake, fled back to Oxford and Bishop Sandys had to explain himself to William Cecil and the Earl of Leicester.[35] On 14 October of the same year, Edward Bacon reported to his brother Nathaniel Bacon of Stiffkey (the eldest son of Sir Nicholas Bacon) that 'ther is continuall preaching at Pawles against the boke, a thing reported to be injoyned etche man that occupieth that place'.[36]

One of the most significant of those who preached 'against the boke' was John Whitgift, who took his turn at Paul's Cross on 2 November 1572.[37] We have no reports of the sermon, and cannot reconstruct it, but we can assume that Whitgift launched at least some of the arguments that would be found in his *Answere to the Admonition*, which he had finished by 21 October and was in print by 21 November of that year.[38] The 'Whitgiftian' position, which would be taken up by other conformists at Paul's Cross also, was that Scripture does not prescribe *all* matters pertaining to public liturgy and Church government, and those matters not prescribed in Scripture were matters for local Church governors.[39] Consequently, ceremonies such as kneeling at communion are not 'faults' to be amended: it is for 'a godly Prince, with the advice of godly and learned Byshoppes' to 'make orders in the Church' (pp. 28–9, 61–2). The history of bishops as superiors and 'overseers' of other ministers is traced back to the Primitive Church, so that they cannot have been 'devised by Antichrist' (pp. 64–76); scriptural warrant for presbyterian elders is not so clear-cut as the authors of the *Admonition* suggest (pp. 112–19, 122–8).

Edwin Sandys, Bishop of London, also preached in the early summer of 1573, but this sermon does survive in a printed version and so it is the first conformist sermon where we can get a clear sense of the place allotted to anti-puritan themes.[40] Sandys's text was Matthew 3:23–4 ('And when he was entred into the ship his disciples followed him. And beholde there arose a great tempest in the sea so that the ship was covered with waves: but he was asleepe'), and Sandys begins by explaining the text as a 'type or figure' to 'set forth the state of the Church' on earth, that is, 'beaten and tossed like a boate, it is disfigured with sharpe and stormie weather' (p. 330). From this, the imperative to follow Christ by rejecting false doctrine and abandoning fleshly lusts is insisted on (p. 332), as is obedience to 'fathers, elders, guides, & teachers' (p. 335). Those who follow Christ will be 'tossed

---

[35] BL Ms Lansdowne 17.f. 43. Wake was deprived not long after this incident (in January 1574) and then emigrated to the Channel Islands, where he was instrumental in the establishment of presbyterianism: A. F. S. Pearson, *Thomas Cartwright and Elizabethan Puritanism, 1535–1603* (Cambridge: Cambridge University Press, 1925), pp. 123, 161–3.
[36] *The Papers of Nathaniel Bacon of Stiffkey*, ed. A. Hassell Smith, Gillian M. Baker, and R. W. Kenny, vol. I (Norwich: Centre of East Anglian Studies, 1979), p. 90.
[37] John Strype tells us that Whitgift's appointment to Paul's Cross had been postponed till later in the term because of his work on the *Answere to the Admonition*: *The Life and Acts of John Whitgift, DD*, 3 vols (Oxford, 1822), vol. 1, p. 96.
[38] Pearson, *Thomas Cartwright*, p. 68. On the wider implications of the *Admonition* controversy, see Lake, *Anglicans and Puritans?*, pp. 28–70.
[39] John Whitgift, *An Answere to a Certen Libel Intituled, An Admonition to the Parliament* (1572), *STC²* 25427, pp. 20–2.
[40] Edwin Sandys, 'The Nineteenth Sermon. A Sermon preached at Pauls Crosse', in *Sermons made by the most Reverende Father in God, Edwin, Archbishop of Yorke* (1585), *STC²* 21713, pp. 330–43.

and greviouslie shaken with a tempest' in this life (p. 335), partly through the enmity of the wicked (p. 337). The 'chiefest members' and 'overseers' (a word that translates 'bishops', 'episcopi') of the church endure the most (pp. 338–9).

From this summary, it is clear that the genre in which Sandys's sermon can be classified is the 'doctrinal' sermon, a type used 'for the information of the mind to a right judgement concerning things to be believed', in the words of William Perkins.[41] Sandys's sermon expounds the nature of the Church militant: that is the 'doctrine' that his hearers are taught. Just as the preachers on political anniversaries incorporated political themes into the 'instructive' sermon through the duty of thanksgiving and obedience, Sandys links his condemnation of puritan agitation to his scriptural text, but only as a particular example of the general truth that the Church on Earth is not at peace. For example, Sandys says that Satan uses every means to upset the Church, including 'the winds of division and contention'. And this lesson is found relevant and 'applied' to the English Church:

A kingdom being at unity in it selfe, though it be smal, yet may be strong: but divided & distracted into factions though it be mighty how should it stand? This is a thing which I wish greatly that we did throughly consider. Hetherto (such is the mercy of almighty God) our enemies have not prevayled against us although they bee many, and wee but fewe; they strong, and wee weake. But if a few sillie weake ones be miserably divided, what may wee looke for but inevitable ruine? It is lamentable that the Gospell of peace should bring forth schisme. This is both slaunderous & undoubtedly perilous to our profession. Unto them whom Satan hath abused as his instruments to worke this evill, I may speake in a maner as the clearke of Ephesus did to the people when they were in an uprore without cause. There is no idolatry no impiety maintained by the lawes and orders of this church.... When they refuse the peaceable meanes wherby strife may be ended, & will followe no course but that which breedeth confusion & raiseth tumultes, may they not justly be accused as clamorous troblers of the church of God, for as much as there can be no just & alowable reason aleaged of these their troublesom & unquiet dealings? Shall we be followers of men in contention & that about frivolous & vaine things, & leave the walking after Christ in peace & love. (pp. 339–40)

As God allows these afflictions to happen to us, Sandys concludes, we must look to him for help when they happen; the sermon ends with a prayer that the Church might be brought through the dangers that afflict her.

As printed, the sermon contains little (beyond the passages quoted) on the controversies caused by the first and second *Admonitions,* but it is probable that the printed version has been revised from that delivered at Paul's Cross, and that the original version had more to say on these matters. An anonymous epistle, 'A friendly caveat to Bishop Sandys' published in *A Parte of a Register*, is prefaced by a note saying that Sandys had complained in his sermon 'the last Sunday at Paules Crosse' about 'the bluntness & plainness of the stile' used by the writer.[42] The

---

[41] *The Arte of Prophecying,* in *Works* (1616–18), *STC²* 19651, vol. 2, p. 668. See also Hyperius (Andreas Gerardus), *De Formandis Concionibus Sacris* (1553), trans. John Ludham, *The Practis of Preaching* (1577), *STC²* 11758, Lib. I, f. 18ʳ.

[42] 'A friendly caveat to Bishop Sandys then Bishop of London, and to the rest of his brethren the Bishops: written by a godly, learned and zealous gentleman, about 1567', in John Udall, *A Parte of a*

printed sermon contains no mention of this letter, but Sandys might well have found space to mention it, in dealing either with the persecutions visited on the 'chief members' and 'overseers' of the church or with the 'troblers of the Church of God'. In an interview that took place on 25 November 1573 between John Stroude, printer of Cartwright's *Reply to the Answer* and *The Second Admonition*, and Sandys in High Commission, Stroude alleged that Sandys said 'in your sermon at Paules crosse, that there were certaine maculats in our ministrye'. Sandys did not deny this, but said that they ought not to be removed except 'by publique authority'.[43] This admission is not included in the sermon as it is printed.

Common to the conformist arguments of the 1570s is the characterization of puritans by their 'disturbing' the Church (rather than by their presbyterianism, for example). This may seem like an insulting diminution of the puritan programme, but it was a tactic that allowed for reconciliation. In the 'Challenge' sermon, John Jewel had done the opposite, widening the division between the two sides so that the laity would be drawn into the arms of the established Church. The conflict between conformists and puritans was not presented as being necessarily permanent: puritans were not essentially 'enemies' whose doctrine differs fundamentally from that established in the English Church, but misled 'disturbers' who must respect ecclesiastical authority. (Puritan answers to conformists did not always maintain the same distinction.) For now, conformist preaching at Paul's Cross kept the division between puritans and conformists permeable, presumably with the intention of siphoning off as much support among the uncommitted as possible.

Another sign that conformist preaching was not intended to make permanent the rift in the Church is the disappearance of anti-puritan digressions in the years after the *Admonition* controversy: complaints about the 'troublers of the Church' and those who contend over trifles vanish in the years between the *Admonition* and Whitgift's campaign for conformity of 1583. Puritan preachers were still invited to take some of the most prestigious slots in the pulpit's schedule: John Knewstub, one of the 'godly' since his time in Cambridge and later a prominent member of the *classis* movement in Suffolk, preached the Passion sermon in 1576.[44] Knewstub's sermon is primarily a meditation on the Passion, as befitted the day, but includes a

---

Register (Middelburg, 1593), *STC²* 10400, pp. 371–81. The letter is dated 1567 but addressed to Sandys as 'then Bishop of London', which he was not until 1570; Collinson dates this letter to July 1573: *Elizabethan Puritan Movement*, p. 149. The writer himself confesses that his style is 'stinging' (p. 371), and indeed it is: Sandys and the bishops are accused of being 'men pleasing mungerelles' (p. 372); the failure of further reformation lies with 'you Mr doctor Drawbacke in the band, with the rest of your mates'. The writer warns them that 'now divers good and godlie men, set too their hand to make an end of the rodde, which I hope, afore it bee long, will make your proude buttockes to smart' (p. 375). Terms such as 'doctor Drawbacke' and the broad and irreverent humour of a rod being taken to the bishops' 'proud buttocks' suggest a writer with much in common in style and opinion with Job Throckmorton, if not Martin Marprelate.

[43] *The Seconde Parte of a Register*, ed. Peel, vol. 1, pp. 112–13.

[44] On Knewstub, see Collinson, *Elizabethan Puritan Movement*, pp. 126–8, 218–19, 232. Knewstub's Paul's Cross sermon was first printed as part 2 of his *A Confutation of Monstrous and Horrible Heresies, taught by H.N.* (1579), *STC²* 15040, and then reprinted separately as *A Sermon preached at Paules Crosse the Fryday before Easter, 1579* [really 1576] (1579), *STC²* 15046. The context

couple of confutational digressions. In these, Knewstub is careful to make the English Church as inclusive as possible: the 'sworne enimies of godlinesse' are 'Papistes, Anabapistes, Libertines, and the Familie of Love' because they all submit the revealed Word to other authorities, be it Tradition or private inspiration (sigs E^v–E2^v). The considerable space between the radical's private inspiration and the Catholic's Tradition can then be occupied by the mainstream Reformed tradition without minute distinctions that might expose the disagreements between the Churches, or within the English Church. Laurence Chaderton returned to Paul's Cross in 1578, and his castigation of the failures of the English included 'dumb' preachers: in the non-political context of an exhortatory sermon, this passed into print without comment.[45] Preaching on 10 May 1579, John Stockwood asked 'what if for hatred of him that rebuketh in the gate, and through abhorring him that speaketh uprightly, we be tearmed by the odious names of Puritans, Presicians, unspotted brethren'. Stockwood's 'we' suggests that he thought himself to be with others to whom those 'odious names' had been applied.[46]

WHITGIFT, MARPRELATE, BANCROFT

The bishops put Paul's Cross to work as the platform from which to defend the Elizabethan Church settlement again in 1584. John Whitgift had been made Archbishop of Canterbury on 23 September 1583. Whitgift had prepared a wide-ranging series of articles to be enquired of by his bishops in the southern diocese; he gained the Queen's approval of them and they were ready for promulgation by 29 October 1584. One of these articles required ministers to subscribe to three propositions (that no foreign power has any jurisdiction, spiritual or temporal, in the Queen's realms; that the Book of Common Prayer contains nothing contrary to the word of God; and that the Thirty-Nine Articles are agreeable to the word of God). The first article presented no problems for puritans, but the second was difficult for those, including many moderates, who thought the Church's ceremonies popish and unscriptural; the third was problematic if agreement was demanded with all, and not merely the thirty-six doctrinal, Articles of Religion.[47] Whitgift preached the accession sermon at Paul's Cross that November.[48] In that sermon he set out his agenda as archbishop, and that agenda was about conformity and obedience. The central theme of the sermon was obedience and those 'conceited, and wayward' people who obey 'when they list, wherein they list, and so long as

---

of the original printing (alongside a tract condemning the Family of Love) may suggest that Knewstub's targeting of Protestant radicals was a deliberate inclusion in the Passion sermon.

[45] Laurence Chaderton, *An Excellent and Godly Sermon* ([1578?]), *STC*² 4924, f. 8^v.

[46] John Stockwood, *A Very Fruiteful Sermon Preached at Paules Crosse* (1579), *STC*² 23285, p. 6.

[47] Collinson, *Elizabethan Puritan Movement*, pp. 243–5.

[48] [John Whitgift], *A Most Godly and Learned Sermon, preached at Pauls Crosse the 17 of November* (1589), *STC*² 25432. Whitgift's sermon was not printed until 1589, when its editor claimed he thought it useful for a time when '*Martyn* and his *Martynistes*, have given so great an offence to the Church of God' (sigs A2^r, A4^v).

they list' (sig. C6ᵛ) are criticized at length. The target for Whitgift's campaign against disobedience is without doubt those who show no respect for bishops. Nicholas Faunt, an ardent puritan, reported to Anthony Bacon that the sermon was 'only som Invectyve against the best professors whom he termed weyward fellowes'.[49]

The puritan movement was not passive in its response to Whitgift's campaign: several lengthy and learned tracts defending their position came from the press. As was the case with anti-Catholic propaganda in the early Elizabethan period, Paul's Cross was one of the venues from which the ecclesiastical authorities sought to win the lay auditors around to their side of the argument. Dudley Fenner, the probable author of *A Counter-poison* (1584), objected to the interpretation of 1 Timothy 5:17 offered by John Copcot in a recent convocation sermon.[50] John Copcot appeared at Paul's Cross the same year with a sermon 'where Answer is made to the Counterpoison'.[51] John Field's publication of William Fulke's *Learned Discourse* was the catalyst for John Bridges' Paul's Cross sermon of 1584/5. No copy of Bridges' sermon is extant, but it is thought to have included material later printed in his *Defence of the Government Established* (1587).[52] It is impossible to reconstruct which elements of Bridges' notoriously long book might have been rehearsed from Paul's Cross.[53] We are luckier with John Copcot's sermon, which survives in manuscript. Like Edwin Sandys's sermon of 1573, Copcot's is a 'doctrinal' sermon on the nature of the Church. His text was Psalm 84:1, on David's longing to see the Lord's tabernacle, and Copcot elaborates on David's grief that 'he could not enjoye

---

[49] Lambeth Palace Library MS 647, f. 162ᵛ.

[50] 'Let the elders that rule well be counted worthy of double honour, especially they who labour in the word and doctrine' (AV). Presbyterians interpreted this text as showing that pastors and doctors were two distinct offices, and conformists interpreted it as referring to bishops as superior ministers. I can find no record of Copcot's convocation sermon except his own reference to it as the context for Fenner's attack (LPL MS 374, f. 155ʳ). This is confirmed by a marginal note in Fenner's *A Counter-poyson Modestly Written for the Time* (1584), *STC²* 10770, p. 134. On Copcot, see Stephen Wright, 'Copcot, John (d. 1590)', *Oxford Dictionary of National Biography* (Oxford: Oxford University Press, 2004); online edn., Jan 2008 <http://www.oxforddnb.com/view/article/6248>, accessed 17 February 2010.

[51] Lambeth Palace Library MS 374, ff. 114ᵛ–153ʳ. There was a reply to Copcot, also probably by Fenner, entitled *A Defence of the Reasons of the Counter-poyson, for Maintenance of the Eldership* ([Middelburg: R. Schilders], 1586), *STC²* 10772. The author speaks of his difficulty in getting a copy of the Paul's Cross sermon (which confirms that it was not printed), but he says that the sermon circulated in manuscript and he has 'since that time . . . fallen upon the whole Sermon in writing' (sig. πʳ). He reproduces 'That part of his Sermon which concerned Discipline' (sigs. π2ʳ–3ᵛ) but it is a short summary compared to the copy in LPL MS 374: Fenner may have not found 'the whole Sermon' as he thought, or he may have summarized Copcot's argument.

[52] *A Briefe and Plaine Declaration, concerning the Desires of all those Faithfull Ministers* (1584), *STC²* 10395. On the authorship of this tract, see Pearson, *Thomas Cartwright*, pp. 272–3; John Bridges, *A Defence of the Government established in the Church of Englande for Ecclesiasticall Matters* (1587), *STC²* 3734; *Register of Sermons*, p. 64; Collinson, *Elizabethan Puritan Movement*, pp. 274–5.

[53] Peter Lake explains that John Bridges moved from a Whitgiftian position (arguing for the antiquity of episcopacy but not claiming it was instituted *jure divino*) to being a supporter of *jure divino* claims for episcopacy between 1573 and 1587. Given that no reports of the sermon at Paul's Cross from 1584 survive, it is unwise to guess which position he might have adopted then: Lake, *Anglicans and Puritans*, pp. 90–1. On the shift towards *jure divino* episcopacy in English conformist thought, see also M. R. Sommerville, 'Richard Hooker and his Contemporaries on Episcopacy: an Elizabethan Consensus', *Journal of Ecclesiastical History*, 35 (1984), 177–87, pp. 178–81.

the fruite of the outward ministerie which the Lord hade planted in his churche'.[54]
This leads Copcot to a consideration of the necessity of belonging to the Church,
and from there to the 'marks' of the true Church (the Word purely preached, the
sacraments duly administered, and discipline; ff. 121ᵛ–122ʳ). Copcot then spends
considerable time arguing that the Catholic Church lacks these 'marks' of the true
Church (ff. 122ʳ–132ᵛ). It is only when he turns to discuss the third 'mark',
discipline, that Copcot digresses to address the puritan claim that the English
Church lacks ecclesiastical discipline because it lacks the system for enforcing
discipline (Church elders) established by God. Copcot denies that there is only
one form of Church government established by God, and he quotes extensively
from Rudolph Gualter, Bullinger's successor in Zurich, to show that separating
from a Church over this question is wrong (ff. 133ʳ–135ʳ). Gualter's moderation is
then contrasted with the inflexibility of those who insist on *jure divino* presbyer-
ianism, and who insist on their reading of 1 Timothy 5:17 as evidence of the
necessity for separate pastors and doctors. Copcot defends the interpretation of this
text that he had offered in his earlier convocation sermon, and he criticizes the
author of the *Counter-poison* for adopting a confutation strategy in answering him:
the author of the *Counter-poison* 'for want of indifferent eares' claimed that Copcot
took his interpretation of the text from 'the Rhemish testament' and the Jesuits
(f. 136ʳ). This allows Copcot to lament the unbrotherly dealings of the author of
the *Counter-poison* and his fellows:

> They be occupied in the worde, but not well, that with great shew of holines crie out, if they
> should holde their peace the stones would crye, yet in truthe, onely by greate pride of heart,
> contend to have their owne honour, satisfied to the great disquiet of the Churche, setting
> men in doubt what church they should sticke unto. To these the Apostle commaunded not
> so muche as single honour to be geven: of them here he speaketh not, but where he saith
> <u>would to god they were even cutt of that disquiet you</u> (ff. 138ʳ⁻ᵛ).

The puritans are again described as 'disturbers' of the Church's peace. The divisions
in the Church, including those caused by men who 'are grieved that others are
preferred before them: and therefore shoote at the estate ecclesiasticall' show
ingratitude to God for the benefits of the Reformation. If these divisions are
widened, with the laity absenting themselves 'from holye assemblies because such
indifferent rites are used', then the English could end up lamenting the loss of
church services altogether (ff. 148ᵛ–149ʳ).

Copcot's sermon does no more than follow the line taken by other defenders of
the Elizabethan settlement in these years: Peter Lake has described how writers like
Richard Cosin, Thomas Cooper, John Bridges, and John Whitgift presented
themselves as 'the defenders of core protestant doctrines and aspirations', emphasizing 'those things which united all English protestants against Rome' in order to
'play down the significance of the presbyterian/conformist split', and to make the
presbyterians' refusal 'to unite with the conformists against the papists . . . the more
heinous'. Only selfish reasons could explain the puritans' refusal to accept the

---

[54] LPL MS 374, f. 115ʳ.

moderate claims made by the conformists. By making the puritans appear to be 'aggressive and unreasonable zealots', the conformists could 'split off this radical presbyterian minority from other more moderate puritans in the ministry and among the laity.[55] This appeal to moderates is even more noticeable from Paul's Cross than from printed books: no argument for *jure divino* episcopacy was made from the Cross, as far as we can tell, even though the conformist argument was moving in that direction. In those cases where the genre of sermon can be ascertained, we see that preachers take a 'doctrinal' approach to their text: they emphasize what is to be taught, and confine their anti-puritan comments to digressions on those who 'trouble' the Church and confuse the laity. One could say that Paul's Cross hosted no 'anti-puritan' sermons in the sense that there were no sermons that used the confutational methods found in anti-Catholic preaching until 1589.

In his *Sermon preached at Pauls Crosse, the 9 of February, being the First Sunday in the Parleament, Anno 1588* (1589),[56] Richard Bancroft broke new ground 'denouncing the puritan movement more forcibly that it had ever been denounced' in Owen Chadwick's words. Patrick Collinson goes further and described the sermon as a 'diatribe' that would 'hardly have been uttered' earlier in Elizabeth's reign.[57] The sermon caused considerable outrage at the time. Sir Francis Knollys, the elderly Privy Counsellor, appealed to John Reynolds in Oxford for answers to the claims about episcopacy made by Bancroft.[58] Robert Beale, an advocate for the puritan movement and Clerk of the Privy Council, thought that Bancroft had accused 'all suche persones as have desired a perfecte reformation of sondrie abuses remayninge in this Churche' with 'disobedience unto hir Majesty yea with treason' and of coupling them 'in a yoke with papistes, Anabaptistes, and Rebelles'.[59] John Penry, writing from Scotland, wrote an answer defending presbyterianism and the English puritan movement.[60] James VI and some of the ministers of his Kirk complained of

---

[55] Lake, *Anglican and Puritans?*, pp. 104–10.

[56] Richard Bancroft, *A Sermon Preached at Pauls Crosse, the 9 of February, being the first Sunday in the Parleament, Anno 1588* (1589), *STC²* 1347.

[57] Owen Chadwick, 'Richard Bancroft's Submission', *Journal of Ecclesiastical History*, 3 (1952), 58–73, esp. 58; Collinson, *Elizabethan Puritan Movement*, p. 397.

[58] Reynolds's original letter to Knollys is British Library MS Lansdowne 61, item 27. The text was printed in 1608 in *Information, or a Protestation, and A Treatise from Scotland, Seconded with D. Reignoldes his letter to Sir Francis Knollis, and Sir Francis Knollis his speech in Parliament*, (1608), *STC²* 14084, pp. 73–87.On this letter, see W. D. J. Cargill Thompson, 'Sir Francis Knollys' Campaign against the *Jure Divino* Theory of Episcopacy', in C. Robert Cole and Michael E. Moddy (eds), *The Dissenting Tradition: Essays for Leland H. Carlson* (Athens: Ohio University Press, 1975), pp. 39–77, pp. 59–60, and notes. Cargill Thompson has also demonstrated that Bancroft's sermon was not the first statement of *jure divino* episcopacy at Paul's Cross, as had been thought: 'A Reconsideration of Richard Bancroft's Paul's Cross Sermon of 9 February 1588/9', *Journal of Ecclesiastical History*, 20(2) (1969), 253–66.

[59] British Library Additional MS 48039, ff. 2ʳ⁻ᵛ.

[60] [John Penry], *A Briefe Discovery of the Untruthes and Slanders (against the True Governement of the Church of Christ) contained in a Sermon, preached the 8 of Februarie 1588 by D. Bancroft* (Edinburgh, 1590), *STC²* 19603.

the representation of the Scottish Reformation in the sermon.[61] But it is only when we compare Bancroft's sermon to those of other conformists at Paul's Cross that we see the reason for the dismay that this sermon caused: Bancroft preached a confutational sermon, a genre hitherto restricted to anti-Catholic (or occasionally anti-separatist) preaching.

The sermon was delivered on the first Sunday of the Parliament of 1589, and was most probably designed to introduce the government's determination to avoid religious controversies in the house and to continue Whitgift's subscription campaign outside it. The publication of the sermon, if not the appointment of Bancroft to preach at the Cross, seems to have been prompted by Whitgift and his ally Lord Chancellor Christopher Hatton.[62] The sermon was preached three days before a royal proclamation against the Marprelate tracts and while the ecclesiastical authorities were searching for the tracts' authors and the press they used.[63] And that public relations disaster for the Elizabethan puritan movement is the immediate context for understanding the kind of sermon that Bancroft preached.

The text of Bancroft's sermon is 1 John 4:1 ('Dearly beloved, beleeve not every spirit, but trie the spirits whether they bee of God: For manie false Prophets are gone out into the world'), which sets heresy and schism as the theme, and not disobedience or the Church's 'troublers'. Bancroft divides his text in three: it contains 'a prohibition *Beleeve not everie spirit*: a commandement, *But trie the spirits whether they be of God*: and a reason of them both, *Because many false Prophets are gone out into the World*' (p. 1). But Bancroft then proceeds to deal with these parts in reverse order, bringing the identification of false prophets immediately to the fore. Bancroft's definition of 'false prophets' is broad enough to include heretics, schismatics, and those merely disobedient to their ecclesiastical superiors. Among the kinds of 'false prophets' described are those 'who do pervert the meaning of the Scriptures for the maintenance, and defence of any false doctrin, schism, or heresie', and one example of this is the puritan campaign for presbyterianism (p. 8). The example is 'as strange . . . as any is to be found in a matter of no greater importance', and the key proof-texts do indeed look strange and unconvincing in the bald summaries that Bancroft gives (pp. 8–9). Bancroft offers the Whitgiftian argument that there is little evidence for presbyerianism in the

---

[61] J[ohn] D[avidson], *D. Bancrofts Rashness in Rayling against the Church of Scotland* (Edinburgh: by Robert Waldegrave, 1590), *STC²* 6322. On James VI's complaint (Bancroft had suggested that James was acting in bad faith while supporting the Kirk and was merely waiting for an opportunity to re-establish episcopacy, pp. 74–5), see Chadwick, 'Richard Bancroft's Submission', and Jenny Wormald, 'Ecclesiastical Vitriol: The Kirk, the Puritans and the Future King of England', in Guy (ed.), *The Reign of Elizabeth I*, pp. 171–91.

[62] Archbishop Whitgift's testimonial on Bancroft, transcribed in Albert Peel, *Tracts ascribed to Richard Bancroft* (Cambridge: Cambridge University Press, 1953), states that Bancroft's sermon was printed 'by direction, from the Lord Chancellor & L. Treasurer' and 'was to special purpose, & did very much abate the edge of the Factious': p. xix.

[63] The first Marprelate tract, the *Epistle*, was printed in October 1588 and the *Epitome* at the end of November of that year. Bancroft's sermon was entered for publication on 3 March. For a full account of the 'anti-Martinist' campaign during and after 1588/9, see Joseph L. Black (ed.), *The Martin Marprelate Tracts: A Modernized and Annotated Edition* (Cambridge: Cambridge University Press, 2008), pp. lvi–lxxiv.

Church's history, and on these grounds asserts that 'for mine owne part I cannot choose but account these Interpreters to be in truth perverters of Christs meaning' (p. 11), placing them firmly among the false prophets.

Unlike the 'doctrinal' sermons of Edwin Sandys and John Copcot, where the puritan movement was dealt with in a discrete digression, Bancroft's sermon is structured around the presentation of puritans as false prophets. The sermon's 'explication' of the text numbers them among the false prophets; its 'application' warns the hearers not to trust them. From the outset, therefore, the puritans are identified as untrustworthy guides in matters of faith, and the lay hearers at Paul's Cross are exhorted to 'believe them not'. This is directly analogous to the method used to present the Catholic clergy as unreliable guides in Jewel's 'Challenge' sermon. And it enables us to show that Bancroft's sermon belongs to the 'confutational' genre: its primary purpose is not to explain his opponents' errors, but to use all necessary means to warn the hearers of the dangers of crediting anything that his opponents say.

Bancroft links the teaching of error (the 'false prophets') with disobedience to the ecclesiastical authorities through his handling of schism. Schism he defines as leaving the Church 'for any imperfections or errours, which do not impugne nor overthrow the substance, and articles of the Christian faith' (p. 13). That the targets of Bancroft's denunciation are not only separatists (those who have 'departed from the congregations of the faithfull accounting them ungodlie, and have gathered to themselves companies agreeable to their owne humors; which they onely esteeme for the Churches of God', pp. 11–12) but also the puritan ministers within the Church becomes evident from what follows. Four causes are given for the false prophets in the world, and of these 'contempt of bishops' is first. The second cause of false prophets is ambition, and here Bancroft relates how Aerius (of Sebaste), thwarted in his ambition to become a bishop, began to claim that bishops and priests were equal in honour (pp. 16–18). Bancroft makes explicit the parallel between this false prophet and another, more recent one:

> The course of which historie I have the rather at large noted unto you, bicause *Martin* would gladly have been as subtill to have deceived you, as he is malicious in depraving his superiours. Who taking upon him with *Aerius* to proove an equality in the ministerie, and that there ought to be no different betwixt a B[ishop]. and a priest, commeth at last to these wordes; *There was never anie but Antichristian popes, and popelings that ever claimed this authoritie* (he meaneth the superiority which Bb. have over the clergie) *especially when the matter was gainsaid &c.* (p. 18)

The equality of ministers, a crucial element of the presbyterians' argument, is presented as one of Marprelate's lies, and here Bancroft says it is motivated by the same 'malicious' attitude to his superiors as that of Aerius (who was accused of heresy by St Jerome on this point). This is the first mention of the parity of ministers in the sermon, and so it is significant that it is associated with the irreverent satire of Marprelate rather than with the scholarly arguments of Cartwright (whose arguments Bancroft will not consider until much later in the sermon). Schism and heresy are all characterized by an irreverent attitude to bishops, and so irreverent behaviour towards bishops becomes the first sign of schism.

To guide his hearers away from heresy and schism, however, Bancroft must explain how the 'spirits' should be 'tried'. 'The meane therfore betwixt both these extremities, of trieng nothing and curious trieng of all things' is 'that when you have attained the true grounds of Christian religion, and are constantly built by a lively faith upon that notable foundation . . . you then content your selves, and seeke no farther' (p. 41). The Scriptures should be read, 'but with sobrietie' and the ordinary Christian should rely on the established church for guidance. 'Now that popery is banished' there is no reason why 'we should not attribute as much to the decrees of our learned fathers in their lawfull assemblies, as other men in time past of as great judgement as we are of, have done' (pp. 42–4). Bancroft then offers the following advice to his hearers in a direct address:

That which hitherto hath been spoken doth contein divers & very sufficient reasons why you ought not to beleeve every spirit. There are many of them false, contemptuous, ambitious, proud, and covetous. Whom if you finde (knowing your selves to be throughly grounded in matters of salvation) to draw you by slanderous speeches, and false collections, into a mislike of other points agreed upon by the church, therby troubling your peace, and feeding your eares with plausible devises, I beseech you with the Apostle in this place, beleeve them not. (pp. 50–1)

As we have seen in the previous chapter, the techniques of confutational preaching are basically two: the association of the opponents' opinions with agreed errors, and the discrediting of the opponents as unreliable authorities. Just as Bancroft has associated puritans with heresy and schism (as 'false prophets') in the first part of the sermon, so in the long, final section, he employs his extensive knowledge about the puritan movement to discredit them as duplicitous and treasonous subversives of Church and government. He targets their opposition to the *Book of Common Prayer*, and from there, he argues for their political unreliability. On all grounds, the puritans are presented as dangerous false prophets, and not believing them is made the 'application', the lesson that the hearers are to take from the sermon and put into practice.

The official consensus about doctrinal formulations (which Bancroft had previously offered as a means by which the laity can judge false prophets) is now used to demolish the credibility of puritan complaints about the *Book of Common Prayer*. Bancroft ranges the names of '*Cranmer, Ridley, Bucer, Peter Martir* and many other' against those who 'are growen to such a hatred of it, as they scarcely have patience to heare the booke once named'. If those opponents are right, then the Reformation's leading figures were 'compassed about belike with such thicke clouds, and mistes of palpable darknes, that they could in a maner see nothing' (p. 57). The different versions of the *Book of the Forme of Prayers* are detailed in order to show that the puritans' unity in denouncing the Prayer Book is not matched by any unanimity about what should replace it. 'About fouer yeares since', he tells his hearers, 'some two or three private men in a corner' compiled this alternative, but this book awards no place to the civil magistrate in the control of the Church, something that is unheard of in 'any true Church in the world' since the conversion of rulers to Christianity. The next year, Bancroft continues, another version 'with the like authoritie, and commendation that the other had' was circulated with 'not so few as 600 alterations'. Among the amendment was the inclusion of the civil magistrates, but 'in the last page' and 'for manners sake' (pp. 62–4). Within another year, Bancroft says, yet another version was published, and the same 'private men' campaigned for it to be allowed by public authority.[64]

The failure to make more explicit provision for the Christian magistrate allows Bancroft to make his most damaging accusation against the puritans: that they are seditious. To do this, Bancroft uses the confutational technique of mixing and selectively quoting from various sources. Among these sources, the satirically exaggerated language of Martin Marprelate proves particularly damaging when quoted out of context. Martin made a mock-syllogism that because 'petty Popes' were not tolerated in the church, bishops, being petty popes, should not be tolerated either.[65] 'But why staied he there', Bancroft asks:

Indeede it was time for him to staie . . . For though he cunningly would seeme to shew his malice onely against bishops; yet hath he left to be implied the very same reasons against the civill magistrate. So that upon his principles a man may frame this rebellious argument; No pettie Pope is to be tollerated in a Christian common-wealth: But her Majestie is a pettie Pope: Therefore her Majestie is not to bee tollerated in a Christian common-wealth. (p. 68)

Bancroft has no real evidence for sedition against the puritans beyond the exclusion of the civil magistrate in the *Booke of the Forme of Prayers* already mentioned.[66] So he employs the confutational device of creating guilt by association. An example of what a presbyterian system would entail for royal authority existed in Scotland, Bancroft claims, and cites the Ruthven Raid as an example. The King's views on the compatibility of his supremacy with presbyerianism were evident in the anti-presbyterian 'Black Acts' of 1584 (pp. 72–5).[67] Quotations from Thomas Cartwright on the civil magistrate's exclusion from decision-making in 'ecclesiastical orders and ceremonies' are equated with the Catholic Thomas Harding's exclusion of the civil magistrate from the government of the Church (pp. 80–1). Bancroft

---

[64] The three versions of *A Booke of the Forme of Common Prayers, Administrations of the Sacraments, &c* referred to here are: *STC²* 16567, printed in London by Robert Waldegrave in 1585; *STC²* 16568, printed by Richard Schilders in Middleburg in 1586; and *STC²* 16569, also printed by Richard Shilders, in 1587. See Collinson, *Elizabethan Puritan Movement*, pp. 286–7, 294, 307–9, and notes.

[65] Martin Marprelate (pseud.), *The Epistle*, in *The Marprelate Tracts*, ed. Black, pp. 9, 10.

[66] The Puritans were understandably wary of doing anything that would appear to contravene the Act of Supremacy, although organizing clandestine *classes* came perilously close: the nine ministers brought before the Star Chamber in 1591 were charged with 'a seditious attempt to supersede the queen's supreme authority in ecclesiastical matters': Collinson, *Elizabethan Puritan Movement*, pp. 420–3.

[67] Bancroft's source for Scottish history was Archbishop Patrick Adamson's *A Declaratioun of the Kings Majesties Intentioun and Meaning Concerning the Late Acts of Parliament* (Edinburgh, 1585), *STC²* 21948, which would be incorporated into Holinshed's *Chronicles* in the 1587 edition. Bancroft's knowledge of the Scottish situation seems to have been rather shallow at this stage: see Gordon Donaldson, 'The Attitude of Whitgift and Bancroft to the Scottish Church', reprinted in *Scottish Church History* (Edinburgh: Scottish Academic Press, 1985), pp. 164–77, pp. 170–1.

warns his hearers that these men will not 'tarry' for the magistrate (pp. 82–3), and once again Martin Marprelate provides him with the best quotation to prove this:

Martin in his first booke threateneth *Fists*: and in his seconde, he wisheth that our Parleament, which is now assembled, would put downe Lord Bishops, and bring in the reformation which they looke for, whether hir Majestie will or no.... Surely whilest he talketh much of treason, I feare he wil be found a traitor himself. (p. 83)

It is only after he has compared England's puritans with papists and rebellious Scottish presbyterians and accused them of plotting treason that Bancroft addresses the arguments for the eldership advanced by Thomas Cartwright. It is placed within a lengthy final exhortation to the hearers to 'believe not' these spirits. Bancroft avoids the intricate arguments used in the *Admonition* controversy; instead, he breaks the debate down into a series of oversimplified propositions easily dismissed as historically inaccurate (pp. 97–103). With confident irony suggestive of a rhetorical victory, he appeals to those who will still follow the puritans to wait 'untill, at the least, they agree among themselves'. This, he assures them, will keep them in 'your old love of the truth' and the 'present reformation' that England enjoys (p. 104).

We might well argue that Bancroft's is the only truly anti-puritan sermon preached at Paul's Cross up until this date. He does not treat 'the godly' as factious members of the Church but as schismatics who have separated from it, and he chose the confutational genre of sermon to enable him to preach against believing the puritans without giving their ideas a fair hearing. The opportunity for such an outright attack on puritanism was created by the publication of the Marprelate tracts. Bancroft deploys the name of Martin strategically throughout the sermon, linking it to the writers of the *Admonition to Parliament* and to Cartwright, effectively tarring the entire puritan movement with the contempt for ecclesiastical authority evidenced by the scurrility of Martinist satire. Bancroft needed to look no further than the Marprelate tracts for apt quotations demonstrating that puritan agitators showed no respect for the Church's government or its officers. The denunciatory tone of the earlier manuscript letters to the conformist bishops, now mixed with a considerable amount of satiric wit, had found its way to the print-buying public, and the ideological rift between the puritans and the bishops was laid bare. Bancroft could metaphorically exclude puritans from the English Church in his Paul's Cross sermon because Marprelate had suggested that the puritans felt no allegiance to it.[68]

Martin Marprelate and the puritan movement were condemned in other sermons at Paul's Cross in the year or so following Bancroft's appearance, but no one followed Bancroft's lead in preaching in a confutational manner and in denying the puritans a place within the English Church. In a rather disorganized sermon of

---

[68] On the Marprelate tracts and their impact, see Joseph Black, 'The Rhetoric of Reaction: The Martin Marprelate Tracts (1588–89), Anti-Martinism, and the Uses of Print in Early Modern England', *Sixteenth Century Journal*, 28 (1997), 707–25; Brian Cummings, 'Martin Marprelate and the Popular Voice', in Kate Cooper and Jeremy Gregory (eds), *Elite and Popular Religion* (Woodbridge: Boydell, for the Ecclesiastical History Society, 2006), pp. 225–39.

9 November 1589, William James stresses the impact on Church revenues and the universities of the puritan programme. He says that greed motivates those 'that under pretence to reforme, seek to overthrowe all'; they are 'with *Martine*' ready to 'offer sacrifice to their god their owne bellie'.[69] But this is in the context of a sermon whose text (1 Corinthians 12:25–37) and argument are dominated by dissuasions from contentions within the Church, and James unambiguously includes puritans within the English Church. Thomas White did much the same in his Accession Day sermon two weeks later. He condemned 'our *Lunaticke libellers*' who foolishly assist the papists' campaign against the English Church, but White's puritans are still within the Church, because 'they are to bee counted our enimies that are *Gods* enimies, and hate out faith, . . . and all the other odds is nothing unto that'.[70] In November 1592, Robert Temple (chaplain to Bishop Aylmer) preached *A Sermon teaching Discretion in Matters of Religion* and in that sermon he lists three groups who imperil the Church: the Jesuits, the Martinists, and the Brownists. Martinists are not treated as typical representatives of the puritan position, as Bancroft had done, however. Martin 'handleth divinitie with scurrilitie, & scripture with laughter', and so 'fie for shame', Temple exclaims against '*Martin* and *Antemartin*' for their handling of this debate.[71] 'Martin' and the Brownists effectively draw fire away from English puritans in Temple's sermon. Around the same time, Richard Turnbull preached at Paul's Cross on slander. He said the 'malicious and mischievous Martins' are guilty of slander because they 'have brought malicious slander upon the Gospell, and given the enemie, by secret suggestions & surmises, occasion to rejoice'. No less guilty of slander are those who 'invey against Princes and Magistrates in presence of a small number of common people, or speake most bitterly against the Bishops and clergy theyr brethren, before a silly congregation'.[72] Once again, the puritans are 'troublers' of the Church's peace, but the bishops and clergy are 'theyr brethren'.

EARLY STUART PURITANISM AND AVANT-GARDE CONFORMITY

A Star Chamber trial of 1591, in which nine puritan ministers barely escaped charges of sedition, brought an end to the politically activist phase of the puritan movement.[73] Puritan ministers diverted their energies into less political dangerous channels, and particularly into the 'practical divinity' for which England became

---

[69] William James, *A Sermon preached at Paules Crosse the IX of November, 1589* (1590), *STC²* 14464, sig. C4ᵛ.
[70] Thomas White, *A Sermon preached at Paules Crosse the 17 of November An. 1589* (1589), *STC²* 25407, pp. 47–8.
[71] Robert Temple, *A Sermon teaching Discretion in Matters of Religion* (1592), *STC²* 23869, sigs B6ᵛ–Cʳ.
[72] Richard Turnbull, *A Exposition upon the XV Psalm Divided into Foure Sermons* (1592), *STC²* 24339.5, ff. 29ᵛ–30ʳ.
[73] Collinson, *Elizabethan Puritan Movement*, pp. 403–47.

famous: through preaching and publication of sermons, prayer books, and catechisms, they sought to evangelize England piece by piece. The households of leading puritan ministers became the training ground for the next generation of the 'godly'.[74] Chaplaincies, benefices with sympathetic patrons, and parish lectureships (a post in which the Prayer Book service could be avoided) became 'safe havens' where puritan preachers could continue their work within the Church but without confrontation with the bishops (some of whom were sympathetic themselves).[75] So puritanism neither died away nor left the Church (although some English puritans did establish separate congregations in the Low Countries). Early Stuart puritanism was a more diffuse sort of 'movement', and, as Tom Webster writes, must be defined differently to its Elizabethan predecessor:

If we look for a collection of reformist demands and efforts as a combination of relatively unchanging priorities, it can be found in the piety, the supportive sociability and the intended proselytisation and social intervention consequent upon that piety. This sits alongside the contingent, conditional loyalties to crown and commonwealth dependent upon their relationship with the parameters of godliness. . . . This is not a matter of looking for continuity in the form of a focused, almost inevitable movement; instead, we should be thinking in terms of changing tensions in relation to both internal and external factors and, perhaps especially marginal, peripheral pressures.[76]

But this pattern of 'supportive sociability' and the 'intended proselytization and social intervention' that went with this style of piety left fewer identifiable marks on the Paul's Cross sermons than the 'movement' for presbyterian church government had. Puritans were not the only preachers who delivered Jeremiads at Paul's Cross, or who mentioned predestination in their preaching, or who denounced England's failures to be as pious, charitable, honest, and serious-minded as she ought to be. We cannot use any of these themes or tropes to identify puritan preaching at Paul's Cross, before or after 1590. Of course, the 'character' of the puritan as a 'precise' and ostentatiously pious figure can be found in the sermons: in 1610, William Holbrooke lamented the pride with which some people 'vex the godly' by swearing. In 1622, Daniel Donne would complain that the hypocrisy of *'Mocke-Christians'* led too many to treat piety as *'precisenesse'* and to 'deride' the godly 'under the name of a *Catharist* or *Puritan'*.[77] After the Hampton Court Conference of 1604, there was no more political agitation for Church reform of the sort seen in the 1570s, and so there was an end to preaching against the puritan movement from Paul's Cross. Neither the Millenary Petition nor the Hampton Court Conference prompted the bishops to appear at Paul's Cross in defence of the established church, as they had

[74] Tom Webster, *Godly Clergy in Early Stuart England: The Caroline Puritan Movement, c. 1620–1643* (Cambridge: Cambridge University Press, 1997).

[75] Paul Seaver, *The Puritan Lectureships: The Politics of Religious Dissent, 1560–1662* (Palo Alto, CA: Stanford University Press, 1970). On the 'preaching pastors' among James I's episcopate, see Kenneth Fincham, *Prelate as Pastor: The Episcopate of James I* (Oxford: Clarendon, 1990).

[76] Tom Webster, 'Early Stuart Puritanism', in Coffey and Lim (eds), *Cambridge Companion to Puritanism*, pp. 48–66, pp. 61–2.

[77] William Holbrooke, *Loves Complaint, for Want of Entertainment* (1610), *STC²* 13564, sig. C3ʳ; Daniel Donne, *A Sub-Poena from the Star-Chamber of Heaven* (1623), *STC²* 7021, pp. 34, 37.

done in 1565–6, 1571–3, and 1588–9. How then do we trace the history of puritanism at Paul's Cross in the years after 1590?

One prominent theme among those 'moderate puritans' appearing at Paul's Cross is Church unity. On 13 May 1591, George Gifford preached on Church unity, taking as his text Psalm 133. He reminds his hearers of the great benefits they have received under Queen Elizabeth's rule, most important of which is their delivery 'out of Idolatrie and blindnesse'.[78] Notwithstanding these benefits there has been 'great discorde and variaunce', not just 'against Papistes and other enemies of the holie religion, but even among brethren, which professe the same holy doctrine and faith of our Lord Jesus Christ'. This disunity is dangerous not least because it gives the advantage to their enemies the Papists (sig. B3ᵛ). As it is 'confessed of all . . . that it is a most necessarie thing in Gods Church and amonge brethren, to eschew discorde and to seek unitie' (sig. B3ᵛ), Gifford encourages his hearers to be 'united with our brethren unto God, otherwise, all shall be dissolved and scattered again in confusion' (sig. B3ʳ). Gifford preached this sermon at the time when the trial of the ministers involved in the *classis* movement was being transferred from High Commission to Star Chamber. His involvement with the movement was known to the Commissioners: he had been forbidden to preach in London in 1589 and was 'harried' by the Church authorities throughout 1590 and 1591.[79] Whatever prompted Bishop John Aylmer of London to appoint Gifford to Paul's Cross at this time, the urgency of Gifford's appeal for unity among brethren needs little explanation. In the next decade, other members of the puritan movement like Richard Stock, Francis Marbury, and Henoch Clapham would preach anti-Catholic sermons at Paul's Cross with similarly vehement appeals to unity in the face of a common enemy. There is a certain irony in the translation of this theme, so central a feature of early conformist anti-puritan preaching, to the puritan ministers who did not separate from the Church and whose position was increasingly under strain from both sides.

Setting the boundaries of the Church as broadly as possible (between the 'papists' and the separatists) is also a feature of puritan preaching at Paul's Cross: we saw John Knewstub do this in 1576. His lead was followed by William Symonds in 1606, William Crashaw in 1607, and Thomas Thompson in 1618: all three preachers delivered sermons on Revelations 18:4, or similar texts, in which they argued for separation from the Roman Catholic Church on the grounds of its faulty doctrine but also against the separatists' allegation that the English Church was similarly flawed. In a 1618 Spital sermon, Roger Hacket identified 'two stinking weeds' to be rooted out by those dressing the Lord's garden, and they are 'Papisme' and 'Puritanisme'. But Daniel Featley, the preacher of the Rehearsal sermon that year, stressed in his summary of Hacket's sermon that puritans are 'not

[78] George Gifford, *A Sermon preached at Pauls Crosse the thirtie day of May, 1591* (1591), *STC²* 11862.3, sig. B2ʳ.

[79] Collinson, *Elizabethan Puritan Movement*, pp. 405, 408. See also, Brett Usher, 'Gifford, George (1547/8–1600)', *Oxford Dictionary of National Biography* (Oxford: Oxford University Press, 2004); online edn., Jan 2008 <http://www.oxforddnb.com/view/article/10658>, accessed 10 November 2009.

those who are usually branded with that name, *but a sect of impure Catharists or Donatists, stiled* The Brethren of the Separation, *who refuse to partake with us in our Prayers and Sacraments*'.[80] By defining the English Church through contrasts with the Church of Rome and the separatist congregations, these preachers leave the maximum room in the Church for 'moderate' puritans: those who had not separated from the Church but whose loyalty was, to quote Tom Webster again, 'contingent' and 'conditional'.

Hacket used the term 'puritan' to refer to those who had fully separated from the Church, but it was also used of those who had not separated.[81] Although 'puritan' was not a term used by Bancroft in his sermon of 1589, his chaplain Samuel Collins used it in a sermon from 1606. The purpose of that sermon was to alienate the laity from the puritan clergy. Arguing from 1 Timothy 6:3–5, Collins alleges that subscription is an extension of the 'consent' to the 'wholesom words' of Christ mentioned in his text, and is necessary 'to maintain good order and keep all from running into endlesse confusion'.[82] The contentions over the Prayer Book and liturgical ceremonies are dismissed as unwarranted (pp. 20–2), and the 'originall of all our woe' is found to be 'the desperate licentiousnesse of the Teacher', whom the 'poor ignorant people' might well accuse of beguiling them into mistrusting the church (pp. 24–7). The hearers must 'make a difference heerafter between Teachers and false Teachers', and Collins (like Bancroft) encourages them to trust the Church authorities in helping them to make this 'trial' (pp. 34–8). The authority being claimed over matters of 'decency and order' was no more than the citizens claimed over their children and apprentices, after all (pp. 45–6). The claims made for the superior piety of the 'godly' ministers are dismissed as a myth by Collins: some may be better than others, but not all are better than their peers, and their readiness to publicize their virtue suggests the opposite (pp. 58–76). Having thoroughly denounced the motives and actions of the puritan ministers, Collins pre-empts a complaint that 'if the puritan smart for it (say they) why not the papist much more?' (p. 77), and answers with a vague invocation of 'reasons of state'.

'Puritan' is used by Collins as a synonym for the puritan clergy, and the lay hearers at Paul's Cross are discouraged from trusting what these 'false teachers' say. Again, we have seen this technique (addressing the laity on the dangers of trusting the 'other' party) in the 'Challenge' sermon and subsequent anti-Catholic sermons. Collins' avoidance of arguments on the ceremonies objected to by puritans and his concentration on their fault (the failure to give consent, as required by his scriptural text) is also a confutational device: it avoids detailed argument in favour of methods that

---

[80] Daniel Featley, *The Spouse her Pretious Borders* in *Clavis Mystica* (1618), *STC²* 10730, p. 437. The word was used in the same way by Joseph Naylor in his 1631 Gunpowder Plot sermon, where he refers to '*Puritanicall New-England Sectaries*', who compare their separation from the Church with Lott's leaving Sodom: St Paul's Cathedral Library MS 52.D.60.01, f. 40ʳ.

[81] It was used in that sense by John Whitgift in his *Answere to the Admonition*: in the preface (p. 10) and on pp. 234–5, where he lists the four groups who 'defaced' the Prayer Book as 'Papists, Anabaptists, and (as you would be compted) Puritanes'. We do not know whether the term was used by Whitgift in the Paul's Cross sermon that he delivered after completing the *Answere*.

[82] Samuel Collins, *A Sermon preached at Paules-Crosse* (1607), *STC²* 5564, p. 13.

merely discredit the opponent. Collins' is an 'anti-puritan' sermon, as Bancroft's was; but both sermons define their target as members of the clergy. By the end of James' reign, the target would not only be these 'false teachers' that Collins complains about, but the culture of sermon-centred piety (with its de-emphasis on liturgy and ceremonies) that had grown popular with the 'godly' laity too. This is suggestive of a larger shift that would take place over the course of James' reign, in which the amorphous term 'puritan' was increasingly co-opted by opponents of the 'movement' and the style of piety that we associate with it. As Lori Anne Ferrell has written:

> Between 1603 and 1625, therefore, governmental displeasure with radical sectarianism metamorphosed into a condemnation of 'Puritanism' that expanded to include those we would now call moderate Puritans. This paved the way for a definition of 'Puritan' in the 1630s that included even those stalwart defenders of the Jacobean Church and faith, Calvinist conformists.

And 'puritan' in this context meant being 'alienable from the established Church'.[83]

Defences of the established Church were included in sermons at Paul's Cross by conformists who were not associated with 'Laudianism',[84] but it was the rise of 'Laudianism', or 'avant-garde conformity' that brought the puritan as a figure 'alienable from the Church' back to Paul's Cross after his first appearance in Richard Bancroft's 1589 sermon.[85] Some of the avant-garde conformist's concerns had been announced from Paul's Cross surprisingly early: most famously, Samuel Harsnett preached a sermon against Calvinist formulations of predestination, claiming that they made God responsible for our sins, in 1584.[86] In 1598 John Howson delivered a sermon insisting that the emphasis on sermons in contemporary religious culture meant the neglect of prayer, and prayer was the proper end of the service of God. And so Howson argues, 'the rule is *Semper finis excellit id quod est ad finem*': there should be less preaching, and more prayer.[87] It was not until Laud's time as bishop of London, however, that this would be a dominant note in the sermons at Paul's Cross. The tightening of control on Paul's Cross by Laud and Juxon brought more men with sympathies towards the 'Laudian' programme to the Cross. Giles

---

[83] Lori Anne Ferrell, *Government by Polemic: James I, the King's Preachers and the Rhetorics of Conformity, 1603–1625* (Palo Alto, CA: Stanford University Press, 1998), pp. 15–16. For some of the reasons behind this shift, see Kenneth Fincham and Peter Lake, 'The Ecclesiastical Policy of King James I', *Journal of British Studies*, 24 (1985), 169–207.

[84] Two examples are William Westerman, 'The Faithfull Subject', in *The Faithfull Subject: or, Mephisboseth, and Salomons Porch* (1608), *STC*[2] 25280, pp. 19–25; and Griffith Williams, *The Resolution of Pilate*, in *The Best Religion* (1636), *STC*[2] 25718, pp. 399–408. Williams's sermon was preached in 1614 (*Register of Sermons*, p. 103), but was substantially expanded for publication in *The Best Religion*, so it is uncertain how much of the anti-puritan material was in the original sermon.

[85] On the term 'avant-garde conformist' see Peter Lake, 'Lancelot Andrewes, John Buckeridge and Avant-Garde Conformity at the Court of James I', in Linda Levy Peck (ed.), *The Mental World of the Jacobean Church* (Cambridge: Cambridge University Press, 1991), pp. 113–33.

[86] Samuel Harsnett, 'A Sermon preached at S. Pauls Cross in London, the 27. day of *October, Anno Reginae Elizabethae 26*', in *Three Sermons preached by . . . Dr Richard Stuart . . . To which is added a Fourth Sermon* (1658), Wing S5527, pp. 121–65. On this sermon, see Nicholas Tyacke, *Anti-Calvinists: The Rise of English Arminianism, c.1590–1640* (Oxford: Clarendon Press, 1987), p. 252.

[87] John Howson, *A Second Sermon, preached at Paules Crosse* (1598), p. 43.

Fleming preached a sermon exhorting the repairing of churches, and St Paul's in particular, and in that sermon he blamed puritan styles of piety for the reluctance of his lay supporters to make monetary contributions to such work. He writes:

> though wee have nice and narrow gullets, to straine at Gnats and Ceremonies, yet we can glibly swallow downe Extortion and Sacrilege; and though we be easily drawne to God enough in hearing of Sermons, yet we will bate him for it, in workes of mercy and *building of Synagogues*.[88]

William Watts did something very similar in a 1637 sermon on the need for fasting: Watt satirized the 'sermon-centred' piety of puritan religious culture in an attempt to pre-empt condemnation of his theme as 'popish': fasting during the plague is neglected but 'without a *Sermon*, the encrease of *Sicknesse* is doomed'.[89]

It was the avant-garde conformists who would insist on the repositioning of puritans from 'disturbers of the church' to the 'alienable from the established Church'. Preaching against heresy and schism, they did not distinguish those who 'troubled' the Church from within from those who had formally separated from it: internal dissent was itself schism. Illustrative of this shift is a sermon by Edward Boughen preached on 18 April 1630. Boughen took as his text 1 John 4:1–3, the text on which Bancroft had preached in 1589.[90] Where Bancroft reversed his text so that he could begin with a definition of 'false prophets', Boughen takes the words as they stand, so that he can begin with a warning not to believe 'though occasions draw you abroad amongst diversitie of *Spirits*' (p. 5). The lengthy discussion of schism and heresy offered by Bancroft is omitted by Boughen, who offers the laity a simpler, and far narrower, definition: 'those, that undertake to be Masters in the Pulpits' will be punished if they 'teach you any thing that contradicts the received Doctrine of the Church' (p. 8). It is the 'received Doctrine of the Church' that should guide the hearers in 'trying the spirits', a point also emphasized by Bancroft. But Bancroft went to considerable lengths to say why the framers of the Elizabethan settlement could be trusted to deliver doctrine to the people. Boughen merely treats their authority to do so as the premise from which he argues for an utterly passive acceptance of the king and bishop's definition of the Church. He tells his hearers of the King's Declaration of 1629, which stated that preachers were not to 'draw the Articles aside any way', or 'put his own sense or comment to be the meaning of the article'.[91] This, Boughen eulogizes, is 'Lords doing, and it

---

[88] Giles Fleming, *Magnificence Exemplified* (1634), *STC²* 11052, p. 28. Fleming's accusation is unwarranted; many London churches were renovated in the Jacobean period: see J. F. Merritt, 'Puritans, Laudians, and the Phenomenon of Church-Building in Jacobean London', *Historical Journal*, 41 (1998), 935–60.

[89] William Watts, *Mortification Apostolicall* (1637), *STC²* 25129, p. 47. Puritans did object to Watt's sermons: Jason Mc Elligott, 'Watts, William (c.1590–1649)', *Oxford Dictionary of National Biography* (Oxford: Oxford University Press, 2004); online edn., Jan 2008 http://www.oxforddnb.com/view/article/28895, accessed 27 February 2010.

[90] Edward Boughen, *A Sermon preached at Saint Paul's Crosse* (1635), *STC²* 3408.

[91] Edward Cardwell (ed.), *Documentary Annals of the Reformed Church of England*, 2 vols (Oxford, 1839), vol. 2, pp. 169–73.

ought to be acceptable in our eyes; this, this is the only way to breed unity and amity, to settle us in that faith, which we have received from the Church' (p. 10).

Where Bancroft assumed some sympathy with puritan ministers in his auditory, a sympathy he tried to diminish by associating the puritans with sedition, Boughen assumes that his auditory distinguish themselves from the Church's troublemakers:

> Give not eare, keepe not company, suffer not any of yours to keep company with Schismatikes or Heretickes; have no Communion with these *spirits* of darkenesse. For by acquainting your selves with them, or seeming to favour such kinde of men, you wrong not your selves onely, but others also. You wrong your selves, by endangering your own soules; for it is an hard matter to *touch pitch, and not be defiled.* And you injure others by your countenance towards these exorbitant persons; for they, that have either dependence upon you, or a good opinion of you, will the sooner give eare to them for your sake. (p. 13)

This avoidance of schism must not simply be a matter of outward conformity: 'if our *bodies* observe the orders of the Church, and our *hearts* encline to Schism, we are liable to this *Nolite,* God will have a saying to us for it' (p. 13). And the identity of these schismatics and heretics who are to be so strenuously avoided is made clear with a reference to King James' *Directions for Preachers.* Where he spoke of 'ungrounded Divines' whose 'unsound, seditious and Dangerous doctrines' were 'disquieting' the Church and state, Boughen tell us: 'at first their malice was at a few Ceremonies and Rites of the Church, but now yee see, what an height they are growne to' (p. 18). The puritan's objection to having every sermon preceded by the Prayer Book service is merely one example of their general unwillingness to obey the king (p. 22). Boughen's account of the puritan position is bluntly polemical and grossly overstates the case:

> Through the cunning of these men our Churches are accounted no better then Synagogues; the Sanctuary of God is denyed to be sacred, *sacramenta non sacra consentur,* the sacraments are scarce held to be holy, and our high festivall dayes are no more reckoned of, then an ordinary work day.... Are not these rotten unsavory fruites sufficient to make us abhorre such *ravening Wolves,* and to cast off these *false Prophets?* Surely, if we meane to keep with Gods house the Church, we must not follow them, for *exierunt, they are gone out,* they are none of this house; that's evident. (p. 39)

When Boughen comes to the final part of his text, in which a definition of 'false prophets' is offered, he again disregards questions of doctrine in favour of the virtue of unity and uniformity per se. The defining characteristic of Christ and his teaching is charity, and those who 'dissolve the unity of the Church' break charity and therefore are false prophets, regardless of their 'sanctified behaviour' and 'zealous protestations'.

Boughen's is the third anti-puritan confutational sermon we encounter from Paul's Cross, after Bancroft's and Collins', and it marks the increasing alienation of avant-garde conformist argument from that of the conformists who preceded them. Bancroft deliberately conflated heresy and schism, and then suggested that the members of the puritan movement were guilty of sedition; Boughen makes dissent from the Church authorities itself schism, heresy, and sedition. Collins distinguished the lay hearers from the puritan preachers with whom they might be in sympathy, and preached against reliance on the latter as spiritual guides. Boughen advises against any association whatsoever with anyone guilty of schism, which he takes to mean dissent from the Church authorities. The puritans are '*gone out*, they are none of this house'. They and their sympathizers are no longer assumed to constitute part of the auditory at Paul's Cross.

Another indication that puritan sympathies were increasingly absent from the Paul's Cross pulpit and auditory in the 1630s is the tendency for sermons of this decade to include a digression on the dangers of schism as frequently as the more conventional digression on the 'evils of popery'. In a sermon on the theme of judgement preached in 1629, Richard Farmer took the time to condemn those whose religion is dominated by 'projects of new formes of government', and who traduce their superiors.[92] In a sermon preached shortly after an outbreak of plague, Oliver Whitbie warns his hearers that schism pulls down the church and will be punished more severely than idolatry, a lesson he wishes 'our Novatian brood' would learn.[93] Walter Stonehouse told his hearers in 1638 that 'schisme & division' would bring down the Church, and so 'it belongs therfore to every good Christian, as farre as he may procure, at least to pray for the peace of Jerusalem'; the peace of the Church was the theme of Henry Vertue's sermon of 9 July 1637.[94] The loss of that peace was evident from one of the last Paul's Cross sermons to discuss the 'troublers' of the Church's peace. On 10 October 1641 Thomas Cheshire made a plea for the Prayer Book service and episcopal government (citing the 1641 *Protestation* to support him). The Church is under attack from the inconstant schismatics who 'clamour' for their conventicles and against 'our *Church* and the government thereof, down with Bishops, down with *Common Prayer,* down with *Organs*, down with the *Golden Idoll in Cheape*'.[95] Cheshire compares England's recent history to 'the apparition to *Elias* on Mount *Horeb*: the 'great *storme* and tempest' of the Wars of the Roses is not where God was found, nor in the '*earth-quake* that shooke down all the *Monasteries and Abbies*', nor the '*fire,* in those *Marian* times'. But in the reigns of 'that second *Deborah*' and 'king *James* of sweet and blessed memory' and of 'our second *Josiah*, our present gracious *Soveraigne*', England had 'the *small* and *still* voyce of the *Gospell of Christ*, a quiet and peaceable enjoyment of *Gods* publique worship' (pp. 18–19). But now, Cheshire continues, 'the *winde* hath begun to *blow*, in a *baulling* and *blustering* of turbulent and unquiet *schismatiques*'. This 'wind' threatened to overthrow 'the sweet harmonious peace, and blessed tranquillity of *Church* and *State*', as indeed it did.

---

[92] Richard Farmer, *A Sermon preached at Pauls Cross* (1629), *STC²* 10699, pp. 10–11.
[93] O[liver] W[hitbie], *Londons Returne, after the Decrease of the Sicknes* (1637), *STC²* 25371, pp. 14–15.
[94] Walter Stonehouse, 'Holy Husbandry. A Sermon preached at St Pauls Crosse in London Aprili 29th 1638', in Bodleian Library MS Eng.th.f.62, p. 538. I would like to thank Richard Webster for alerting me to this manuscript. Henry Vertue, *A Plea for Peace* (1637), *STC²* 24691.
[95] Thomas Cheshire, *A True Copy of that Sermon* (1641), Wing C3782, p. 17.

Epilogue

We have traced several changes to the Paul's Cross sermons over the eighty-four years from Elizabeth I's accession to the outbreak of civil war in 1642 which suggest that the sermon series reached the height of its prestige and influence under James I but then saw a contraction in audience and supporters. After John Alymer's bequest reached the City Chamberlain in 1606, the Paul's Cross sermons became more financially secure because of generous bequests administered by the Chamber of London; this encouraged preachers to undertake a Paul's Cross sermon, and there was some competition for appointments 'to the Cross'. But the senior avant-garde conformists had no interest in preaching at Paul's Cross, and William Laud is the only one that we know who did appear there. This meant that Paul's Cross saw fewer 'court preachers' and bishops in the 1630s than at any other time after 1558. The organization of the sermon series improved over Elizabeth's reign too, with the arrangements for the preacher's visit (his accommodation and his meeting with the bishop's chaplain before the sermon) becoming more formalized. This meant that the bishop of London gained far more control over the sermons, especially after William Laud introduced the rule that preachers supply a copy of their sermon in advance of preaching.

Paul's Cross had been a pulpit where unscripted things might be said (as happened with Arthur Wake and Richard Crick preaching in favour of presbyer-ianism in 1572), but this tendency diminished in James' reign, especially after the 1622 *Directions for Preachers*. One suspects that part of the audience for the sermons diminished with their increasing predictability. The narrowing political range of the Paul's Cross sermons may also have affected the numbers in its auditory: the tendency to criticize both papists and puritans as comparable, if not equal, enemies of the Church, and the conflation of separatism with all forms of puritan opposition can hardly have made the Paul's Cross sermons an 'edifying' occasion for London's godly. The decline of the political anniversary sermons, in which political obedience was encouraged within a celebration of God's care for England, meant that there were fewer occasions for formal attendance at Paul's Cross by the livery companies, and the appeal of this sermon series to the civic community beyond the aldermanic bench diminished.[1]

---

[1] Members of the livery companies attended fast sermons and thanksgiving sermons in the cathedral, and their account books reveal payment for the benches ('forms') on which they sat for these sermons. But records for attendance on a weekly basis and references to the 'Paul's Cross' sermons

We can assume a shrinking auditory for the Paul's Cross sermons for two reasons: the first is the transfer of the sermons into the choir of the cathedral in 1634 without any protest by auditors. The choir was a smaller space than the Cross Yard and had designated seating only for the lord mayor and aldermen (along with the cathedral staff of course, not all of whom would be present every week). Yet we have no records of complaints about a lack of room or about the unsuitability of the space. The second reason for assuming that fewer people took an interest in Paul's Cross at the end of the 1630s is the lack of comment on the pulling down of the pulpit cross itself, which probably happened in 1634 or 1635. Were it not for Henry Peacham's pamphlet that mentions Paul's Cross having been demolished by 1641, we would be reliant on historians like William Dugdale and Thomas Fuller, writing in the 1650s and 1660s, who thought that the pulpit cross was taken down under the 1643 ordinance against idolatry.[2] There were vociferous complaints about the building work on the cathedral, but they concerned the orders to pull down the buildings abutting the cathedral, including the parish church of St Gregory's under St Paul's (which the Long Parliament ordered to be rebuilt).[3] The texts documenting this furore make no mention of the demolition of the Paul's Cross pulpit.

Paul's Cross was a very different preaching venue in the 1630s than it had been in the 1610s, 1590s, or 1560s and 1570s: this may have made Laud's opponents less likely to lament its destruction. The sermons were less newsworthy: far fewer were being printed, and the calibre of the people preaching there had diminished. The men in charge of appointing the preachers, Laud and Juxon, felt an antipathy to Paul's Cross, and this contributed to the decline of the sermon series before anything was done in the Cross Yard. Controversy did rage about preaching in London in the 1630s, but it was over the parish lectureships (preaching posts funded by parishioners that circumvented the process of approval by bishops and that allowed ministers to opt out of delivering the Prayer Book services). In these cases, Laud and Juxon came into conflict with parishioners who fought back against his encroachment on what they saw as their right to maintain lectureships and appoint lecturers. Why did the Corporation of London not do the same for Paul's Cross?

The London Corporation before 1641 had no interest in contradicting royal policy. The Corporation was dominated by monopolist traders and customs farmers who relied on the King for the maintenance of the privileges that allowed them to trade profitably. They had nothing to gain from alienating the King over a pet project like the rebuilding of St Paul's. Some of them were Arminians, like the

---

are rarer. I am grateful to Lucy Bates for alerting me to this material: her thesis on 'days of prayer', 1640–60, will add greatly to our knowledge of this subject.

[2] C. H. Firth and R. S. Rait (eds), *Acts and Ordinances of the Interregnum*, 3 vols (London: HMSO, 1911), vol. 1, pp. 265–6; William Dugdale, *The History of St Pauls Cathedral in London*, (1658), Wing D 2482, p. 173; Thomas Fuller, *History of the Worthies of England* (1662), Wing F2440, pp. 71–2.

[3] 'History of the Trouble and Trials of Archbishop Laud', in *Works*, ed. James Bliss (Oxford, 1854), vol. 4, pp. 92–180; *The Journal of Sir Simonds D'Ewes*, ed. Wallace Notestein (New Haven: Yale University Press, 1923), pp. 38, 223.

Lord Mayor Christopher Clitherow, and some also contributed to the rebuilding work on St. Paul's, which was the reason for the pulling down of Paul's Cross in 1634.[4] But the Common Council elections of December 1641 were decisive in changing the balance of power in the city from the conservative, often Laudian and sometimes Royalist, Court of Aldermen to their political opponents.[5] This shift in power was completed on 11 July 1642 when Lord Mayor Gurney was impeached, and on 16 August his place was taken by Isaac Penington. This new ruling elite were very active in rescuing the Paul's Cross sermons and taking control of them in a way that was never possible with a functioning bishop of London or dean of St Paul's.

The process began even before the mayoralty had changed hands. In June 1642, the Court of Aldermen ordered a letter to be sent to the bishop of London to 'acquaint him how of late the pulpitt in St Paules on Sundays hath byn furnished with meane Preachers', and desiring 'that some care be taken that they said Place may hereafter bee supplied with learned and true orthodoxall Teachers'.[6] (As William Juxon was one of only five bishops to avoid impeachment proceedings in 1641, he may still have been functioning as bishop in some capacity at this point.[7]) In August 1642, the Corporation set up a committee to review the bequests and find out 'in whome of right is and hath byn the appointment of those preachers' and to put together a petition to the House of Commons 'that henceforth the nominacon and appointment of the said preachers may bee in this court', which they did; the petition was read in the House of Commons on 24 September; the Commons ordered that the Corporation be given the right to appoint, and in May 1643 an ordinance to the same effect was passed.[8] It is not clear who administered the Paul's Cross rota before May 1643, or whether the sermons were being preached regularly: Richard Gardiner's Royalist Accession Day sermon of 1642 suggests that supporters of the king could still control appointments at that stage. Thomas Morton, Bishop of Durham, preached in St Paul's on 19 June 1642 a sermon entitled *The Presentation of a Schismaticke*, which uses many of the defences of conformity and anti-puritan arguments discussed in Chapter 7. If this is a 'Paul's Cross' sermon (Morton does not mention whether the sermon was preached in the morning) then Royalist and conformist control over the pulpit lasted until the end of Gurney's mayoralty.[9]

---

[4] Valerie Pearl, *London and the Outbreak of the Puritan Revolution: City Government and National Politics, 1625–43* (Oxford: Oxford University Press, 1961), pp. 91–4; Robert Brenner, *Merchants and Revolution: Commercial Change, Political Conflict, and London's Overseas Traders, 1550–1653* (1993; repr. London: Verso, 2003), pp. 290–7.

[5] Pearl, *London and the Outbreak of the Puritan Revolution*, pp. 132–57; Brenner, *Merchants and Revolution*, pp. 396–400.

[6] City of London, London Metropolitan Archive, Corporation of London Rep. 55, f. 445.

[7] Juxon avoided trouble during the Civil War period remarkably well: see Brian Quintrell, 'Juxon, William (*bap*.1582, *d*.1663)', *Oxford Dictionary of National Biography* (Oxford: Oxford University Press, 2004); online edn., Jan 2008 <http://www.oxforddnb.com/view/article/15179>, accessed 3 March 2010.

[8] LMA, Corporation of London Rep. 56, f. 8ᵛ (30 August 1642); f. 168ᵛ (4 May 1643); *Commons Journal* vol. 2, pp. 768, 782, 789; vol. 3, pp. 82, 105.

[9] Thomas Morton, *The Presentment of a Schismaticke* (1642), Wing M2846.

Thomas Gage's *The Tyranny of Satan* was preached on 28 August 1642, and it was printed by October with a dedication to the new Lord Mayor Isaac Penington.[10] Gage's sermon is an old-fashioned anti-Catholic recantation sermon, which suggests that practical control of the pulpit was moving to the Corporation. Corporation accounts for September 1641 to September 1642 record payments to fifty-four Paul's Cross preachers, but the accounts for September 1642 to June 1643 record payments to only three preachers,[11] indicating that the sermon series collapsed temporarily in the winter and spring of 1642–3. This may be the point at which control finally passed from the bishop's former chaplains.

The Corporation's original plan appears to have been to restore the pulpit in the Cross Yard: on 16 May 1643, they sent a delegation 'to consider of a convenient and fitt place within the said yard for a pulpitt to stand in and also of a convenient place for the Lord Mayor Aldermen to sitt to heare the word of God preached as heretofore hath byn accustomed upon the Lords day'.[12] By December 1643, however, the Corporation were planning to petition the House of Commons that 'all things offensive in Paules Church may bee removed and the same fitted and liberty granted for sermons to bee preached in Paules Church every Sunday att the assembly of the Lord Mayor and Aldermen by such ministers as the Lord Mayor or this court shall for that purpose appoint', and by February they had appointed two aldermen to view the chancel and see what was needed to make a place suitable for meeting 'to hear the word of god preached there every lords day in the forenoone' (the traditional time of the Paul's Cross sermons).[13] The area modified to make a suitable space for the sermons was the east end (the Lady Chapel and the choir). William Dugdale writes in his *History of St Paul's* that 'part of the Quire, with the rest of the building East-ward from it, is by a new partition Wall, made of brick, in *Anno* 1649, now disposed of for a *Preaching place*'.[14] It was here that the displaced Paul's Cross sermons were delivered.

Accounts of Paul's Cross usually end in the 1642, but it is now clear that the sermon series continued through the 1640s and 1650s. Dozens of sermons paid for

[10] Thomas Gage, *The Tyranny of Satan* (1642), Wing G116. The copy of the sermon purchased by George Thomason bears the date 'Octo.3d'.
[11] LMA, City Cash Book 4, ff. 141ᵛ, 215ᵛ. There may be two more sermons from 1642–3. The entry on f. 215ᵛ mentions that Thomas Goodwin and Edmund Calamy were paid for sermons 'which they should have preached at Paul's Cross' but which were preached in the Mercers' Chapel on 11 June and 18 June 1643. The payment was 'by vertue of an order of the Comons house of Parliament of the xith day of May 1643'. The accounts for 1642–3 are from Michaelmas to the Feast of John the Baptist because of a change of chamberlain; the accounting period is usually Michaelmas to Michaelmas.
[12] LMA, Corporation of London Rep. 56, f. 173ᵛ. The same entry notes the petition for 'stones rubbish pales and Shedds that are erected lyeing and beeing in the said Church yard' to be removed as they block the light to the parishioners' houses. This suggests that the Cross Yard had simply been abandoned by the masons when work on the cathedral stopped.
[13] LMA, Corporation of London Rep. 57, ff. 27ʳ⁻ᵛ, 55ʳ. The aldermen were also commissioned to check the scaffolding in the church.
[14] William Dugdale, *History of St Pauls*, p. 173. Dugdale says that this modification was for the benefit of Cornelius Burges who was appointed preacher to St Paul's with a stipend of £400 pa in 1644: Firth and Rait (eds), *Acts and Ordinances of the Interregnum*, vol. 1, pp. 672–3. These sermons are separate from the Paul's Cross sermons, which continued to be financed by the Corporation out of the endowments for the Paul's Cross sermons.

from the Paul's Cross endowments were preached before the lord mayor and aldermen on Sunday mornings in the cathedral from 1643 until the Great Fire; many of them were printed, and almost all carried dedications to the lord mayor or Corporation. To name only the most notable: in the mayoralty of Thomas Adams (Michaelmas 1645–6) the prominent Presbyterian ministers Simeon Ashe, Joseph Caryl, and Matthew Newcomen all preached to the Corporation in St Paul's and dedicated their sermons to the lord mayor, sheriffs, and aldermen of the city.[15] Stephen Marshall (famous for his sermons to Parliament, and the 'Sm' of the composite Presbyterian writer Smectymnuus) preached *A Thanksgiving Sermon* on 28 July 1648, celebrating the collapse of the English risings in the second civil war. The sermon was dedicated to Lord Mayor John Warner.[16] On 3 October 1651, the diarist Ralph Josselin preached before the lord mayor and aldermen at St Paul's, and this was the first time that Josselin had preached in London. He records that 'the audience was great, my text was Luke. 21.v.28. I dined with the Lord Mayor, and by his intreaty preached before him, at his owne church', and Josselin thanked God for this success.[17] William Spurstowe (the 'uus' of Smectymnuus) preached on *The Magistrates Dignity and Duty* in 1654 and dedicated the sermon to Thomas Viner, Lord Mayor.[18] In December of the same year Richard Baxter and Edmund Calamy (the 'ec' of Smectymnuus) preached to the Corporation in St Paul's and both dedicated their sermons to the new lord mayor, Christopher Pack.[19] These examples serve to illustrate the conservative, Presbyterian religious politics of the Corporation in the 1650s. The preachers were all Presbyterian, in the sense that they believed in a non-episcopal national church organized on presbyterian principles and opposed religious toleration for Protestant sects as well as for Roman Catholics. Further study of these texts, which have not been recognized as Paul's Cross sermons until now, is needed to get a clearer sense of how the series reflected and affected the politics of London. After the Restoration, the Paul's Cross sermons were transferred to St Mary Le Bow, probably in the wake of the Great Fire, and then, in 1687, were moved to the Guildhall Chapel.[20] Where they began as sermons to the London community, the Paul's Cross series ended up as sermons preached to the London government.

[15] Simeon Ashe, *Reall Thankfulnesse* (1645), Wing A3964; Joseph Caryl, *The Present Duty and Endeavour of the Saints* (1646), Wing C786; Matthew Newcomen, *The Duty of such as would Walke Worthy of the Gospel* (1646), Wing N909. Ashe preached again in 1655 (*The Doctrine of Zeal Explained*, Wing A3952), and this sermon was also dedicated to the Lord Mayor (Christopher Pack) and aldermen.

[16] Stephen Marshall, *A Thanksgiving Sermon . . . in Pauls Church London, July 28, 1648* (1648), Wing M791.

[17] *The Diary of Ralph Josselin, 1616–1683*, ed. Alan MacFarlane (London: for the British Academy by Oxford University Press, 1976), p. 258.

[18] William Spurstowe, *The Magistrates Dignity and Duty* (1654), Wing S5095.

[19] Richard Baxter, *A Sermon of Judgement* (1655), Wing B1408; Edmund Calamy, *The Monster of Sinful Self-seeking* (1655), Wing C259.

[20] One of the Newdigate newsletters, dated 12 January 1687, refers to the sermons 'formerly preached at Paulls Cross & lately at Mary Le Bow' being transferred to the Guildhall Chapel: Folger Shakespeare Library MS L.c.1907. I would like to thank Professor Stephen Taylor for this reference.

Once they were confined to the cathedral choir in 1634, the Paul's Cross sermons lost not just part of their auditory, but the element of unpredictability that had made them so newsworthy in the earlier period. This did not change when control of the pulpit and appointment of preachers passed from the bishops of London to the Corporation. Now the sermons were very clearly a vehicle for the presentation of the religion approved by the city government (who had a level of control over funding, appointments, and the preaching space unmatched by any of the competing authorities of the pre-war period), and the dominance of Presbyterian preachers among those who printed sermons in the 1640s reflects this control. The printed texts describe themselves simply as 'sermons preached before the lord mayor and Aldermen on Sunday mornings in the cathedral'; it is only in the City Cash Books that they are referred to as 'Paul's Cross' sermons (as a way of identifying the fund that should pay the preachers, presumably). And so there is, I think, a paradox in the control of Paul's Cross: the fewer, or the better coordinated, the regulatory forces were, the more predictable the resulting oration was, and the smaller the auditory that bothered to listen.

Although the demolition of the pulpit was quickly forgotten, some memory of the outdoor pulpit cross seems to have lingered. And the associations of the outdoor pulpit were with a more 'disorderly' kind of preaching than that found in the cathedral choir. On 7 May 1640, James Hunt, a 'fanatic and frantic person, a husbandman, and altogether illiterate' had been 'taken absurdly preaching on a stone in St. Paul's Churchyard', one imagines because of the association with Paul's Cross.[21] On 4 February 1644, the antinomian preacher John Simpson clashed with the more conservative Presbyterian Cornelius Burges over control of the pulpit in St Paul's. Having been denied access to the cathedral pulpit, Simpson preached 'at *Pauls* Cross', where he delivered the 'tenets of the Antinomians'. The next day, he was 'sent for, as a Delinquent' by the House of Commons, who ordered him to refrain from preaching (without effect).[22]

Thereafter, Paul's Cross almost disappears from our records.[23] It is not until John Strype's revised version of John Stow's *Survey of London* was printed in 1720 that Paul's Cross began to figure in narratives of London and the Reformation.[24]

---

[21] *Acts of the Court of High Commission*, in *CSPD, 1640*, p. 415.

[22] *Mercurius &c*, 31 Jan–6 Feb. 1644 (Thomason, E 31/18), p. 16; *Commons Journal*, vol. 3, p. 389. On this incident, see also Keith Lindley, *Popular Politics and Religion in Civil War London* (Aldershot: Scholar, 1997), p. 287; R. L. Greaves, *Saints and Rebels: Seven Nonconformists in Stuart England* (Macon, GA: Mercer University Press, 1985), p. 101.

[23] Although not conclusive, a search of Early English Books Online (http://eebo.chadwyck.com/) by title keyword and subject with 'Paul's Cross' (and alternative spellings) date-limited 1660–1720 resulted in three entries: the 1672 edition of Mark Franks *LI Sermons* (Wing F2074A), which includes a Paul's Cross sermon preached in 1641, and the 1677 and 1684 editions of Robert Johnson's *Dives and Lazarus*, a sermon preached at Paul's Cross in 1623.

[24] John Strype, *Survey of London* (1720), Book 3, Chapter 8, p. 149. Available online at 'The Stuart London Project, Humanities Research Institute, University of Sheffield, http://www.hrionline.ac.uk/ strype, accessed 2 March 2010. On Strype's version of Stow's *Survey*, see John J. Morrison, 'Strype's Stow: The 1720 edition of "A Survey of London"', *London Journal*, 3 (1977), 40–54, and J. F. Merritt, 'The Reshaping of Stow's "Survey": Munday, Strype, and the Protestant City', in J. F. Merritt (ed.), *Imagining Early Modern London: Perceptions and Portrayals of the City from Stow to Strype, 1598–1720* (Cambridge: Cambridge University Press, 2001), pp. 52–88.

The accounts of London that appeared between the 1633 revision of Stow (by Anthony Munday and Humphrey Dyson) and Strype's 1720 edition had diminished the amount of information offered about Paul's Cross: Thomas De Laune's *The Present State of London* (1681), a book heavily indebted to Stow's *Survey*, says nothing of Paul's Cross, and James Howell's *Londinopolis* (1657), which lifts whole passages from Stow, reproduces Stow's description of St Paul's Churchyard but leaves out the passage on Paul's Cross.[25] It is tempting to say that the Paul's Cross sermons had been forgotten about by mid-century, and that it was Strype's *Survey of London* and his *Annals of the Reformation* (in four volumes, 1709–38) that reminded people of them. But Paul's Cross appears to have been remembered as a prestigious pulpit for much longer in New England. In a letter of 1729, Samuel Sewall wrote about Edward Taylor, whom he had known at Harvard. Sewall remarks: 'I have heard him preach a Sermon at the Old South upon short warning which, as the phrase in England is, might have been preached at Paul's Cross.'[26]

Whether or not this phrase did survive 'in England', it seems most likely that Strype's publications reminded the English reading public of Paul's Cross and its significance to the history of London and England between the Reformation and the Civil War. One of the earliest post-Strype texts to make reference to Paul's Cross is an anonymous tract, entitled *The Layman's Sermon, Occasioned by the Present Rebellion; which was (or ought to have been) preached at St Paul's Cross* (1745), which calls for a defence of English Protestantism against the Jacobites. It 'ought to have been' preached at Paul's Cross because 'it was from this Place the great and good *Wickliff*, un-awed by the Frowns of Power, and Fury of Persecution, first laid the Foundation of that Reformed Religion'.[27] The writer's history may not be accurate, but his sense that Paul's Cross was crucial to England's Protestant Reformation is correct.

---

[25] John Stow, *The Survey of London...And now completely finished by the Study and Labour of A.M. H.D. and Others* (1633), *STC*[2] 23345; Thomas De Laune, *The Present State of London* (1681), Wing D894; James Howell, *Londinopolis* (1657), pp. 312–13.

[26] 'Letter-Book of Samuel Sewall', *Collections of the Massachusetts Historical Society*, 6th series, 2 vols (Boston, 1888), vol. 2, p. 274.

[27] *The Layman's Sermon, Occasioned by the Present Rebellion; which was (or ought to have been) preached at St. Paul's Cross, on the 1st of October, 1745* (1745), p. 3. The pamphlet was also printed in Belfast and Dublin: see 'Eighteenth Century Collections Online', http://find.galegroup.com/ecco/, accessed 2 March 2010.

Bibliography

MANUSCRIPT SOURCES

London

British Library
BL Additional MS 48039, Papers of Robert Beale relating to religious affairs, c, 1584–1591.
BL Harleian MS 353, Copies of 16th century letters and papers.
BL Additional MS 20,066, Notes for sermons by Robert Sanderson.
BL Lansdowne MS 84, Burghley Papers.
BL Additional MS 32092, State papers and historical documents, 16th and 17th centuries.
BL MS Lansdowne 17, Diplomatic correspondence and letters from courtiers to Burghley, 1573.
BL Harleian MS 425, Notes of John Foxe's 1570 sermon at Paul's Cross.
BL Harleian MSS 389 and 390, Correspondence of Joseph Mede.
BL Harleian MS 417, Papers relating to John Foxe.

City of London, London Metropolitan Archive
Repertory of the Court of Aldermen, vols 13–57.
Corporation of London, Letter Book Q.
City Cash Books 1–5.
Corporation of London Remembrancia, vols 1 and 7.
P. E. Jones, 'St Paul's Cross and Preachers', Corporation of London Record Office Research Papers 4.13 (1934).
Diocese of London, Vicars General Books, 'Stanhope', vols I and II.
Consistory Court of London, Act Books, 1583.

Guildhall Library
GL MS 34048 (Merchant Taylors Company, Master and Wardens Account Books) vols 15, 16, and 17.
GL MS 25630 (Dean's Registers), vols 5 and 8.
GL MS 9537, vol. 9, Records of the 1598 episcopal visitation.
GL MS 25,473/2, Accounts for the rebuilding of St Paul's, 1635.
GL MS 36,711, Dr Mapletoft's letter of appointment to Paul's Cross, 1638.

Lambeth Palace Library
LPL MS 447, Sermons and sermon notes, incl. John Harris' accession day sermon, 1619.
LPL MS 113, Copy of a sermon by Dr Jegon, preached at Paul's Cross.
LPL MS 374, Sermons and sermon notes, including John Copcot's sermon on *The Counter-poison,* 1584.
LPL MS 647, Papers of Anthony Bacon.
LPL MS 739, Sermon notes, including notes on Paul's Cross sermons by John Bullingham and by John Mullins.
LPL MS 2004, Papers, including the answers of John Richardson about his Paul's Cross sermon of 1599.

LPL MS 931, Papers, including notes of William Barlow's sermon on the Earl of Essex' execution.

St Paul's Cathedral Library
MS 52.D60.01, Copy of Dr Joseph Naylor's sermon at Paul's Cross.
MS 38.F.22, The Passion sermon and Spital sermons for 1588.

Inner Temple Library
MS Petyt MS 538, vol. 47, Response to Paul's Cross Sermon by Thomas Cowper, Bishop of Lincoln in 1572, and answers of Richard Crick to accusations made against his Paul's Cross sermon of 1573.

Dr Williams Library
MS 12.10, ff. 7^r–16^r, Copy of a sermon by William Goodwin, preached at Paul's Cross on 5 November 1614.

Oxford

Bodleian Library
Bodl. MS Tanner 50, Sermon notes from Paul's Cross, 1565–6.
Bodl. MSS Eng.th.b.4–7, Sermon notes by John Warner, Bishop of Rochester.
Bodl. MS Eng.th.e.14, Sermons, including a copy of a sermon by Mr Lambe, preached at at Paul's Cross in 1629.
Bodl. MS Rawlinson D. 399, Papers, including a letter appointing to Paul's Cross and the order of the sermons in St Paul's Cathedral, 1661.
Bodl. MS Selden Supra 44, ff. 48–52, Response to John Jewel's Paul's Cross sermon of 1571.
Bodl. MS Rawlinson D.274, Theological commonplace book of John Rogers.
Bodl. MS Rawlinson D.1350, Papers and notes, including notes on Thomas Walkington's *Rabboni* (1620).
Bodl. MS Rawlinson D. 719, Papers, including notes on William Barlow's sermon on the Earl of Essex's execution.
Bodl. MS Eng.th.f.62, Copy of a sermon by Walter Stonehouse, preached at Pauls Cross in 1638.

Cambridge

Cambridge University Library
CUL MS Add. 3177, Robert Saxby's notes and sermon notes.

Christi College Cambridge
MS 119, item 14, Letter to Matthew Parker appointing him to preach at Paul's Cross.

San Marino, California

Henry E Huntington Library
MS Ellesmere 1172, Copy of the rehearsal sermon by R. Barlow, 1605.

Washington, DC

Folger Shakespeare Library
Folger MS V.b.317, Collection of historical papers, including a letter from Archbishop Tobie Matthew to the Earl of Leicester (1576–7).

Folger MS V.a.1. Copy of a sermon by an unknown preacher, preached at Paul's Cross in 1636.

Folger MS V.a.251, Copy of a sermon by John Dove, preached at Paul's Cross, 1606.

County Record Offices

Hampshire Record Office
MS 44M/F2/15/2, Transcription of the diary of Sir Richard Paulet by Dr Eric Lindquist.

Hertfordshire Records Office
ASA 5/5 No. 201, 2 January 1594/5, Instructions from Bishop John Fletcher to the archdeacons of the London diocese.

Centre for Kentish Studies
MS CKS–U350/Q5, Richard Carpenter's complaint against Samuel Baker.
MS CKS-U350/C2/53, Letter by Richard Carpenter to Sir Edward Dering, *c.*1635.

PRINTED PAUL'S CROSS SERMONS

Adams, Thomas, *The Temple. A Sermon preached at Pauls Crosse the Fifth of August 1624* (1624), *STC²* 129.

Anderson, Anthony, *A Sermon Preached at Paules Crosse, the 23. of Aprill* (1581), *STC²* 570.

Andrewes, John, *The Brazen Serpent* (1621), *STC²* 591.

Aylesbury [Ailesbury], Thomas, *The Passion Sermon at Pauls-Crosse* (1626), *STC²* 999.

——, *A Sermon Preached at Paules Crosse* (1623), *STC²* 1000.

Bancroft, Richard, *A Sermon Preached at Pauls Crosse, the 9 of February, being the first Sunday in the Parleament, Anno 1588* (1589), *STC²* 1347.

Barlow, William, *A Sermon preached at Paules Crosse, on Martii I, 1600* (1601), *STC²* 1454.

——, *The Sermon preached at Paules Crosse, the Tenth day of November* (1606), *STC²* 1455.

Barne, Thomas, *A Sermon Preached at Pauls Cross* (Oxford, 1591), *STC²* 1464.8.

Barrell, Robert, *The Spiritual Architecture* (1624), *STC²* 1498.

Bedford, Thomas, *The Sinne unto Death* (1621), *STC²* 1788.

Bedingfield, Robert, *A Sermon Preached at Pauls Crosse the 24. of October. 1624* (Oxford, 1625), *STC²* 1792.

Benson, George, *A Sermon Preached at Paules Crosse* (1609), *STC²* 1886.

Bilson, Thomas, *The Effect of Certaine Sermons Touching the Full Redemption of Mankind* (1599), *STC²* 3064.

Bolton, Robert, *A Discourse about the State of True Happinesse* (1611), *STC²* 3228.

Boughen, Edward, *A Sermon Preached at Saint Pauls Crosse* (1635), *STC²* 3408.

Bourne, Immanuel, *The True Way of a Christian to the New Jerusalem* (1622), *STC²* 3419.

Boys, John, *An Exposition of the Last Psalme* (1615), *STC²* 3464.

Bridges, John, *A Sermon Preached at Paules Cross* ([1571]), *STC²* 2726.

Brookes, Matthew, *The House of God* (1627), *STC²* 3836.

——, *A Sermon preached at Pauls-Crosse, May 30. 1626* (1626), *STC²* 3837.

Buggs, Samuel, *Davids Strait* (1622), *STC²* 4022.

B[unny], E[dmund], *A Sermon Preached at Pauls Cross on Trinity Sunday, 1571* (1576), *STC²* 4183.

Burt, Thomas, *A Nicke for Neuters* (1604), *STC²* 4132.

B[ury], G[eorge], *The Narrow Way, and the Last Judgement* (1607), *STC²* 4179.5.

Chaderton, Laurence, *An Excellent and Godly Sermon* ([1578?]), *STC²* 4924.

Chaloner, Edward, *Pauls Peregrinations*, in *Six Sermons* (1622), STC² 4936.

Cheshire, Thomas, *A True Copy of that Sermon* (1641), Wing C3782.

Clapham, Henoch, *A Description of New Jerusalem* (1601), *STC²* 5336.5.

Collins, Samuel, *A Sermon preached at Paules Crosse* (1607), *STC²* 5564.

Crakanthorpe, Richard, *A Sermon at the Solemnizing of the Happie Inauguration or our Most Gracious and Religious Soveraigne King James* (1609), *STC²* 5979.

Crashaw, William, *The Sermon preached at the Crosse, Feb. xiiii.1607* (1608), *STC²* 6027.

Creswell, George, *The Harmonie of the Lawe and the Gospell* (1607), *STC²* 6038.

Curteys, Richard, *The First Sermon preached at Paules* Crosse in *Two Sermons preached by the Reverend Father in God the Bishop of Chicester* (1576), *STC²* 6140.

Deios, Laurence, *That the Pope is that Antichrist* (1590), *STC²* 6475.

Delaune [Delawne], Nathaniel, *The Christians Tryumph* (1617), *STC²* 6550.5.

Denison, Stephen, *The New Creature* (1619), *STC²* 6607.

——, *The White Wolfe* (1627), *STC²* 6608.3.

Donne, Daniel, *A Sub-poena from the Star-Chamber of Heaven* (1623), *STC²* 7021.

Donne, John, 'Preached at Paul's Cross, March 24, 1616/1617, on *Proverbs* 22.11', in *The Sermons of John Donne*, ed. G. R. Potter and E. Simpson, 10 vols (Berkeley: University of California Press, 1953–62), vol. 1.

——, 'Preached at St Paul's Cross on September 15, 1622 on *Judges* 5.20', in *The Sermons of John Donne*, ed. G. R. Potter and E. Simpson, 10 vols (Berkeley: University of California Press, 1953–62), vol. 4.

——, 'The Anniversary Celebration or our Deliverance from the Powder Treason. Intended for Paul's Cross, but by reason of the weather, preached in the Church, November 5, 1622, on *Lamentations* 4.20', in *The Sermons of John Donne*, ed. G. R. Potter and E. Simpson, 10 vols (Berkeley: University of California Press, 1953–62), vol. 4.

——, 'Preached at St Paul's Cross, May 6, 1627, on *Hosea* 3.4', in *The Sermons of John Donne*, ed. G. R. Potter and E. Simpson, 10 vols (Berkeley: University of California Press, 1953–62), vol. 7.

——, 'Preached at St Paul's Cross, November 22, 1629, on *Matthew* 11.6', in *The Sermons of John Donne*, ed. G. R. Potter and E. Simpson, 10 vols (Berkeley: University of California Press, 1953–62), vol. 9.

Dove, John, *A Sermon preached at Pauls Cross the 3. of November 1594* (1594), *STC²* 7086.5.

Downame, George, *A Treatise on John 8.36 concerning Christian Liberty* (1609), *STC²* 7124.

Drant, Thomas, *The Divine Lanthorne* (1637), *STC²* 7164.

——, *A Fruitfull and Necessary Sermon* (1572), *STC²* 7166.

Duport, John, *A Sermon preached at Paules Crosse on the 17. day of November 1590* (1591), *STC²* 7365.5.

Dyos, John, *A Sermon preached at Paules Crosse the 19. of Juli 1579* (1579), *STC²* 7432.

Evans, William, *The Christian Conflict, and Conquest* (1636), *STC²* 10595.

Farmer, Richard, *A Sermon preached at Pauls Cross* (1629), *STC²* 10699.

Fawkner, Anthony, *Comfort to the Afflicted* (1626), *STC²* 10718.

Featley, Daniel, 'The Spouse Her Pretious Borders', in *Clavis Mystica* (1636), *STC²* 10730.

Fenton, R[oger], *The Necessity of the Passion* and *The Wisdome of the Rich* in *A Treatise.... With 6 Certaine Sermons Preached in Publike Assemblies* (1617), *STC²* 10805.

Fisher, William, *A Godly Sermon Preached at Paules Crosse the 31. day of October 1591* (1592), *STC²* 10919.

Fleming, Giles, *Magnificence Exemplified* (1634), *STC²* 11052.

Fosbroke, John, 'England's Warning', in *Six Sermons* (Cambridge, 1633), *STC²* 11199.

Foster, William, *The Means to Keep Sinne from Reigning* (1629), *STC²* 11204.

Fotherby, Martin, *The Third Sermon,* in *Foure Sermons lately preached* (1608), *STC²* 11206.

Foxe, John, *A Sermon of Christ Crucified* (1570), *STC²* 11242.3.

Fuller, Thomas, *A Sermon Intended for Paul's Crosse* (1626), *STC²* 11467.

Gardiner, Richard, *A Sermon Appointed for Saints Pauls Crosse ... March 27, 1642* (1642), Wing G231.

Gardiner, Samuel, *The Foundation of the Faythful* (1611), *STC²* 11577.

Gee, John, *Hold Fast* (1624), *STC²* 11705.

Gibson, Abraham, *The Lands Mourning, for Vaine Swearing* (1613), *STC²* 11829.

Gifford, George, *A Sermon preached at Pauls Crosse the thirtie day of May, 1591* (1591), *STC²* 11862.3.

Gore, John, *The Oracle of God* (1635 [1636]) Wing G 1294.

Gosson, Stephen, *The Trumpet of War* (1598), *STC²* 12099.

Gravet, William, *A Sermon Preached at Paules Crosse ... Intreating of the Holy Scriptures* (1587), *STC²* 12200.

Greenwood, Henry, *Tormenting Tophet, or a Terrible Description of Hel* (1615), *STC²* 12336.

Gumbleden, John, *Gods Great Mercy to Mankinde* (Oxford, 1628), *STC²* 12514.

Hales, John, 'Of Dealing with Erring Christians', in *Golden Remains* (1659), Wing H267.

Hall, Joseph, *An Holy Panegyrick. A Sermon preached at Pauls Crosse* (1613), *STC²* 12673.

——, *The Passion-sermon* (1609), *STC²* 12693.7.

Harnsett, Samuel, 'A Sermon preached at S. Pauls Cross in London, the 27. day of *October, Anno Reginae Elizabethae* 26', in *Three Sermons preached by ... Dr Richard Stuart ... To which is added a Fourth Sermon* (1658), Wing S5527.

Harris, Robert, *Gods Goodnes and Mercy* (1622), *STC²* 12831.

Hayward, John, *God's Universal Right Proclaimed* (1603), *STC²* 12984.

Higgons, Theophilus, *A Sermon preached at Pauls Crosse the Third of March, 1610* (1611), *STC²* 13455.7.

Holbrooke, William, *Loves Complaint, for Want of Entertainment* ([1610?]), *STC²* 13564.

Holland, Thomas, [[H] -e paneguris] *D. Elizabetha* (Oxford, 1600), *STC²* 13596.5; 2nd edn, *Paneguris D. Elizabethae* (Oxford, 1601), *STC²* 13597.

Holyday, Barten, *A Sermon preached at Pauls Crosse, August the 5. 1623* (1626), *STC²* 13615.

——, *A Sermon preached at Pauls Crosse, March the 24. 1624* (1626), *STC²* 13616.

Hooke, Christopher, *A Sermon Preached in Paules Church in London* ([1603]), *STC²* 13703.

Howson, John, *A Second Sermon, preached at Paules Crosse* (1598), *STC²* 13883.

Jackson, Thomas, *Londons New-yeeres Gift* (1609), *STC²* 14303.

Jackson, William, *The Celestiall Husbandrie* (1616), *STC²* 14321.

James, William, *A Sermon preached at Paules Crosse the IX of November, 1589* (1590), *STC²* 14464.

Jewel, John, *The Copie of a Sermon Pronounced by the Byshop of Salisburie at Paules Crosse,* part 2 of *The True Copies of the Letters betwene the Reverend Father in God John Bisshop of Sarum and D. Cole* ([1560]), STC² 14612.

——, [On Joshua 6:1-3], in *Certaine Sermons preached before the Queenes Majestie, and at Paules Crosse* (1583), *STC²* 14596.

Johnson, Robert, *Davids Teacher* (1609), *STC²* 14694.

——, *Dives and Lazarus* (4th edn., 1623), *STC²* 14694.3.

Jones, John, *Londons Looking Backe to Jerusalem* (1633), *STC²* 14722.

King, Henry, *A Sermon Preached at Pauls Crosse, the 25 of November. 1621* (1621), *STC²* 14969.

King, Henry, *A Sermon preached at St Pauls March 27 1640* (1640), *STC²* 14970.

King, John, *A Sermon at Paules Crosse, on Behalfe of Paules Church, March 26. 1620* (1620), *STC²* 14982.

[Latimer, Hugh], *A Notable Sermon . . . preached in the Shroudes at Poules Church in London*, in *27 Sermons preached by the Right Reverende . . . Hugh Latimer* (1562), *STC²* 15276.

Laud, William, *A Commemoration of King Charles his Inauguration* (1645), Wing L579.

Lawrence, John, *A Golden Trumpet, to Rowse up a Drowsie Magistrate* (1624), *STC²* 15325.

Lever, Thomas, *A Fruitfull Sermon made in Paules Church at London in the Shroudes* ([1551]), *STC²* 15543.

Ley, Roger, *The Bruising of the Serpents Head* (1622), *STC²* 15568.

——, *The Scepter of Righteousnesse* and *A Sermon upon Saint Stephens Day* in *Two Sermons* (1619), *STC²* 15569.

Lynch, John, *Pascha Christianum*, in John Squire and John Lynch, *Three Sermons: Two of them appointed for the Spittle* (1637), STC² 23120.

Marbury [Marburie], Francis, *A Sermon preached at Paules Cross the 13. of June. 1602* (1602), *STC²* 17307.

Milles, Robert, *Abrahams Suite for Sodome* (1612), *STC²* 23503.

Milward, John, *Jacobs Great Day of Trouble and Deliverance* (1610), *STC²* 17942.

Mosse, Miles, *Justifying and Saving Faith* (Cambridge, 1614), *STC²* 18209.

Myriell, Thomas, *The Christians Comfort* (1623), *STC²* 18321.

——, *The Devout Soules Search* (1610), *STC²* 18323.

Pelling, John, *A Sermon of the Providence of God* (1607), *STC²* 19567.

Petley, Elias, *The Royall Receipt* (1623), *STC²* 19801.

Price, Gabriel, *The Laver of the Heart* (1616), *STC²* 20306.

Purchas, Samuel, *The Kings Towre and Triumphant Arch of London.* (1623), *STC²* 20502.

Rainbow, Edward, *Labour Forbidden, and Commanded* (1635), *STC²* 20603.

Rawlinson, John, *Vivat Rex. A Sermon Preached at Pauls Crosse* (1619), *STC²* 20777.

Sanderson, Robert, *A Sermon preached at St. Paul's Crosse, Aprill. 15*, in *Two Sermons preached at Paules-Crosse* (1628), *STC²* 21708.5.

Sandys, Edwin, *A Sermon preached at Pauls Cross at what time a Maine Treason was Discovered*, and *The Nineteenth Sermon. A Sermon preached at Pauls Crosse* in *Sermons Made by the Most Reverende Father in God, Edwin, Archbishop of Yorke* (1585), *STC²* 21713.

Sclater, William, *A Threefold Preservative against Three Dangerous Diseases of these Latter Times* (1610), *STC²* 21847.

Sheldon, Richard, *A Sermon preached at Paules Crosse Laying open the Beast, and its Marke* (1625), *STC²* 22395.

Sonibancke [Sonnibank], Charles, *The Eunuches Conversion* (1617), *STC²* 22927.

Spenser, John, *A Learned and Gracious Sermon Preached at Paules Crosse* (1615), *STC²* 23096.

Stock, Richard, *A Sermon Preached at Paules Crosse, the Second of November 1606* (1609), *STC²* 23276.

Stockwood, John, *A Sermon Preached at Paules Crosse on Bartholomew Day* ([1578]), *STC²* 23284.

——, *A Very Fruiteful Sermon Preched at Paules Crosse* (1579), *STC²* 23285.

Stoughton, John, *The Love-sicke Spouse* in *XV Choice Sermons Preached upon Select Occasions* (1640), *STC²* 23302.

Sutton, Thomas, *Englands First and Second Summons: Two Sermons preached at Paules Crosse* (1616), *STC²* 23502.

Sydenham, Humphrey, *Jacob and Esau. Election. Reprobration Opened and Discussed* (1626), *STC*² 23567.

Symonds, William, *A Heavenly Voyce* (1606), *STC*² 23591.

Temple, Robert, *A Sermon Teaching Discretion in Matters of Religion* (1592), *STC*² 23869.

Thompson, Thomas, *Antichrist Arraigned in a Sermon at Pauls Crosse* (1618), *STC*² 24025.

Tynley, Robert, *Two Learned Sermons* (1609), *STC*² 24472.

Vase, Robert, *Jonah's Contestation about his Gourd* (1625), *STC*² 24594.

Vertue, Henry, *A Plea for Peace* (1637), *STC*² 24691.

Wakeman, Robert, *Jonahs Sermon, and Ninivehs Repentance* (1606), *STC*² 24948.

Walkington, Thomas, *Rabboni; Mary Magdalens Teares* (1620), *STC*² 24970.

Walsall, John, *A Sermon preached at Pauls Crosse. 5 October, 1578* ([1578]), *STC*² 24995.

Ward, Samuel, *Balme from Gilead to Recover Conscience* (1617), *STC*² 25035.

Watts, William, *Mortification Apostolicall* (1637), *STC*² 25129.

Webbe, George, *Gods Controversie with England* (1609), *STC*² 25162.

Westerman, William, *The Faithfull Subject: or, Mephisboseth, and Salomons Porch* (1608), *STC*² 25280.

Westfailing, Herbert, 'Two Sermons touching the Supper of the Lorde', in *A Treatise of Reformation in Religion* (1582), *STC*² 25285.

Whalley, John, *Gods Plentie Feeding True Pietie* (1616) *STC*² 25294.

Whitbie, Oliver, *Londons Returne, after the Decrease of the Sicknes* (1637), *STC*² 25371.

White, John, *A Sermon Preached at Paules Crosse upon the Foure and Twentieth of March, 1615* in *Two Sermons* (1615), *STC*² 25392.

White, Thomas, *A Sermon preached at Pawles Crosse on Sunday the ninth of December 1576* (1578), *STC*² 25405.

———, *A Sermo[n] preached at Pawles Crosse on the Sunday the Thirde of November 1577 in the Time of the Plague* (1578), *STC*² 25406.

———, *A Sermon preached at Paules Crosse the 17. of November An. 1589* (1589), *STC*² 25407.

[Whitgift, John], *A Most Godly and Learned Sermon, preached at Pauls Crosse the 17 of November* (1589), *STC*² 25432.

Wigmore, Michael, *The Way of All Flesh: A Sermon Prepared for Pauls Crosse* (1619), *STC*² 25618.

Wilkinson, Robert, *Lots Wife. A Sermon Preached at Paules Crosse* (1607), *STC*² 25656.

Williams, Griffith, *The Delight of the Saints and The Resolution of Pilate in The Best Religion* (1636), STC² 25718.

Worship, William, *The Patterne of an Invincible Faith* (1616), *STC*² 25995.

OTHER PRIMARY SOURCES

Alley, William, *Ptochomuseion: The Poore Mans Library* ([1565]), *STC*² 374.

Ames, William, *The Marrow of Sacred Divinity* (1642), Wing A 3000.

Ainsworth, Henry, *Counterpoison* ([Amsterdam], 1608), *STC*² 234.

Arber, Edward, *A Transcript of the Registers of the Company of Stationers of London, 1554–1640* (1875–94).

Bacon, Francis, *The Letters and Life of Francis Bacon*, ed. James Spedding, 7 vols (London: Longman, 1862–74).

Bacon, Nathaniel, *The Papers of Nathaniel Bacon of Stiffkey*, ed. A. Hassell Smith, Gillian M. Baker, and R. W. Kenny, vol. 1 (Norwich: Centre of East Anglian Studies, 1979).

Bibliography

Bernard, Richard, *The Faithfull Shepheard* (1607), *STC²* 1939; (1621 edn), *STC²* 1941.
——, *Thesaurus Biblicus* (1644), Wing B2035.
Birch, Thomas (ed.), *The Court and Times of Charles I* (1848).
Bowyer, Robert, *The Parliamentary Diary of Robert Bowyer, 1606–1607*, ed. David Harris Willson (Minneapolis: University of Minnesota Press, 1931).
Bray, Gerald (ed.), *Records on Convocation*, 20 vols (Canterbury, 1509–1603), vol. 7.
Brinsley, John, *A Consolation for our Grammar Schooles* (1622), *STC²* 3767.
——, *Ludus Literarius: or, The Grammar Schoole* (1612), *STC²* 3768.
——, *The Preachers Charge. And Peoples Duty (1631), STC²* 3790.
Cabala, sive Scrinia Sacra, Mysteries of State and Government (1654), Wing C184.
'The satisfaction of Laurence Caddey, touching his frailties, and fall from the Catholike Church, at his retorne into England', printed in [William Allen], *A True Report of the late Apprehension and Imprisonment of John Nichols Minister* (Rhemes, 1583), ARCR 13.
Cardwell, Edward (ed.), *Documentary Annals of the Reformed Church of England*, 2 vols (Oxford, 1839).
—— (ed.), *Synodalia, A Collection of Articles of Religion, Canons, and Proceedings of Convocation in the Province of Canterbury, from the year 1547 to the year 1717*, 2 vols (Oxford, 1842).
Chamber Accounts of the Sixteenth Century, ed. Betty R Masters (London Record Society, for the Corporation of London, 1984).
Chamberlain, John, *The Letters of John Chamberlain*, ed. Norman Egbert McClure, 2 vols (Philadelphia: American Philosophical Society, 1939).
Chappell, William, *The Preacher* (1656), Wing C1957.
Chronicle of the Grey Friars of London, ed. John Gough Nichols (1852).
Clarke, John, *Holy Oyle for the Lampes of the Sanctuarie* (1630), *STC²* 5359.
Clarke, Samuel, *The Lives of Thirty-Two English Divines,* 3rd ed. (1677), Wing C4539.
Clarke, Thomas, *The Recantation . . . made at Paules Crosse* (1593), *STC²* 5366.
Clay, William Keatinge, *Liturgies and Occasional Forms of Prayer set forth in the Reign of Queen Elizabeth* (Cambridge, 1847).
Cooke, Richard, *A White Sheete, or A Warning for Whoremongers* (1629), *STC²* 5676.
[Cooper, Thomas], *An Admonition to the People of England* (1589), *STC²* 5682.
Cosin, John, *The Correspondence of John Cosin*, ed. George Ornsby, 2 vols (Durham, 1869).
Crosfield, Thomas, *The Diary of Thomas Crosfield*, ed. F. S. Boas (Oxford: Oxford University Press, 1935).
D[avidson], J[ohn], *D. Bancrofts Rashness in Rayling against the Church of Scotland* (Edinburgh, 1590), *STC²* 6322.
Dekker, Thomas, *The Guls Horne-booke* (1609), *STC²* 6500.
D'Ewes, Simonds, *The Diary of Sir Simonds D'Ewes (1622–1624)*, ed. Elisabeth Bourcier (Paris: Didier, 1974).
Donne, John, *Letters to Severall Persons of Honour* (1651), Wing D1865.
Dorman, Thomas, *A Disproufe of M. Nowelles Reproufe* (Antwerp, 1565), ARCR 168.
——, *A Proufe of Certeyne Articles in Religion, denied by M. Juell, sett furth in Defence of the Catholyke Beleef therein* (Antwerp, 1564), ARCR 169.
Dugdale, William, *The History of St Pauls Cathedral in London, from its Foundation until these times* (1658), Wing D 2482.
Earle, John, *Microcosmographie, Or A Piece of the World Discovered* (1628; 1633 edn), *STC²* 7444.
Fitzherbert, Thomas, *A Defence of the Catholyke cause . . . Written by T[thomas] F[itzherbert] With an apology, or defence, of his innocency* ([Antwerp], 1602), ARCR 279.

Floyd, John, SJ, *The Overthrow of the Protestants Pulpit-Babels* (1612), ARCR 297.

Frere, Walter Howard (ed.), *Visitation Articles and Injunctions of the Period of the Reformation*, 3 vols (London: Longmans, 1910).

Fuller, Thomas, *The Church History of Britain; from the Birth of Jesus Christ untill the year M.DC.XLVIII* (1655), Wing F 2416.

Gage, Thomas, *The Tyranny of Satan* (1642), Wing G116.

Gairdner, James (ed.), *Three Fifteenth-Century Chronicles, with Historical Memoranda by John Stow, the Antiquary, and Contemporary Notes of Occurrences written by him the Reign of Queen Elizabeth* (1880).

Gardiner, Stephen, *A Declaration of such True Articles as George Joy hath gone about to Confute as False* (1546), *STC²* 11588.

Gardiner, S. R. (ed.), *Letters and Documents Illustrating the Relations between England and Germany at the Commencement of the Thirty Years' War* (1868).

——, *Reports of Cases in the Court of Star Chamber and High Commission* (1886).

Gataker, Thomas, *A Discours Apologetical* (1654), Wing G319.

Goff, Thomas, *Deliverance from the Grave* (1627), *STC²* 11978.

Grindal, Edmund, *The Remains of Edmund Grindal, D.D.*, ed. Revd William Nicholson (Cambridge, 1843).

Harding, Thomas, *An Answere to Maister Juelles Chalenge* (Louvain, 1564), ARCR 371.

——, *A Briefe Answere of Thomas Harding* (Antwerp, [1565]), ARCR 373.

——, *A Rejoindre to M. Jewels Replie* (Antwerp, 1566), ARCR 376.

Harington, Sir John, *Nugae Antiquae*, ed. Henry Harington, 2 vols (1804), vol. 2.

Hatton, Christopher, *Memoirs of the Life and Times of Sir Christopher Hatton, K.G.*, ed. Sir Harris Nicolas (1847).

Heylyn, Peter, *Cyprianus Anglicus* (1668), Wing H1699.

Hieron, Samuel, *The Dignity of Preaching*, in *Works* ([1620?]), *STC²* 13377.5.

Higgons, Theophilus, *A Briefe Consideration of Mans Iniquitie* (1608), *STC²* 13453.

——, *The Apology of Theophilus Higgons lately Minister* (Roan, 1609), ARCR 432.

——, *The First Motive of T.H. . . . to Suspect the Integrity of his Religion* ([Douai], 1609), ARCR 433.

Hoby, Sir Edward, *Letter to Mr T.H. late Minister, now Fugitive* (1609), *STC²* 13541.

Holinshed, Raphael, *et al.*, *The Third Volume of Chronicles* (1586), *STC²* 13569.

——, *Holinshed's Chronicles of England, Scotland and Ireland*, ed. Sir Henry Ellis, 6 vols (London, 1807–8), vol. 4.

Hollybrand, Claudius, *The French Schoolemaster* (1573; 1649 edn.), Wing S293B.

Horne, Robert, *An Answeare made by Rob. Horne, Bishoppe of Wynchester, to a Booke entituled The Declaration of suche Scruples, and Staies of Conscience touchinge the Othe of Supremacy, as M. John Fekenham, by writinge did deliver unto the L. Bishop of Winchester, with his Resolution made thereunto* (1566), *STC²* 13818.

Howson, John, *A Sermon preached at St Maries Oxford* (1602), *STC²* 13884.

Hughes, Paul L., and James F. Larkin (eds), *Tudor Royal Proclamations*, 3 vols (New Haven: Yale University Press, 1969), vol. 2.

Hutt, Cecilia A. (ed.), *English Works of John Fisher, Bishop of Rochester. Sermons and Other Writings 1520–1535* (Oxford: Oxford University Press, 2002).

Hutton, Matthew, *The Correspondence of Dr Matthew Hutton, Archbishop of York* (1843).

Hyperius (Andreas Gerardus). *De Formandis Concionibus Sacris* (1553), trans. John Ludham, *The Practis of Preaching* (1577), *STC²* 11758.

James I of England, *His Majesties Declaration Concerning his Proceedings with the States Generall of the United Provinces of the Low Countreys, in the cause of D. Conradus Vorstius* (1612), *STC²* 9233.

——, 'Speech to Parliament of 9 November 1605' in *King James VI and I, Political Writings*, ed. Johann P. Sommerville (Cambridge: Cambridge University Press, 1994).

Jewel, John, *The Works of John Jewel*, ed. Rev. John Ayre, 4 vols (Cambridge, 1845–50).

——, *A Replie unto Hardinges Answere* (1565), *STC²* 14606.

Jonson, Ben, *Everyman Out of his Humour*, in *Works*, ed. C. H. Herford and Percy Simpson (Oxford: Clarendon Press, 1925–52).

Kenyon, J. P. (ed.), *The Stuart Constitution: Documents and Commentary*, 2nd edn., (Cambridge: Cambridge University Press, 1986).

Knight, William, *A Concordance Axiomaticall: Containing a Survey of Theologicall Propositions* (1610), *STC²* 15049.

Knollys, Sir Francis, *Information, or a Protestation, and A Treatise from Scotland, Seconded with D. Reignoldes his letter to Sir Francis Knollis, and Sir Francis Knollis his speech in Parliament,* (1608), *STC²* 14084.

Laud, William, *The Works of Archbishop Laud*, ed. James Bliss, 8 vols (Oxford, 1847–60).

McCullough, Peter (ed.), *Lancelot Andrewes: Selected Sermons and Lectures* (Oxford: Oxford University Press, 2005).

Machyn, Henry, *The Diary of Henry Machyn, Citizen and Merchant-Taylor of London, from A.D. 1550 to A.D. 1563*, ed. John Gough Nichols (1848).

Manningham, John, *The Diary of John Manningham of the Middle Temple, 1602–3*, ed. Robert Parker Sorlein (Hanover, NH: University Press of New England, 1976).

The Martin Marprelate Tracts: A Modernized and Annotated Edition, ed. Joseph L. Black (Cambridge: Cambridge University Press, 2008).

Martiall, John, *A Treatyse of the Cross gathred out of the Scriptures, Councelles, and Auncient Fathers of the Primitive Church* (Antwerp, 1564), ARCR 513.

Middleton, Thomas, *The Black Book*, ed. G. B. Shand, in *Thomas Middleton: The Complete Works*, gen. eds Gary Taylor and John Lavagnino (Oxford; Oxford University Press, 2007).

——, *Michaelmas Terme*, ed. Theodore B. Leinwand, in *Thomas Middleton: The Complete Works*, gen. eds Gary Taylor and John Lavagnino (Oxford; Oxford University Press, 2007).

——, *The Triumphs of Truth*, ed. David M. Bergeron, in *Thomas Middleton: The Complete Works*, gen. eds Gary Taylor and John Lavagnino (Oxford; Oxford University Press, 2007).

N., N., *Maria Triumphans* (Saint Omer, 1635), ARCR 563.

Narratives of the Days of the Reformation, chiefly from the Manuscripts of John Foxe the Martyrologist, ed. John Gough Nichols (1859).

Newcourt, Richard, *Repertorium Ecclesiasticum Parochiale Londiniense*, 2 vols (1708).

Nichols, John, *A Declaration of the Recantation of J. Nichols* (1581), *STC²* 18533.

Nichols, John, *The Progresses and Public Processions of Queen Elizabeth,* 3 vols (1823).

Northbrooke, John, *Spiritus est Vicarius Christi in Terra* (1571), *STC²* 18663.

Nowell, Alexander, *A Reproufe, written by Alexander Nowell, of a Booke entituled, A Proufe of Certayne Artices in Religion denied by M. Juell* (1565), *STC²* 18740.

——, *The Reproufe of M. Dorman his Proufe of Certaine Articles in Religion &c.* (1566) *STC²* 18742.

Officium Concionatoris (1655), Wing O157.

The Ordre of my Lord Mayor, the Aldermen & the Shiriffes, for their Metings and Wearynge of theyr Apparel Throughout the Yeare (1568), *STC²* 16705.7; (1621 edn), *STC²* 16728.

Overall, W. H. and H. C. Overall (eds.), *Analytical Index to the Series of Records known as the Remembrancia* (1878).

Owen, John, *John Owen's Latine Epigrams Englished by Thom. Harvey, Gent.* (1677), Wing O825E.

Parker, Matthew, *Correspondence of Matthew Parker*, ed. John Bruce and Revd Thomas Thomason Perowne (Cambridge, 1853).

[Peacham, Henry], *A Dialogue between the Crosse in Cheap and Charing Crosse . . . by Ryhen Pameach* (1641), Wing P944.

Peel, Albert (ed.), *The Seconde Parte of a Register: Being a Calendar of Manuscripts under that Title Intended for Publication by the Puritans about 1593, and now in Dr Williams's Library, London*, 2 vols (Cambridge: Cambridge University Press, 1915).

——, *Tracts ascribed to Richard Bancroft* (Cambridge: Cambridge University Press, 1953).

[Penry, John], *A Briefe Discovery of the Untruthes and Slanders (against the True Governement of the Church of Christ) contained in a Sermon, preached the 8 of Februarie 1588 by D. Bancroft* (Edinburgh, 1590), *STC²* 19603.

Perkins, William, *The Art of Prophecying*, in *Works*, 3 vols (1616–18), *STC²* 19651, vol. 2.

'Memoirs of Fr Persons S.J., 1581-84 (contd)', ed. J. H. Pollen, S.J., *Catholic Record Society, Miscellanea*, 4 (1907).

Pilkington, James, *The True Report of the Burnyng of the Steple and Church of Poules in London* ([1561]), *STC²* 19930.

Platter, Thomas, *Thomas Platter's Travels in England, 1599*, trans. and intro. Clare Williams (London: Jonathan Cape, 1937).

Playfere, Thomas, *The Pathway to Perfection* (1596), *STC²* 20020.

Rastell, John, *A Confutation of a Sermon, pronounced by M. Juell, at Paulles Crosse* (Antwerp, 1564), ARCR 671.

Robinson, Hastings (ed.), *The Zurich Letters, AD 1558–1579*, 2 vols (Cambridge, 1842–5).

Rous, John, *Diary of John Rous, 1625–1642* ed. Mary Anne Everett Green (London, 1856).

Shakespeare, William, *Henry IV, Part II*, ed. A. R. Humphreys (London: Routledge, for Arden, 2nd ser., 1966).

Smith, Henry, *Thirteene Sermons upon Severall Textes of Scripture* (1592), *STC²* 22717.

Sparrow Simpson, W., *Registrum Statutorum et Consuetudinum Ecclesiae Cathedralis Sancti Pauli Londiniensis* (1873).

Stepney, William, *The Spanish Schoole-master. Containing Severall Dialogues, According to Every Day in the Weeke* (1591), *STC²* 23256.

Stow, John, *Annales, or A General Chronicle of England. Begun by John Stow, continued . . . by Edward Howes, Gent.* (1631 [1632]), *STC²* 23340.

——, *A Survey of London by John Stow*, ed. Charles Lethbridge Kingsford, 2 vols (Oxford: Clarendon Press, 1908).

——, *The Survey of London . . . Inlarged by the Care and Diligence of A.M. . . . Finished by the Study and Labour of A.M. H.D. and others* (1633), *STC²* 23345.

Strype, John, *Annals of the Reformation*, 4 vols (Oxford, 1824).

——, *Historical Collections of the Life and Acts of the Right Reverend Father in God, John Aylmer* (Oxford, 1821).

——, *The Life and Acts of Matthew Parker*, 3 vols (Oxford, 1821).

——, *The Life and Acts of John Whitgift, DD*, 3 vols (Oxford, 1822).

——, *A Survey of the Cities of London and Westminster . . . by John Stow . . . Now Lastly Corrected, Improved and very much Enlarged . . . by John Strype* (London, 1720).

Sutcliffe, Matthew, *De Recta Studii Theologici Ratione* (1602), *STC²* 23459.

Tesimond, Oswald, *The Gunpowder Plot: The Narrative of Oswald Tesimond alias Greenway*, ed. Francis Edwards, SJ (Chatham: Folio Society, 1973).

Tedder, William, and Anthony Tyrrell, *The Recantations as they were severally pronounced by W. Tedder and A. Tyrrell* (1588), *STC²* 23859.

'The Fall of Anthony Tyrrell', ed. John Morris, S.J., in *The Troubles of our Catholic Forefathers, related by themselves*, 2nd ser. (1875).

Udall, John, *A Parte of a Register* (Middelburg, 1593), STC² 10400.

Verstegan, Richard, *A Declaration of the True Causes of the Great Troubles, presupposed to be intended against the Realme of England* ([Antwerp, 1592]), ARCR 760.

Walton, Izaak, *The Lives of John Donne, Sir Henry Wotton, Richard Hooker, George Herbert, and Robert Sanderson*, ed. George Saintsbury (Oxford: Oxford University Press, 1927).

Wapull, George, *The Tide Tarrieth No Man* (1576), in *English Morality Plays and Moral Interludes*, eds. Edgar T. Schell and J. D. Shuchter (New York: Rinehart and Winston, 1969).

Ward, Samuel, *A Coal from the Altar* (1615), STC² 25039; (1616), STC² 25040.

Whitgift, John, *The Works of John Whitgift*, ed. Revd John Ayre, 3 vols (Cambridge, 1851–3).

——, *An Answere to a Certen Libel Intituled, An Admonition to the Parliament* (1572), STC² 25427.

[Whittingham, William], *A Brief Discours off the Troubles begonne at Franckfort* ([Heidelberg], 1574), STC² 25442.

Wilkins, John, *Ecclesiastes* (1656), Wing W2188.

Wright, Abraham, *Five Sermons, in Five Sundry Styles* (1656), Wing W3685.

SECONDARY SOURCES

Almond, Philip C., *Demonic Possession and Exorcism in Early Modern England* (Cambridge: Cambridge University Press, 2004).

Anstruther, Godfrey, *The Seminary Priests: A Dictionary of the Secular Clergy of England and Wales, 1558–1850* (Ware: St Edmund's College, 1969–77).

Arbuckle, W. F., 'The Gowrie Conspiracy', *Scottish Historical Review*, 36 (1957), 1–27, 89–110.

Archer, Ian, 'The Charity of Early Modern Londoners', *Transactions of the Royal Historical Society*, 12 (2002), 223–44.

Armstrong, Catherine, '"Error Vanquished by Delivery": Elite Sermon Performance in Jacobean England', D.Phil. thesis, University of Oxford, 2007.

Aston, Margaret, *The King's Bedpost: Reformation and Iconography in a Tudor Group Portrait* (Cambridge: Cambridge University Press, 1993).

——, 'Puritans and Iconoclasm, 1560–1660', in Christopher Durston and Jacqueline Eales (eds), *The Culture of English Puritanism, 1560–1700* (London: Macmillan, 1996), pp. 92–121.

Atherton, Ian, and David Como, 'The Burning of Edward Wightman: Puritanism, Prelacy and the Politics of Heresy in Early Modern England', *English Historical Review*, 120 (2005), 1215–50.

Bald, R. C., 'Dr. Donne and the Booksellers', *Studies in Bibliography*, 18 (1965), 70–80.

Barnard, John, 'Introduction', in John Barnard, D. F. McKenzie with Maureen Bell (eds), *The Cambridge History of the Book in Britain*, vol. IV: *1557–1695* (Cambridge: Cambridge University Press, 2002), pp. 1–25.

Barron, Caroline M., *London in the Later Middle Ages: Government and People, 1200–1500* (Oxford: Oxford University Press, 2004).

——, 'London and St Paul's Cathedral in the Later Middle Ages', in Janet Backhouse (ed.), *The Medieval English Cathedral: Papers in Honour of Pamela Tudor-Craig* (Donington: Shaun Tyas, 2003), pp. 126–49.

Bellany, Alastair, *The Politics of Court Scandal in Early Modern England: News Culture and the Overbury Affair, 1603–1660* (Cambridge: Cambridge University Press, 2002).

——, '"Railinge Rymes and Vaunting Verse": Libellous Politics in Early Stuart England, 1603–1628', in Kevin Sharpe and Peter Lake (eds), *Culture and Politics in Early Stuart England* (London: Macmillan, 1994), pp. 285–371.

Bentley, G. E., 'Sunday Performances in the London Theatres', in *The Jacobean and Caroline Stage*, 7 vols (Oxford: Clarendon Press, 1968), vol. 7.

Berry, Herbert, 'Where Was the Playhouse in Which the Boy Choristers of St Paul's Cathedral Performed Plays?', *Medieval and Renaissance Drama in England*, 13 (2001), 101–16.

Bidwell, William B., and Maija Jannson (eds), *Proceedings in Parliament, 1626*, vol. 2 (New Haven: Yale University Press, 1992).

Black, Joseph, 'The Rhetoric of Reaction: The Martin Marprelate Tracts (1588–89), Anti-Martinism, and the Uses of Print in Early Modern England', *Sixteenth Century Journal*, 28 (1997), 707–25.

Blayney, Peter W. M., *The Bookshops in Paul's Cross Churchyard* (London: Bibliographical Society, 1990).

——, 'The Alleged Popularity of Playbooks', *Shakespeare Quarterly*, 56(1) (2005), 33–50.

——, 'John Day and the Bookshop That Never Was', in Lena Cowen Orlin (ed.), *Material London, ca. 1600* (Philadelphia: University of Pennsylvania Press, 2000), pp. 322–43.

——, 'The Publication of Playbooks', in John D. Cox and David Scott Kasten (eds), *A New History of Early English Drama* (New York: Columbia University Press, 1997), pp. 383–422.

Blench, J. W., *Preaching in England in the Late Fifteenth and Sixteenth Centuries* (Oxford: Blackwell, 1964).

Booty, John E., *John Jewel as Apologist of the Church of England* (London: SPCK, 1963).

Bossy, John, *The English Catholic Community, 1570–1850* (London: Darton, Longman & Todd, 1975).

——, 'The Character of Elizabethan Catholicism', *Past and Present*, 21 (1962), 39–59.

Bowers, Roger, 'The Playhouse of the Choristers of Paul's, c. 1575–1608', *Theatre Notebook*, 54 (2000), 70–85.

Braddick, Michael, *God's Fury, England's Fire: A New History of the English Civil Wars* (London: Allen Lane, 2008).

Bridgen, Susan, *London and the Reformation* (Oxford: Clarendon Press, 1989).

——, 'Religion and Social Obligation in Early Sixteenth-Century London', *Past and Present*, 103 (1984).

Cargill Thompson, W. D. J., 'Sir Francis Knollys' Campaign against the *Jure Divino* Theory of Episcopacy', in C. Robert Cole and Michael E. Moddy (eds), *The Dissenting Tradition: Essays for Leland H. Carlson* (Athens: Ohio University Press, 1975), pp. 39–77.

——, 'A Reconsideration of Richard Bancroft's Paul's Cross Sermon of 9 February 1588/9', *Journal of Ecclesiastical History*, 20(2) (1969), 253–66.

Carlson, Leland H., *Martin Marpelate, Gentleman: Master Job Throckmorton Laid Open in his Colors* (San Marino, CA: Huntington Library, 1981).

Chadwick, Owen, 'Richard Bancroft's Submission', *Journal of Ecclesiastical History*, 3 (1952), 58–73.

Clark, Andrew (ed.), *Register of the University of Oxford*, vol. 2 (Oxford Historical Society, 1887).

Clark, John Willis (ed.), *Endowments of the University of Cambridge* (Cambridge, 1904).

Clegg, Cyndia Susan, *Press Censorship in Elizabethan England* (Cambridge; Cambridge University Press, 1997).

——, *Press Censorship in Jacobean England* (Cambridge: Cambridge University Press, 2001).

Coffey, John, and Paul C. H. Lim, 'Introduction', in John Coffey and Paul C. H. Lim (eds), *The Cambridge Companion to Puritanism* (Cambridge: Cambridge University Press, 2008), pp. 1–15.

Cogswell, Thomas, *The Blessed Revolution: English Politics and the Coming of War, 1621–1624* (Cambridge: Cambridge University Press, 1989).

——, 'The Politics of Propaganda: Charles I and the People in the 1620s', *Journal of British Studies*, 29 (1990), 187–215.

Colclough, David, *Freedom of Speech in Early Stuart England* (Cambridge; Cambridge University Press, 2005).

Collinson, Patrick, *The Birthpangs of Protestant England: Religious and Cultural Change in the Sixteenth and Seventeenth Centuries* (London: Macmillan, 1988).

——, *The Elizabethan Puritan Movement* (London: Jonathan Cape, 1967; repr. Oxford: Clarendon Press, 1990).

——, *The English Captivity of Mary Queen of Scots* (Sheffield: Sheffield History Pamphlets, 1987).

——, *The Puritan Character; Polemics and Polarities in Early Seventeenth-Century English Culture* (Los Angeles: William Andrews Clark Memorial Library, University of California, 1989).

——, 'Ecclesiastical Vitriol: Religious Satire in the 1590s and the Invention of Puritanism', in John Guy (ed.), *The Reign of Elizabeth I: Court and Culture in the Last Decade* (Cambridge: Cambridge University Press, 1995), pp. 150–70.

——, 'Elizabethan and Jacobean Puritanism as Forms of Popular Culture', in Christopher Durston and Jacqueline Eales (eds), *The Culture of English Protestantism, 1560–1700* (London: Macmillan), pp. 32–57.

——, Arnold Hunt and Alexandra Walsham, 'Religion Publishing in England, 1557–1640', in John Barnard, D. F. McKenzie with Maureen Bell (eds), *The Cambridge History of the Book in Britain*, vol. 4: *1557–1695* (Cambridge: Cambridge University Press, 2002), pp. 29–66.

Como, David R., 'Predestination and Political Conflict in Laud's London', *Historical Journal*, 46 (2003), 263–94.

Croft, Pauline, 'Libels, Popular Literacy and Public Opinion in Early Modern England', *Historical Research*, 68 (1995), 266–85.

Cressy, David, *Bonfires and Bells: National Memory and the Protestant Calendar in Elizabethan and Stuart England* (London: Wiedenfeld and Nicolson, 1989).

——, 'Book Burning in Tudor and Stuart England', *Sixteenth Century Journal*, 26(2) (2005), 359–74.

Cummings, Brian, *The Literary Culture of the Reformation: Grammar and Grace* (Oxford: Oxford University Press, 2002).

——, 'Martin Marprelate and the Popular Voice', in Kate Cooper and Jeremy Gregory (eds), *Elite and Popular Religion* (Woodbridge: Boydell, for the Ecclesiastical History Society, 2006).

Devlin, Christopher, 'An Unwilling Apostate: The Case of Anthony Tyrrell', *The Month*, n.s., 6 (1951), 346–58.

Doran, Susan, and Christopher Durston, *Princes, Pastors and People: the Church and Religion in England, 1500–1700* (London: Routledge, 2003).

Donaldson, Gordon, 'The Attitude of Whitgift and Bancroft to the Scottish Church', reprinted in *Scottish Church History* (Edinburgh: Scottish Academic Press, 1985), pp. 164–77.

Durston, Christopher, and Jacqueline Eales, 'Introduction: The Puritan Ethos, 1640–1700', in Christopher Durston and Jacqueline Eales (eds), *The Culture of English Puritanism, 1560–1700* (London: Macmillan, 1994), pp. 1–31.

Ferrell, Lori Anne, *Government by Polemic: James I, the King's Preachers and the Rhetorics of Conformity, 1603–1625* (Palo Alto, CA: Stanford University Press, 1998).

Freeman, Thomas, 'Demons, Deviance and Defiance: John Darrell and the Politics of Exorcism in late Elizabethan England', in Peter Lake and Michael Questier (eds), *Conformity and Orthodoxy in the English Church, c. 1560–1660* (Woodbridge: Boydell Press, 2000), pp. 34–63.

——, 'Providence and Prescription: The Account of Elizabeth in Foxe's "Book of Martyrs"', in Susan Doran and Thomas S. Freeman (eds), *The Myth of Elizabeth* (London: Palgrave Macmillan, 2003), pp. 27–55.

Fincham, Kenneth, *Prelate as Pastor: The Episcopate of James I* (Oxford: Oxford University Press, 1990).

——, 'Prelacy and Politics: Archbishop Abbot's Defence of Protestant Orthodoxy', *Historical Research*, 61 (1988).

——and Nicholas Tyacke, *Altars Restored: The Changing Face of English Worship, 1547–c.1700* (Oxford: Oxford University Press, 2007).

—— and Peter Lake, 'The Ecclesiastical Policy of King James I', *Journal of British Studies*, 24 (1985), 169–207.

Fox, Adam, 'Ballads, Libels and Popular Ridicule in Jacobean England', *Past and Present*, 145 (1994), 48–83.

——, 'Rumour, News and Popular Political Opinion in Elizabethan and Early Stuart England', *Historical Journal*, 40 (1997), 597–620.

Fraser, Antonia, *The Gunpowder Plot: Terror and Faith in 1605* (1996; repr. London: Arrow Books, 1999).

Gair, Reavley, *The Children of Paul's: the Story of a Theatre Company, 1553–1608* (Cambridge: Cambridge University Press, 1982).

Gants, David L., 'A Quantitative Analysis of the London Book Trade, 1614–1618', *Studies in Bibliography*, 55 (2002), 185–213.

Gardiner, S. R., *History of England from the Accession of James I to the Outbreak of the Civil War, 1603–1642* (1883–4; repr. New York: AMS Press, 1965), vol. 10.

Graves, M. A. R., 'The Management of the Elizabethan House of Commons: The Council's "Men-of-Business"', *Parliamentary History*, 2 (1983), 11–38.

Green, Ian, *The Christian's ABC: Catechisms and Catechizing in England c. 1530–1740* (Oxford: Clarendon Press, 1996).

——, *Print and Protestantism in Early Modern England* (Oxford: Oxford University Press, 2000).

Green, Ian, 'Continuity and Change in Protestant Preaching in Early Modern England', Friends of the Dr Williams's Library Sixtieth Lecture (London: Dr Williams's Trust, 2009).

Gurr, Andrew, 'Henry Carey's Peculiar Letter', *Shakespeare Quarterly*, 56(1) (2005), 51–75.

Haigh, *English Reformations: Religion, Politics and Society under the Tudors* (Oxford: Clarendon Press, 1993).

Haigh, *The Plain Man's Pathways to Heaven: Kinds of Christianity in Post-Reformation England, 1570–1640* (Oxford: Oxford University Press, 2007).

——, 'The Character of an Antipuritan', *Sixteenth Century Journal*, 35 (2004), 671–88.

——, 'The Recent Historiography of the English Reformation' *Historical Journal*, 25 (1982), 995–1007.

Hammer, Paul E. J., *The Polarisation of English Politics: The Political Career of Robert Devereux, 2nd Earl of Essex, 1585–1597* (Cambridge: Cambridge University Press, 1999).

——, 'Shakespeare's *Richard II*, the Play of 7 February 1601, and the Essex Rising', *Shakespeare Quarterly*, 59 (2008), 1–35.

Hartley, T. E. (ed.), *Proceedings in the Parliaments of Elizabeth I*, vol. 1: *1558–1581* (Leicester: Leicester University Press, 1981).

Heinemann, Margot, *Puritanism and Theatre: Thomas Middleton and Opposition Drama under the Early Stuarts* (Cambridge: Cambridge University Press, 1980).

Heltzel, Virgil B., 'Young Francis Bacon's Tutor', *Modern Language Notes*, 63(9) (1948), 483–8.

Herr, Alan Fager, *The Elizabethan Sermon: A Survey and a Bibliography* (Philadelphia: University of Pennsylvania Press, 1940).

Hoffer, Peter C., and N. E. H. Hull, *Murdering Mothers: Infanticide in England and New England 1558–1803* (New York: New York University Press, 1981).

Hunt, Arnold, 'The Art of Hearing: English Preachers and Their Audiences, 1590–1640, Ph.D. thesis, University of Cambridge, 2001.

——, 'Licensing and Religious Censorship in Early Modern England', in Andrew Hadfield (ed.), *Literature and Censorship in Renaissance England* (London: Palgrave Macmillan, 2001), pp. 127–46.

——, 'Tuning the Pulpits: the Religious Context of the Essex Revolt', in Lori Anne Ferrell and Peter McCullough (eds), *The English Sermon Revised: Religion, Literature and History, 1600–1750* (Manchester: Manchester University Press, 2000), pp. 86–114.

Ingram, Martin, *Church Courts, Sex and Marriage in England, 1570–1640* (Cambridge: Cambridge University Press, 1987).

James, Mervyn, 'At a Crossroads of the Political Culture: the Essex Revolt, 1601', in *Society, Politics and Culture: Studies in Early Modern England* (Cambridge: Cambridge University Press, 1986), pp. 416–65.

Jenkins, Gary W., *John Jewel and the English National Church: The Dilemma of an Erastian Reformer* (Aldershot: Ashgate, 2006).

Jones, Norman, *Faith by Statute: Parliament and the Settlement of Religion, 1559* (London: Royal Historical Society, 1982).

Keene, Derek, Arthur Burns and Andrew Saint, eds., *Saint Pauls: The Cathedral Church of London 604–2004* (New Haven: Yale University Press, 2004).

King, John, 'Fiction and Fact in Foxe's *Book of Martyrs*', in David Loades (ed.), *John Foxe and the English Reformation* (Ashgate: Scholar Press, 1997), pp. 26–31.

Kirby, W. J. Torrance, 'The Public Sermon: Paul's Cross and the Culture of Persuasion in England, 1534–1570', *Renaissance and Reformation / Renaissance et Réforme*, 31(1) (2008), 3–29.

Lake, Peter, *Anglicans and Puritans?: Presbyterianism and English Conformist Thought from Whitgift to Hooker* (London: Unwin Hyman, 1988).

——, *The Boxmaker's Revenge: 'Orthodoxy', 'Heterodoxy' and the Politics of the Parish in Early Stuart London* (Manchester: Manchester University Press, 2001).

——, 'Anti-popery: The Structure of a Prejudice', in Richard Cust and Ann Hughes (eds), *Conflict in Early Stuart England: Studies in Religion and Politics, 1603–1642* (London: Longmans, 1989), pp. 72–106.

——, 'Calvinism and the English Church, 1570–1635', *Past and Present*, 114 (1987), 32–76.

——, 'Lancelot Andrewes, John Buckeridge and *Avant-Garde* Conformity at the Court of James I', in Linda Levy Peck (ed.), *The Mental World of the Jacobean Church* (Cambridge: Cambridge University Press, 1991), pp. 113–33.

——with Michael Questier, *The Antichrist's Lewd Hat: Protestants, Papists and Players in Post-Reformation England* (New Haven: Yale University Press, 2002).

—— and ——, 'Agency, Appropriation and Rhetoric under the Gallows: Puritans, Romanists and the State in Early Modern England', *Past and Present*, 153 (1996), 64–107.

—— and ——, 'Introduction', in Peter Lake and Michael Questier (eds), *Conformity and Orthodoxy in the English Church, c. 1560–1660* (Woodbridge: Boydell Press, 2000).

—— and ——, 'Puritans, Papists and the "Public Sphere" in Early Modern England: The Edmund Campion Affair in Context', *Journal of Modern History*, 72 (2000), 587–627.

——and Steve Pincus, 'Rethinking the Public Sphere in Early Modern England', *Journal of British Studies*, 45 (2006), 270–92.

Lares, Jameela, *Milton and the Preaching Arts* (Cambridge: James Clarke, 2001).

Larkin, James F. (ed.), *Stuart Royal Proclamations*, 2 vols (Oxford: Clarendon Press, 1983).

McCaffrey, Wallace, *Elizabeth I* (London: Edward Arnold, 1993).

McCullough, Peter, *Sermons at Court: Politics and Religion in Elizabethan and Jacobean Preaching* (Cambridge: Cambridge University Press, 1998).

MacDonald, Alan, *The Jacobean Kirk, 1567–1625: Sovereignty, Polity and Liturgy* (Aldershot: Ashgate, 1998).

McKitterick, David, '"Ovid with a Littleton": The Cost of English Books in the Early Seventeenth Century', *Transactions of the Cambridge Bibliographical Society*, 11 (1997).

McLaren, A. N., *Political Culture in the Reign of Elizabeth I: Queen and Commonwealth, 1558–1585* (Cambridge: Cambridge University Press, 1999).

MacLure, Millar, *The Paul's Cross Sermons* (Toronto: University of Toronto Press, 1958).

——, *Register of Sermons Preached at Paul's Cross, 1534–1642*, rev. by Peter Pauls and J. C. Boswell (Ottawa: Dovehouse, 1989).

Maltby, Judith, *Prayer Book and People in Elizabethan and Early Stuart England* (Cambridge: Cambridge University Press, 1998).

Marsh, Christopher, *The Family of Love in English Society, 1550–1630* (Cambridge: Cambridge University Press, 1994).

Matthews, W., 'Shakespeare and the Reporters', *The Library*, 4th ser. 15 (1935), 381–498.

Mayer, J. E. B. (ed.), *Early Statutes of the College of St John the Evangelist in Cambridge.* (Cambridge, 1859).

Mears, Natalie, *Queenship and Political Discourse in the Elizabethan Realms* (Cambridge: Cambridge University Press, 2005).

——, 'Council, Public Debate, and Queenship: John Stubbs's *The Discoverie of a Gaping Gulf,* 1579', *Historical Journal*, 44 (2001), 629–50.

Merritt, J. F., 'Puritans, Laudians, and the Phenomenon of Church-Building in Jacobean London', *Historical Journal*, 41 (1998), 935–60.

Milton, Anthony, *Catholic and Reformed: The Roman and Protestant Churches in English Protestant Thought 1600–1640* (Cambridge: Cambridge University Press, 1995).

——, 'Licensing, Censorship, and Religious Orthodoxy in Early Stuart England', *Historical Journal*, 41 (1998), 625–51.

Milward, Peter, *Religious Controversies of the Elizabethan Age: A Survey of Printed Sources* (London: Scholar Press, 1978).

——, *Religious Controversies of the Jacobean Age: A Survey of Printed Sources* (London: Scholar Press, 1978).

Mitchell, W. T. (ed.), *Register of Congregations, 1505–1517* (Oxford Historical Society, 1948).

Moore, Jonathan D., *English Hypothetical Universalism: John Preston and the Softening of Reformed Theology* (Grand Rapids, MI: Eerdmans, 2007).

Morrissey, Mary, 'John Donne as a Conventional Paul's Cross Preacher' in David Colclough (ed.), *Professional Donne*, (Cambridge: D. S. Brewer, 2003), pp. 159–78.

——, 'Presenting James VI and I to the Public: Preaching on Political Anniversaries at Paul's Cross', in Ralph Houlbrooke (ed.), *James VI and I: Ideas, Authority, and Government* (Aldershot: Ashgate, 2006), pp. 107–121.

——, 'Rhetoric, Religion and Politics on the St Paul's Cross Sermons, 1603–1625', PhD thesis, University of Cambridge, 1998.

——, 'Scripture, Style and Persuasion in Seventeenth-century English Theories of Preaching', *Journal of Ecclesiastical History*, 53(4) (2002), 686–706.

Mulholland, P. A., 'The Dating of *The Roaring Girl*', *Review of English Studies*, ns, 28 (1977), 18–31.

Mullinger, J. B., *The University of Cambridge, From the Earliest Times to the Royal Injunctions of 1535*, 3 vols (Cambridge, 1873), vol. 1.

Murphy, Kathryn, 'The Date of Edwin Sandys's Paul's Cross Sermon, " . . . at which time a maine treason was discouered" ', *Notes and Queries* (December 2006), pp. 430–2.

Neale, J. E., *Elizabeth I and her Parliaments, 1558–1581* (London: Jonathan Cape, 1953).

——, *Queen Elizabeth* (London: Jonathan Cape, 1934).

——, 'November 17th', in *Essays in Elizabethan History* (London: Jonathan Cape, 1958), pp. 9–20.

Olsen, V. Norskov, *John Foxe and the Elizabethan Church* (Berkeley: University of California Press, 1973).

Owen, H. Gareth, 'The London Parish Clergy in the Reign of Elizabeth I', Ph.D. thesis, University of London, 1957.

——, 'Paul's Cross: The Broadcasting House of Elizabethan London', *History Today*, 11 (1961), 836–42.

Parry, Graham, *The Arts of the Anglican Counter-Reformation: Glory, Laud and Honour* (Woodbridge: Boydell and Brewer, 2006).

Peacock, George, *Observations on the Statutes of the University of Cambridge* (London, 1841).

Pearl, Valerie, *London and the Outbreak of the Puritan Revolution: City Government and National Politics, 1625–43* (Oxford: Oxford University Press, 1961).

Pearson, A. F. S., *Thomas Cartwright and Elizabethan Puritanism, 1535–1603* (Cambridge: Cambridge University Press, 1925).

Penrose, F. C., 'On the Recent Discoveries of Portions of Old St Paul's Cathedral', *Archaelogia*, 47 (1883), 381–92.

Pettegree, Andrew, *Reformation and the Culture of Persuasion* (Cambridge: Cambridge University Press, 2005).

Questier, Michael, *Catholicism and Community in Early Modern England: Politics, Aristocratic Patronage and Religion, c. 1550–1640* (Cambridge: Cambridge University Press, 2006).

——, *Conversion, Politics and Religion in England, 1580–1625* (Cambridge: Cambridge University Press, 1996).

——, 'The Phenomenon of Conversion: Change of Religion to and from Catholicism in England, 1580–1625', D.Phil. thesis, University of Sussex, 1991.

——, 'John Gee, Archbishop Abbot, and the use of converts from Rome in Jacobean Anti-Catholicism', *Recusant History*, 24 (1993), 347–60.

Read, Conyers, *Mr Secretary Walsingham and the Policy of Queen Elizabeth*, 3 vols (Oxford: Clarendon Press, 1925), vol. 2.

Riehl Leader, Damien, *A History of the University of Cambridge*, vol. I, to 1546 (Cambridge: Cambridge University Press, 1988).

Russell, Conrad, *The Causes of the English Civil War* (Oxford: Clarendon Press, 1990).

Seaver, Paul, *The Puritan Lectureships: The Politics of Religious Dissent, 1560–1662* (Palo Alto, CA: Stanford University Press, 1970).

Shagan, Ethan, *Popular Politics and the English Reformation* (Cambridge: Cambridge University Press, 2003).

Shami, Jeanne, *John Donne and Conformity in Crisis in the late Jacobean Pulpit* (Cambridge: D. S. Brewer, 2003).

——, *John Donne's 1622 Gunpowder Plot Sermon: A Parallel-text Edition* (Pittsburgh, Duquesne University Press, 1996).

——, 'Donne's 1622 Sermon on the Gunpowder Plot: His Original Presentation Manuscript Discovered', *English Manuscript Studies, 1100–1700*, 5 (1995), 63–86.

Sharpe, Kevin, *The Personal Rule of Charles I* (New Haven: Yale University Press, 1992).

Shell, Alison, *Oral Culture and Catholicism in Early Modern England* (Cambridge: Cambridge University Press, 2007).

Shriver, Frederick, 'Orthodoxy and Diplomacy: James I and the Vorstius Affair', *English Historical Review*, 85 (1970), 449–74.

Skinner, Quentin, *Reason and Rhetoric in the Philosophy of Hobbes* (Cambridge: Cambridge University Press, 1996).

Slack, Paul, *The Impact of Plague in Tudor and Stuart England* (Oxford: Clarendon Press, 1985).

Smuts, Malcolm, *Court Culture and the Origins of a Royalist Tradition in Early Stuart England* (Philadelphia: University of Pennsylvania Press, 1987).

Sommerville, M. R., 'Richard Hooker and his Contemporaries on Episcopacy: an Elizabethan Consensus', *Journal of Ecclesiastical History*, 35 (1984), 177–87.

Southern, A. C., *English Recusant Prose, 1559–1582* (London: Sands, 1950).

Southgate, W. M., *John Jewel and the Problem of Doctrinal Authority* (Cambridge, MA: Harvard University Press, 1962).

Sparrow Simpson, *Chapters in the History of Old S. Paul's* (1881).

——, *Documents Illustrating the History of S Paul's Cathedral* (1880).

——, *Saint Paul's Cathedral and Old City Life* (1894).

Sparrow, John, 'John Donne and Contemporary Preachers: Their Preparation of Sermons for Delivery and for Publication', *Essays and Studies*, 16 (1931), 144–78.

Stanwood, P. G., 'John Donne's Sermon Notes', *Review of English Studies*, 29 (1978), 313–20.

Strong, Roy, 'The Popular Celebration of the Accession Day of Queen Elizabeth I', *Journal of the Warburg and Courtauld Institutes*, 21 (1958), 86–103.

Todd, Margo, *Christian Humanism and the Puritan Social Order* (Cambridge: Cambridge University Press, 1987).

Towers, S. Mutchow, *Control of Religious Printing in Early Stuart England* (Woodbridge: Boydell Press, 2003).

Tudor-Craig, Pamela, and Christopher Whittick, *'Old St Paul's': The Society of Antiquaries' Diptych, 1616* (London: London Topographical Society, 2004).

Tyacke, Nicholas, *Anti-Calvinists: The Rise of English Arminianism, c.1590–1640* (Oxford: Clarendon Press, 1987).

——(ed.), *The History of the University of Oxford, vol. IV: Seventeenth-Century Oxford* (Oxford: Oxford University Press, 1997).

Usher, Roland G., *The Rise and Fall of the High Commission*, with introduction by Philip Tyler (1913; Oxford: Oxford University Press, 1968).

Ussher, Brett, *William Cecil and Episcopacy, 1559–1577* (Aldershot: Ashgate, 2003).

——, 'The Deanery of Bocking and the Demise of the Vestiarian Controversy', *Journal of Ecclesiastical History*, 52(3) (2001), 434–55.

Venn, John (ed.), *Grace Book [Delta]: containing the Records of the University of Cambridge for the years 1542–1589* (Cambridge: Cambridge University Press, 1910).

Wabuda, Susan, *Preaching during the English Reformation* (Cambridge: Cambridge University Press, 2002).

——, 'Equivocation and Recantation during the English Reformation: The "Subtle Shadows" of Dr Edward Crome', *Journal of Ecclesiastical History*, 44 (1993), 224–42.

Walsham, Alexandra, *Church Papists: Catholicism, Conformity and Confessional Polemic in Early Modern England* (Woodbridge: Boydell, 1993).

——, '"A Very Deborah?": The Myth of Elizabeth as a Providential Monarch', in Susan Doran and Thomas S. Freeman (eds), *The Myth of Elizabeth* (London: Palgrave Macmillan, 2003), pp. 143–68.

——, '"The Fatal Vesper": Providentialism and Anti-Popery in Late Jacobean London', *Past and Present*, 144 (1994), pp. 37–87.

Watts, Tessa, *Cheap Print and Popular Piety, 1550–1640* (Cambridge: Cambridge University Press, 1991).

Webster, Tom, *Godly Clergy in Early Stuart England: The Caroline Puritan Movement, c. 1620–1643* (Cambridge: Cambridge University Press, 1997).

——, 'Early Stuart Puritanism', in John Coffey and Paul C. H. Lim (eds), *The Cambridge Companion to Puritanism* (Cambridge: Cambridge University Press, 2008), pp. 48-66.

Wooding, Lucy, *Rethinking Catholicism in Reformation England* (Oxford: Clarendon Press, 2000).

Wormald, Jenny, 'Ecclesiastical Vitriol: the Kirk, the Puritans and the Future King of England', in John Guy (ed.), *The Reign of Elizabeth I: Court and Culture in the Last Decade* (Cambridge: Cambridge University Press, 1995), pp. 171–91.

ELECTRONIC RESOURCES

Early Stuart Libels: An Edition of the Poems from Manuscript Sources, ed. Alistair Bellany and Andrew McRae, *Early Modern Textual Studies*, Texts Series I (2005), http://purl.oclc.org/emls/texts/libels/.

Foxe's Book of Martyrs Variorum Edition Online, Humanities Research Institute, University of Sheffield, http://www.hrionline.shef.ac.uk/foxe/.

An electronic edition of John Strype's A Survey of the Cities of London and Westminster, The Stuart London Project, Humanities Research Institute, University of Sheffield, http://hrionline.ac.uk/strype.

CCEd: Clergymen of the Church of England database, http://www.theclergydatabase.org.uk/index.html.

Index

Abbot, George, Bishop of London, later
    Archbishop of Canterbury 93–5, 117
Abbot, Robert 33
accession of Charles I 33, 73
accession of Elizabeth I 130, 135–6, 139–43
accession of James I 5, 141
accession of Mary Tudor 171
Act of Uniformity 172; *see also* Supremacy and
    Uniformity
Adams, Thomas 46, 226
Admonition controversy 202 n. 38, 205, 213;
    see also *Admonition to Parliament*
Admonition to Parliament 64, 78, 192, 197, 200
Ainsworth, Henry 186
aldermen of London 32–3, 104, 157, 224–7
    attending Paul's Cross 12–13, 16–17, 19–22,
        131, 180, 223
    control of sermons 72–3, 80–2, 84
Alley, William 103
Allington, Sir Giles 127–9
Anabaptists 95, 113, 189, 208
Anderson, Anthony 36, 49, 180
Andrewes, John 47
Andrewes, Lancelot 38, 59, 142, 150
Anne, Queen of England 21–2
Aristotle 165
Arminianism 97–101, 165, 183–4, 223
Articles of Religion 95, 98, 198, 205
Ashe, Simeon 226
atheist 183
Atherton, Ian 109
Atkinson, William 116–17
auditors 10–12, 18, 25, 142, 206, 223
    Anti-Catholicism and 160–1, 179, 181
    complaints and 85
    controlling the pulpit and 102–3, 110,
        114, 127
    Elizabethan settlement and 160
    Gunpowder Plot and 145, 147, 149, 151
    Henry Smith and 39
avant-garde conformist 91, 218–20, 222
Aylesbury, Thomas 97
Aylmer, John, Bishop of London 24, 45, 50,
    216
    control of sermons 26–7, 80, 87
    funding preachers and 30–2

Babington Plot 76, 115–16
Bacon, Lady Anne 166, 177
Bacon, Anthony 206
Bacon, Edward 202
Bacon, Sir Francis, Lord Keeper, later viscount
    St. Albans 18, 84

Bacon, Nathaniel 202
Bacon, Sir Nicholas 202
Baker, Samuel 119
Ballard, John 115
Bancroft, Richard, Bishop of London, later
    Archbishop of Canterbury 1, 26
    Admonition to Parliament and 78, 192, 197,
        200, 213
    anti-puritanism and 214, 217, 218, 220
    Book of Common Prayer and 211–12
    sermon control and 85–6, 88–9, 128
    A Sermon preached at Paul's Cross (1589) 192–3,
        208–10, 218, 219
Barlow, William 1, 71, 89–91, 134, 148–50
Barnes, Robert 27
Barton, Elizabeth 113
Barrow, Henry 65
Bates, Thomas 106
Bartholomew's Day xi, 178
Battle of White Mountain 92
Baxter, Richard 226
Bayly, Lewis 92
Beale, Robert 208
Beaufort, Lady Margaret 28
Becanus, Martin 109
Becon, Thomas 74, 113
Bedingfield, Robert 97
Bentham, Thomas 71–2
Berkeley, Gilbert, Bishop of Bath and
    Wells 122
Bernard, Richard 36, 50–1, 55–7, 60, 110, 165
Beza, Theodore 198
Bible 36, 49–55, 59, 110, 137, 140, 198
    Joshua 136
    Psalms 23, 51, 139, 144, 148, 150, 152
    Jeremiah 51, 147, 186, 199
    Ezekiel 150
    Matthew 51–2, 54, 89, 140, 170, 202
    Luke 180, 226
    Acts 199
    Romans 52, 56, 139, 141, 171, 188
    1 Corinthians 163, 199–200, 214
    2 Corinthians 54
    1 Timothy 52, 138, 157, 206–7, 217
    2 Timothy 56
    Titus 141
    Hebrews 183
    1 John 209, 219
    Revelations 118, 173, 185, 187–8, 216
Bickley, Thomas 170
Bill, Dr William 70–1
Bilson, Thomas, Bishop of Winchester 65–6,
    103

Bishop of London, *see* George Abbot, later
 Archbishop of Canterbury; John Aylmer;
 Richard Bancroft, later Archbishop of
 Canterbury; Edmund Bonner; Richard
 Fletcher; Edmund Grindal, later
 Archbishop of Canterbury; William
 Juxon, later Archbishop of Canterbury;
 John King; William Laud, later
 Archbishop of Canterbury; George
 Montaigne, later Archbishop of York;
 James Pilkington; Thomas Ravis;
 Nicholas Ridley; Edwin Sandys, later
 Archbishop of York; Richard Vaughan.
Bishops' Wars 154–6
Black Acts of 1584 212
Blackal, John 122
Blayney, Peter W. M. 4–5
Blench, J. W. 58–9
Blood of Hales 113, 160
Boleyn, Anne 110
Bolton, Robert 60, 82
Bonner, Edmund, Bishop of London 17, 29, 70
Book of Common Prayer 72, 176, 198–200, 205,
 211, 217
 Prayer Book service 182, 215, 220–1, 223
Bossy, John 180
Boughen, Edward 219–21
Bourne, Dr Gilbert 7, 17, 87, 102
Bourne, Immanuel 54
Boys, John 148, 151–2
Brent, Sir Nathaniel 121
Bridges, John 63, 206–7
Briggs, Agnes 123
Brinsley, John 39–40, 53, 55
Bristow 178
Brocas, Sir Pexall 125, 128
Brookes, Matthew 98, 188–90
Browne, Sir William 17, 118
Brownists 186–7, 189, 214
Buckeridge, John, Bishop of Ely 114
Bullingham, John 41, 195
Bunny, Edmund 176
Burges, Cornelius 227
Burgess, Anthony 37
Bury, George 44
Bynneman, Henry 47

Caddey, Lawrence 114–15
Cadiz raid 90
Calfhill, James 73, 75, 194
Calvinists 96–9, 183–4, 191, 218
Cambridge, University of 28–9, 86, 100–1,
 153, 170, 204
 Corpus Christi College 29 n. 132
 Thomas Cartwright and 192, 198
 St John's College 28 n. 129
Campion, S.J., Edmund 174, 180
Carew, Sir Griffin 125
Carleton, Dudley 38, 126, 131

Carlyle, Thomas 4
Carpenter, Richard 119
Cartwright, Thomas 66, 78–9, 198, 204,
 210, 212–13
 praise for 201
Caryl, Joseph 226
catechism 94–6, 215
Cecil, Robert, 1st Earl of Salisbury 26, 81, 85–6,
 88–9, 104, 116–17, 145
Cecil, William, 1st Baron Burleigh 26–7, 70,
 72, 74, 78, 202
censors 44–5
censorship 107, 111
 appointment of preachers 26–7, 33, 201,
  224–5, 227
 book burning 102, 107–9, 112, 130
 complaints against preachers 18, 31, 64, 95,
  100
 control of preaching 26, 68–101, 119, 222,
  224
 Laudian 99, 102, 218
 licensing for publication 44, 112, 199
 pre-publication censorship 112
 punishment of preachers 82–3, 121–4, 174
 see also *Directions for Preachers*; Stationers'
  Company
Chaderton, Laurence 63, 201, 205
Chadwick, Owen 208
'Challenge' sermon 1, 72, 162–75, 179, 193,
 195, 204, 210, 217
Chamberlain, John 5–6, 16, 38, 143
 on acoustics 10, 111
 on attendance of sermons 16–17
 on book burning 108
 on public penance 123, 125–7
Chappell, William 59
charitable causes 7–8; *see also* collections
Charles I, King of England 6, 16, 34, 46, 92,
 97–8, 143, 156–9
 attending Paul's Cross 130, 132–4
 see also accession of Charles I
Charles II, King of England 16, 132
Cheshire, Thomas 221
Children of Paul's 3, 4 n. 12
Church courts 120–1, 123, 125, 128
Church Fathers 51, 53, 57, 164
Civil War 118, 154, 156
Clapham, Henoch 45, 182–3, 216
Clarke, Thomas 114–15
Claydon, John 93
Clegg, Cyndia Susan 108, 112
Clitherow, Christopher, Lord Mayor of
 London 33, 224
Closse, George 81–2
Clough, William 69
Cogswell, Tom 93, 100
Coke, Sir Edward, Chief Justice 128–9
Coke, Frances 129
Cole, Henry, Dean of St. Paul's 164

Cole, Dr Thomas 73–4, 194
Colet, John 28
collections 7–8, 22, 39
Collins, Samuel 217–18, 220
Collinson, Patrick 137, 182, 192, 194, 200, 208
communion 163–4, 202, 220
Como, David 109
conformity 72, 79, 163, 175, 182
    ecclesiastical vestments and 192–3
    Puritan movement and 194, 199, 220, 224
    see also *avante-garde* conformist; non-conformity
convocation 30, 113, 161, 189, 195, 198
    house 11
    sermon 206–7
Cooke, Richard 124
Cooke, Tobie 44
Cooper, Thomas, Bishop of Winchester 27, 130, 200–1, 201
Copcot, John 206–7, 210
Cornford, Margaret 11
Corporation of London, *see* London
Corpus Christi College, Oxford 28
Cosin, John 31–2, 101
Cosin, Richard 207
Cotton, William 30
court, royal 18, 28, 30, 72, 83–4, 130, 133, 141, 142, 150
    accusation of idolatry in 104
    Earl of Essex and 87
    pulpit 2, 70, 72, 184
Court of Common Pleas 128
Court of High Commission 81, 86, 108, 120–9, 137, 204, 216
Coventry, Sir Thomas, Attorney General 126
Coverdale, Miles 72
Cox, Richard, Bishop of Ely 72, 176
Crakanthorpe, Richard 137, 143–4
Cranmer, Thomas, Archbishop of Canterbury 26, 198, 211
Crashaw, William 82, 186–9, 216
Cressy, David 107, 112, 135, 139, 154
Creswell, George 38, 47
Crick, Richard 78, 201, 222
Crome, Edward 113
Crowley, Robert 74, 194–6
Curteys, Richard 177

Dalton, Dorothy 127
Day, William 195
Dean of St Paul's 87, 131, 166, 224; *see also* Henry Cole; John Donne; John Feckenham; Alexander Nowell; John Overall
Deios, Laurence 50, 55, 80
De Laune, Thomas 228
Delaune, Nathaniel 63, 184
Delaune, William 184
Denison, Stephen 114
Dent, Arthur 160
Dering, Edward 199

Devereux, Robert, 2nd Earl of Essex 90 n. 82, *see also* Earl of Essex
Devick, William 12
D'Ewes, Simonds 12, 16, 19
Digby, Sir Everard 106
Directions for Preachers 12, 79, 94–5
disobedience 89, 120–1, 206, 208–10
Doctors of Civil Law 13
Donne, Daniel 48, 49 n. 60, 93 n. 90, 215
Donne, John, Dean of St. Paul's 1, 5, 25, 28, 34, 58
    on copying out sermons 38–9
    'Doctrine and use' and 59
    gesture and 62
    last sermon at Paul's Cross 98
    sermon division and 53–5
    see also *Directions for Preachers*; sermons, genres, accession day; sermons, genres, Gunpowder Plot
Dorman, Thomas 167, 171–2
Drapers' Company 32
Drope, John 85
Ducie, Mr Robert 38
Duffy, Eamon 160
Dugdale, William 1, 34, 133, 223
Duport, John 140
Dyos, John 178–9
Dyson, Humphrey 228

Earl of Essex 7, 26, 86–93, 102
    execution of 1, 134
Earl of Tyrone 88–9
Earle, John 3, 33, 61
Ecclesiastical Commissioners 73, 194
Edward VI 18, 28, 68, 113
Elizabeth, Queen of England 26, 71, 75, 106, 148, 183
    attending sermons at Paul's Cross 16, 130, 132–3, 135
    censorship and 107
    government of 7, 161
    illness of 5
    see also accession of Elizabeth; Elizabethan Settlement
Elizabeth of Bohemia, daughter of James I 92
Elizabethan Settlement 24, 160, 163, 192, 205, 207, 219
Elton, Edwards 111–12
Essex rebellion 91, 93, 102; *see also* Earl of Essex
Etherington, John 114
Eucharist, *see* communion
execution of Mary, Queen of Scots 76
executions 106–7, 124
Evans, William 32
Everard, John 82, 93

Falstaff, Sir John 3
Farmer, Richard 221

Faunt, Nicholas 206
Featley, Daniel 19, 59, 111–12, 216
Feckenham, John, Dean of St. Paul's 172
Felton, John 106–7
Fenner, Dudley 206
Ferrell, Lori Anne 141, 148, 150, 218
Field, John 199, 206
Firth, Mary 123–5
Fisher, John, Bishop of Rochester 28, 107
Fisher, William 30
Fleming, Giles 218
Fleming, John 32
Fletcher, Richard, Bishop of London 31
Floyd, S.J., John 181–2, 186–8
Fotherby, Martin 148–9, 151–2
Fourth Lateran Council 164
Foxe, John 1, 24 n. 106, 49, 139,
         185, 198
   complaint against 85
   on Catholics 175–6
   Foxe's Book of Martyrs and 107 n. 24, 112
   Sermon on Christ Crucified 59
French Match 111
Fulke, William 206
Fuller, Thomas 33, 62, 223

Gage, Thomas 119–20, 225
Gataker, Thomas 19, 43, 46, 101
Gardiner, Richard 1, 52, 155–9, 224
Gardiner, S. R. 156
Gardiner, Samuel 184
Gardiner, Stephen 26–7
Garnet S.J., Henry 106–7
Gee, John 97, 117, 188
Gibson, Abraham 48
Gifford, George 44, 160, 182, 216
Gipkyn, John 8–9, 14
Goodwin, William 149–50
Gore, John 33
Gosson, Stephen 25
Gorges, Sir Arthur 106
Gowrie Conspiracy 22, 134, 146; *see also*
         sermons, genres, Gowrie Conspiracy
Grant, John 106
Gravet, William 64
Great Fire 226
Greenwood, Henry 38, 63, 65
Grindal, Edmund, Bishop of London, later
         Archbishop of Canterbury 17, 24, 26,
         71–4, 135, 176
   Accession Day liturgy and 139
   appointment of preachers and 27
Gualter, Rudolph 107
Guildsmen 17, 22
Gumbleden, John 97
Gunpowder Plot 22, 106–7, 142, 147, 183;
         see also sermons, genre, Gunpowder Plot
Gurney, Richard, Lord Mayor of London 157,
         224

Hacket, Roger 216–17
The Hague 126
Haigh, Christopher 160
Hales, John, of Eaton 10
Hall, Joseph, Bishop of Norwich 58–9, 137, 143
Hammond, Henry 37
Hampton Court Conference 193, 215
Hapsburgs 92
Harding, Thomas 61, 212
   'Challenge' controversy and 162, 166–72,
         174, 195, 197
Harington, Sir John 103
Harsnett, Samuel 218
Hatton, Sir Christopher 87, 209
Hayward, John 88–9
Heath, Sir Robert, Solicitor General 126
Henry VIII, King of England 110
Herbert, George 60
heresy 56, 68, 161, 170
   burned for 106, 109
   recantation of 120–1
   and schism 98, 190, 209–11, 219–20
heterodoxy 105, 109, 113, 183
Higgons, Theophilus 12, 17, 117–18
High Commission, *see* Court of the High
         Commission
Hilton, John 113
History of St Paul's 133, 225; *see also* William
         Dugdale
Hoby, Sir Edward 118
Holbrooke, William 48, 215
Holland 92
Holland, Thomas 92, 136–8, 140–1, 143, 157
Hollybrand, Claudius 17
Holy Communion, *see* communion
Holyday, Barten 143, 147
Hooker, Richard 1, 62
Horne, Robert, Bishop of Winchester 71,
         172–3, 186, 196–7, 199–201
House of Commons 84–5, 127, 224–5, 227;
         see also parliament
Howard, Sir Charles 121
Howard, Sir Robert 126–8
Howell, James 228
Howson, John 140, 218
humanist 29, 52
Humphrey, Laurence 73–4, 201
Hunt, Arnold 26
Hunt, James 227
Hurlebutt, John 8–9, 12, 103
Hussey, Vincent 89
Hutton, Matthew 27
Hyperius of Marburg 56, 138, 165
hypothetical universalism 99

iconoclasm 158 n. 89
idolatry 34, 46, 104, 203, 211
   1643 ordinance against 223
   Catholicism and 136, 163

Inns of Court
  members of 19
  sermons at 24

Jackson, Thomas 62, 183
Jackson, William 64
Jacobs, Henry 66
James I, King of England 92–3
  when James VI of Scotland 208
  attending sermons at Paul's Cross 5, 16, 22,
    130–4
  censorship and 108–11
  Protestant calendar and 141–53
  see also accession of James I
James, William 214
Jeremiads, *see* sermons, genres
Jesuits 17, 40, 110, 149, 153, 183, 189, 207,
    214
  mission to England 114, 179, 181
  Society of Jesus 117
Jesus Guild 29
Jewel, John 1, 23, 61–2, 75, 136, 174
  anti-popery and 174–7, 181
  as conformist 195
  controversy with Harding 197, 199–201
  see also 'Challenge' sermon
Jews 150, 186
Johnson, Robert 31–2
Josselin, Ralph 226
Juxon, William, Bishop of London, later
    Archbishop of Canterbury 100, 154,
    218, 223–4

Kenyon, J. P. 129
Frederick V, King of Bohemia 92, 131
King, Henry 34, 58, 65, 154, 156, 184
King, John, Bishop of London 5, 17, 22, 65,
    132, 184
Knewstub, John 204–5, 216
Knight, John 108, 110
Knight, William 50
Knollys, Sir Francis 208

laity 166, 169–71, 198, 204, 207–8, 211,
    217, 219
  Catholic 181
  English 163–4, 184
  interpreting scripture 65
Lake, Arthur 33, 59
Lake, Peter 69, 75, 83, 91, 207
Latimer, Hugh 1, 11 n. 49
Laud, William, Bishop of London, later
    Archbishop of Canterbury 5, 34, 99,
    104–5, 119, 154
  appointment of preachers 223
  avant-garde conformism and 218, 222
  High Commission and 128
  letters 100–01
  see also sermons, genres, accession day

Laudianism (Laudians) 34, 21, 119, 158–9,
    218, 224
  censorship 91, 99
  Laudian authorities 21, 102, 154,
    Richard Gardiner as 156
Law, Matthew 33
Lawrence, John 62
Legate, Bartholomew 109
Lestrange Morduant, Sir and Lady 38
Lever, Thomas 73, 194–5, 199
Ley, Roger 38, 61
libel 87, 104, 151, 214
  publishing 4, 103, 105
licensing for publication, *see* censorship,
    licensing for publication
livery companies 12, 16, 22, 222
London, *see also* aldermen of London; livery
          companies; Guildsmen; Merchant Taylors;
    Stationers' Company; Saddlers' Company;
          Drapers' Company
  Cheapside 3, 112, 122
  Cheapside Cross 108, 113 n. 46
  Corporation of London 104, 132–3, 157
    anti-Catholicism and 179
    appointment of preachers and 26–33, 227
    accommodation at Paul's Cross sermons 16
    attending Paul's Cross 19–21, 24, 61
    control of sermons 25, 69, 73–4, 80–4, 87
    Court of Alderman 13, 19, 73, 180, 224
    Court of Orphans 82
    financial support of Paul's Cross 22
    in managing Paul's Cross 6, 12–13, 119,
      223–6
  Guildhall 21, 25, 226
  Ludgate Hill 3, 108 n. 26
  St Mary's Spital 21–2; *see also* sermons,
    genres, Spital; sermons, genres, Rehearsal
  New churchyard 77 n. 37
  Paul's Alley 4
  Paul's Cross
    accommodation for preachers 32, 46, 222
    acoustics 10
    pulpit built 8
    pulpit location 1
    pulpit renovated 8, 16
    pulpit closed 22
    pulpit demolished 2, 34, 223, 227
    sermon house 13, 14, 20, 103, 131–2
    sermon house demolished 34
    sermon house renovated 12–13
  St Faith under St Paul's 10
  St Paul's Cathedral 2–3
    almonry 4 n. 12
    chapter 3, 18, 29, 132
    chapter house and undercroft 4 n. 12, 11
    choir 2, 7, 11, 20–1, 34, 100, 131–2, 155,
      223, 225, 227
    great north door 3
    great west door 3, 107, 131–2

London, (cont.)
  nave 11, 21
  St Dunstan's chapel 13 n. 64, 20 n. 87,
    n.90
  Lady chapel 225
  see also Dean of St Paul's
  St Paul's Churchyard 2–8, 10–12, 20–2,
    67, 227
    Bishop's Palace 106, 131–2, 176
    book burning in 108
    display of government power and 102, 107
    north 3–4, 105
    public penance in 105–6
    St Faith under St Paul's 2, 10–11
    St Gregory's by St. Paul's 223
    St Paul's School 4
    Stationers' Hall 108
    Stow's description of 228
    south 3, 105 n. 15
    west 106, 108 n. 26, 131, 176
    see also London, Paul's Cross
  Virginia Company 25
  Westminster, see Westminster Disputation;
    parliament; royal court
Lord Mayor of London 4, 6, 24, 32, 131
  appointment of preachers 104, 119
  attending Paul's Cross 7, 12–13, 17–20, 22,
    223, 225–7
  control of sermons 72, 74, 80–4, 88
  sponsorship of Paul's Cross 25, 33
  see also Christopher Clitherow; Richard
    Gurney; Sir Edward Osborne; Isaac
    Penington; Thomas Rowe
Louvainists 166–7
loyalty 22–3, 69, 135–6, 141, 155, 181, 217
Luther, Martin 107, 185

McCullough, Peter 72, 141
Machyn, Henry 17, 22, 106
MacLure, Millar 1–2, 68, 99
Magisterial Reformers 51, 53, 178
Manningham, John 19, 39–41, 181
Markham, Lady Anne 125
Markham, Griffin 125
Marshall, Stephen 226
Mary, mother of Jesus 136
Mary, Queen of Scots 18, 68, 75–8, 85, 91
Marbury, Francis 49, 182–3, 216
Marprelate, Martin 63, 141, 182, 205, 210,
    212–13
  Martinists 213–14
Marprelate Tracts (pamphlets) 27, 192, 209,
    213; see also Martin Marprelate
Martyn, Sir Henry 127
Matthew, Tobie, Archbishop of York 76
Mede, Joseph 79, 99–100, 128
Merchant Taylors' Company 22
Middleton, Thomas 22–3, 82
Millenary Petition 215

Milles, Robert 83
Millington, Thomas 4, 104
Milton, Anthony 99
Milward, John 146–7, 153
Montagu, Henry 127
Montague, Richard 97, 101
Montaigne, George, Bishop of London, later
    Archbishop of York 99, 100, 110–11
Morton, Thomas, Bishop of Durham 118,
    153, 224
Mosse, Miles 36, 62
MPs (Members of Parliament) 18–19, 84–5, 93,
    127, 200; see also Richard Strickland
Munday, Anthony 228
mutilations 106
Myriell, Thomas 64, 96

Naylor, Joseph 153–4
Nethersole, Sir Francis 131
Newcomen, Matthew 226
Nichols, John 115
Nicolson, George 145
nonconformity 69, 194
Northbrooke, John 122
Northern Rebellion 148, 176
Nowell, Alexander, Dean of St Paul's 5, 24, 28,
    72–3, 162
  anti-Catholicism and 167, 170–2
  anti-Puritanism and 194–5

Oath of Allegiance 109, 118, 134, 149, 172, 184
obedience 69, 89–91, 182, 187, 202–3, 205
  Homily of 94
  political 52, 134, 135–8, 141, 143, 145,
    155–7, 222
  see also disobedience
Osborne, Sir Edward, Lord Mayor of
    London 83
Overall, John, Dean of St Paul's 20
Overbury trials 104
Owen, H. Gareth 4
Oxford, University of 100; see also St John's
    College, Oxford; Corpus Christi, Oxford

Pack, Christopher 226
Page, Dr Samuel 92
Paget, Thomas 174
Palatinate 92, 131
Palyn, George 32
panegyric 137, 143, 156
Pareus, Davis 108, 110
Parker, Matthew, Archbishop of Canterbury 26,
    72–4, 123, 193–4, 199
Parker, Roger 84–5
parliament 27, 66, 114, 156, 176, 223
  abolition of Court of High Commission and 129
  trial of Mary Queen of Scots and 76
  anti-catholic laws and 179
  of 1559 161

Gunpowder plot and 142, 148–9, 152
James' address to 93
mentioned in sermons 104, 108
privilege 126–7
Puritanism and 192, 198–9, 209
sermons to 18, 226
see also MPs; *Admonition to Parliament*;
    Supremacy and Uniformity
Paul's Cross, *see* London, Paul's Cross
Paul's Cross sermons
appointments 33, 70, 73–4, 222, 224, 227
    of Richard Bancroft 209
    of John Gee 188
    of Laurence Humphrey 201
    letters of 26–7, 100
    of Arthur Wake 79
bequests to 29, 32, 222, 224
financing of 22, 24, 30–1, 222
end of 225–6
prestige of 21, 25, 42, 134, 222, 228
timing of 21
Paulet, Sir Richard 11
Peacham, Henry 34, 223
Pelling, John 33, 45
penance 102, 113–14, 120–8, 130
Pendleton, Dr Henry 103
Penington, Isaac, Lord Mayor of London 119,
    224–5
Penry, John 208
Perkins, William 53, 58–9, 160, 203
Persons, Robert 115–16, 151
Petley, Elias 47
Piers, John, Bishop of Salisbury 131
Pilkington, James, Bishop of London 3
Pincus, Steven 69, 75, 91
Pinder, Rachel 123
plague 6, 56, 82–3, 183, 185, 219, 221
plain style 57
Platter, Thomas 8, 10, 23
Playfere, Thomas 44, 48
Prayer Book service, see *Book of Common Prayer*
Pormort, Thomas 106
preaching style 52, 58, 60, 147, 181; *see also*
    plain style; rhetoric; sermons, parts of
predestination 94, 96–9, 165, 184
    Puritan movement and 191, 215, 218
presbyterianism 78, 91, 191, 198, 201–2, 204
    and conformists 207–8
    equality of ministers and 210
    George Glifford and 182
    ministers 226
    puritan campaign for 209, 215–17
    Scottish 213
    see also Black Acts of 1584
press 5, 83, 111, 185, 206, 209
    printing of Paul's Cross sermons and 37,
        43–8, 63–5
priest 112–19, 140, 177, 181, 196, 210
    and Jesuits 183

missionary 187
Thomas Pormort as 106
Privy Council 3, 61, 135, 142, 198, 208
    appearing at Paul's Cross 7, 16–19, 22, 130, 132
    appointment of preachers and 26, 30–1
    control of sermons and 69, 71–2, 81, 83–5,
        90, 100
    financial management of Paul's Cross and 24
    in regulation of Paul's Cross 6, 8
    propaganda 68, 71–2, 86–7, 91, 102, 134
        anti-Catholic 110, 114, 116–19, 122, 206
        Catholic 177, 180, 184
        parliamentary 198
Prynne, William 112
Public Sphere 69
Purbeck, Viscountess Frances 126–7, 129
Purchas, Samuel 147
Puritanism 80, 95, 150, 187, 190–3, 196, 213
    early Stuart 214–16, 218
    Jacobean 39, 137
    radical 111

Questier, Michael 185

Ravis, Thomas, Bishop of London 45 n. 45
Rawlinson, John 144
recusant 117, 149, 174–7, 180–1, 183, 187
Reformation 20, 95, 113, 115, 176, 186–7
    book burning and 107
    narratives of 166, 227
    puritans and 207, 211
    Paul's Cross and 228
repentance 51, 57, 96, 114
restrictions (of the pulpit) 92, 94–6
Reynolds, John 208
rhetoric 55, 57, 59
    anti-Catholic 150, 153, 181
    Rich, Richard 137
Richardson, Charles 64
Richardson, John 86
Ridley, Nicholas, Bishop of London 211
Ridolfi Plot 76
riot 7, 22, 102
Robinson, Edward 84–5
Robinson, Nicholas 170
Rogers, John 39
Roman Catholicism
    attitudes to, before 1580 161
    anti-popery 150, 152–4, 181–3, 185, 187–8,
        190, 192
    clergy 17, 161, 164, 170, 173, 181, 210;
        see also priest
    conversion from 72, 93, 97, 113–19
    conversion to 17, 65, 117
    see also Jesuit; recusant
Rood of Boxley 113
Rowe, Thomas, Lord Mayor of London 25 n.
    112, 77 n. 37
royal court, *see* court, royal

Russell, Thomas 32
Ruthven, Alexander 145–6
Ruthven, John, Earl of Gowrie 145
Ruthven Raid 212

sacraments 111, 163, 178–9, 207, 217, 220;
  see also communion
Saddlers' Company 12, 22
St John's College, Oxford 28
St Paul's Churchyard, *see* London
Sampson, Thomas 70, 72–4, 199
Sanderson, Robert 34, 37, 51, 58, 98
Sandys, Edwin, Bishop of London, later
    Archbishop of York 24, 27, 71–2, 76–9
  conformist sermon 202–4, 206, 210
  preaching on Mary, Queen of Scots 85
Sandys, Sir Edwin, author of *A Relation to the
    State of Religion* 108
Saxby, Robert 23, 39
scandal 54, 104, 121, 123, 125, 128
schism 98, 190, 203, 209–13, 219–21
  schismatics 186–9, 224
Scory, John 71–2
Scottish Reformation 209
Seaver, Paul 25, 32, 79
sedition 212, 214, 220
separatists 182, 185–90
  Henry Barrow and John Greenwood as 65
  Henoch Clapham as 45, 182
  semi-separatist 66, 103
sermon notes 36–8, 47–8, 57–8, 63, 66, 169
  hearers' notes in manuscript 23, 25, 39–41,
    43–4, 67, 181
  in preachers' manuscripts 29, 37, 43, 169–72,
    197
  printed 37–8, 43–4, 48
  in shorthand 30 n. 22
sermons, genres 56
  accession day 7, 16–17, 22, 134–41, 143,
    154
  by John Donne 5, 16, 38, 143
  by John Duport 140
  elements of 144–5, 147–48
  by Richard Gardiner 2, 52, 155, 224
  by Joseph Hall 143
  by John Jewel 136
  by Henry King 156
  by William Laud 143, 155–6
  by John Whitgift 137–8, 141, 157, 205
  by John White 157, 214
  by Thomas White 48, 139
  confutation 56, 161–2, 165–6, 187–8,
    198, 217
  anti-Catholic 114, 151, 174–5, 178, 181,
    190, 192–3
  Bancroft and 209–13
  Jewel and 169–70
  puritans and 200, 204, 207–8, 217, 220
  consolation 56

doctrinal 56, 59, 94, 97, 161, 175
  Copcot and 206, 210
  Sandys and 203, 210
  exhortation, *see* sermons, parts, exhortation
Gowrie Conspiracy 46, 142, 145, 147–8, 153
Gunpowder Plot 22, 134, 145, 147–54
  by John Donne 11, 39, 152–3
instructive 56, 138, 203
Jeremiad 6, 51, 56, 105, 151, 183, 215
passion 7, 21, 97, 136, 175, 201, 204
recantation 12, 93, 114, 117–20, 225
rehearsal 7, 21, 39, 70, 101, 201, 216
Spital 7, 18, 21, 39, 73–4, 101
  by Thomas Bilson 65
  by Roger Hacket 216
  by Samuel Page 92
  by Thomas Playfere 44
sermons, parts of
  application 55–60, 78, 80, 85, 155, 210–11
    in Accession Day sermons 144, 156
    in Gowrie Conspiracy sermons 146–7
  delivery 35, 51, 56, 66, 102
    printing after 38, 46, 118, 152
    style of 44, 49
  division 40–1, 53–9, 148, 180
  'doctrine and use' 59
  exhortation 51, 56–8, 77–8, 90, 156–9,
    175, 179
    about blessings of peace 93
    to godliness 96, 182–3
    the king and 147, 159
    to maintain church unity 200
    to thankfulness 78, 139, 150–3, 157
    to virtue 137
  explication 48, 53, 155, 157–8
    Accession Day and 137
    and the application 56–8, 60, 144, 210
    Barlow and 89
    Gowrie Conspiracy and 146
    Sandys and 77–8
  gesture 58, 61–2, 104, 146, 158
  proof-text 52, 57, 157, 170, 185, 209
  text (choice of biblical) 23, 51–2, 55, 77,
    139–40
  voice 58, 61–2, 64, 66, 111
sermons, printed 6, 11–12, 35, 132
  Calvinist 99
  difference from sermon notes 40–1
  division in 55, 58–9
  motives for publication 33, 48–9, 52, 63–7,
    82
  permission for 35–6
  publication rates 1, 5, 33, 42–3, 97, 134,
    223, 226
  sermon-book 37
  unauthorised publication 44
  see also censorship, appointment of preachers;
    censorship, licensing for publication
Sewall, Samuel 228

Shaxton, Nicholas 113
Sheldon, Richard 93, 118–19, 188
Simpson, John 227
Smith, Arbella 121
Smith, Edward 121
Smith, Henry 39, 46
Smith, Richard 113
Smithe, Anne 39
sola Scriptura 53
Southern, A. C. 162
Spain 5, 46, 89, 94
Spanish Armada 5, 16, 106, 130, 136
Spanish Infanta 92
Spanish Match 5, 70, 92, 131, 184, 188
Sparrow Simpson, Dr. William 2
Spenser, John 40
Spurstowe, William 226
Stapleton, Thomas 174
Star Chamber 88, 193, 214, 216
Stationers' Company 22
Stepney, William 18, 23
Stock, Richard 81, 183, 216
Stockwood, John 18, 49, 82, 178, 205
Stokesley, John 26
Stonehouse, Walter 221
Stoughton, John 37, 42
Stow, John 1, 21–2, 29, 73, 171, 227–8
    on monarchs 130–1, 133
    on penance 123, 125
Strickland, Richard, MP 198
Stroude, John 204
Strype, John 11, 70–1, 227–8
Stubbs, Philip 87
Stutevile, Sir Martin 128
Suárez, Francisco 110
Supremacy and Uniformity, Acts of 70, 172
Survey of London 21, 227–8; *see also*
        John Stow
Sutton, Thomas 83, 183
Sydenham, Humphrey 96, 165
Symonds, William 185, 189, 216
Synod of Dort 99, 184

Tanner 50, 41, 170–2, 174, 193, 197
tax 81, 84, 89, 157
Taylor, Edward 228
Tedder, William 114
Temple, Robert 45, 214
theatres 82–4; *see also* Children of Paul's
Thirty-nine Articles, *see* Articles of Religion
Thirty Years' War 92 n. 86
Thompson, Thomas 187, 189, 216
Throckmorton, Sir John 125
Throckmorton, Job 200–1
Tower of London 71, 89
treason 76–8, 88–9, 106, 149, 152–3, 208, 213
Trumbull, William 118, 125
Turnbull, Richard 214
Tyacke, Nicholas 99

Tynley, Robert 148–9, 151
Tyrrell, Anthony 114–16

Vase, Robert 51, 97
Vaughan, Richard, Bishop of London 142
Veron, John 72
Verstegan, Richard 182
Vertue, Henry 221
vestments 72–4, 193–7, 199
Vestiarian controversy 192, 196–7, 201
Villiers, George, Duke of Buckingham 6, 100,
        104, 126–7
Villiers, John 126, 129
Vorstius, Conrad 108–10

Wake, Arthur 79, 202, 222
Wakeman, Robert 23, 49
Walgrave, Sir William 44
Walsall, John 177
Walsingham, Francis 174
Walton, Izaak 37, 53, 60
Wapull, George 23
Ward, Samuel 43–4, 46, 99, 101
Warner, John, Bishop of Rochester 36, 226
Wars of the Roses 221
Watson, Dr Thomas 7, 17, 22
Watts, William 219
weather (inclement) 10–12
Webbe, George 32
Webster, Tom 215, 217
Westminster Disputation 71–2, 84
Weston, Richard, Lord Treasurer 105
Whalley, John 48
Whately, William 59
Whitbie, Oliver 221
White, John 83, 157
White, Thomas 47–8, 64, 139, 176–7, 214
White, William 199–201
Whitgift, John, Archbishop of Canterbury 10, 31, 65,
        campaign for conformity 202, 204–7, 209
        controversy between Thomas Cartwright
            and 192
        see also sermons, genres, Accession Day
Whitsunday 17, 19–20, 22, 25, 63, 77, 104
Wightman, Edward 109
Wigmore, Michael 44
Wilcox, Thomas 199–201
Wilkins, John 59
Wilkinson, John 41
Wilkinson, Robert 52
Williams, Griffith 59, 65
Williams, John, Lord Keeper and Bishop of
        Lincoln 126–7
Winter, John 106
Wisdom, Robert 113
Wood, Ambrose 43
Woollock 171
Worship, William 33
Wright, Robert 137